Sheffield Hallam University
Learning and IT Services
Adsetts Centre City Campus
Sheffield S1 1WS

D0420368

SHEFFIELD HALLAM UNIVERSITY
LEARNING CENTRE
WITHDRAWN FROM STOCK

Teaching and Learning Pragmatics

KEY TEXT

REFERENCE

SHEFFIELD HALLAM
LEARNING CENTRE
WITHDRAWN FROM STOCK

Teaching and Learning Pragmatics

Where Language and Culture Meet

Noriko Ishihara and Andrew D. Cohen

Longman
is an imprint of

Harlow, England • London • New York • Boston • San Francisco • Toronto • Sydney • Singapore • Hong Kong
Tokyo • Seoul • Taipei • New Delhi • Cape Town • Madrid • Mexico City • Amsterdam • Munich • Paris • Milan

PEARSON EDUCATION LIMITED

Edinburgh Gate
Harlow CM20 2JE
United Kingdom
Tel: +44 (0)1279 623623
Fax: +44 (0)1279 431059
Website: www.pearsoned.co.uk

KTPS
401.4507
IS

First edition published in Great Britain in 2010

© Pearson Education Limited 2010

The rights of Noriko Ishihara and Andrew D. Cohen to be identified
as authors of this work have been asserted by them in accordance
with the Copyright, Designs and Patents Act 1988.

ISBN: 978-1-4082-0457-3

British Library Cataloguing in Publication Data
Ishihara, Noriko.
Teaching and learning pragmatics : where language and culture meet / Noriko
Ishihara and Andrew D. Cohen — 1st ed.
   p. cm.
   Includes bibliographical references and index.
   ISBN 978-1-4082-0457-3 (pbk.)
   1. Pragmatics. 2. Interlanguage (Language learning) 3. Second language
acquisition. 4. Language and culture–Study and teaching. 5. Speech acts
(Linguistics) I. Cohen, Andrew D. II. Title.
   P99.4.P72I85 2010
   401'.45071–dc22

Library of Congress Cataloging in Publication Data
A CIP catalog record for this book can be obtained from the Library of Congress

All rights reserved; no part of this publication may be reproduced, stored
in a retrieval system, or transmitted in any form or by any means, electronic,
mechanical, photocopying, recording, or otherwise without either the prior
written permission of the Publishers or a licence permitting restricted copying
in the United Kingdom issued by the Copyright Licensing Agency Ltd,
Saffron House, 6–10 Kirby Street, London EC1N 8TS. This book may not be lent,
resold, hired out or otherwise disposed of by way of trade in any form
of binding or cover other than that in which it is published, without the
prior consent of the Publishers.

10 9 8 7 6 5 4 3 2 1
14 13 12 11 10

Set in 9/13.5pt Stone Serif by 35
Printed and bound in Malaysia, CTP-KHL

The Publisher's policy is to use paper manufactured from sustainable forests.

Contents

Acknowledgments

First and foremost, we would like to express our deep gratitude to the participants of our Center for Advanced Research on Language Acquisition (CARLA) five-day institute courses held in summer of 2005–2009 at the University of Minnesota. These participants made invaluable contributions to chapters under development in this book. Their voices and their reactions to materials, coming from their own expertise and experience, greatly enhanced the book. We are also grateful to both the Director of CARLA, Elaine Tarone, and to the Coordinator, Karin Larson, for agreeing to offer this new institute on pragmatics and for their feedback on this practically oriented resource, especially with respect to Chapters 5 and 14.

In addition, we would like to acknowledge the contributions made by several colleagues to the shaping of specific chapters. Rachel Shively generously shared her expertise in technology and the teaching of Spanish of pragmatics, and her input is reflected in Chapter 13. Thanks also go to Kim Johnson and Anne Dahlman for their brilliant insights from a teacher educator's perspective for Chapter 2. We also thank our current and former graduate students at American University and at the University of Minnesota for helping to make this book more readable and accessible to practicing teachers.

We would also like to thank the series editor for Pearson Education, Chris Candlin, for his solid support of our effort to create this book and for his insights in preparing the book for publication. Our heartfelt thanks go to Mayuko Onda for her original illustrations. We also wish to acknowledge Kumiko Akikawa for her meticulous work in coordinating the references for this book. We are grateful to the Pearson Education editorial staff as well for their assistance in this endeavor. Last but not least, special thanks go to our families for their support and encouragement during the preparation of this manuscript.

Publisher's acknowledgements

We are grateful to Oxford University Press for permission to reproduce the extracts on pp. 158–60 from Bardovi-Harlig, K., Hartford, B. S., Mahan-Taylor, R., Morgan, M. and Reynolds, D. W., 'Developing pragmatic awareness: closing conversation', *ELT Journal*, 45(1), 4–15, 1991. Reproduced by permission of Oxford University Press.

In some instances we have been unable to trace the holders of copyright material, and we would appreciate any information that would enable us to do so.

Introduction

The theme of interlanguage pragmatics and, in particular, the link between language and culture has gained wide appeal internationally, and has enjoyed attention in the field of language education for the last 30 years at least. This has resulted in a growing number of applied-linguistics books with pragmatics in the title and several international journals which encompass this field, such as the *Journal of Pragmatics* and *Intercultural Pragmatics*. It is probably fair to say that pragmatics has increasingly become mainstream in second/foreign-language (L2) teaching and learning.

The writing of this book was prompted by what we perceived as a gap between what research in pragmatics has found and how language is generally taught today. As of the present time, research in cross-cultural and interlanguage pragmatics has delved into a number of topics with direct relevance to language instruction. For example, there are now numerous studies available exploring speech acts such as *requesting, refusing, apologizing, complimenting,* and *complaining* in various languages. There are also many studies on how L2 speakers of those languages comprehend and behave pragmatically in their first language (L1) and in their L2. On the other hand, not much of this empirical work has as yet been systematically applied to the L2 classroom and few commercially available textbooks offer research-informed instruction. In addition, few teacher education programs seem to deal with the practical application of pragmatics theories. In putting together the book we have attempted to help fill this gap by illustrating a number of ways in which empirically validated pragmatics material can become a mainstream part of teacher development and can assume a more prominent place in L2 instruction. Accordingly, this bridging work in support of *instructional pragmatics* constitutes a key theme of the book.

This book is intended as a guidebook for teachers with various hands-on activities. As such, the book may be of interest to pre- and in-service language teachers and graduate students, as well as teacher educators. Our primary concern is to show how pragmatics interfaces with culture in human interaction and to underscore this link in language teaching. So, the book is primarily focused on classroom practice, and we see this research-informed, pedagogically oriented approach to pragmatics as a relatively new contribution to the field. Special attention is afforded to instructional approaches and classroom processes, as well as to modes of assessment in this context. We are also concerned with curriculum writing and the incorporation of online pragmatics material. At the same time the book addresses issues of language learning and teaching in terms of discourse and interaction. Although speech acts are given major attention in the guide, we neither equate them with pragmatics nor suggest that speech acts should dominate the L2 curriculum that incorporates pragmatics. Speech acts are only one component of pragmatics, and much of our discussion applies to the pragmatics of written language as well to spoken discourse. Because speech acts have been well-studied, research findings about them are readily applicable to instruction. Indeed it is our intention to call for further research and instruction in other areas of pragmatics.

We view the learning of pragmatics not only as a cognitive process but also as a social phenomenon, looking into how L2 speakers construct and negotiate their identities as they become socialized into the L2 community. We see the pragmatic norms of a community as constructed not by native speakers of the language, but by pragmatically competent expert speakers, native or non-native. Because non-native speakers can be as pragmatically effective as (or at times, more so than) some native speakers, we wish to depart from the misleading dichotomy of native vs non-native speakers wherever possible. In fact, especially with regard to English, the demarcation between native and non-native speakers is becoming increasingly blurred with the spread of English as an international language. Rather than relying on this questionable distinction, we view one's pragmatic ability as contextually constructed in interaction, often negotiable in context. This is why we emphasize the speaker's goals and intentions, the way that they are interpreted by the listener, and the likely consequences of the interaction, whoever the speaker and the listener may be. We intend to highlight the social aspects in the learning of L2 pragmatics and invite teacher readers to consider how learners' social being relates to the instructional and evaluative practices of the teachers.

In our view, language teachers need to have specific guidance in how to teach and assess pragmatics systematically in order to feel comfortable incorporating empirically based pragmatics more into their teaching. In this book we provide guidelines, practical steps, and examples for classroom practice, along with hands-on activities intended for enhancing teachers' (and their students') pragmatic awareness and reflective teaching. Even though teacher readers of this book may not conduct formal research, we provide suggestions for how both teachers and their students can conduct informal investigation by gathering data on pragmatics. Such classroom-based research can contribute both to students' language learning and to teachers' professional development. We see classroom teachers as primarily engaged in instruction while at the same time exploring student learning in the authentic classroom and analyzing language use in and outside of the classroom. In this sense, practitioners have access to knowledge and insights about real language classrooms that are not available to researchers. We would welcome, as a consequence of reading and using this book in their instruction, teachers' contribution of their own insights for the teaching and assessing of pragmatic ability to future volumes of this kind, in order to further inform theory and research in this domain. For example, many of the examples provided in this book revolve around material for adult or adolescent learners; we invite readers' innovations for enhancing instructional pragmatics for young learners in particular.

The following is a brief description of the book. In Part One, we provide some grounding in the teaching and learning of L2 pragmatics. In Chapter 1, we discuss terminology in L2 pragmatics and related fields, including a discussion of what we mean by "culture" and how that interfaces with pragmatics. In Chapter 2, we consider teachers' reflections on language learning and teaching, especially with regard to how they experience pragmatic development and how that, along with their professional development, influences their knowledge, beliefs, and practices. Chapter 3 looks at various methods for obtaining language samples to be used for pragmatics-focused instruction and at the advantages and disadvantages of each method. Chapter 4 describes and promotes the development of a link between classroom practice and research-established information by introducing an online database for L2 pragmatics. Chapter 5 identifies potential sources of learners' pragmatic divergence, provides numerous examples, and offers explanation for the divergence, which can be both unintentional and intentional.

Part Two constitutes the "nuts and bolts" of pragmatics-focused instruction. The common thread that weaves through this section is the idea that pragmatic norms vary across languages, cultures, and various other social contexts, as well as across individuals. Thus, we argue that pragmatics would be best taught in (sometimes imagined) interactional social contexts. Chapter 6 gives brief theoretical underpinnings for current instructional approaches to L2 pragmatics. We discuss the learning of pragmatics not only from a cognitive point of view but also from social, cultural, psychological, and emotional perspectives, and consider their implications on classroom practices. Chapter 7 offers guidelines for how to observe instruction that focuses on a pragmatics component, as well as simulated demonstrations for teaching L2 speech acts. Chapter 8 deals with the assessment of textbook materials and possible ways to adapt these materials or to design instruction for the purpose of teaching pragmatics to complement them. Chapter 9 considers the contributions of both discourse analysis and language corpora in understanding L2 pragmatics, and looks at the potential contribution that these insights can lend to language instruction. Chapter 10 offers some guidelines for constructing pragmatics-focused lesson plans, as well as inviting teacher readers to engage in reflective activities for learning and teaching L2 pragmatics. Finally, Chapter 11 draws on an L2 pragmatics-focused curriculum that is both web-based and classroom-based to offer principles for curriculum development and examples that illustrate these principles.

Part Three of the book considers further issues in the learning, teaching, and assessing of L2 pragmatics. Chapter 12 looks at what might constitute successful strategies in speech act performance and offers a proposed taxonomy of learner strategies for acquiring pragmatics. Chapter 13 deals with the application of instructional technology to the teaching and learning of pragmatics. Chapter 14 engages the reader in the issue of how to approach the assessment of learners' pragmatic ability, and offers suggested strategies for assessing pragmatics. Chapter 15 takes a more close-up view of classroom-based assessment of pragmatics, and provides samples of assessment materials, learner language, and teacher feedback. The concluding chapter first reviews key issues covered in the book, and then asks readers to reflect on these topics and to set goals for future instruction related to pragmatics instruction.

The chapters are for the most part relatively short in order to keep them accessible to teacher readers. Each chapter includes hands-on activities designed to provide an experiential connection with the material in the chapter, as well as to offer models for activities that teachers could be using with their own students. Because interaction among participants would effectively enhance teacher learning, activities are written for a group audience. Most of the activities have been field-tested in a summer institute on teaching L2 pragmatics offered since the summer of 2006 at the University of Minnesota through the CARLA. It is our intention that this book be an ongoing source of practical ideas for classroom instruction that provides a strong presence for pragmatics in the curriculum.

Grounding in the teaching and learning of L2 pragmatics

CHAPTER 1

Coming to terms with pragmatics

Andrew D. Cohen

Pragmatic ability

The notion of *pragmatics* has numerous meanings depending on the context. When we say that someone is taking a "pragmatic approach" to something, for example, the implication is that the person is being practical. Yet, the word assumes a more specialized meaning in applied linguistics. The term *pragmatic ability* as used in this volume refers both to knowledge about pragmatics and to the ability to use it.[1]

Pragmatic ability actually encompasses the four main channels for communication, the receptive ones, listening and reading, and the productive ones, speaking and writing. Whether the reception or production is pragmatically successful in the given L2 depends on various factors, such as: (1) our proficiency in that L2 and possibly in other (especially related) languages, (2) our age, gender, occupation, social status, and experience in the relevant L2-speaking communities, and (3) our previous experiences with pragmatically competent L2 speakers and our multilingual/multicultural experiences in general. Let's look at the different skill areas:

1   As **listeners**, we need to interpret what is said, as well as what is not said, and what may be communicated non-verbally. These verbal and non-verbal cues transmit to us just how polite, direct, or formal the communication is and what the intent is (e.g., to be kind, loving, attentive, or devious, provocative, or hostile). The input could be

---

[1] As indicated in the introductory chapter, we will generally be characterizing pragmatic ability in terms of situational competence, rather than native or non-nativeness.

through language (e.g., through words, phrases, or extended discourse), though gestures, or through silence.

2   As **readers**, we need to comprehend written messages, identifying the rhetorical structure of the message and catching sometimes subtle indications of tone or attitude in the communication (e.g., anything from a humorous, sincere, sympathetic, or collaborative tone to one that is teasing, sarcastic, angry, threatening, patronizing, or sexist).

3   As **speakers**, we need to know how to say what we want to say with the proper politeness, directness, and formality (e.g., in the role of boss, telling employees that they are being laid off; or in the role of teacher, telling students that their work is unacceptable). We also need to know what not to say at all and what to communicate non-verbally. What do we as speakers need to do in order for our output to be *comprehensible* pragmatically to those interacting with us, and what do we need to know about the potential consequences of what we say and how we say it? What do we need to know as learners in order to accommodate to the local speech community's norms for pragmatic performance, such as in, say, making an oral request? There are various factors that can stand in the way of pragmatically appropriate performance (see Chapter 5 on pragmatic divergence).

4   As **writers**, we need to know how to write our message intelligibly, again paying attention to level of politeness, directness, and formality, as well as considering issues of rhetorical structure (e.g., in the role of concerned tenant, composing a message to post in an apartment building warning neighbors not to exit the parking lot too fast; or in the role of employee, requesting a promotion and a raise, or a paid vacation from the boss).

It is worth mentioning at this juncture that pragmatics has conventionally focused on the spoken medium and has paid little attention to writing, so that we know little about how learners acquire the ability to be functionally appropriate in their written language.[2] Though some efforts have been made in the research literature to focus on the pragmatics of written language,[3] this is still more the exception than the rule. Given that issues relating to pragmatics are relevant to written language, we will make an effort in this book to include this focus. There are, of course, various hybrid genres of

---

[2] Ellis (1994: 187–8).
[3] See, for example, Cohen and Tarone (1994).

written language, such as e-mail messages, which contain elements of both oral and written language.

Having pragmatic ability means being able to go beyond the literal meaning of what is said or written, in order to interpret the intended meanings, assumptions, purposes or goals, and the kinds of actions that are being performed.[4] The interpretation of pragmatic meaning can sometimes pose a challenge – even to natives of the language – since speakers do not always communicate directly what they mean and listeners do not always interpret the speakers' meaning as it was intended. So, the speakers and the listeners need to collaborate to assure that genuine communication takes place. In fact, pragmatics deals with meaning that the speaker needs to *co-construct* and negotiate along with the listener within a given cultural context and given the social constraints.[5] Inevitably, learners will relate the pragmatic ability that they have in their first language (L1), the language other than their first one which is currently their dominant one, or perhaps some other language (if they are multilinguals) to the pragmatics of the target language community. In part, it entails drawing on the latent knowledge that they already possess to help sort out the pragmatics of the L2, and in part, it calls for the acquisition of new knowledge.

Why are messages not communicated directly? One reason is that members of the given speech community may find it inappropriate and even rude to come right out and ask point blank, "Why haven't you gotten married yet?" In that speech community, the shared knowledge may be that it is necessary to be indirect and to make innuendos, and then see if the other person wishes to comment on his or her personal situation. In another language community, it may be perfectly acceptable to ask this question. The direct question was the approach that the Aymara Indians used with co-author Cohen when he was a Peace Corps Volunteer in rural community development on the high plains of Bolivia in the mid-1960s.

Another reason why members of a given speech community do not always communicate messages directly is that it might sometimes be considered more appropriate in that community to hint about the matter rather than to spell it out. For example, there may be rules about "being on time" which are largely left unsaid. So if someone is too early or too late, according to expectations, a hint is made to that effect (e.g., "Oh, you're here in time to help us finish preparing the hors d'oeuvres"), and it would be rude to spell it out. This leaves the listener or reader to intuit what is probably meant.

---

[4] Yule (1996: 3–4).
[5] LoCastro (2003); Thomas (1995).

While correctly interpreting the innuendo may even be difficult for highly competent speakers, it may be a far more daunting task for less competent learners – both to perceive the hint and to interpret the meaning of the message correctly. There are also instances where what someone says is not what they mean. So, for example, in American English, "We must get together" is usually not to be taken seriously, and a reply like "OK, let's make a firm date" would be met with surprise. It is often just a polite way to end an encounter in a friendly way.

The field of pragmatics is broad and encompasses matters of reference, presupposition, discourse structure, and conversational principles involving implicature and hedging.[6] This volume will focus primarily on speech acts, since they are have an important role to play in L2 communication, and are teachable and learnable. In addition, they are among the most rigorously researched of the areas in pragmatics, which was what motivated us to demonstrate how to draw on this empirical resource in the teaching of L2 pragmatics.

Speech acts

Within the realm of pragmatic ability, the ways in which people carry out specific social functions in speaking such as apologizing, complaining, making requests, refusing things/invitations, complimenting, or thanking have been referred to as *speech acts*. Speech acts have a basic meaning as conceived by the speaker ("Do you have a watch?" = do you own a watch?) and an **intended** or *illocutionary* meaning (e.g., "Can you tell me what time it is?"), as well as the **actual** illocutionary force on the listener, also referred to as the *uptake* (i.e., a request to know the time, and hence, a reply like "It's 10:30 AM right now."). In this instance, a young child or a facetious adult might respond to "Do you have a watch?" with "Yes, I do." If so, the uptake would not work for the speaker, who might then need to ask, "What is the time, then?" While sometimes speech acts are accomplished by a single word like "thanks," at other times they involve complex and indirect speech over a series of conversational turns.

Many of these speech acts tend to follow regular and predictable patterns for members of the given community. In the case of "greetings," for example, let us say that in a US context you are greeted in English by an associate at work with something on the order of "How're ya' doing?" You are expected to say, "Fine, thanks," "OK, thanks," or something of that sort,

---

[6] Mey (2001).

FIGURE 1.1 Asking for the time

rather than delving into a litany of woes, given that you have a bad knee and will be having surgery in a few weeks, and that one of your kids just lost her job. To actually go into detail about how you are doing would be unexpected, to say the least. In fact, the person who asked how you were probably kept on walking and had no intention of engaging you in genuine conversation. Members of a given speech community know how to perform such greetings and how to interpret them as well.

For learners, the presumably easy task of performing greetings and leave-takings may be difficult. In fact, learners may simply translate what they would say in their native language in such a situation. It is easier than trying to determine how best to say it in a way that conforms with patterns for the target language and culture, given the respective ages, social status, and roles of the speaker and listener in that situation. So, the learner's version of leave-taking from a professor may come out far too informal for that culture. With regard to the interpretation of pragmatics – which may pose a real challenge to learners of a language – a learner may not perceive that leave-taking is simply ritualistic, and may inappropriately respond to "Let's get together sometime" with a challenge, "So, when will we do it?" which may in the given instance come across as a bit pushy and even rude.

Speech act sets

The performance of common speech acts usually involves choosing from a set of possible strategies, some of which may involve the use of what could be viewed as other distinct speech acts, and for this reason the term *speech act set* has been introduced.[7] For example, in complaining, you could include a threat, which constitutes a speech act distinct from complaining (e.g., "OK, then. If you won't turn your music down, I'll call the police!"), or in apologizing, you could also add criticism (e.g., "Sorry I bumped into you, lady, but look where you're standing!").

The realization of a given speech act in a given context, then, involves the use of a minimum of one strategy from the speech act set to the selection of numerous strategies from that set. In the case of the apology, for example, the strategy of expressing an apology could be performed just through the strategy of expressing an apology ("I'm sorry," "excuse me," or "I apologize") or offering repair ("Here, let me pick these up.") or could involve a combination of them, such as expressing apology, acknowledging responsibility, and offering repair. In fact, there is a set of at least five *speech act strategies* or *semantic formulas* which seem to apply to apologizing in a variety of different languages:[8]

1 *Expression of an apology*: A word, expression, or sentence containing a verb such as "sorry," "excuse," "forgive," or "apologize." In American English, "I apologize . . ." is found more in writing than it is in oral language. An expression of an apology can be intensified – in American English, usually by adding intensifiers such as "really," "terribly," "awfully," "so," "very," or some combination of them – for example, "I'm really very sorry."

2 *Acknowledgment of responsibility* – degree of recognition of fault. This strategy includes a continuum: accepting the blame: "It's my fault"; expressing self-deficiency: "I was confused/I didn't see/You are right";

---

[7] Olshtain and Cohen (1983).
[8] Cohen and Olshtain (1981); Olshtain and Cohen (1989). *Semantic formulas/speech act strategies* alone or combined with other strategies constitute the speech act. Since semantic formulas are often not formulaic (Bardovi-Harlig, 2006: 4), we will refer to these strategies as *speech act strategies*.

lack of intent: "I didn't mean to"; implicit expression of responsibility: "I was sure I had given you the right directions"; not accepting the blame/denying responsibility: "It wasn't my fault"; or even blaming of the listener: "It's your own fault."

3 *Explanation or account* – a description of the situation which led to the offense, serving as an indirect way of apologizing. This explanation is intended to set things right. At times it is interpreted as an excuse.

4 *Offer of repair*: the apologizer makes a bid to carry out an action or provide payment for some kind of damage which resulted from his/her infraction (e.g., "Let me pick those up for you" "I'll be there in half an hour"). This strategy is situation-specific and is only appropriate when actual damage has occurred.

5 *Promise of non-recurrence*: the apologizer commits him/herself to not having the offense happen again (e.g., "I'll never forget our anniversary again."). This strategy is situation-specific and less frequent than the other strategies.

At least one of these strategies needs to be selected for use in the perform-ance of a speech act in a given speech community for the speech act to take place. Whether strategy 3, "explanation or account," is sufficient in a given context depends on the speech community. In some cultures this may be a more acceptable way of apologizing than in others. In cultures where public transportation is unreliable (such as in Israel), arriving late to a university course session and telling the professor that the bus was late (without an expression of apology as in #1) might be perfectly acceptable. Some might argue more universally that it is unacceptable to use an explanation (= excuse) as the sole strategy for apologizing, even in a culture such as that of Israel. While we might argue that strategy 1, expression of an apology (e.g., through "I'm really sorry"), is the most core member of the speech act set, we could also envision situations in which saying it would be unnecessary. Rather, the student would use strategy 2, acknowledging responsibility ("I really should have allowed more time for the bus ride") and strategy 4, offering repair ("I'll get notes on what I missed from a classmate").

Looking closely at speech acts, we see that there are some strategies which are relatively unique to that particular speech act set, such as the offer of repair in an apology. In addition, there are strategies that can be applied to various speech acts, such as an opener consisting of a greeting like "Hi" serving as an attention getter. This opener might be found in requests, complaints, and numerous other speech act sets. We will be using the term "speech act" to refer to what is actually a **speech act set** or a potential component of the set.

Speech acts across languages

What makes the study of speech acts across languages all the more interesting is that while these core strategies tend to exist in most languages, knowing whether they are applied in the given language context, and if so, determining when, how, and why they say what they say can be challenging. The tendency to use a particular configuration of these strategies in a given situation depends on the language and culture. The following is an example of one such situation:

> You completely forget a crucial meeting at the office with your boss to go over the final draft of an important document. Two hours later you realize what you have done, and you call him to apologize.

In such a situation, an Israeli Hebrew speaker may select *expression of apology* and *explanation* as the strategies from the speech acts set of apologizing. For example:

> אני מצטער בקשר לפגישה, אבל הייתי צריך לקחת את הבן
> רופא, ו... [1]
>
> *Ani mitsta-er bekesher lap'gisha, aval haiti tsarix lakaxat et haben sheli larofe, ve. . . .* "Sorry about not making the meeting but I had to take my kid to the doctor and . . ."

Speakers from this cultural background have actually been found to avoid the strategy of *repair*, because in the Israeli culture, the boss determines the next step. For the speaker to suggest what comes next would be equivalent to committing a second infraction aside from missing the meeting.[9]

The Israeli situation is in stark contrast to the typical formal Japanese situation where offering the boss an unsolicited explanation for being late would be considered inappropriate. Unlike the Israeli situation, in Japan the employee would most likely be expected to offer an expression of apology repeatedly and profusely, and not to give a detailed explanation unless the boss calls for it.[10] For example, a Japanese worker might say:

---

[9] Cohen and Olshtain (1981).
[10] Kondo (1997); Kumagai (1993); Nonaka (2000).

えー、あの、先程欠席してしまいましたミーティングの件ですが、誠に申し訳ありませんでした。全く私の不注意で、本当に申し訳ありません。 *Ee, ano, sakihodo kessekishite shimaimashita miitinguno kendesuga, makotoni moushiwake arimasen deshita. Mattaku watakushino fuchuuide hontouni moushiwake arimasen.* "Uhm . . . about the missed meeting earlier today, I am *really* sorry. It was completely due to my carelessness. I really have no excuse."

The speaker is likely to intentionally avoid providing an explanation, as that may sound as if s/he were providing an excuse and requesting the boss's forgiveness which is undeserved.

Within other speech communities, the apology might play itself out with an overlapping but different set of strategies specific to the given context. It may be imperative for the apologizer to offer repair so as to appear dutifully apologetic. In the US context, for example, the speaker may say something like, "Oh, no! I guess I really had my head screwed on backward! Please let me make it up to you. I can rush those papers to you within the hour, or how about meeting on it first thing tomorrow?"

But what if an Israeli and a Japanese speaker without much cross-cultural experience were interacting in English in a business context in, say, London? Let us also assume that they have made a dinner meeting to negotiate a business matter. If the two speakers were to behave consistent with stereotypic expectations, then the Israeli might arrive 30 minutes late and the Japanese counterpart would be there right on time or even a few minutes early. So, presumably the Japanese businessman might expect an apology from the Israeli. Let us imagine that the Israeli makes an excuse about the bus being late, since that excuse works in Israeli society. An empirical question would be whether the Japanese business associate would be understanding and not take offense. Beyond the basic speech acts specific strategies, there may or may not be modifications according to the following:

1 **The relative social status of the speakers (writer) and listener (reader):** Is the listener of higher status? If so, the speaker may need to show deference by adding extra markers of politeness (such as the use of "Sir" or "Ma'am" in English).

2 **The level of social distance and psychological distance:** How distant or close are the speaker/writer and listener/reader socially or feel to each

other? Is it someone they know well or even intimately or is it someone they have only slight acquaintance with or none at all?

3   **The intensity or severity of the act**: How serious or important is the issue?[11]

The following is a relatively severe offense and the recipient of the apology is a friend:

> In a cafeteria, you accidentally bump into a person who is holding a cup of hot coffee. A little coffee spills on the person's clothes, and the person suffers a slight burn.

It would be necessary to know whether the response within the given speech community varies according to how well the person is known by the person committing the infraction. It would also be necessary to determine how severity of infractions is measured in a given culture (e.g., what spilling coffee on someone else's clothing actually means). Finally, the speaker needs to know the language conventions for performing the apology in deference to the relative social status of the speaker and listener, their familiarity with each other, and the perceived severity of the incident. The point is that we cannot assume that the incident will be interpreted in the same way across languages and cultures. In fact, the spill itself may be a cause for alarm in one culture and a cause for mirth in another, producing different verbal and non-verbal responses. This shows how the setting itself, the behavioral environment, the choice of speech acts and the language used, and the background knowledge of those in the situation all contribute to the pragmatics associated with the event.

Social, cultural, and pragmatic norms

Accurate interpretation of the pragmatics behind human behavior relies on both social and cultural norms. *Social norms* can be viewed as explicit or implicit statements or rules for when something should or could be said and the manner in which it would be expected to be said. These norms influence societal behavior, and are usually based on some degree of group consensus. Attempting to define *cultural norms* is not easy because traditions, customs,

---

[11] Brown and Levinson (1987).

beliefs, values, and thought patterns all contribute to such norms.[12] Culture has, in fact, been defined as "a fuzzy set of attitudes, beliefs, behavioural conventions, and basic assumptions and values that are shared by a group of people, and that influence each member's behaviour and each member's interpretation of the 'meaning' of other people's behaviour."[13]

Since even native speakers vary among themselves as to how they perform pragmatic routines in a given discourse situation, there is not necessarily language behavior which would be deemed absolutely "right" or "wrong" in a given case. Rather, the norms of the community tend to make certain pragmatic behavior more or less preferred or appropriate in a given context by speakers in that community.[14] So *pragmatic norms* refer to a range of tendencies or conventions for pragmatic language use that are not absolute or fixed but are typical or generally preferred in the L2 community.

Objective vs subjective culture and explanatory pragmatics

A distinction has been made between *objective culture* and *subjective culture*.[15] Objective culture refers to the institutional aspects of culture, such as political and economic systems, and to its products such as art, music, and cuisine. Subjective culture refers to the learned and shared patterns of beliefs, behaviors and values of groups of interacting people, or in other words, the philosophical, psychological, and moral features that define a group of people. An explanatory approach to pragmatics builds on the notions of subjective culture. In this approach, pragmatic use of language is characterized in terms of a range of pragmatic norms or tendencies of L2 communities rather than absolute prescriptive rules.[16]

An explanatory approach to pragmatics has as its goal to alert learners as to why L2 speakers commonly use the language as they do, why there are differences in how meaning is conveyed in the L2, and how underlying cultural values, beliefs, and assumptions influence L2 speakers' pragmatic behavior. If learners just study the language material without analysis of its cultural meaning, they may not notice the underlying material that can shape the behaviors, roles and ethics of participants in the culture.[17]

[12] Prosser (1978).
[13] Spencer-Oatey (2000: 4).
[14] Ishihara (2006).
[15] Berger and Luckmann (1967).
[16] Meier (1999, 2003); Richards and Schmidt (1983).
[17] Meier (1999, 2003).

Informed explanations by teachers can help to provide an "insider's" perspective.

However, at least three caveats are in order with regard to this explanatory approach to pragmatics.[18] First, instruction must clearly differentiate a stereotypical view of cultures from generalizations or general tendencies.[19] In addition, it is beneficial for teachers to characterize culture as being variable, diverse, and changing over time, not as a monolithic, homogeneous, or static entity.[20] Secondly, the degree to which learners actually shift in their interpretation of social and cultural norms in the L2 is an empirical question and one that could be explored as a classroom-based research project. Lastly, it is up to the learners themselves as to whether they will choose to be pragmatically appropriate. Even if they gain an understanding of the social and cultural norms, they could still resist accommodating to L2 norms in their own pragmatic performance.[21]

Learning how to be pragmatically appropriate in the L2 culture

Since the focus of pragmatics in the real world involves the use of language in a host of social and cultural contexts, learners of a language invariably have a lot to learn if they do choose to avoid cross-cultural misunderstandings. They need to be aware of social norms for when speech acts are likely to be performed (e.g., knowing if and when to ask the boss about a raise or moving to another office), cultural reasoning as to why they are performed that way, and knowledge about the consequences of utterances in that particular culture. In other words, they can benefit from knowing something about the norms of behavior for realizing the given speech act in a given context, taking into account factors such as: (1) the culture involved, (2) the relative age and gender of the speaker and listener(s), (3) their social class and occupations, and (4) their social status and roles in the interaction.[22] So, for example, is it appropriate to ask the other person his/her age (since in some cultures, advanced age brings with it added status) or how much s/he makes a month (since in some cultures, a higher salary brings with it higher social status)? Is it appropriate by way of "small talk" to ask whether the

---

[18] Ishihara (2006).
[19] See Paige *et al.* (2006: 57–61) for a practical treatment of this distinction.
[20] McKay (2002).
[21] Ishihara (2006).
[22] Thomas (1983, 1995).

listener is married? And what about asking how much the listener paid for the new car? What might be innocuous questions in one culture may be insulting, intrusive, or otherwise offensive in another culture.

Along with having social and cultural knowledge about the speech community, it is important to know the language forms to use in a host of sometimes delicate cross-cultural situations, depending on who is being spoken to, the relative positions of authority of the conversational partners, and the context of the communication. For example, assuming that it is acceptable in the given culture to ask how much someone paid for a new car, it would still be necessary to know what acceptable language for requesting that information would be. You would want to know, for instance, whether you could just come out and ask directly, "How much did you get that new car for, George?" or whether you would need to be more indirect, "Boy, that car must have set you back a pretty penny!"

In addition, the way that you offer *back-channeling* (i.e., giving feedback as a listener) to demonstrate that you are in fact engaged in the conversation may vary dramatically depending on your role in the interaction. So while it may be less pronounced in English than in other languages, using "yeah" as a way of saying you are listening can be too informal when interacting with an individual of significantly higher status (e.g., the CEO of a company or a leading national politician). Rather than responding to "This report has major implications for policy" with "Yeah," it may be more appropriate to respond with "Yes, I understand fully." So, making the appropriate language choices in performing a given speech act calls for selecting those language forms that best express the intent of the speech act in that context. This involves taking into account the norms of behavior relevant to the given situation in the given speech community.[23]

Here is a final example of somewhat inappropriate language use that could possibly lead to pragmatic failure. Cohen received the following e-mail message from a Japanese colleague who was acknowledging receipt of feedback from an anonymous reviewer on a chapter for a volume that Cohen was co-editing:

> I certainly received the feedback. Thanks a lot.

---

[23] Morgan and Cain (2000: 5–7).

His colleague's terse response made it sound as if he had received much more feedback than he had bargained for and that he was even perhaps a bit annoyed. It is all because of the word "certainly." His intention was to simply let Cohen know that he had received the reviewer's feedback and appreciated it. He was using "certainly" as an intensifier. The translation equivalent of "certainly" in Japanese, *tashikani*, works as an intensifier in formal contexts. The implication is that since he received it for sure, if there is any glitch afterwards, it is his fault and not Cohen's. Given the use of "certainly" in the first sentence, the demonstration of gratitude "Thanks a lot" could be construed as facetious. Although initially taken aback by the message, Cohen ultimately interpreted the message as intended to acknowledge receipt of the chapter and as a vehicle for sending his thanks for the feedback he received, so in this case pragmatic failure was averted.

Discussion

This chapter started by defining *pragmatic ability* in terms of listeners, speakers, readers, and writers of a language. We pointed out that having pragmatic ability means being able to go beyond the literal meaning of what is said or written, in order to interpret the intended meanings, assumptions, purposes or goals, and the kinds of actions that are being performed. We noted reasons why speakers of a language in a given speech community may purposely be indirect in their communication and in their behavior in general, and that consequently learners may need to find out how to be effective pragmatically in those given situations. We then considered what speech acts consist of, using the example of the apology speech act set and the strategies that tend to characterize it – namely, expression of an apology, acknowledgment of responsibility, explanation or account, offer of repair, and promise of non-recurrence.

The chapter then looked at social, cultural, and pragmatic norms, paying particular attention to the distinction between objective and subjective culture, and the notion of explanatory pragmatics. It was noted that the explanatory approach to pragmatics informs learners as to why L2 speakers commonly use the language as they do, why there are differences in how meaning is conveyed in the L2, and how underlying beliefs and values with regard to culture influence L2 speakers' pragmatic behavior.

The chapter ended by looking at what it takes to learn how to perform L2 pragmatics. It was noted that since pragmatics in the real world involves the use of language in a host of social and cultural contexts, learners have a lot to learn if they wish to avoid cross-cultural misunderstandings. They need to be aware of social norms for when something should or could be said and the manner in which it would be expected to be said (e.g., knowing if and when to ask the boss about a raise or about a need to move to another office) and cultural reasoning as to why they are performed that way.

The activity below is intended to provide users of this guide with an opportunity to observe their ability to make pragmatically appropriate judgments, according to the contextual factors such as status, level of acquaintance, and the stakes in the situation. You will be asked to appraise the level of formality, directness, and politeness of a scripted complaint interaction and to see how your own behavior might shift in an apology situation with an acquaintance as opposed to a close friend.

Activity 1.1 Enhancing awareness of pragmatic behavior

Objectives

1   You will be able to identify what constitutes appropriate pragmatic behavior, according to the contextual factors such as status, level of acquaintance, and the stakes in the situation.

2   You will be able to appraise the level of formality, directness, and politeness of a scripted complaint interaction and to identify that your own behavior might shift in an apology situation with a working associate as opposed to a close friend.

Suggested time: 45 minutes.

Materials: Task sheet: "Pragmatic meaning in role-play situations" (see below).

Directions

Part I

1   Form groups of three in which one person reads the part of the chair, Francine, one the part of the employee, Charlie, and the third serves as observer. The two role-players are to focus on doing the best job that they can to portray their given characters (and to pay attention to how consistent the roles that they play are with their own personality). The observer is to pay attention to the ways that the boss and the employee convey pragmatic meaning, both verbally (including tone of voice) and non-verbally.

2   After the dialogue has been role-played, the observer is to provide an evaluation of the interaction according to the level of formality of the speaker and listener (highly formal, formal, more informal, very informal), their directness (totally

blunt, somewhat blunt, indirect, very indirect), and the level of politeness (very polite, polite, rude, very rude). The observer is also to comment on the tone or attitude projected by each of the two participants in the dialogue (e.g., angry, pugnacious, conciliatory, etc.).

3   Next the two role-players are invited to analyze the speech acts that they performed in this role-play (e.g., complaint, request, denial, threat, etc.) and to consider how effective they think each of these speech acts was (i.e., in terms of the uptake from it).

4   The following group activities are also suggested:

- Determine if there were any instances of pragmatic failure in the interaction (i.e., a participant not succeeding in having the intended uptake from what they say).

- Speculate how this interaction might have unfolded if the participants had been close friends, age mates, and both having the same gender. Do the interaction several more times, changing the dialogue accordingly (possibly with the observer assuming one of the roles).

- Consider how this interaction might be different if it were taking place between the same people but over beers after hours, at a local pub.

- Consider the situation if the young employee were the child of a long-time friend? Again, modify the interaction accordingly (possibly with the observer assuming one of the roles).

- Speculate as to how this situation might unfold if it were taking place in another language and cultural context, for example, where standards for what is considered "teasing" are different, and where females may not be taken as seriously as males.

5   The various groups are to share their insights from this task with the whole group.

Part II

1   Participants are to form a new group of three, again with two doing the role-plays and a third participant serving as an observer, watching the role-plays and making comments.

2   The first time through this role-play, Harry is an intimate friend of yours. You see each other almost every weekend.

3   The second time through this role-play, Harry is a working associate of yours – a colleague that you need to interact with regularly – but not a close friend.

4   While two members of the group are performing the role-play, the observer pays attention to the level of familiarity between the role-players and the severity of the infraction (e.g., Harry is a close friend and a full apology is more crucial to maintaining the friendship vs Harry is a colleague and the apology is for the sake of maintaining a working relationship). The observer also pays attention to the conventions used (i.e., the level of familiarity, formality, and seriousness), indicated by the way the role-play is handled.

5   As in the first task, the groups then are to share their insights from the second task with the whole group.

Discussion/wrap up

Look at ways that this exercise has helped to provide a clearer understanding of pragmatic ability, speech acts, and social and cultural norms of behavior. It may also be of value to go back through the chapter in order to identify the concepts in this chapter that are important to convey to learners and how a teacher might do that.

Task sheet: Pragmatic meaning in role-play situations

Part I Dialogue between a boss and a young employee

Assume that the following conversation takes place between a department chair and a member of staff. The chair, Francine, has been at the head of the language instruction unit for 20 years and the employee has been teaching for just two years. The chair has had some doubts about this instructor for some time, and this encounter is possibly the "straw that breaks the camel's back." Below are segments of this imagined dialogue between the chair and the staff member.

Francine (F): Hi, Charlie. Come on in and have a seat.

Charlie (C): Thanks.

F: You probably know why I've called you in here today. It is because I received complaints about your teaching. Some women in your class are saying that you are making fun of them. Do you have anything to say for yourself?

C: Can you tell me who said that?

F: No. I'd rather not mention any names.

C: Oh, I see. Well, I'm not aware that I've teased anyone. I use humor in class, but it certainly isn't at anyone's expense, and especially not aimed at women. I just want the students to have a good time in class.

F: Look, Charlie. I've been getting reports on your teaching style from more than one student and not just recently. If you are teasing anybody, it's gotta stop now. We can't have this kind of thing going on here because . . .

C: Listen, Francine. I resent your just accepting whatever the students said to you. How do you know they were telling the truth? It's unfair to me to make assumptions when you don't know . . .

F: Charles. You're still relatively new here and in my opinion you have a lot to learn. I have watched how you make quips at faculty meetings. You think you're being funny, but sometimes people get offended. You really need to be more careful about what you say if you want to continue to work here and . . .

C: Well, maybe I should look for another job then – one where I am more appreciated just the way I am.

Part II Varying the pragmatics in an apology situation

Assume that in a luncheon with colleagues, you said something negative behind the back of another colleague, Harry – namely, that he lacked tact. Unfortunately, it got back to him. Over a cup of coffee, he confronts you with what he heard you had said:

Harry: Hey, I just was talking with Bethany, and she said you were saying things about me behind my back. I guess I want to hear it directly from you. . . .

You:

CHAPTER 2

Teachers' pragmatics: knowledge, beliefs, and practice

Noriko Ishihara

Introduction

Now that we have discussed the basics – what pragmatics is, how it is intertwined with culture, and why it is important to teach it in the L2 classroom – we would like to shift the focus to what the teacher brings to the learning and teaching of pragmatics. Therefore, this particular chapter may be of interest to teacher educators, as well as to teachers and prospective teachers. We know that teachers' backgrounds, knowledge, experiences, and beliefs have an impact on what and how they teach. As stated earlier, a primary intention of this book is to help narrow the gap between what is currently known about how language is pragmatically used and how that information is (or is not) taught in the classroom. In doing so, it is quite clear that the teacher is the main agent in creating this bridge. In our view, this bridging work can be achieved in part by making available to teachers research-based information about how language is used pragmatically, as well as by demonstrating effective approaches to the teaching of pragmatics (a theme we will come to in upcoming chapters). A recent nationwide survey has found that the treatment of pragmatics in teacher development courses in the US centers on theoretical models (e.g., those relating to linguistic politeness and to speech acts) rather than on practical applications (e.g., how to teach L2 pragmatics).[1] It may be assumed that if given an appropriate theoretical framework, language teachers can devise

---

[1] Vasquez and Sharpless (2009).

instructional strategies on their own. However, the knowledge and skills necessary to do an effective job of teaching L2 pragmatics[2] may not come automatically to all language teachers, and specific preparation focused on instructional pragmatics would probably benefit them in their professional development.

It is also our view that only teacher readers themselves can decide how the information provided in this book would actually be used in their respective classrooms in their own institutional contexts. It is for this reason that in this chapter we first encourage readers – if they are language teachers – to reflect critically, for example, on their language learning and teaching experiences, what they have learned from their initial teacher preparation and further professional development, and what they believe are effective instructional strategies in general and for the teaching of pragmatics in particular. Readers will also be invited to engage in *exploratory practice*,[3] in which they incorporate systematic reflection into their day-to-day instructional routine. These reflective tools have been known to empower teachers as they gain explicit knowledge of their own teaching that otherwise remains tacit and inaccessible to the teachers themselves. Teachers can also be empowered by becoming better able to make sense of their beliefs and practice, and better able to make decisions about whether or how to change their practice when necessary. Below we begin by briefly discussing the nature and components of teachers' knowledge, beliefs, and practice. Although this type of information is often made available to teacher educators rather than teachers themselves, this awareness can also help teachers develop an analytic eye as to their own nature and process of professional development.

Teacher knowledge, beliefs, and practice

As a background to the teacher-led reflection proposed at the end of the chapter, this section discusses what constitutes teacher knowledge especially with regard to the teaching of pragmatics, areas in which these knowledge and beliefs are generated, potential sources of these knowledge and beliefs, and their relation to what teachers do in the classroom.

---

[2] Qualifications of effective teachers of pragmatics would include: a) an awareness of diverse pragmatic norms in a speech community, b) the ability to provide metapragmatic information about target language pragmatic norms, c) the ability to develop and assess L2 learners' pragmatic competence (Bardovi-Harlig [1992]; Meier [2003]), and d) a sensitivity to learners' subjectivity and cultural being.

[3] Allwright (2001, 2003).

Teacher knowledge

Through teacher education, classroom practice, and experiences inside and outside of the classroom, teacher's knowledge is, for example, acquired, shaped, refined, modified, reinforced, transformed, used, and revised. So in order for a language teacher to teach effectively, what exactly do they need to know? The components of language teacher knowledge have been argued to include the following:

- subject-matter knowledge (e.g., how English grammar works);

- pedagogical knowledge (e.g., how to teach and assess);

- pedagogical-content knowledge (e.g., how to teach writing);

- knowledge of learners and their characteristics (e.g., how they tend to respond to group and individual tasks);

- knowledge of educational contexts (e.g., whether the L2 is a **second** or **foreign** language at the elementary, secondary, or post-secondary level); and

- knowledge of the curriculum and educational ends (e.g., whether/how the content is integrated into language learning).[4]

So how would these categories be applied to the teaching of L2 pragmatics in particular? It is important to identify what specifically teachers of pragmatics need to know to help learners understand others' intentions and express themselves as intended in the given sociocultural context. The following chart shows a preliminary attempt to answer this question:

Selected components of teacher knowledge for teaching L2 in general	Components of teacher knowledge specifically required for teaching of L2 pragmatics*
Subject-matter knowledge	Knowledge of pragmatic variation.
	Knowledge of a range of pragmatic norms in the target language.
	Knowledge of meta-pragmatic information (e.g., how to discuss pragmatics).
Pedagogical-content knowledge	Knowledge of how to teach L2 pragmatics.
	Knowledge of how to assess L2 pragmatic ability.

[4] Adapted from Borg (2003); Freeman (2002); Freeman and Johnson (1998); Johnston and Goettsch (2000); Shulman (1987).

Selected components of teacher knowledge for teaching L2 in general	Components of teacher knowledge specifically required for teaching of L2 pragmatics*
Knowledge of the learners and local, curricular, and educational contexts	Knowledge of learners' identities, cultures, proficiency, and other characteristics.
	Knowledge of the pragmatics-focused curriculum.
	Knowledge of the role of L2 pragmatics in the educational contexts.

*A preliminary attempt adapted from Bardovi-Harlig (1992); Ishihara (2007a); Kasper (1997); Meier (2003).

When teachers intend to teach pragmatics, naturally they need to know what it is (subject-matter knowledge). This would include knowing that pragmatic norms vary depending on, for example, the regional, generational, gender and ethnic backgrounds of the speakers, as well as various contextual factors[5] (knowledge of pragmatic variation), knowing how the L2 is typically used (knowledge of the range of L2 pragmatic norms to be taught), and knowing how to explain pragmatics in the way learners can relate to (knowledge of meta-pragmatic information). In order to actually teach L2 pragmatics in the classroom, teachers would need to know instructional and evaluative strategies specifically as they relate to pragmatics (pedagogical-content knowledge). It would be a teachers' immediate concern, for instance, to know how to communicate to their students the importance of having pragmatic ability in the L2, how to direct learners' attention to features of sociocultural context, and how to elicit and assess learners' pragmatic use of language. In addition, effective and culturally sensitive teachers of pragmatics would be well aware of such things as the characteristics of the learners (e.g., their cultural identities and levels of proficiency), the scope and educational objectives of the curriculum, and the limits of the institutional contexts in which they are teaching pragmatics (e.g., the flexibility of the curriculum and the time allowed for pragmatics instruction). Teacher education in the area of L2 pragmatics has only started to be researched, and this list of components of teacher knowledge for teaching L2 pragmatics is a preliminary effort intended to open up more discussion on this topic.

---

[5] These variations are termed *macro-social variation* and *intra-lingual/micro-social variation* (Barron 2003, 2005; Schneider and Barron 2008).

Teacher knowledge and beliefs[6]

Teachers usually have certain ideas that they know or believe to be true generally about learning and teaching. This following list shows specific areas of teachers' knowledge and beliefs and can stimulate teacher readers' reflection as they explore their own beliefs related to learning and teaching. Teachers' beliefs can be their implicit theories of, for example:

- learning in general;
- the subject matter (e.g., the nature and characteristics of the target language; and the nature of pragmatics in our case);
- the nature of knowledge (e.g., how knowledge is generated or acquired);
- (language) learning;
- (language) teaching;
- learners and their characteristics;
- learning to teach;
- self (e.g., self-identity and self-esteem);
- teacher efficacy (e.g., teachers' perception of their own influence on student learning);
- the teacher's role;
- the curriculum; and
- teaching contexts.[7]

Past research has found that the teacher beliefs that were formed early tend to self-perpetuate and may be difficult to change, and that teacher beliefs tend to be largely influenced by experience from their own learning, professional training, and previous teaching experiences.[8] Teacher beliefs are also likely to affect teachers' perceptions, thinking processes, and decision-making in the classroom. In the next section, we briefly touch on the potential link between teacher beliefs and practice.

---

[6] Because teacher knowledge and beliefs are inextricably intertwined, some researchers in teacher education see it as rather unproductive to attempt to draw a clear line between the two (e.g., Borg 2006; Meijer et al. 1999). We share this approach and discuss teacher cognition more broadly.

[7] Adapted from Calderhead (1996); Pajares (1992); Richards and Lockhart (1996).

[8] Pajares (1992).

Teacher beliefs and practice

In many cases teachers draw on their knowledge base in ways that influence or determine their instructional, evaluative, and curricular decisions.[9] For example, how teachers view the nature of language or that of learning may translate into how they believe language can best be learned. If a teacher believes that there is a "correct" way to use language that everyone should follow, she may rely only on a standard variety (and teach an expression, for instance, *Do you want to come with me?*) and focus on accurate production of it by her students, rather than exposing them to local pragmatic variation (such as an often-heard Midwestern variety, *Do you wanna come with?*). What another teacher believes about how children and adults learn in general can also affect the choice of his instructional strategies for young learners and college students (e.g., using smiley face icons or narrative comments for giving feedback). If still another language teacher believes that students learn language through repetition and memorization, she may select simple drills of a request phrase, "Can you . . . ?" as her preferred activity for lower-level learners to learn to make a request.

Teacher beliefs reflect their personal, cultural, educational, and political values and are known to influence and be influenced by a range of experiences in and outside of the classroom. Teachers' investigation of these sources of their own beliefs is likely to promote critical reflection of their experiences, which can trigger a deeper understanding of their teaching. For instance, in the above case of teaching the pragmatics of requests through role-memorization, what is the basis of this particular belief? Is it based on the instruction in some language textbook the teacher has been exposed to, or is it perhaps traceable to her past language learning experience? If another teacher believes that a feature film is a rich source of pragmatics instruction, is it because he has read a paper written by a pragmatics expert about its positive effects? Or is it because he learned a great deal of L2 pragmatics through film himself? Or if teacher learners read about the benefits of computer-assisted language learning in their teacher preparation course, does it tend to influence their method of teaching pragmatics?

Teacher beliefs and practices are not always consistent with each other because they are most likely to be affected in complex ways by a combination of (but not limited to) the following:

- experiences as a (language) learner in the classroom;
- experiences outside the classroom;

[9] Graves (2000); Wright (2005).

▪ established instructional practices in the educational community;

▪ theories, approaches, methods, or techniques informed through teacher preparation and other professional development opportunities;

▪ personality factors (e.g., being extroverted or introverted); and

▪ classroom teaching experiences.[10]

In other words, teaching practices are typically influenced by the teachers' knowledge and beliefs in an intricate manner; this relationship may not be a linear cause and effect, but a dialectic one.[11] Even if teachers believe in X, it does not simply follow that across the board they all do Y; what they do in the classroom may be different precisely because other factors (such as those noted above) may intervene. Classroom practice and teachers' knowledge construction are often constrained by the instructional context (e.g., the available time and the number of students). Teachers' knowledge, beliefs, and practice are also affected by the larger context of curriculum, community concerns, policies, and educational institutions.[12] Classroom practice may often be guided by teacher beliefs. At the same time, perhaps because teachers see various situational factors as beyond their control, a mismatch between a stated belief and actual practice has sometimes been found in studies investigating this link.[13]

Because teachers' knowledge and beliefs are linked to multiple layers of their experiences in complex ways, we first encourage readers – and teacher readers in particular – to better understand their own beliefs and practices by asking why they decide to teach what they teach and why they teach it the way that they do in the classroom. In order to make sense of their beliefs and practices, the above lists of potential sources of teacher beliefs and practices may be useful in prompting thought about various factors associated with teaching and learning.

To give an example, imagine that we have an EFL teacher who knows that speakers vary in the way that they greet people in different English-speaking countries, or even within the same culture, depending on who the conversational partner is and what the occasions are. Let us say, however, that she teaches her beginning-level students only one formal greeting routine that appears in the EFL textbook. Here, we see a gap between her knowledge and practice. Does she teach that way because it is an established

[10] Borg (2003); Calderhead (1996); Pajares (1992); Richards and Lockhart (1996).
[11] Thompson (1992).
[12] Richards and Lockhart (1996); Shulman and Shulman (2004).
[13] Borg (2006).

practice in the institution or in the textbook? Is it because when she learned another language, she was taught only one example of a greeting routine herself? Is it because she believes that mastering one routine is a sufficient start for beginning learners? Was it because she did not have much time to spend on the first chapter and did not wish to overload her learners with too many forms? Why does she teach the way she does? It is important to ask this question because if she does not teach according to what she believes and is actually a bit uncomfortable with how she currently teaches and why she teaches that way, she may consider changing her practices.

So if readers of this book are already knowledgeable about instructional pragmatics and see the value in enhancing L2 learners' pragmatic ability, then we would recommend that they attempt to align their practice as much as possible with their knowledge and beliefs ("teaching by principles"[14]), or if there are inconsistencies, that they try to identify the reasons why. If their exposure to instructional pragmatics has been somewhat limited until now, then hopefully reading and working through this book will help them become more familiar with current thinking in this field. Then if they feel pragmatics is important to teach in the L2 classroom, this opportunity in turn could contribute to the further development of their beliefs and to classroom practices that are consistent with these beliefs.[15]

Let us go back to the case of the English teacher above. If her way of teaching greetings is based on mere habits, then identifying the discrepancy between her knowledge, beliefs, and practice may offer an opportunity for this teacher to rethink and perhaps introduce the notion of pragmatic variation into classroom practice. This could be done, for example, by exposing learners to another, more informal greeting routine (see Activity 8.2 in Chapter 8 for an example). But if her decision to limit instruction to one standard greeting was based on a lack of instructional time, it helps to have that explicit realization; she may be more likely to incorporate variation when more instructional time is available. If this teacher were to participate in a professional development workshop on instructional pragmatics and came to believe that pragmatics can be incorporated in a manner that beginners can benefit, she might change her future curriculum to allow more time for pragmatics. Of course, if the teacher thought that while teaching pragmatic variation might be important, beginning learners benefit most from attaining accuracy in one greeting routine, her beliefs would in

[14] Brown, H. D. (2001).
[15] As indicated in the introduction to the volume, teachers can be seen as creators, rather than just recipients of knowledge. Teachers' pedagogical insights gained through real classroom experience are valuable and can inform further research and knowledge in the area.

fact be consistent with her classroom practice, and there would not be a need for action.

While knowledge and beliefs that teachers have with regard to their teaching may escape conscious attention or analysis, focused critical reflection can help make the knowledge and beliefs accessible to the teachers themselves.[16] This explicit awareness can be beneficial to teaching if there is a connection between what teachers know, believe, and do in the classroom. When there is this connection, then teachers are more likely to make conscious and informed decisions in their instructional contexts. On various occasions during the instruction, teachers also send consistent messages to their students about how language can be learned effectively.

Discussion

Teacher knowledge and beliefs are recognized as a dynamic system that is subject to change in relation to, for instance, teachers' professional development and experience. Because various events happen simultaneously at multiple levels in the classroom, much of teachers' knowledge of their own teaching may remain below the level of consciousness. Their beliefs may be an outgrowth of this implicit knowledge or may be traceable to experiences they have had in their own learning or teaching decades ago. Because teachers' experience may have occurred unconsciously or subconsciously or may be buried deeply in the past, their knowledge and beliefs may not be easily articulated.

For this reason in this chapter we have encouraged teacher readers to take a close look at their current knowledge and beliefs about L2 pragmatics, monitor how they may develop while reading this book, and examine how the knowledge and beliefs relate to their classroom practice by engaging in a reflective activity such as the one offered in this chapter (Activity 2.1). An explicit awareness of teachers' knowledge, beliefs, and practice makes what is tacit in their knowledge base more accessible to themselves and facilitates its analysis, modification, or refinement. We recommend that teachers routinely engage in reflective practice for further *reasoning*[17] of their own teaching. Because learning through reflection can be enriched, supported, and furthered by dialoguing with oneself or with colleagues,[18] teachers are encouraged to use written reflections and interactive discussions as much as possible. In working with this book, teacher readers can independently

[16] See Lazaraton and Ishihara (2005) for an example of the benefits of collaborative and focused teacher reflection.
[17] Teachers' reasoning refers to the complex ways in which they understand, explain, and respond to their experience in and outside of the classroom (Johnson 1999).
[18] Vygotsky (1978).

and collaboratively revisit the prompts in Activity 2.1 below (see Part II of Activity 2.1) to think through and discuss how they interpret the information and ideas presented, how they might help refine or alter their original knowledge, beliefs, and practice related to the teaching and learning of pragmatics. We will revisit this point occasionally in this book.

In the area of language teacher education, teachers' reflective practice has been promoted through various means, such as narrative inquiry,[19] action research,[20] and exploratory practice.[21] These reflective tools can empower teachers when knowledge of their own beliefs and practice becomes more accessible to them. With this explicit knowledge, teachers can be more powerful agents who know the reasons for their own instructional decisions and whether to change or how to change their practice when they deem it necessary. Drawing on this body of literature, Activity 2.1 will provide an opportunity for teacher readers to engage in exploratory practice for their selected inquiries more extensively.[22] Once again, teachers' knowledge, beliefs, and practice can shift dynamically throughout their career as their understanding of language learning and teaching develops. Teachers can explore these developments in their knowledge and beliefs, and contemplate on how these relate to the principles that govern their classroom practice, primarily in the area of pragmatics.

Activity 2.1 Reflecting the knowledge and beliefs about the learning and teaching of pragmatics

Objectives

1   You will have an enhanced awareness of how your beliefs relate to your past experiences in both learning and teaching pragmatics.

2   You will become more aware of specific issues in instructional pragmatics and critically reflect on your own beliefs and potential sources of such beliefs.

Suggested time: initially 40 minutes and more as needed.

---

[19] Teachers' inquiries into their knowledge and experience can be pursued through reflection using narratives and can promote professional development. See Barkhuizen (2008); Bell (2002); Johnson and Golombek (2002), for examples.

[20] For example, in action research, teachers engage in reflective practice and implement an action for change for enhanced instruction and professional development (Burns 1999; Haley 2005; Nunan 1992; Wallace 1998).

[21] For example, exploratory practice is action for understanding, which primarily aims at gaining a better understanding of the classroom practice in the teacher's local context (Allwright 2001, 2003; Johnson 2002; see Activity 2.2 for more information).

[22] Also see Chapter 7 for a story-based approach to the teaching of pragmatics.

Materials:

- Task sheet: "Reflective prompts";
- blank sheets of paper.

Directions

1   Use prompts meant to stimulate reflection, as listed in Part I of the Task sheet, "Reflective prompts." Work individually to choose one or more of the prompts and put down your ideas.

2   Break into small groups of approximately three according to the choice of the prompts. Share your beliefs and experience related to the teaching and learning of pragmatics, and then with the whole group.

3   Use the Part II prompts and repeat the steps 1–2 above. Alternatively, use these prompts as you read through the chapters specified for each prompt. Gain an awareness of your implicit beliefs or critically reflect on what you now believe. There is no right or wrong answer for any of these, but you can use these questions as a guide to stimulate your thoughts as you read on the upcoming chapters designed to help you shape, modify, or refine your knowledge and beliefs in instructional pragmatics.

Discussion/wrap-up

While other teachers share their views in this activity, try to stay as open as possible to different ideas and beliefs that they might disclose. Be nurturing and facilitate others' ideas and growth rather than being overly critical. In principled teaching where there is a firm connection between teachers' theory and practice, teachers' explicit knowledge and beliefs are likely to help them teach and assess pragmatics the way that they intend. Monitoring developments in teacher beliefs assists in principled teaching, allowing teachers to make informed decisions and to send consistent messages to learners about how pragmatics can be learned effectively.

Later in this book, you will be asked occasionally to reflect on your thoughts and see if any of your beliefs have undergone scrutiny, have become explicit, have been reinforced or refined, or have been challenged and changed. What are some implications that this may have for classroom practice? For example, could new insights (such as the ways that you best learned pragmatics yourself) lead to any change in your teaching? Or perhaps you already teach pragmatics that way and through this focused reflection and articulation of your beliefs, you would justify the way you teach it and gain an enhanced awareness of the sources of your beliefs and actual practice.

Task sheet: Reflective prompts

Part I Exploring experience related to the learning and teaching of pragmatics

1   Describe your interest in the learning or teaching of pragmatics. What brought you to this book?

2   Describe your experience learning L2 (or L1) pragmatics. What aspects of L2 pragmatics do you remember learning? How did you learn them? Does/will it affect the way you teach pragmatics?

3   What surprised you in the learning of L2 pragmatics? Any joys or plights of learning pragmatics that way? Can you think of a cultural blunder you experienced? How might this possibly traumatic experience have affected the way you teach pragmatics?

4   Describe your experience teaching pragmatics, even if you were not clearly aware of it at that point. How does pragmatics come up in your teaching? How do your students usually react? Why do you teach pragmatics that way?

Part II Exploring beliefs about specific issues in instructional pragmatics

1   How important is it to teach appropriate language use in the language classroom? Why do you believe so? (Chapters 1, 2, 5)

2   Based on what you already know, what do you want to know more about the teaching/learning of pragmatics? What questions do you have? (Chapters 2, 4, Conclusion)

3   Who is best qualified to teach pragmatics? What teacher factors and qualifications are important in the teaching of pragmatics? Why do you think so? (Chapters 1, 2, 3, 5, 6)

4   How should samples of the modeling of L2 pragmatics as well as samples of learner language be obtained (e.g., from teacher-generated dialogues based on teacher intuitions, from language as represented in textbooks, from recordings of natural speech, or from other sources)? Why do you believe so? (Chapters 3, 8, 9)

5   Taking into account, for example, your learners' goals, age, proficiency levels, how much do you think your learners need pragmatics instruction? What teaching approaches and exercises are likely to appeal to them and why? (Chapters 5, 6, 7, 10, 11, 12, 13)

6   In pragmatics instruction, should learners be given pragmatics-related information first and then practice using language appropriately (deductive approach)? Or should learners be guided to self-discover pragmatic norms (inductive learning)?

Which approach, inductive or deductive, or a combination of both would you use for your students and why? (Chapters 6, 7, 10, 11, 12)

7   Whose pragmatic norms should be viewed as a model in L2 pragmatics instruction and assessment? Why? (Chapters 5, 6, 7, 15)

8   What does culturally sensitive pragmatics instruction and assessment look like? (Chapters 7, 15)

9   How might your knowledge and beliefs about second language acquisition in general apply to the learning and teaching of pragmatics? (Chapters 2, 6)

10 How can learners' pragmatic ability be assessed in the classroom? What testing procedures or classroom tasks could be used? Why would you use them? (Chapters 14, 15)

Activity 2.2 Engaging in exploratory practice for teaching pragmatics

Objectives

1   You will be able to identify an issue to be investigated in your teaching of L2 pragmatics.

2   You will be able to engage in your selected inquiries extensively by collecting classroom-based data and critically reflecting on these data.

3   You will be able to gain greater understanding of the selected issue, possibly identify areas for modification, and then take action to introduce a change in your teaching if necessary.

Suggested time: 30 minutes initially and then more as needed.

Materials:

- Information: "Guide for exploratory practice";
- blank sheets of paper.

Directions

1   Exploratory practice is "action for understanding,"[23] which is intended to help teachers to gain a better understanding of some aspect of their instructional

---

[23] Allwright (2001, 2003).

behavior. It deals with a real issue (a *puzzle*, rather than a *problem*) in the teacher's local context. Although improvement of instruction through change may result from the newly gained understanding, action for change is neither required nor promoted. After your initial reflection on your beliefs and practice in Activity 2.1 above, use the information, "Guide for exploratory practice," and conduct further reflection individually or with a colleague. Identify an area of inquiry related to your teaching based on this reflection.

2   Following the "Guide for exploratory practice," design your data collection, collect, and analyze your data individually or collaboratively with your students or colleagues if applicable.

3   If your newly gained understanding of your classroom practice warrants any change in practice, make an action plan for change, and implement it in your classroom. Observe how it might affect student learning, attitude, or motivation.

4   Reflect on how you feel about your initial beliefs and practice, given your current, deepened understanding of classroom practice and the potential role of pragmatics.

5   Share your inquiry and findings with the whole group.

6   Go back to the original cycle. Find another inquiry and follow steps 1–5, above.

Discussion/wrap-up

Because the guide for exploratory practice provided below is rather brief, interested teachers are invited to read more about exploratory practice and action research[24] and see actual examples in the literature.[25] Exploratory practice is a reflective tool with which teachers can gain a more explicit, and often more sophisticated, understanding of their beliefs and practice. Teachers' knowledge and expertise are likely to expand as they engage in the recursive cycle of reflection promoted in exploratory practice.

Information: Guide for exploratory practice[26]
Steps involved in exploratory practice

1   Observe, reflect, and contemplate on your current teaching independently or collaboratively with your colleague. Identify an area of inquiry you wish to further explore.

---

[24] See for example, Allwright (2001, 2003); Burns (1999); Richards and Lockhart (1996); Wallace (1998).
[25] Examples conducted by actual classroom teachers include: Haley (2005); Johnson (2002); Tsui (1993); and various others in Richards and Lockhart (1996).
[26] Adapted from Allwright (2001).

2 Design a doable study that you can conduct in your classroom, involving the collection and analysis of data. Depending on the nature of your inquiry, your data may be drawn from just one portion of a lesson, or they may be drawn from a series of sessions over time. That will depend on what you choose to explore with regard to your practice. You may wish to collaborate with your colleague in this process and also to involve your students if appropriate.

3 If applicable, implement change that was found to be suitable through your exploration. Further observe and reflect on any positive or negative consequences that your enhanced understanding or the change may bring about in your classroom.

4 Reflect on this newly gained explicit knowledge of your teaching or on the change brought to your practice. Then revisit your initial beliefs and practice in light of this deepened understanding.

5 Discuss or write about your exploratory practice for professional development (e.g., newly gained explicit knowledge of your briefs and practice, and possibly a conference presentation/dissemination).

6 You are invited to repeat this recursive cycle of processes 1–5 as a means of professional development.

Examples of exploratory practice[27]

1 *A teacher's initial reflection.* How can my students best learn pragmatics? Should I teach them pragmatic norms directly (deductive learning) or lead them to self-discover them (inductive learning)? Selected inquiry: Which approach to L2 pragmatics do my students prefer for learning about how to make requests – a deductive or inductive one?

2 *Study designed and implemented by the instructor.* Find two comparable segments in the teaching of requests; one to be taught deductively, the other to be taught inductively. Teach these two sections with the different approaches and conduct an informal learner survey or interview in order to discover their preferences. The teacher's findings: Learners found it more time-consuming to learn inductively but for most, it was a more enjoyable and memorable approach.

3 *Action plan for the teacher.* Try incorporating inductive learning into the teaching of pragmatics to the extent that it is deemed appropriate. Observe students' reactions and reflect on their motivation and development.

---

[27] Adapted from exploratory practice/action research conducted by an anonymous teacher learner (Ishihara 2008*a*).

4   *Reflections on the findings from this classroom-based exploratory study.* Reflect on the newly gained explicit knowledge or the change brought to the practice. Revisit initial beliefs and practice in light of this process.

5   *Demonstration of newly gained knowledge.* Discuss, write, and possibly present the findings in and outside of the teachers' local institutional context for dissemination and professional development.

6   *Further professional development.* Identify another area for inquiry in the further exploration of ways to improve classroom practice.

CHAPTER 3

Collecting data reflecting the pragmatic use of language

Noriko Ishihara

Introduction

In teaching pragmatic language use in either spoken or written discourse, teachers need some language data (e.g., dialogues or examples of writing) to be used as learners' input. How should we obtain authentic data that are reasonably natural and appropriate for classroom purposes? Teachers also need to investigate learners' pragmatic use of language in natural or elicited discourse in order to provide effective instruction. In this section, we will discuss several means of obtaining samples of language data reflecting pragmatic use of language – language use both from fluent speakers to be used as a model and from L2 learners to be used for diagnostic purposes. The data sources include:

- intuition and introspection;
- discourse completion tasks (DCTs);
- role-plays;
- recording of natural conversation; and
- field observation of natural conversation.

First we will look briefly at these data collection methods along with some examples of possible instruments. Then, we will study examples of data obtained by means of such methods. Finally, we will discuss some pros and cons of the various methods and instruments associated with each method.

Intuition and introspection

If we create a dialogue based on what we think people tend to say or how they speak, these data would then be an example of the use of intuition. Many L2 textbooks are, in fact, written based on the curriculum writers' intuition. In later chapters, we will have a chance to take a closer look at language use in currently available textbooks (Chapter 8) and in naturally occurring conversations (Chapter 9). For now, let us more broadly discuss the use of intuition in the teaching of pragmatics.

Here is an example of how introspective data may be used that draw on the teacher's intuition:

> Imagine that a student of yours comes to you and asks how you would compliment someone in the language you teach. You think of what you would say and respond to this student.

We often find textbook language unnatural and stilted. Given that many textbooks are written based on the writer's intuition, introspection is rarely an effective means for producing pragmatic language samples. What we believe we say is not necessarily consistent with what we actually say. Even native speakers' intuition about their own pragmatic use of language is not always accurate because much of the language use is unconscious and automatic.[1] The use of intuition has in fact been characterized by sociologists as "notoriously unreliable"; even though we think we are aware of societal norms, we are "under the mistaken impression that these norms represent the actual speech patterns of the community."[2]

Pragmatic language use is in fact very complex, with a number of contextual factors influencing actual language use. For example, average native speakers would most likely have difficulty providing a thorough description of how they express politeness through intonation, pauses, hedges, word choice, grammar, and discourse structures, for example. A full picture of how pragmatics works cannot be obtained through quick introspection of our own language behavior.

For this reason, we strongly discourage teachers from relying solely on their intuition, even if they are native or fluent speakers of the language they teach. Simply being a fluent speaking teacher does not qualify someone

---

[1] Judd (1999); Kasper (1997).
[2] Manes and Wolfson (1981: 16).

to be an effective teacher of pragmatics. Rather, it is awareness about pragmatics (*meta-pragmatic awareness*), intercultural experience and sensitivity, and a repertoire of teaching and assessment strategies in this area that qualify us as competent teachers of pragmatics.[3]

The research literature is a fruitful source of information for learning about pragmatics-focused aspects of language use across various cultural contexts. Given that research articles are not always accessible to practicing teachers, one online resource may be useful. A website on speech acts housed under the Center for Advanced Research on Language Acquisition (CARLA) at the University of Minnesota (http://www.carla.umn.edu/index.html[4]) has compiled descriptions of speech acts (http://www.carla.umn.edu/speechacts/descriptions.html[5]). This site carries research-based information on how six speech acts are performed in multiple languages, which we will take a closer look at in Chapter 4. In addition, teachers (and students alike) can collect pragmatics data in their own communities through procedures such as those described below.

Elicited data: discourse completion tasks (DCTs) and role-plays

Another way to collect samples of pragmatic language is to elicit language use from learners or pragmatically competent speakers of the language (typically native-speaking or highly fluent speakers). Speakers can be given a scenario describing a situation and asked to write down or role-play what they would say in that situation as in the following examples.

Examples of DCTs

You are enrolled in a large class at a major university in Minneapolis. A week before one of your course papers is due, you notice that you have three more major papers due the same week. You realize that it is not possible to finish them all by their respective due dates and decide to go to one of the instructors, Professor Johnson, to ask for an

▶

---

[3] Judd (1999); Kasper (2001); Meier (2003).
[4] Accessed on December 20, 2009.
[5] Accessed on December 20, 2009.

extension on the paper for her course. She is a senior professor in her 50s teaching a large lecture course and this is your first time talking to her in private. You approach her after the class session is over and say:

Single-turn DCT

You:

Multiple-turn DCT

You:

Prof. Johnson: But the deadline was made clear in the syllabus.

You:

Prof. Johnson: Well, OK, but only two extra days.

You:

While the single-turn DCT may elicit an expression of request alone, the multiple-turn DCT most likely prompts speakers to engage in a more extended dialogue.[6] Speakers are also required to attend to what their conversational partner says and make their response fit into the context (see more discussion about this point in Chapter 9). A DCT is often written but can be conducted using oral language (hence, an oral DCT).[7] The description of the situation can be enhanced with detailed information about the context or with some visual aids (e.g., picture-enhanced DCT[8]). Another creative use of DCT in the classroom is the *student-generated DCT*[9] in which learners, instead of teachers, develop DCT scenarios based on their needs and past experiences.

[6] Cohen and Shively (2003).
[7] As in Brown, J. D. (2001); Ishihara (2003*b*).
[8] Yamashita (2002).
[9] McLean (2005).

Examples of role-plays

Role A: Employee

You have a part-time job at a local convenience store. One day, your boss and the store owner, who is about 20 years older than you, invites all the employees to a staff appreciation party. You know it would be fun to go, especially since everyone else will be there. The problem is that you have dinner planned and theater tickets that evening with an old friend just in town for the day. So while there is a sense of obligation to your boss, you're going to need to skip the party. You feel you need to tell your boss.

Role B: Boss

You are a store owner of a local convenience store. One day, you send out a notice to all your employees about a staff appreciation party requesting RSVP. While you are in the process of spreading the word, one of your part-time employees (about 20 years younger than you) comes up to you to ask you about something else. Since s/he has not responded to your message yet, you decide to invite him/her personally. Since you value this employee's work highly, you especially want him/her to attend so you can express your appreciation:

Boss:

Employee:

Boss:

Employee:

(Role-play can continue to its logical conclusion, however many conversational turns it takes.)

When we speak or write, we adjust our language use according to the situation, for example, whom we are speaking to and what we are discussing. Language use is influenced by a number of extra-linguistic contextual factors. The following three are known to be major elements (see also the discussion in Chapter 1):

(a) *Social status* (S). Relative social status of the speaker/writer and the listener/reader.

(b) *Distance* (D). Level of social distance and psychological distance (how distant or close the speaker/writer and listener/reader feel to each other).

(c) *Intensity* (I). Intensity of the act (e.g., the magnitude of the imposition in a request or the severity of the infraction in an apology).[10]

A primary advantage of a language elicitation procedure is that we can manipulate these contextual factors across items and analyze how they affect language use – for instance, in terms of level of politeness, directness, and formality. To give a more specific example, let's compare a small request from a student to a new teacher with the same request by the student when directed at a close friend. This task allows us to focus on the impact that two contextual factors – social status (S) and distance (D) – have on language use. In Figure 3.1, below, if the Xs are more to the left, the language is expected to be less polite, less formal, and more direct; when they are more to the right, then the language is anticipated to be more polite, formal, and indirect.

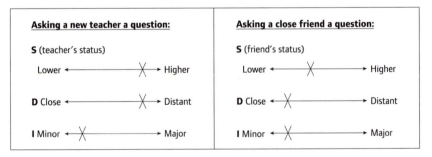

FIGURE 3.1

The language of requesting would also be different depending on the magnitude of the imposition involved in the request (e.g., borrowing a close friend's pen for a minute vs asking the same friend to use his/her car for a week). In this case, we can observe how the intensity of the act (I) (magni-

[10] Adapted from Brown and Levinson (1987).

tude of the imposition in this case) may affect the way that the request is crafted (see Figure 3.2, below).

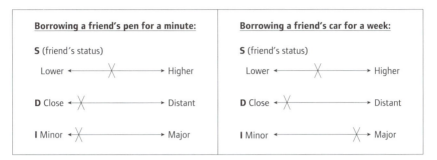

FIGURE 3.2

Data elicitation, such as through DCTs and role-play, tends to be a quick and convenient way to collect a relatively large amount of language data. At the same time, pragmatics researchers have pointed out repeatedly that elicited data, particularly written tasks such as the written DCT, do not accurately reflect the way we actually speak.[11] For example, the speakers providing language data may not be familiar with the situations described in the scenarios. Or even if they are, real-life consequences (*consequentiality*[12]) are lacking in such imagined contexts, and we may be testing their acting skills along with pragmatic ability. The number of studies that researched effects of the DCT in fact have questioned the validity of DCT-elicited data and have recommended caution in using these data.[13] Data collected from DCTs may reflect the speakers' knowledge of pragmatics rather than their online productive skills.[14] Speakers providing pragmatic language use might consider the social desirability of what should be said and how it should be said, and demonstrate more of what they perceive as appropriate behavior than what they would actually say in interactive contexts. Also, DCTs may be a valid source of pragmalinguistic[15] (language-focused) data, but might not be reflective of the sociopragmatic (culture-focused) aspects of the speech act.[16] Some have argued that the effects of the DCT may differ depending on

[11] Kasper and Dahl (1991); Kasper and Rose (2002). Also see Golato (2003); Kasper (2000) for more discussion.
[12] Bardovi-Harlig and Hartford (2005).
[13] See for example, Beebe and Cummings (1996); Golato (2003); Hartford and Bardovi-Harlig (1992); Kasper and Rose (2002).
[14] Golato (2003).
[15] Though somewhat overlapping, *sociopragmatics* deals with sociocultural norms for linguistic behavior in a given context while *pragmalinguistics* refers to the actual language forms used to convey the intended meaning (Thomas, 1983).
[16] Nelson *et al.* (2002).

the language or the culture of the speakers.[17] Compared to a written DCT, a role-play tends to be more interactive and spontaneous, and thus is likely to yield more naturalistic discourse.[18]

For the purpose of language teaching, we would first encourage you to be familiar with the potential pros and cons of elicitation measures (which will be discussed in Activity 3.1, below). Having this awareness would allow you to select suitable procedure(s) from a range of data collection strategies, including recording or field observation of naturally occurring conversations, which we now discuss.

Field observation or recording of natural conversation

Because elicited data lack spontaneity and may come across as contrived, you may say that natural speech would serve best as the source of pragmatic language samples in the classroom. Collecting tape- or video-recordings of natural conversation may be simpler and yield more accurate data than trying to take down the language verbatim. Transcribed examples of natural data can be found in Chapters 8 and 9. A downside of this procedure would be that we usually need to obtain permission for recording ahead of time and need to make sure that the speakers talk naturally without being overly self-conscious. We will discuss organization of natural conversation and the suitability of naturally occurring data in Chapter 9. Examples of natural conversations can be found in Activity 3.1 (below).

Making use of field observation techniques, we could carefully record natural conversations we overhear or engage in. We could take notes on, for example:

- what people say;
- their tone of voice;
- their gestures; and
- their eye-contact.

We would also record relevant contextual factors such as those appearing below, to the extent that they can be known or guessed from the context:

- the physical location/situation;
- the age of the speakers;

[17] Hinkel (1997); Rose (1994a); Rose and Ono (1995).
[18] Kasper and Dahl (1991).

- their gender;

- their relative social status; and

- the level of distance between them.

The choice of factors to consider when observing would depend, of course, on the purpose of the observation, the learners' awareness about pragmatics, their level of proficiency, and so forth.

Using these field observation techniques, a research team collected over 1,200 naturally occurring compliments in the early 1980s.[19] The data can still serve today as a foundation of pragmatics-focused instruction on how to give and respond to compliments in American English. Observation of the language and context can be made based on the observer's memory or audio-/video-recording. Below are two examples (Figures 3.3 and 3.4) of a field observation instrument and data collected using audio-recording.

Teachers may also decide to have learners collect their own data on how target language speakers use language.[20] Learners may even decide what sort of data they are going to collect. For example, they might want to know how one can invite someone on a date and how to accept or refuse such an

Situation/Location			
Contextual factors	**Social status (S)** Relative status (e.g., age, gender, role in conversation) ←————→ Low High	**Distance (D)** Level of social/ psychological distance ←————→ Close Distant	**Intensity (I)** Intensity of act (e.g., imposition) ←————→ Less intense Intense
Interaction	A: B: A: B: (continues)		
Other notes (e.g., tone, gestures, eye-contact)			

FIGURE 3.3 Example of field observation instruments
Adapted from Kakiuchi (2005b).

---

[19] See Manes and Wolfson (1981).
[20] See Tatsuki and Houck (in press) for more details about this procedure.

Situation/Location	At Brett's part-time job; an informal setting		
Contextual factors	**Social status (S)** Relative status (e.g., age, gender, role in conversation)	**Distance (D)** Level of social/ psychological distance	**Intensity (I)** Intensity of act (e.g., imposition)
	Brett Ken ←——X X——→ Low High	←——— X ———→ Close Distant	←— X ————→ Less intense Intense
	Ken: male, late 30s, employer Brett: male, early 20s, employee	Employer-employee relationship, interact with each other a little bit at work	Refusing to go to a staff appreciation party
Interaction	Ken: Hey, Brett, you know about the party, right? Brett: I do, but uh, I'm gonna have a hot date that night. I don't think I'll be able to make it. Ken: Oh, come on! Bring her over to it, man. Everyone's gonna be there. I don't mind. Brett: Yeah, but well, it's just that it's the first time, and we had already made some plans, so, you know how it is. Ken: All right, if you can stop by, please do, but if you can't, that's okay.		
Other notes (e.g., tone, gestures, eye-contact)	Ken's invitation is getting rejected, but he maintains a positive outlook by inviting both Brett and his girlfriend and letting him off the hook at the end.		

FIGURE 3.4 Example of data collected

invitation. Authentic language use in such situations may not be in their language textbooks and warrant collection of naturally occurring (or at least reasonably naturalistic) data. Below is an example, an assignment in which data on giving and responding to compliments were collected by high intermediate ESL learners as part of awareness-raising instruction.[21] The learner language is quoted verbatim in the following table.

For the next few days, pay attention to any compliments that you give, receive, or overhear and jot them down in your notepads as accurately as possible after the conversation. Observe carefully the circumstances in which these compliments were given and responded to in terms of gender, age, role, distance/closeness, and compliment topics. Fill out the following form and bring it to your next class.

[21] Adapted from Ishihara (2003a, 2004).

Contextual factors	Social status (S) Relative status (e.g., age, gender, role in conversation)	Distance (D) Level of distance	Intensity (I) Compliment topic
Dialogue 1	Equals (same age group, females, classmates)	Close	T-shirt (appearance/ possession)
	Jenny: Nice T-shirt! Steph: Well, Jenny, I bought it at a thrift store. Jenny: But it looks new! Steph: Oh, no, it's used, I bought it for $1. Jenny: That's really cheap. Steph: Thanks you.		
Dialogue 2	Equals (same age group, males, roommates)	Close	Cooked meal
	Jeff: You really did a nice work. You made a delicious food. Ricardo: Do you really think so?		
Dialogue 3	Equals (same age group, male to female, classmates)	Somewhat close	Watch (appearance/ possession)
	John: I like your watch. Aisha: Thanks, my fatehr [father] give to me in my birthday. John: I think is really cool.		

Although learner-collected data (as seen above) may not accurately reflect the details of language use, the collected samples can still serve certain purposes in pragmatics instruction. In the example above, for instance, learner data may not always be grammatically correct, but can be useful for the analysis of appropriate topics of compliments, the syntactic structures of compliments, and the compliment response strategies in each context.

Discussion

Every data collection procedure has its advantages and disadvantages. This chapter has stressed the value of using authentic data in the teaching of pragmatics as much as possible instead of relying solely on introspection or intuition. Teachers can weigh the advantages and disadvantages of different data collection procedures and select the most appropriate one(s) for their own purposes. Examining various procedures and sample data can help us determine how we might collect pragmatic language samples for our students. Or teachers might wish to have students collect pragmatic data themselves for the purpose of awareness-raising, even though the collected data may fall short in accuracy. The data collection activities at the end of this chapter provide a hands-on opportunity to collect pragmatics data that may serve as a language model in pragmatics instruction.

Activity 3.1 Evaluating the pragmatics of language samples

Objectives

1   You will be able to evaluate the authenticity of different types of data collected through various means: a) intuition and introspection, b) DCTs, c) role-plays, d) recording of natural conversation, e) field observation.

2   You will be able to compare pros and cons of different types of data and select suitable data collection procedures for your instructional purposes and contexts.

Suggested time: 30 minutes.

Materials:

- ◼ Information: "Samples of language data";

- ◼ Task sheet: "Pros and cons associated with different types of data";

- ◼ internet access to websites offering audio files and transcripts of the sample data.

Directions

1   In a group of about four, familiarize yourself with selected samples of language data and discuss the authenticity (e.g., naturalness and spontaneity of the speech).

2   Within your group, fill in the task sheet, "Pros and cons associated with different types of data." Consider the following points (and anything else) for each data sample.

- ◼ *Interactivity*: Are the data interactive or limited in turn-taking?

- ◼ · *Consequentiality*: Is there a real-world outcome for the speakers? (Natural conversation with real-life consequence or imagined situation?)

- *Comparability*: Are these language samples comparable? (Are these samples useful for teaching students the influence of contextual factors on language form?)[22]

- *Accuracy*: How linguistically accurate are the data collected?

- *Ease/convenience*: How easy or convenient is it to collect data this way?

3 Share your discussion with the whole group.

Discussion/Wrap-up

To conclude, discuss what type(s) of data you would use for teaching pragmatics in your instructional context and why. Considering your students' needs, what features of your data are important to you? How would you compensate for any drawbacks associated with the type(s) of data that you choose to use?

Information: Samples of language data

1 Intuition and introspection-based data

Sample[23]

Chip: Hey there.

Catherine: Hi.

Chip: Cool party, isn't it?

Catherine: Yeah, you bet.

Chip: So, how's it going?

Catherine: Um, OK, I guess.

Chip: By the way, I just want you to know I think you're really cute.

Catherine: Oh, um, thanks.

Chip: So what's your name?

Catherine: Catherine.

Chip: Catherine what?

Catherine: Just Catherine.

Chip: OK. I'm Chip.

---

[22] Interactivity, consequentiality, and comparability from Bardovi-Harlig and Hartford (2005).
[23] Adapted from Robins and MacNeill (2007: 85).

Catherine: Hi.

Chip: So, Catherine, you having a good time?

Catherine: Yeah. I am. Great music, I love it.

Chip: Do you live around here?

Catherine: Yeah, sort of.

Chip: So, where do you live? In the city or in the . . . ?

Catherine: Um, actually, I'd rather not say.

Chip: Well, listen, it's nice meeting you wherever you live.

Catherine: Um . . .

Chip: So what's your phone number? You think I could call you sometime?

Catherine: No, sorry. I don't like to give out my phone number.

Chip: How about your e-mail address? Maybe I could write you an e-mail.

(*continues*)

2 DCT data

Sample 1[24]

Karen: So you know where the restaurant is?

Jeff: Yeah, oh, Karen, I meant to talk to you about that. I've got a big test Friday morning, so I'll probably stay home and study.

Karen: You don't have to stay for the whole thing, but why don't you stop by just a bit?

Jeff: Well, I'll try, but I think I'll probably be studying all night Thursday. Sorry.

Sample 2

Karen: So you know where the restaurant is?

Jeff: Yeah, I know, but I don't think I can make it this weekend. It's just I got tons of work to do, and yeah, I don't think I can make it.

Karen: You don't have to stay for the whole thing, but why don't you stop by just a bit?

Jeff: Um, yeah, I'll see what I can do, I'll try my best. Maybe I'll just stop by for a while. See what'll happen.

---

[24] Samples 1 and 2 from oral DCT data in Ishihara (2003*b*).

3 Role-play data

Sample 1[25]

Alex: Hey, Keith! Are you excited about the big tennis match coming up?

Keith: Ah, you know, I was wondering if there's room in your car for me to hop in and ride with you guys?

Alex: Oh, well, uh, I already got four people. I don't know. It may be too tight.

Keith: Oh, geez, well, the thing is, I talked to everybody else and nobody else seems to be able to do it, and you live, you're closer to me. I just can't miss this match.

Alex: Oh, well, I don't know. I, I guess it might be all right.

Keith: I could, I could ride in the trunk here.

Alex: Yeah, man, that'd be cool. Ah, I tell you what. Uh, give me a call, and if one of these people cancels or something, uh, we'll try to work something out.

Keith: Great, cool. Sounds good! I'll see you then.

Sample 2

Alice: Hi Christine, this is my friend, Rachel. Um, she also plays basketball very well.

Rachel: Hey, it's nice to meet you, Christine.

Christine: (Christine smiles)

Rachel: Yeah, I'm Rachel. Um, I'm not on the team, but yeah, I love basketball.

Alice: Rachel's really good, Christine.

Christine: (Christine nods)

Rachel: Oh, come on, now. I'm not that good. You guys are awesome.

Alice: (Alice talks to Christine) We should play two-on-one sometime while she is still in town.

Rachel: That'll be cool, yeah. So what position do you play, Christine?

Christine: . . .

Sample 3[26]

Listen to the audio and view a transcript of complaints in English: http://www.indiana.edu/~discprag/spch_complaints.html[27]

---

[25] Samples 1 and 2 from Ishihara (2003*b*).

[26] Samples 3 and 4 from Félix-Brasdefer (2005: available online). To listen, go to the window at the bottom of the page. At the top right corner of the window, scroll down to choose an English version and click on the speaker icon.

[27] Accessed December 10, 2009.

Sample 4

Listen to the audio and view a transcript of compliments in English: http://www. indiana.edu/~discprag/spch_compliments.html[28]

4 Transcribed data of recorded natural conversation

The spelling in the samples below is phonetic, following some of the transcription conventions commonly used in conversation analysis.

Sample 1[29]

A: Hi Carol.

B: Hi.

C: (overlapping with B) Carol, Hi.

A: You didn't get an ice cream sandwich.

B: I know, hh I decided that my body didn't need it.

A: Yes but ours did. hh heh-heh-heh heh-heh-heh hhih

B: (overlapping with A) heh-heh-heh

A: hh Awright gimme some money en you c'n treat me one an I'll buy you all some too.

B: (overlapping with A) I'm kidding, I don't need it.

A: (in an emphatic tone) I want one.

C: ehh heh-hu h

A: (overlapping with C) hheh-uh hhh No, they didn't even have any Tab.

C: (overlapping with A) hheh

B: This is all I c'd find.

(Audio-recording of this conversation is accessible at: http://www.sscnet.ucla. edu/soc/faculty/schegloff/RealSoundFiles/papersounds.php?directory=Getting_ Serious)[30]

---

[28] Accessed December 10, 2009.
[29] Samples 1 and 2 from Schegloff (2001: 1948, 1951) on the use of discourse marker *no* that marks a transition from non-serious to serious talk (p. 1948). Some of the transcription conventions were removed or adapted for readability. Teachers may wish to consider modifying the spelling for classroom use or incorporating more of the features of natural conversation such as pauses and overlaps.
[30] Accessed December 10, 2009.

Sample 2

A: Where were we?

B: I dunno. 've you been studying lately?

A: No, not et aw – not et all. I hafta study this whole week. Every night. hhhh en then I got s'mthing planned on Sunday with Laura. She, she wen – she 'n I are gonna go out 'n get drunk et four o'clock in the afternoon.

B: huh-huh hhhh

A: (overlapping with B) It's a religious thing we're gonna have. I d'know why, b't. Uhm. No, her ex-boyfriend's getting married en she's gunnuh be depressed so.

B: She wasn't invited d'the wedding?

A: (overlapping with B) I'm g'nuh take 'er out.

(Audio-recording of this conversation is accessible at: http://www.sscnet.ucla. edu/soc/faculty/schegloff/RealSoundFiles/papersounds.php?directory=Getting_ Serious)

5 Data collected through field observation

Sample 1[31]

Have a productive evening. Get lots of homework graded.

Sample 2

Good luck with everything.

Sample 3

[*To the listener's dog*] Tillie, take care of her.

Sample 4

Have a good weekend. Don't work it away.

Sample 5

Well, have safe travels, then.

Sample 6

You go, girl!

---

[31] Samples 1–10 from Burt (2001: 4–9) on blessings.

Sample 7

I'm not going to wish you luck, because you're not going to need it.

Sample 8

Have a good trip and summer and everything.

Sample 9

If I don't talk to you before Monday, have a wonderful trip.

Sample 10

Have a good day. I may see you at noon and I may not.

Task sheet: Pros and cons associated with different types of data

	Pros	Cons
Intuition and introspection		
DCT		
Role-play		
Recording of natural conversation		
Field observation of natural conversation		

Activity 3.2 Collecting data for pragmatics-focused instruction

Objectives

1   You will be able to construct instructions and scenarios required for collecting language data that are feasible and appropriate for your instructional contexts, and collect language samples for your future teaching of pragmatics.
2   You will be able to evaluate your collected data and identify ways to minimize the potential drawbacks associated with the type of data.

Suggested time: 30 minutes.

Materials:

■   blank sheets of paper;
■   tape/digital-recording device or a camcorder (optional).

Directions

1   Choose one or two data collection procedure(s) that are most useful and feasible in your instructional setting.
2   Write out instructions and/or a scenario for your data collection, if appropriate. Get in a group of about three, ideally with those who speak the language you teach. Have the other participants provide language data, and revise your instructions and/or scenarios if necessary.
3   If you have a recording device, such as a tape recorder, a digital voice recorder, or a camcorder, have your teammates role-play orally and transcribe the dialogue.
4   As an assignment, collect your data outside of the classroom and transcribe them if necessary.
5   Share your (transcribed) data along with the audio/video with the rest of the group.

Discussion/Wrap up

Analyze the pros and cons of your collected data as you did in Activity 3.1. Would your data serve your purpose in your teaching of pragmatics? If there are any drawbacks associated with the type of data, think of how you would compensate for them while teaching pragmatics. For example, if your data were elicited and somewhat unnatural, would you consider making them more authentic? If so, how? If your data were collected naturally and have various features that you think may distract your learners, what would you do? (See also Chapters 7, 8, and 9 for ways to incorporate naturally occurring data into pragmatics instruction.)

CHAPTER 4

Describing speech acts: linking research and pedagogy

Noriko Ishihara and Andrew D. Cohen

Introduction

Natural discourse often includes hedges, fillers, repetitions, overlaps, and repairs, woven in the frequent turn-taking, and the structure of naturally occurring conversation can be highly complex. As we have seen in Activity 3.1 in the previous chapter, the pragmatic use of language found in natural conversations reminds us that natural conversations often fail to be neatly packaged interchanges. One current view holds that if we truly wish to understand the complex organization of natural discourse, we should rely on naturally occurring data alone. An oft-mentioned shortcoming of such data, however, is the difficulty involved in collecting comparable data (see Chapters 3 and 9 for further discussion).

In addition to natural data, empirical research in pragmatics thus far has also utilized various elicited means of data collection (as discussed in Chapter 3). As they are elicited, these data may not provide a mirror image of authentic language use. However, it is our view that dismissing this massive body of collective knowledge at this point is like "throwing the baby out with the bath water." We feel that these data can supplement natural data and are valuable research-based information applicable to teaching L2 pragmatics. The vast amount of such data currently available includes descriptions of language structures and a range of norms for pragmatic behavior in the communities where the target language is used.

This chapter is intended to serve as a guide to the basic shape of some of the well-researched speech acts. A more comprehensive version of the majority of information offered here is posted on the CARLA Speech Act website introduced in Chapter 3 (available at: http://www.carla.umn.edu/speechacts/descriptions.html[1]). This database was originally developed with the intention of supporting teachers and curriculum writers in their efforts to share this information with learners. And in some cases learners have gone directly to the site in order to obtain material to use in performing speech acts in and out of class.[2]

The CARLA Speech Acts website has descriptions of six speech acts (apologies, complaints, compliments and responses to compliments, requests, refusals, and thanks), with examples from various languages (e.g., English, Spanish, German, Chinese, Japanese, and Hebrew). The amount of information on a given speech act varies greatly depending on the availability of research articles that investigate that speech act. In the remainder of this chapter, we will look at the information on several speech acts in American English, as well as on conversational implicature, with an eye to its application to language instruction. The speech acts are compliments and responses to compliments, refusals, apologies, and requests. We end this chapter with an activity intended to provide teacher readers with an opportunity to explore resources on the CARLA website and elsewhere for certain pragmatic features that they choose to teach.

Compliments and responses to compliments

Compliments in English often function as a "social lubricant," helping the social relationships to go smoothly. How are compliments used, for example, in US culture? What strategies are used to give and respond to compliments? Are there any taboos in giving or responding to compliments? How do these norms of behavior vary across languages and cultures?

Functions and strategies for complimenting

According to past research, compliments in English are often used to:

- express admiration or approval of someone's work/appearance/taste;
- establish/confirm/maintain solidarity;[3]
- serve as an alternative to greetings/gratitude/apologies/congratulations;[4]

---

[1] Accessed on December 10, 2009.
[2] ESL students have accessed the website online and taken material from the speech act descriptions for requesting in order to perform role-plays (Jernigan *et al.* 2007).
[3] Herbert (1990); Manes (1983).
[4] Manes and Wolfson (1981); Wolfson (1989).

- soften face-threatening acts such as apologies, requests and criticism;[5]
- open and sustain conversation (conversation strategy);[6] and
- reinforce desired behavior.[7]

Topics of compliments

The major referents of compliments include attributes of the conversational partner, such as:

- appearance/possessions (e.g., *You look absolutely beautiful!*)
- performance/skills/abilities (e.g., *Your presentation was excellent.*)
- personality traits (e.g., *You are so sweet.*)

Grammatical structures and word choice for compliments

In the 1980s, researchers found that 97% of compliments use one of the structures listed below.[8] More recent studies investigating compliments appearing in the current US media also found roughly comparable distribution of these grammatical structures.[9]

1 *Your blouse is/looks (really) beautiful.* (NP is/looks (really) ADJ).
2 *I (really) like/love your car.* (I (really) like/love NP).
3 *That's a (really) nice wall hanging.* (PRO is (really) a ADJ NP).
4 *You did a (really) good job.* (You V a (really) ADV NP).
5 *You really handled that situation well.* (You V (NP) (really) ADV).
6 *You have such beautiful hair!* (You have (a) ADJ NP!).
7 *What a lovely baby you have!* (What (a) ADJ NP!) (See Figure 4.1 below).
8 *Nice game!* (ADJ NP!).
9 *Isn't your ring beautiful!* (Isn't NP ADJ!).

The most commonly used adjectives in compliments were *nice, good, pretty, great*, and *beautiful*,[10] although the list undoubtedly varies for other varieties of English. It could be a student activity to collect the expressions that are

[5] Brown and Levinson (1987); Wolfson (1983).
[6] Billmyer (1990); Dunham (1992); Wolfson (1983).
[7] Manes (1983).
[8] Manes and Wolfson (1981).
[9] Rose (2001); Tatsuki and Nishizawa (2005).
[10] Manes and Wolfson (1981).

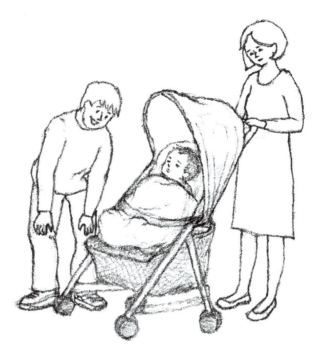

FIGURE 4.1 Compliment for a baby

in fashion in the given speech community or sub-community, especially among youth (e.g., "sweet," "da bomb," "phat," and "ill" in English in the US).

Strategies for responses to compliments

Semantically, common responses to compliments can be categorized into acceptance, mitigation, and rejection. Each category has sub-categories:[11]

1 Accept:

- Token of appreciation (*Thanks/Thank you.*)
- Acceptance by means of a comment (*Yeah, it's my favorite, too.*)
- Upgrading the compliment by self-praise (*Yeah, I can play other sports well too.*)

2 Mitigate:

- Comment about history (*I bought it for the trip to Arizona.*)
- Shifting the credit (*My brother gave it to me/It really knitted itself.*)

[11] Nelson *et al.* (1996); Herbert and Straight (1989).

- Questioning or requesting reassurance or repetition (*Do you really like them?*)

- Reciprocating (*So's yours.*)

- Scaling down or downgrading (*It's really quite old.*)

3   Reject:

- Disagreeing (A: *You look good and healthy.* B: *I feel fat.*)

4   No response.

5   Request interpretation:

- Addressee interprets the compliment as a request (*You wanna borrow this one too?*)

All of the information about giving and responding to compliments as described above can be directly applied to pragmatics instruction in the L2 classroom. Sample lesson materials designed for intermediate ESL learners based on this information can be found in Chapter 7.[12] For further information (e.g., statistical information, gender differences in giving and responding to compliments, compliments in other varieties of English and other languages, and teaching tips), visit the site available at: http://www.carla.umn.edu/speechacts/compliments/index.html.[13]

Refusals

In making a refusal, the speaker/writer is typically communicating a potentially undesirable message as far as the listener/reader is concerned. What strategies can be used to mitigate refusals in English? What pragmatic norms prevail in making and interpreting refusals in English?

Functions and strategies for refusing

Refusals are often made in response to requests, invitations, offers, and suggestions. The direct and indirect strategies of refusals can be described as follows:[14]

---

[12] The effects of this instruction were studied and reported in Ishihara (2004).
[13] Accessed on December 10, 2009.
[14] Beebe *et al.* (1990).

I Direct

1 Using performative verbs (*I refuse.*)

2 Non-performative statement:

- ■ "No"

- ■ Negative willingness/ability (*I can't.*)

II Indirect

1 Statement of regret (*I'm sorry.*)

2 Wish (*I wish I could help you.*)

3 An excuse, a reason, an explanation (*I have a headache.*)

4 Statement of alternative:

- ■ I can do X instead of Y (*I'd rather . . .*)

- ■ Why don't you do X instead of Y? (*Why don't you ask someone else?*)

5 Set condition for future or past acceptance (*If you had asked me earlier, I would have . . .*)

6 Promise of future acceptance (*I'll do it next time.*)

7 Statement of principle (*I never do business with friends.*)

8 Attempt to dissuade the listener:

- ■ Threat or statement of negative consequences to the requester (*I won't be any fun tonight.*)

- ■ Guilt trip (waitress to customers who want to sit a while: *I can't make a living off people who just order coffee.*)

- ■ Criticism of the request/requester (statement of negative feeling, opinion, or insult/attack: *Who do you think you are?*)

- ■ Request for help, empathy, and assistance by dropping or holding the request (*Imagine the situation I'm in.*)

- ■ Letting the listener off the hook (*Don't worry about it.*)

- ■ Self-defense (*I'm trying my best.*)

9 Acceptance that functions as a refusal:

- ■ Unspecific or indefinite reply

- ■ Lack of enthusiasm

10 Avoidance

■ Non-verbal:

   ■ Silence

   ■ Hesitation

   ■ Doing nothing

   ■ Physical departure

■ Verbal:

   ■ Topic switch

   ■ Joke

   ■ Repetition of part of request, etc. (*Monday?*)

   ■ Postponement (*I'll think about it.*)

   ■ Hedge (*Gee, I don't know.*)

Adjuncts to refusals

In addition to the refusals themselves described above, other elements may accompany the refusal:[15]

1 statement of positive opinion/feeling or agreement (*I'd love to come*);

2 statement of empathy (*I realize you are in a difficult situation*);

3 pause fillers (*um, well*); and

4 gratitude/appreciation (*thanks so much for the invite*).

Again, this research-based information can be woven into pragmatics instruction. For further information and examples of refusals in American and British English, Arabic, Chinese, German, Japanese, and Spanish, visit the site at: http://www.carla.umn.edu/speechacts/refusals/index.html.[16] A video demonstration of an innovative ESL lesson plan[17] that has visualized mitigating refusal strategies can be found at: http://www.teachertube.com/uprofile.php?UID=20621.[18]

Apologies

In apologizing, the speaker/writer recognizes the infraction or offense caused through his/her fault and attempts to repair the relationship with the

---

[15] Beebe *et al.* (1990).
[16] Accessed on December 10, 2009.
[17] Archer (in press).
[18] Accessed on December 10, 2009.

listener/reader. The situation may be fairly tense if the infraction is large or if the listener is in a more powerful position on the social scale than the speaker. What are some routinized patterns in apologies in English and what strategies work most effectively to repair and maintain a good relationship with the listener/reader?

Functions for the speech act of apologizing

In American English people typically use apologies for a variety of reasons such as:

- to say that they are sorry;
- to explain why the offense happened; and
- to make a repair for the offense and maintain a good relationship with the addressee.

Strategies for apologizing

Complex speech acts like apologies actually consist of a set of strategies that are used by competent speakers of the language with some regularity. There are five relatively typical strategies for making an apology:[19]

1 **An expression of an apology.** The speaker/writer uses a word, expression, or sentence containing a verb such as "sorry," "excuse," "forgive," or "apologize." Languages have certain words that are used to express an oral apology more than others. For example, in American English, "I apologize . . ." is found more in writing than it is in oral language. An expression of an apology can be intensified whenever the apologizer feels the need to do so. Such intensification is usually accomplished by adding intensifiers such as "really" or "very" – e.g., "I'm really sorry."

2 **Acknowledgment of responsibility.** The offender recognizes his/her fault in causing the infraction. The degree of such recognition on the part of the apologizer can be placed on a scale. The highest level of intensity is full acceptance of the blame: "It's totally my fault." At a somewhat lower level would be an expression of self-deficiency: "I was confused/I didn't see/You are right." At a still lower level would be the expression of lack of intent: "I didn't mean to." Lower still would be an implicit expression of responsibility: "I could be wrong, but I was sure

[19] Cohen and Olshtain (1981: 119–25).

I had given you the right directions." Finally, the apologizer may not accept the blame at all, in which case there may be a denial of responsibility: "It wasn't my fault," or even blaming of the listener: "It's your own fault."

3   **An explanation or account.** The speaker/writer describes the situation which caused him/her to commit the offense and which is used by this speaker/writer as an indirect way of apologizing. The explanation is intended to set things right. In some cultures this may be a more acceptable way of apologizing than in others. Thus, in cultures where public transportation is unreliable, coming late to a meeting and giving an explanation like, "The bus was late," might be perfectly acceptable.

4   **An offer of repair.** The apologizer makes a bid to carry out an action or provide payment for some kind of damage resulting from his/her infraction.

If someone is late for an appointment with a friend s/he might say something like:

   How can I make it up to you? Can I buy you lunch on Friday?

Or someone who fails to make it to an appointment might say:

   Would you be willing to reschedule the meeting?

5   **A promise of non-recurrence.** The apologizer commits him/herself to not having the offense happen again, which is situation-specific and less frequent than the other strategies. For example, if you bump into a stranger, you are not going to promise you will never do it again, but you might if it is a co-worker who you don't pick up on time.

The five major patterns or strategies that make up the apology speech act are almost universally available to speakers/writers, regardless of the language in which they are speaking or writing. Nonetheless, preference for any one of these strategies or for a combination of them will depend on the specific situation a speaker/writer is in within the given language and culture group.

Additional strategies for apologizing[20]

■   Expression of trait of self-deficiency, e.g.,

   I'm so forgetful. You know me, I'm never on time.

---

[20] Blum-Kulka and Olshtain (1984).

■ Explicit self-blame, e.g.,

What an idiot I am!

■ Denial of fault (rejecting the need for apologies), e.g.,

It's not my fault that it fell down.

Interjections and intensifiers

Not only could an intensifier play an important role, but even an interjection like "Oh!" could have an important role. In fact, there could be times when a well-placed "Oh!" and an offer of repair could take the place of an expression of apology in American English: e.g., "Oh! Here, let me help get something on that burn and clean up the mess," as opposed to, "I'm very sorry that I bumped into you."

Other ways of intensifying apologies include expressing explicit concern for the listener and using multiple intensifying strategies. So apologies can be intensified in the following ways:[21]

1   Intensifying the apology expression:

(a) Use of adverbials, e.g.,

I'm really sorry.

(b) Use of repetition or multiple intensifiers, e.g.,

I'm really very sorry.

In American English, there is a difference between "very" and "really," with "really" implying more regret and "very" more etiquette.[22]

2   Expressing explicit concern for the listener, e.g.,

Have you been waiting long?

3   Using multiple intensifying strategies, e.g.,

I'm so sorry. Are you all right? I'm terribly sorry.

Curricular materials for L2 apologies can be found at http://www.carla. umn.edu/speechacts/japanese/apologies/apologies.htm (for Japanese) and http://www.carla.umn.edu/speechacts/sp_pragmatics/Apologies/apologies_ home.html (for Spanish).[23]

---

[21] Blum-Kulka and Olshtain (1984).
[22] Cohen *et al.* (1986: 66–7).
[23] Both sites accessed on December 10, 2009.

Requests

By making a request, the speaker/writer infringes on the listener's freedom from imposition. The recipient may feel that the request is an intrusion on his/her freedom of action or even a power play. As for the requester, s/he may hesitate to make requests for fear of exposing a need or out of fear of possibly making the recipient lose face.[24] In this sense, requests are face-threatening to both the requester and the recipient.

Functions and strategies for making requests

Because requests have the potential to be intrusive and demanding, there often is a need for the requester to minimize the imposition involved in the request.[25] One way for the requester to minimize the imposition is by employing *indirect strategies* rather than *direct* ones (see below). The more direct a request is, the more transparent it is and the less of a burden the recipient bears in interpreting the request. The scale of directness can be characterized according to the following three strategies:[26]

1 **Direct strategies** (marked explicitly as requests, such as imperatives):

> *Clean up the kitchen.*
>
> *I'm asking you to clean up the kitchen.*
>
> *I'd like to ask you to clean the kitchen.*
>
> *You'll have to clean up the kitchen.*
>
> *I really wish you'd clean up the kitchen.*

2 **Conventionally indirect strategies** (referring to contextual preconditions necessary for its performance as conventionalized in the language):

> *How about cleaning up?*
>
> *Could you clean up the kitchen, please?*

3 **Non-conventionally indirect strategies (hints)** (partially referring to the object depending on contextual clues):

> *You have left the kitchen in a total mess.*
>
> *I'm a nun.* (a request to someone to stop trying to pick her up)

---

[24] Blum-Kulka *et al.* (1989: 11).
[25] See also Brown and Levinson (1987).
[26] Blum-Kulka and Olshtain (1984: 201–2).

Both situational and cultural factors influence the selection of these request strategies. Still, there may be consensus across a number of cultures with regard to requesting strategies. For example, a big favor usually comes with more indirect and/or polite strategies than a low-imposition request in various cultures. Friends use more casual requests than acquaintances, provided that the content of the request is the same. However, the specific directness levels appropriate for given situations might differ cross-culturally. A certain language (like German) may tend to use more direct-level requests than other languages (like Japanese) equally in an appropriate manner within the culture. Conventional indirectness may be universal and in fact, generally the most commonly employed level of directness.[27]

The typical request sequence

The request sequence in English (Australian/American/British), French (Canadian), Danish, German, Hebrew, Japanese, and Russian has been divided in the literature into the following three segments:[28]

For a request, *"Danny, can you remind me later to bring the book for you on Monday? Otherwise, I'm sure to forget."*

1   Attention getter/alerter (e.g., address terms):

   Danny,

2   Head act (core of the request sequence, the request proper):

   can you remind me later to bring the book for you on Monday?

3   Supportive move(s) (before or after the head act):

   Otherwise, I'm sure to forget.

Request mitigators/upgraders

Mitigating the face-threatening nature of requests can also be achieved by use of *downgraders*.[29] The requester might indicate being pessimistic with regard to the outcome of the request (negative usage) or hesitant about making the request (interrogative and modal usage "might"). Use of the past tense or embedded *if*-clause might also serve as a distancing element.

---

[27] Blum-Kulka *et al.* (1989); Blum-Kulka and Olshtain (1984).
[28] Blum-Kulka and Olshtain (1984).
[29] Blum-Kulka and Olshtain (1984: 204).

- *Could you do the cleaning up?*

- *Could you remind me later . . . ?*

- *Look, excuse me. I wonder if you wouldn't mind dropping me off at home?*

- *I wanted to ask for a postponement.*

- *I would appreciate it if you left me alone.*

Some examples of other softening downgraders are:

- **Do you think** *I could borrow your lecture notes from yesterday?*

- *Could you tidy up* **a bit** *before I start?*

- **It would really help if** *you* **did** *something about the kitchen.*

- **Will you be able to perhaps** *drive me?*

- *Can I use your pen for a minute,* **please?**

On the other hand, the speaker/writer may wish to increase the compelling force of the request. This function of aggravating the request can be achieved through *upgraders*.

- *Clean up this mess,* **it's disgusting.**

- *You still haven't cleaned up that* **bloody** *mess!*

Supportive moves

A supportive move appears either before or after the head act and affects the context in which the request is embedded, and thus indirectly modifies the request.[30] Some examples are:

> **Are you going in the direction of town?** *And if so, is it possible for me to join you?* (checking on availability)

> **Will you do me a favor?** *Could you perhaps lend me your notes for a few days?* (getting a pre-commitment)

> *Excuse me,* **I've just missed my bus and you live on the same road.** *I wonder if I could trouble you for a lift?* (grounder)

---

[30] Blum-Kulka and Olshtain (1984: 204–5).

You have the most beautiful handwriting I've ever seen! Would it be possible to borrow your notes for a few days? (sweetener)

*Excuse me, **I hope you don't think I'm being forward**, but is there any chance of a lift home?* (disarmer)

*Pardon me, but could you give a lift, **if you're going my way?** I just missed the bus and there isn't another one for an hour.* (cost minimizer)

Request perspectives

Requests usually include reference to the requester, the recipient of the request, and/or the action to be performed. The speaker/writer can manipulate requests by choosing from a variety of perspectives in making requests:[31]

1 **Listener-oriented** (emphasis on the role of the listener):

  *Could **you** clean up the kitchen, please?*

2 **Speaker-oriented** (emphasis on the speaker's role as the requester):

  *Can **I** borrow your notes from yesterday?*

3 **Speaker- and listener-oriented** (inclusive strategy):

  *So, could **we** tidy up the kitchen soon?*

4 **Impersonal:**

  So it might not be a bad idea to get it cleaned up.

Conventionally indirect substrategies

The following substrategies for indirect request are commonly found in Australian English, Canadian French, Hebrew, and/or Argentinean Spanish (see http://www.carla.umn.edu/speechacts/requests/strategies.html for examples in these languages):

1 reference to the listener's ability (used in all of the four languages);

2 reference to the listener's willingness;

3 predicting the listener's doing the act; and

4 formulaic suggestions.

---

[31] Blum-Kulka *et al.* (1989); Blum-Kulka and Olshtain (1984: 203).

Non-conventionally indirect strategies (requestive hints)

In making requestive hints, the speaker/writer uses a lack of clarity as a way of getting the listener to carry out the act that is implicitly requested.[32] There is a gap between the requester's intended meaning and the literal meaning, and the recipient is not expected to process the requester's utterance word-for-word but rather to infer the intended message. The lack of clarity leaves the recipient uncertain as to the requester's intentions, and at the same time leaves the requester the option of denying the recipient's interpretation of the request. The recipient also has the option of rejecting the interpretation that the requester has in fact made a request.

Some examples of hints are:[33]

It's cold in here. (when uttered as a request to close the window)

I love this chocolate but it's so expensive I could not afford it. (when used as a request that the recipient of the remark buy chocolate for the speaker)

Do you have any money on you? (when used as a request for a loan)

You must have had a beautiful party. (when used as a request to clean up the kitchen the morning after)

Husband: *Do you know where today's paper is?*

Wife: *I'll get it for you.*

Requests are among the most researched speech acts, and the empirical information, such as that cited above, has been utilized in recent L2 teaching. You can see some of them in Chapter 7 and on the *Teaching Pragmatics* website.[34]

Conversational implicature

Conversational implicature is an inferential message or the process through which the speaker/writer and the listener/reader derive meaning. The meaning of an utterance is understood through inference in terms of the context, rather than through direct reference.[35] While most utterances are expected to be truthful, appropriately informative, relevant, and clear,[36] at times

---

[32] Blum-Kulka *et al.* (1989).
[33] Blum-Kulka *et al.* (1989: 73).
[34] Bardovi-Harlig and Mahan-Taylor (2003: available online).
[35] Bouton (1994*a*: 88).
[36] Grice (1975).

speakers/writers choose not to abide by these principles and convey meaning indirectly. In such cases, listeners look for another non-literal interpretation for this conversational implicature that fits the context.[37] Below are several classifications and examples of conversational implicature:[38]

1 Irony

Example: Bill is referring to his best friend Peter who danced with Bill's wife while Bill was away:

Bill: Peter knows how to be a really good friend. (*Implying that Peter is not acting the way a good friend should.*)

2 Relevance maxim

This is based on the principle that the intended message must be relevant to the ongoing conversation despite its literal meaning.

Example: Frank talks to his wife, Helen:

Frank: What time is it, Helen?

Helen: The mail carrier has been here. (*Telling Frank approximate time based on the regularity of the mail carrier's deliveries.*)

Frank: Okay. Thanks.

3 Minimum requirement rule

Example: Mr Brown is applying for a loan at the bank to build a new barn:

Banker: Do you have 50 cows, Mr Brown?

Mr Brown: Yes, I do (*Indicating that he has at least 50 cows and maybe more, which is the minimum he needs to apply for a loan*).

---

[37] Bouton (1994*a*, 1994*b*).
[38] The classification and examples are from Bouton (1994*a*) and (1994*b*). See these articles for more details of each context.

4 Indirect criticism through implicature

Example: Teachers A and B are discussing a student's paper:

A: Have you finished with Mark's term paper yet?

B: Yeah, I read it last night.

A: What did you think of it?

B: Well, I thought it was well typed (*Implying that he did not like the paper*).

5 The POPE Q implicature

The name is based on the prototype, *Is the Pope Catholic?*

Example: Two roommates are discussing their plans for the summer:

Fran: My mother wants me to stay home for a while, so I can be there when our relatives come to visit us at the beach.

Joan: Do you have a lot of relatives?

Fran: Are there flies in the summertime? (*Implying that she has a lot of relatives*).

While conversational implicature is part of everyday interaction, understanding implied meaning requires cultural knowledge and its interpretation can be difficult to L2 learners who have lived in the **second-language** context for several years.[39] Studies show, however, that explicit classroom instruction can accelerate the learning of conversational implicature.[40] A description of a suggested instructional procedure on conversational implicature appears in Chapter 8.

Discussion

This chapter has given an introduction to the CARLA Speech Acts website, where descriptions of speech acts are posted as a resource for teachers, curriculum writers, and learners alike. The website is meant to provide

[39] Bouton (1994*a*, 1994*b*); Kasper and Rose (2002).
[40] Bouton (1994*a*, 1999); Kubota (1995).

bare-bone details for six of the major speech acts appearing in the research literature. The following activity will give you an opportunity to explore in greater detail the speech act of your choice, using a larger database housed on the CARLA website. Our view is that if teachers have an explicit know-ledge of the "anatomy" of a given speech act, they would more effectively share that information with learners. The activity at the end of this chapter provides an opportunity to familiarize yourself with the research-based information regarding speech acts in the language(s) taught.

Activity 4.1 Exploring research-based descriptions of speech acts

Objectives

1   You will be able to identify descriptions of speech acts as derived from research in cross-cultural and interlanguage pragmatics.

2   You will be able to gain more explicit awareness of the cross-cultural similarities and differences regarding the pragmatic use of the target language you teach.

Suggested time: 40 minutes.

Materials:

- computers with access to the internet;
- alternatively, research articles on speech acts or other pragmatic features that you wish to investigate.

Directions

1   Form groups according to the speech act(s) of your interest. Ideally your group has speakers of different languages. Sit next to them in the computer lab.

2   Read the portion of this chapter that contains information about the speech act(s) of your choice. This serves as an introduction to the CARLA website.

3   Then, go online and explore your speech act(s) listed in: http://www.carla.umn.edu/speechacts/descriptions.html. Make sure to click on "research notes" links for more detailed information.

4   Save the link or copy down the cultural and linguistic information that you think will be beneficial to you and your colleagues. At some later point you may decide to utilize this information to build pragmatics-focused tasks or a lesson plan.

5   Discuss in your small group what you have found out about the speech act(s) you have studied, comparing descriptions across languages. Evaluate how credible the

information seems to be to you. If the information does not appear to reflect authentic language use, discuss why that might be the case and how you would adapt the information.

6   Report to the whole group what your small group has found out about the speech act(s). Make sure to discuss both cultural and linguistic aspects of the speech act(s).

Discussion/wrap-up

Discuss the utility of research-based information in pragmatics-focused instruction. What are the pros and cons of such data? Start considering how you might use the information in teaching speech acts.

CHAPTER 5

Learners' pragmatics: potential causes of divergence[1]

Noriko Ishihara and Andrew D. Cohen

Introduction

When interacting with people who are not native speakers of our language, we may notice that their pragmatic behavior does not always follow expected patterns. This may be true even if they are relatively advanced-level learners. There could be a number of reasons for this phenomenon, and we will explore five of them in this chapter. Take, for example, the relatively sensitive interaction between an advisor, a fluent speaker of English, and a graduate student who is an L2 speaker of English new in the target culture. Imagine that the student is in her advisor's office and she doesn't agree with the advisor's suggestions regarding the line-up of the classes she should take in the upcoming semester. Refusing the advisor's recommendation could be a frightening proposition and in this face-threatening situation the advisee's pragmatic skills become crucial for her academic success and for maintaining good rapport with her advisor. Research has shown that the speech of even advanced L2 speakers is found to differ from native speakers in ways that could be misleading to an advisor.[2]

We may wonder if learners – especially those living in the L2 community – are able to take advantage of their exposure to authentic language. Even without explicit instruction in pragmatics in the classroom, they might

---

[1] The term, *divergence* or *to diverge*, in this book is descriptive in nature. No pejorative connotation is attached to this term (as in for example, Barron (2003); Beebe and Giles (1984); Beebe and Zuengler (1983)).

[2] Bardovi-Harlig (2001); Bardovi-Harlig and Hartford (2005).

eventually improve their pragmatic ability. However, if no formal instruction is provided, it is said to generally take at least 10 years in a **second-language** context (as opposed to a foreign-language context) to be able to use the language in a pragmatically nativelike manner.[3] Even if learners are immersed in the L2 environment, it is possible that they are not exposed to enough – or appropriate kind of – language exposure. For instance, advising sessions are usually kept private and even if the student in the example above happened to overhear the same advisor with another student on a similar issue, that conversation might not provide the best language model for her due to the differences in relationship. Learners may not receive constructive feedback about their pragmatic language use. In addition, they are not always required or expected to use the language in a native-like manner.[4] Indeed, pragmatic ability is one of the most complex and challenging aspects of communicative competence.

It may seem surprising, but learners might not always be striving for native-like pragmatic use. Research indicates that learners' sense of identity is intertwined with how they use the language, and for this reason they sometimes choose not to behave in a native-like fashion.[5] It is also interesting to note that nonnative-like language use is not always seen as negative; it can be considered innovative, creative, or even charming. This is especially true if natives are willing to "cut learners some slack," rather than coming down hard on them for not performing in the expected way. The issue of who our learners are – namely, their cultural and social identity – needs to be taken into account in our teaching of pragmatics (see Chapters 6, 8, 12, 15 for more discussion on this issue).

Even so, there are cases in which nonnative-like pragmatic use can be misinterpreted and lead to unwanted consequences that could be avoided, which is why it is important to focus on teaching pragmatics in the classroom. Language teachers can support learners when they attempt to produce pragmatically appropriate language and interpret meaning as intended by others in the L2 community. What keeps learners from understanding cultural norms as they are expressed in the L2? What prevents learners from using language exactly as they intend to communicate their meaning?

In this chapter we will look at five common causes of learners' divergence from native-like pragmatic language use. The first four reasons for pragmatic divergence can lead to *pragmatic failure* and are related primarily to cognitive

[3] Cohen and Olshtain (1993); Olshtain and Blum-Kulka (1985); Wolfson (1989).
[4] Barron (2003); Iino (1996); Kasper and Rose (2002); Siegal and Okamoto (2003).
[5] For further reading about this topic, see for example, Ishihara (2006, 2008c); LoCastro (2003); and Siegal (1996).

functioning in language learning and use. Here you might notice that they can have some overlap with each other, as learners sometimes have difficulties in multiple areas. Also, it may be difficult to pinpoint exact source(s) of an instance of pragmatic divergence by just analyzing surface manifestations. The fifth category is distinctively different in that it concerns cases where learners are aware of the pragmatic norms and linguistically capable of producing native-like forms, but make a deliberate choice not to use them on a particular occasion.

Five common causes of learners' divergence from pragmatic norms[6]

Pragmatic divergence due to insufficient pragmatic ability:

1 negative transfer of pragmatic norms;

2 limited grammatical[7] ability in the L2;

3 overgeneralization of perceived L2 pragmatic norms;

4 effect of instruction or instructional materials.

Pragmatic divergence due to learner choice:

5 Resistance to using perceived L2 pragmatic norms.

Divergence due to insufficient pragmatic ability

Sometimes learners may simply not know what is typically said on certain occasions and as a result, inadvertently produce divergent language forms. Or, because their pragmatic awareness has gaps, they decide to take a guess according to what they think most speakers would say, which turns out to be not quite typical in that particular context. On other occasions, they may rely on the sociocultural norms and language behavior associated with another community with which they are familiar. Learners may also obtain material from the teacher or from language textbooks which mislead them, resulting in a cultural *faux pas* when they use it in authentic interaction. So, a partial lapse in pragmatic awareness, insensitivity to pragmatic norms

---

[6] See the references in each individual section below.
[7] Grammar refers broadly to formal linguistic knowledge that includes not only syntax and morphosyntax, but also lexis and phonology (Canale and Swain 1980; Kasper and Rose 2002).

of the L2, or insufficient linguistic ability may very often be the reason for learners' pragmatic failure.

In the following, we will look at each of these sub-categories in order to identify a potential cause or combination of causes of pragmatic divergence. This needs assessment will assist you in making an educated guess as to why students fail to communicate what they intend to convey, or why they deliberately diverge from the range of L2 norms. Knowing about the sources of pragmatic divergence is one of the first steps towards designing effective pragmatics instruction.

1 Negative transfer of pragmatic norms

When learners do not know pragmatic norms in the target language or when they assume that their own pragmatic norms apply in the given situation in the target culture, they may consciously or unconsciously depend on the norms that apply for that situation when using their first, dominant, or some other language. This influence of the learners' knowledge of other languages and cultures on their pragmatic use and development on the use of the L2 is referred to as *pragmatic transfer*.[8] Although pragmatic transfer may produce positive results, when learners' pragmatic norms are similar and applicable to the L2 (referred to as *positive* transfer), our focus here on divergence will have us focus just on what has been referred to in the literature as *negative* transfer.[9]

Let us take the case of a Korean learner of Japanese who receives a compliment on her class presentation from her friend. Although she is not sure of what to say in response in Japanese, she depends on her first-language-based intuition and says an equivalent of "no, that's not true" in Japanese. This is likely to be perceived as an appropriately modest behavior in the target culture where the pragmatic norm is similar to that in the learner's L1.

In a community where the L2 norms are quite different, however, the transfer of behavior consistent with L1 norms may cause awkwardness, misunderstanding, or even a temporary communication breakdown. This is especially the case when the listener is not familiar with learners' language or culture. Let us suppose that the above-mentioned Korean learner, speaking English this time, responds to the same friend's compliment saying "no, that's not true" in English. This language behavior may make it sound as if she were flatly rejecting or questioning the peer's evaluation, and hence

---

[8] Kasper (1992).
[9] The term, *transfer*, in this book is descriptive in nature. It is equivalent to *L1 influence*, a phrase intended to be seen as non-pejorative.

create a somewhat awkward situation or even sound insulting. An ESL teacher with knowledge of Korean pragmatics would most likely understand the source of this response to the compliment, but other listeners may be mystified or offended.

The following are some more examples of negative transfer of L1 pragmatic norms in spoken interactions with members of the L2 community:

- An American hitchhiking in Israel feels the need to entertain the driver by talking non-stop after being given a ride, whereas, depending on the driver, it may be preferable for the hitchhikers to remain completely silent unless asked a question.

- An American asks an Arab married man in Gaza to say how many children he has and to describe each one. The Arab may feel it is a jinx on his family if he provides that information.

- When invited to a birthday party of a friend in Mexico, an American says precisely why he cannot make it, rather than saying he will make an effort to be there, which is a typical refusal in Mexico.[10]

If the reason for learners' pragmatic failure is transfer from another language, you may wish to incorporate some awareness-raising tasks in your pragmatics instruction. Your message to students in such tasks would be that what is appropriate in one culture may or may not be so in the second. For example, in teaching ESL learners how to give and respond to compliments, learners' knowledge of their L1 can be used:

> What do people say in your country when they give and receive compliments on a nice-looking possession or a presentation that is well done? Provide a literal translation of some examples.[11]

This activity is likely to help make similarities and differences across the learners' cultures more apparent, effectively demonstrating the risk involved in inadvertently transferring L1 pragmatic norms into the second. An Arabic-speaking student commented; "Even if I know it [how to give compliments] in my native language, if I translate it, it won't work."[12] It is this awareness of pragmatic norms that would most likely prevent negative pragmatic transfer.

[10] This example comes from Félix-Brasdefer (2003).
[11] Adapted from Ishihara (2003a).
[12] Ishihara (2004: 54).

2 Limited L2 grammatical ability

Learners' grammatical control and pragmatic ability are not necessarily on a par with each other. Learners who can understand and produce highly accurate language forms from a grammatical point of view are not necessarily able to use language in a pragmatically appropriate manner. Even if they have flawless control of grammar, they may fail to understand the listener's intended meaning. Conversely, learners who demonstrate very little grammatical accuracy may still be able to interpret messages as intended and produce pragmatically appropriate utterances.[13]

Nonetheless, learners' grammatical ability may well have an impact on their L2 pragmatic competence. They may be able to comprehend others' messages better when these messages use the grammar that they best understand. Likewise, they are most likely to produce structures that are within their grammatical control. For example, learners whose grammatical ability is limited to simple sentences may understand single-clause requests such as *Could I use your pen for a second?* But if they are yet to master compound sentences, they may not be able to comprehend accurately or produce bi-clausal requests (e.g. *Would you mind if . . .* or *I was wondering if . . .*).[14]

So, if learners' underdeveloped grammatical ability is a cause of pragmatic failure, teachers might decide to include some grammar-focused activities. In teaching bi-clausal requests, for example, it would be important to direct learners' attention to the **form** through either learner discovery or more directive teaching. The subjunctive use of the verb and modal in the *if*-clause, for instance,

*Would you mind if I **borrowed** your notes?* or

*I was wondering if you **could** possibly lend me your car for a few minutes.*

would need to be explicitly addressed. At the same time, it is important to link learners' knowledge of the **meaning** of these constructions, as well as the **use** (when and why they are used). This form–meaning–use approach is advocated in a well-known grammar reference.[15]

Form: subjunctive form in the *if*-clause.

Meaning: the meaning of the verbs *mind* and *wonder*, the intended
           request these formulaic structures convey.

---

[13] For an example of such a learner, see Schmidt (1983).
[14] See Bardovi-Harlig (1999, 2003), and Takahashi (2001, 2005), for further discussion.
[15] Celce-Murcia and Larsen-Freeman (1999).

Use: the level of politeness, formality, and directness of these
             expressions; the reason why these expressions were used in
             terms of the speaker–listener relationship and other situational
             context.

In this teachers' resource book, we suggest sample grammar-focused activities that have bearings on pragmatics for a variety of grammatical structures.

3 Overgeneralization of perceived L2 pragmatic norms

When L2 speakers develop a hypothesis about L2 grammar, they are known
to *overgeneralize* a certain rule to other language situations where the rule
does not apply.[16] For instance, the general rule of forming past tense verbs
by adding -*ed* is often incorrectly applied to irregular verbs (e.g., *eated, taked,*
and *telled*) due to the function of overgeneralization.

We can draw a parallel here in the area of L2 pragmatics. When learners
have only a rudimentary understanding of the target culture and the nature
of its pragmatic norms, they may depend on their preconceived notions
about L2 norms and wrongly apply them to different contexts. Pragmatic
failure may occur as a result. In such a case, the cause of the pragmatic failure
stems from *overgeneralization* of pragmatic norms of the L2, which may draw
on preconceived cultural stereotypes as well. Learners could be neglecting
the social, geographical, and situational variability in the L2. For example,
apologizing by simply saying *I'm sorry* or *Excuse me* works in some situations
but not in others, depending on the listener and magnitude of the offense.
Learners may induce from their own intercultural experiences that, for
instance, Asian language speakers tend to be more indirect in their use of
language compared to English speakers, and may apply this stereotypical
notion inappropriately to another situation in which Asian language speakers
would indeed speak rather directly.

Misconceptions can occur at a more linguistic level as well. Learners may
inappropriately associate linguistic forms with a given level of politeness or
formality. For example, they might look at a range of request expressions
and generate a hypothesis that the longer an expression is, the more polite
or formal the expression must be. So, since the expression, *May I . . . ?*, is
relatively short, they inappropriately associate the structure with extreme
informality, when it actually implies greater formality.[17]

---

[16] See Selinker (1972).
[17] This example comes from Matsuura (1998).

One way to support learners in avoiding such overgeneralizations would be to present a general pragmatic norm and then a few counter-examples. Here is an example of an exercise on refusals in Japanese from the web-based materials.[18]

> **Situation**: Your roommate is a good friend of yours, but she sometimes asks you to loan her some money and does not necessarily pay it back promptly. Today again, she asks you to lend her 3,000 yen. Because she has not yet paid you back from the last few times you loaned her money, you want to decline her request this time. Besides that, you don't really have extra money you can give her at this point.

Here is a sample dialogue between two female friends as it was presented to learners in the web-based unit. This dialogue was elicited through a role-play and reflects authentic language use. By attending to the refusal strategies in **bold** below, you may notice how indirect and polite B's responses are in general. Given that learners are likely to have generalized that refusals in Japanese are more indirect than in English, this example would be consistent with that generalization.

> A: ねえ、みか、ちょっとお金貸してもらえないかな、今日。 "Hey, Mika, can you lend me some money today?"
>
> B: **えー、いくら？** "Um, how much?"
>
> A: あの、3000円なんだけど。 "Well, 3,000 yen."
>
> B: **うーん、今月はね、私もちょっと厳しいの。** "Well, my budget is a little tight this month, too."
>
> A: うーん、そこをなんとかならないかな。 "Well, can you help me at all somehow?"

---

[18] Ishihara and Cohen (2004: available online). The entire exercise, as well as audio files and transcripts for both dialogues, is available at: http://www.carla.umn.edu/speechacts/japanese/Refusals/Ex2.html. See also Chapter 11 for more about this curriculum.

B: えー、でも先月の 2000 円もまだ返してくれてないじゃない。"Well, but you haven't paid the 2,000 yen back from last month yet either."

A:　うん、そうだったね。来週、ほら、あの、お給料入るから、全部一緒に払えるから。だめかな。"You are right. Well, I'll get paid next week, so I can pay everything back at that time."

B:　うーん、ともこさんには聞いてみた？　"Well, have you asked Tomoko?"

A:あー、そうだね、聞いてみるよ。"Ah, that's right. I'll ask her."

B:うん、その方が嬉しいな。"Yeah, I'd be happier that way."

A:うん、わかった。じゃあ。"All right. See you, then."

B:ごめんね。"I'm sorry,"

A:いいよ、いいよ、気にしないで。"That's OK. Never mind."

The exercise goes on to present another sample dialogue, this time with two male speakers. Again, this example was obtained through a role-play but the exchange reflects authentic language use. Note how the refusals are presented in a direct fashion (in **bold**).

A:　あ、けんじ、ちょっと頼みがあるんだけどさ。"Oh, Kenji, I have a favor."

B: えー、何、何？ "Oh, what is it?"

A: あの、3000 円貸してくれない？ "Um, can you lend me 3,000 yen?"

B: え、また？だってさ、この間貸したけどさ、返ってきてないよ。"What, again? I lent you some the other day, but you haven't paid me back yet."

A: うん、返すからさ、月末には。"Yeah, I'll pay you back at the end of the month."

B:　いやー、そんなこと言っておまえ、いつも返してくれないじゃん。　"No way, you say that, but you never pay me back."

A: いやー、返すよ、ほらこの間返したじゃん、一回。"Oh, no, I will pay you back. See, I paid you back the other day."

▶

B: いや、うそ、うそ。ちょっとだめだよ。だって全然返してくれないんだもん。 "No, way, you liar! [lit. that is a lie.] I can't. You never pay it back."

A: いやー、困ってるんだよ。頼むからさ、今回だけ。 "Well, I'm in trouble. Please. Just this time."

B: だめ、だめ、もう癖になるからね。だめ、だめ。 "No, no. You'd always say that. No, no!"

You may have noticed that speaker B even characterizes his friend's utterance as a lie (although doing so has less of a shock value in Japanese than in English)! This particular sample could work as a counter-example to the learners' generalization that Japanese speakers tend to be indirect. Learners can be asked to compare these two dialogues and consider what factors have led to the pragmatic differences. They may notice the impact of gender and perhaps also personal speech styles. So, showing contrastive examples such as these helps to illustrate the variability found in authentic discourse and why learners' dependence on generalizations may be a bit risky, however convenient it is to be able to simplify speech patterns.

4 Effect of instruction or instructional materials[19]

Learners' pragmatic divergence can sometimes be attributed to the effect of the instruction or the instructional materials, rather than being a result of insufficient pragmatic awareness or incomplete pragmatic control on the learners' part. So what distinguishes this category from the three previous ones is that the responsibility for the divergence actually lies with the instruction, not with the learner. It is as if divergence is simply "waiting to happen."

For example, classroom instruction may put an emphasis on having learners produce complete sentences. However, sometimes when learners apply this pattern to real-life conversations, the communication is viewed as inefficient, irritating, or lacking tact. It in fact violates the *principle of economy* where repetitive information tends to be omitted in natural conversation.[20] For example, when asked, "Have you already had a chance to go canoeing on the beautiful Lake of the Isles this summer?" a learner replies,

---

[19] Selinker (1972) referred to teacher- or materials-induced errors as *transfer of training*.
[20] Thomas (1983).

"Yes. I have already had a chance to go canoeing on the beautiful Lake of the Isles this summer." This response would show up as too lengthy and redundant in the spoken discourse.

Similarly, generalizations found in instructional materials may be misleading. For instance, a cultural note in a language textbook that says that Americans tend to speak directly may induce learners' overgeneralization of this tendency. Learners may assume that there are few (or no) indirect expressions in English.[21] Such a misconception neglects the complexity of pragmatic norms in a language, and disregards how much language can vary across situations. So a learner who remembers this misleading piece of information could possibly ask too direct a question in the situation of getting to know a colleague at work. For example, if that learner turns to this colleague and asks, "What is your religion?" the American listener's interpretation might be that the learner is being too direct and personal.

One way for teachers to avoid negative consequences of instruction itself would be to check just how well what is taught reflects the reality found in different situations. While the instructional materials may not be "wrong," they might be purposefully simplified to accommodate learners' levels of proficiency. You may wish to make sure that the information presented is not misleading. If it is, you may choose to avoid or adapt it accordingly. It may also be beneficial to point out to your students how textbook exercises may use language in a way that is not consistent with the pragmatic norms of the target community.

In the above example, we discussed a case of learners instructed to produce complete sentences for the sake of structural practice. For pragmatics-focused instruction, teachers might use transcripts of formal and informal exchanges and have learners analyze how frequently complete and incomplete responses are chosen. The class could also discuss what pragmatic effects both types of sentences have in the particular contexts. Depending on the context, complete sentences could be interpreted as anywhere from appropriately formal/well-articulated to inefficient, repetitive, tactless, or even rude or sarcastic. Similarly, incomplete sentences may sound appropriately informal/efficient, uncooperative in conversation, or overly informal. Learners can be encouraged to consider these pragmatic effects in interpreting and using complete and incomplete utterances. This awareness-raising task would help guard against the inappropriate use of instructional content by allowing learners to grasp pragmatic meaning more accurately and make a more informed decision as to how they choose to express themselves.

---

[21] Ishihara (2009).

Pragmatic divergence due to the learners' choice

Thus far we have looked at causes of pragmatic failure or nonnative-like pragmatic behavior that are the result of gaps in basic language proficiency or in knowledge about L2 pragmatics. What the instances of divergence that we have looked at so far have in common is that they are *unintended*. But what about instances where learners deliberately choose to resist pragmatic norms for the community? Let us now take a look at this type of learner behavior.

5 Resistance to using perceived L2 pragmatic norms

As discussed above, another possible cause for learners' pragmatic divergence may be their sense of resistance, or their intentional divergence from the perceived range of pragmatic norms of the L2. As you may well imagine, learners are not a blank slate free from preconceptions of the world. Rather, they are social beings replete with their own cultural values, beliefs, and worldview. Their subjective disposition – social identity, attitudes, personal beliefs, and principles – is likely to influence how they present themselves in their L2 pragmatic behavior. On the one hand, they may adjust to L2 norms so as to communicate effectively or attain social approval in the community. On the other, they may deliberately diverge from L2 norms to accentuate their linguistic differences.[22] They may even elect to isolate themselves from the L2 group and to maintain their subjectivity (e.g., their cultural identity, personal principles, sense of value, and integrity that were in conflict with a perceived L2 norm). Learners may refuse to learn certain language forms that conflict with their own subjective position (in which case, the cause of their pragmatic divergence would be insufficient pragmatic ability). However, on other occasions learners may choose – as a way of asserting their subjectivity – **not** to use the forms that they have control over linguistically and are capable of producing (see Chapter 6 for more theoretical discussion of this pragmatic choice).[23]

This issue of learner resistance has important pedagogical implications for language teaching. First of all, we need to make sure that teachers do not impose the adoption of L2 norms on learners. This could be interpreted as cultural imposition or exercise of power.[24] It is the prerogative of the learners

---

[22] See the Speech Accommodation Theory (Beebe and Giles 1984).
[23] Examples of such learner behavior can be found in LoCastro (1998); Ishihara (2008c), (in press, b); Ishihara and Tarone (2009); and Siegal (1996), among others.
[24] Kasper and Rose (2002).

to decide when they will accommodate to the perceived range of pragmatic norms and to what extent they will do so under each set of circumstances. So rather than attempting to eliminate learners' resistance, teachers could use culturally sensitive instructional strategies.

For example, a learner of Japanese in a research study chose to use the higher level of *keigo* (exalted and humble forms of honorifics) in casually conversing with a much younger employee, when he knew that he was not expected to use it at all. His rationale was that he believed in equality among all human beings and that he did not want to seem discourteous to anyone by using a less respectful speech style.[25] Thus, his personal beliefs and principles conflicted with what he knew as the pragmatic norm of behavior in the L2. This personal conflict caused him to deliberately diverge from the perceived norm. While our view would be that this learner's pragmatic choice deserves to be respected, we would then need to ensure that learners have *receptive* pragmatic skills so that they are able to recognize common interpretations of L2 pragmatic norms in the target community. With this particular learner, teachers could use the following discussion prompts for pragmatic awareness-raising:

> What positive, negative, or neutral impression might your employee have of you and your speech style? How might s/he define his/her relationship with you as a result? What are some consequences – potential pros and cons of your developing this type of relationship with him/her?

In order to ensure that learners are able to *produce* the appropriate honorific forms in the Japanese language classroom, teachers could do so by asking learners:

> What would **most people** in Japan say in this situation?

---

[25] Ishihara and Tarone (2009).

rather than:

> What would **you** say in Japanese in this situation?

While the difference may strike you as subtle, in this way teachers could evade the issue of how learners personally choose to express themselves, while teaching the language-focused side of pragmatics (pragmalinguistics) – in this case, honorific forms. Similarly, learners' pragmatic choice would be evaluated in light of their *intention*, rather than how native-like it is. We will take a more in-depth look at the assessment issues in Chapters 14 and 15.

In any case, teachers can play an important role in helping learners to interpret the L2 as intended and express themselves as they please. Whether learners choose to conform to perceived native-speaker norms or diverge from them, it is important for language teachers to ensure that learners recognize the shared interpretation of their utterances in the community and potential *consequences* of their pragmatic behavior.[26] In the above example, most Japanese speakers do not use a higher level of *keigo* honorifics addressing a much younger employee in an informal setting. So the shared understanding of deliberately using them would be that the employer is being overly polite and perhaps a bit alienating, or sarcastic and playful. Or, if the employer is perceived as an L2 speaker not fully competent in the target language, the relationship may not be affected at all, or he may be seen as trying to be respectful in his own way. While accommodation to L2 norms may open doors to cultural integration, resisting L2 norms in a given situation may lead to alienation from the community (a negative repercussion), or freer expression of learners' cultural identity and negotiation of the community norms (positive consequences).[27]

Discussion

In this chapter, we have explored potential causes of learners' pragmatic behavior that is different from L2 norms. When we encounter such behavior in the classroom, teachers of L2 pragmatics might first wish to differentiate between what is likely to be problematic and what is not. "Unproblematic"

---

[26] Siegal and Okamoto (2003).
[27] See further examples and interpretations in Ishihara (2006, 2008c).

behavior may not exactly correspond to what most target language speakers say, but is likely to communicate learners' intentions. So perhaps it is safe to leave this type of learners' pragmatic use alone. For example, although "I am Ken" on the phone is not exactly native-like, it is unlikely to cause offense for the listener especially if the speaker is viewed as a beginning language learner. On the other hand, potentially "problematic" language behavior is another type that tends to cause misunderstanding on the listeners' part, and thus, most likely warrants instruction. If the same learner on the phone goes on to say, "who are you?" in a rather sharp tone of voice, the likelihood that this sounds unpleasant to the listener increases. This may be when a teacher decides to intervene to teach a more pragmatically appropriate behavior.

Learners' potential pragmatic failure that is unintended can stem from their limited pragmatic and/or grammatical ability and can be attributed to several factors:

- inappropriate transfer of norms from another language;

- limited grammatical ability which precludes their understanding or producing native-like forms;

- their misapplication of what they think is a target pragmatic norm to a wrong context; and

- their obtaining misleading information from the teacher or the instructional materials about the pragmatic norms of the L2.

These factors are not mutually exclusive and can occur sometimes in combination. The causes of pragmatic divergence are not always crystal clear, and the teacher may need to observe learners further or ask them why they said what they said. In another case of pragmatic *choice*, even knowing pragmatic norms in the L2 community, learners may intentionally resist such perceived norms to assert their identity.

In any case, teachers conducting needs assessment – analyzing and identifying a potential reason or a combination of sources for learners' pragmatic divergence – may have a head start in effectively teaching and assessing learners' development of pragmatic skills. For instance, when the cause of a pragmatic error is learners' limited grammatical control, reinforcement of necessary structures would meet learners' needs more efficiently than revising pragmatic awareness that learners already have demonstrated. Teachers sensitive to learners' pragmatic choice might make their assessments based on how well learners' intended meaning is expressed rather than how native-like they sound (see Chapters 14 and 15 for more information). The following activity will show authentic examples of pragmatic divergence.

The activity will provide readers with an opportunity to analyze potential causes of learners' pragmatic divergence and brainstorm about effective teaching strategies.

Activity 5.1 Determining the sources of learners' pragmatic behavior

Objectives

1   You will be able to identify the potential source or combination of sources for this divergence.

2   You will be able to analyze the factors that might have influenced your pragmatic use through reflection on your own experience learning and using an L2.

Suggested time: 40 minutes.

Materials:

■   Information: "Source of pragmatic divergence" (List 1), with five potential sources for learners' divergent pragmatic behavior;

■   Task sheet: "Examples of learners' divergent pragmatic behavior" (List 2);

■   Possible answers (List 3).

Directions

Part 1

1   Form into groups of four to five participants.

2   Each group is to get a copy of the list of potential sources for pragmatic divergence (List 1) and a copy of task sheet, "Examples of pragmatic divergence" (List 2).

3   Look at each example of learners' pragmatic L2 use included in the scrambled set of examples of pragmatic behavior and determine the factors that may have contributed to that particular pragmatic behavior. Match each example with one or more of the five possible sources. Note that there could potentially be more than one source for a certain pragmatic behavior and it may be difficult or impossible to identify only one. Place the corresponding letter(s) representing the source of the divergence in the blank for each situation. If you are not sure about a source, put parentheses around the letter(s).

4   After matching all examples with potential reasons, refer to the possible answers (List 3), comparing them with the results obtained by your group.

5   As a whole group, share the highlights of your small-group discussion.

Part 2

1   Get back into your small group.

2   Brainstorm about your own previous experiences learning and using an L2 – particularly with regard to cases of pragmatic failure and pragmatic resistance. Sample discussion questions:

   (a) What pragmatic difficulties or failures have you experienced? How did your partner for the interaction respond to you?

   (b) Have you felt resistant to any L2 pragmatic norms? In what situations and why? How did you behave in that situation, and how did the listener react to your pragmatic choice?

3   For each example of pragmatic failure and pragmatic choice, determine what factors/sources might have contributed to the communicative difficulties, misunderstandings, and sense of resistance.

4   As a whole group, share some of the examples and highlights of your discussion.

Discussion/wrap-up

Brainstorm about the instructional tasks you would design for helping learners overcome each type of pragmatic failure. If your list of reasons for divergence includes learners' resistance to perceived L2 norms, consider prompts that you might use with your students in order to probe the level of their pragmatic awareness. (Observation alone may not tell you how aware they are of the L2 norms and of the potential consequences resulting from their resistance.) If they are well aware, you might remain respectful of their pragmatic choice. If they are unaware, consider a classroom task or activity that you would provide them that would raise their pragmatic awareness (for examples, see the tasks suggested for each cause of pragmatic divergence in this chapter).

Information: Sources of pragmatic divergence (List 1)

Negative transfer of pragmatic norms	NT
Limited L2 grammatical ability	G
Overgeneralization of perceived L2 pragmatic norms	O
Effect of **instruction or instructional materials**	I
Resistance to using perceived L2 pragmatic norms	R

Task sheet: Examples of pragmatic divergence (List 2)

1 An American learner of Spanish has a sense that Spanish speakers are more formal in their requests so if she wants a glass of water from the mother of her host family, she asks for it in a most polite way, "Would you be able to give me a glass of water, please." The host mother finds her style overly formal since in their Barcelona home they just say the equivalent of "Water, please" or "Give me a glass of water, please."

Potential reasons for pragmatic divergence: _____

2 An L2 speaker of Japanese starts teaching English in a Japanese junior high school. A Japanese colleague approaches him and asks in Japanese if he wants to clean the school with the students, a customary daily routine in most schools there. Knowing that a Japanese teacher would probably say yes, he chooses to decline, because he believes that he did not go to college to clean a school.[28]

Potential reasons for pragmatic divergence: _____

3 A learner of English who reads in an ESL textbook: *Americans say "thank you" to a compliment received*,[29] starts responding that way to *all* compliments she receives and expects all fluent English speakers to react that way.

Potential reasons for pragmatic divergence: _____

4 Unaware of grounds for refunds in Japanese society, an American insists that his niece complain to the receptionist at a public bath resort in Tokyo after she is expelled from the bath because she has a small rose tattoo on the back of her shoulder (which, according to the bath house rules, is grounds for expulsion). He insists that they refund her $29 entrance fee.[30]

Potential reasons for pragmatic divergence: _____

5 A Japanese learner of English is invited to a concert on the weekend, but wants to decline because he would rather spend the night with his children at home. He literally translates what he would say in Japanese into English and says, "I have something to take care of at home."[31]

Potential reasons for pragmatic divergence: _____

6 A Japanese speaker writes an email message in English, acknowledging feedback from an anonymous reviewer on a chapter: "I certainly received your feedback. Thanks a lot." The writer's intention was simply to indicate that he had received

---

[28] An example from Ishihara (2006).
[29] A textbook commentary reported in Coulmas (1981).
[30] This actually happened to Cohen and his niece at the Utopia Bath House in Tokyo.
[31] An example from Beebe *et al.* (1990).

the feedback and appreciated it. He used "certainly" as an intensifier since *tashikani* would work in formal contexts in Japanese. But the effect in English was to sound as if he had gotten more feedback than he had bargained for and that he is even perhaps a bit annoyed. Even the "Thanks a lot" could be interpreted as facetious.

Potential reasons for pragmatic divergence: _____

7 An English-speaking learner of Indonesian hears an expression, *Did you eat yet?* as a regular greeting used among native speakers but avoids using it herself because it does not really seem like a greeting to her.[32]

Potential reasons for pragmatic divergence: _____

8 An English-speaking learner of Japanese is offered some more food at an informal dinner table by a close friend. The learner knows an expression, *Iie, kekkoudesu*, an equivalent of "no thanks" in Japanese and uses it.[33] However, the learner is unaware that this expression is usually used in formal situations and sounds funny or awkward if directed to a close friend.

Potential reasons for pragmatic divergence: _____

9 A Western learner of Japanese hears a female Japanese speaker use a combination of higher-level honorifics (humble and polite forms) to an elderly male and says to herself: "I'll play it safe with the polite form. She sounds too humble for me."[34] Although she gets a perfect score in a quiz on humble forms in her Japanese language class, she decides not to use it in speaking to the elderly male.

Potential reasons for pragmatic divergence: _____

10 A beginning learner of English asks a good friend to help him/her with a course paper written in English. The friend says: "If you'd told me earlier, I could've helped you." The learner catches the ". . . I could . . . help" portions of the message and is somewhat confused about what the friend means: Can s/he help or not?

Potential reasons for pragmatic divergence: _____

11 When invited to a special office party of a friend in Mexico, an American checks her calendar and sees she has a conflict, so she declines the invitation straight away – causing her friend to respond with surprise and disappointment since an acceptance, however reluctant, would be expected (regardless of actual intention to attend).

Potential reasons for pragmatic divergence: _____

[32] An example reported in DuFon (1999).
[33] An example reported in Ikoma and Shimura (1993).
[34] An example reported in Siegal (1996).

12 A beginning learner of English requests that a clerk in a repair shop fix an item, with "Do this for me now" because the learner has not yet learned how to be more indirect and consequently sound more polite (E.g., "I was wondering how soon you might be able to repair this for me").

Potential reasons for pragmatic divergence: _____

13 A Korean visitor to the US heard that Americans tend to be friendly, so she is surprised when the middle-aged man next to her on the bus seems unwilling to have a conversation with her. In response to her question, "What can I see in this town?" he just responds with, "Oh, lots of things", and goes back to reading his novel. The visitor is put off by this response.

Potential reasons for pragmatic divergence: _____

14 An American learner of Japanese is taught to fill a pause with *eeto* (more informal) or *ano* (more formal) in his Japanese class, and so does his best to fill as many pauses as he can that way, only to be told by a Japanese teacher that he is filling his pauses too much – that they prefer to use silence or non-verbal cues more.

Potential reasons for pragmatic divergence: _____

15 An American learner of Italian heard that Italians talk with their hands a lot, so he made an effort to use a lot of hand gestures to make his points in Italian while studying in Rome. An Italian friend took him aside and told him that he was gesturing too much, and also that some of his gestures meant something different from what he intended.

Potential reasons for pragmatic divergence: _____

16 An Israeli asks an American colleague how much she makes a month, assuming that it is fine to ask this question because it would indeed be reasonable in his home community. The American colleague is put off by the question since she takes it as unacceptable prying.

Potential reasons for pragmatic divergence: _____

17 A male Spanish learner of English gives an inappropriate compliment (*piropo*) to a female English speaker (e.g., "My god! So many curves and me without brakes!" – a literal translation from the Spanish: *¡Dios mio, tantas curvas y yo sin frenos!*[35]) This Spanish speaker isn't aware that such *piropos*, which are likely to be socially

---

[35] An example from Campo and Zuluaga (2000). The acceptability and interpretation of *piropos* much depends on various factors like the listener's regional variety of Spanish, age, occupation, and education. A more socially acceptable example of a *piropo* is: *La flor por ser flor no necesita mil colores un hombre para ser hombre no necesita mil amores.* "A flower, to be a flower, doesn't need a thousand colors; a man, to be a man, doesn't need a thousand lovers."

acceptable in a certain subculture of Spanish speakers, are much less so in English-speaking culture. In this case, the female English speaker in fact interpreted his utterance as rude and chauvinistic.

Potential reasons for pragmatic divergence: _____

Possible answers (List 3)

Note that for each of the scenarios above, there may be more than one source of learners' pragmatic divergence. The causes of divergent pragmatic behavior may result from multiple sources that are intertwined with each other. It may be difficult to determine a single cause, especially just by observing learners' pragmatic behavior. However, it is still valuable for language teachers to raise the issue as to the possible combination of reasons that might have caused learners to diverge from pragmatic language use. You can also ask the learners themselves for their explanations since they may be the best judge of whether a particular divergence was a result of negative transfer or overgeneralization, for example. Such analysis of learners' pragmatic use can lead to better informed language instruction. In addition, teachers and learners can make it a joint goal to support the learners in avoiding pragmatic divergence when they do not want it and to deal with it gracefully when they do.

1 Overgeneralization; possibly instruction or instructional materials, if the learner's source of belief is classroom instruction or instructional materials.

2 Resistance.

3 Instruction or instructional materials; overgeneralization, if instruction or instructional material is seen as a sub-category of over-generalization.

4 Negative transfer.

5 Negative transfer.

6 Negative transfer.

7 Resistance.

8 Negative transfer; possibly instruction or instructional materials, if the learner's language was misguided through instruction; possibly overgeneralization, if the learner assumed the polite expression to be appropriate based on the stereotype of the culture being polite.

9 Resistance.

10 Limited grammatical ability.

11 Negative transfer.

12 Limited grammatical ability; possibly negative transfer, if the learner's L1 allows this type of direct request in a service encounter.

13 Overgeneralization; possibly instruction or instructional materials, if the generalization was misguided through instruction.

14 Instruction or instructional materials; possibly negative transfer, if the learner guesses or assumes that pause fillers must occur as frequently in Japanese as in his L1 English.

15 Overgeneralization; possibly instruction or instructional materials, if the source of his information is instruction or instructional materials; possibly negative transfer, if he uses many hand gestures in his L1, which may be fine in that language but comes across as too much in Italian.

16 Negative transfer.

17 Negative transfer.

The nuts and bolts of pragmatics instruction

CHAPTER 6

Theories of language acquisition and the teaching of pragmatics

Noriko Ishihara

Introduction

Although the bulk of this teachers' guide is practical in orientation, this chapter takes a brief look at theoretical underpinnings for L2 pragmatics instruction. Because teachers' knowledge, beliefs, and practice are interconnected, (re)visiting a current understanding of pragmatics-focused language learning and teaching can reinforce this link and facilitate principled teaching (see Chapter 2). Since language learning is a complex phenomenon, it is a challenge to explain the multiple layers involved. Here, an Indian fable about nine blind men[1] may be relevant.

Once there were nine inquisitive blind men who did not know what an elephant was. They went to make acquaintance with this animal in order to understand what it was like. Each one touched only one part of the elephant and on that basis made an observation. The blind man who touched only the ears thought that an elephant was like a large, thin fan. The man who touched the tail thought that an elephant was like a rope. Another man who touched the trunk associated an elephant with a snake. The one who touched the legs likened the elephant to a tree trunk. The man who touched the elephant's side thought the animal was like a tall wall . . .

This fable illustrates the relationship between the parts and the whole (Figure 6.1). Observation of just one component part – the spotlight on only

---

[1] Cited in Patton (2002: 62).

FIGURE 6.1 Elephant in the spotlights

one part of a complex phenomenon – may not tell the whole story and, in fact, may be misleading. We need to group together the observations for each component in order to arrive at a comprehensive understanding of the phenomenon in question.

As language educators, we generally do not have access to what is going on inside our students' heads and do not follow them around to check out how they actually use the L2 in their social network. We are in some ways like the blind men when it comes to understanding the phenomenon of language learning. While a probe that we make to understand learners' cognitive processing can be of value, at best it provides only a limited picture of this multi-faceted phenomenon. A more holistic approach to understanding the development of pragmatic ability would entail shining a spotlight on more aspects involved in language learning and consider, among other things, how learners' sociocultural being is linked to their pragmatic use.

Researchers in second language acquisition (SLA) have offered theoretical frameworks that facilitate our understanding of how language learning works. Let us first look at the basic tenets of one of them, which has come to be called the Noticing Hypothesis. This hypothesis helps us explain an important cognitive learning of L2 pragmatics, and suggests how teachers can assist in this process. In addition, given the social and cultural nature of language learning and use, we will consider three other interdisciplinary frameworks, those related to identity, speech accommodation, and second language socialization. These theoretical frameworks are useful in attempting to account for social, cultural, psychological, and affective (emotional) factors that can influence L2 pragmatic learning and use. This chapter will also make a brief reference to other frameworks that can help to explain pragmatics-focused language learning.

Cognitive frameworks relating to L2 pragmatic development

Among the theoretical frameworks relevant to L2 language development are the noticing hypothesis,[2] the output hypothesis,[3] the interaction hypothesis,[4] and sociocultural theory.[5] We will now briefly discuss the basics of each of them below in this order with a focus on the first. These frameworks help us justify the awareness-raising approach currently being promoted in L2 pragmatics instruction.

Noticing, awareness, and attention

The noticing hypothesis in second language acquisition (SLA) has been extended to its sub-discipline, the realm of L2 pragmatics learning.[6] According to this framework, *attention* and *awareness* can be viewed as inseparable, like two sides of the same coin. Attention is seen as a variety of mechanisms or subsystems that control access to awareness. Attention is limited and selective in nature, managing access to consciousness and leading to the control of action and learning.[7] According to this framework, pragmatic information must be consciously attended to for the learning of pragmatics to take place. When pragmatic information is noticed, whether attended to deliberately or inadvertently, the input has the potential to become intake and may be stored in long-term memory.[8]

Then what pragmatic aspects should learners attend to? Does each of the specific attributes need to be attended to in processing, or is global attention sufficient? In this framework, attention must be directed not only to global attributes but also to specific, focused aspects of the L2. So with regard to the

---

[2] Schmidt (1990, 1993, 2001).
[3] Swain (1998); Swain and Lapkin (1995).
[4] Long (1985, 1996); Long *et al.* (1998).
[5] Vygotsky (1978).
[6] Kasper and Schmidt (1996); Schmidt (1990, 1993, 2001).
[7] Schmidt (2001).
[8] Kasper and Schmidt (1996); Schmidt (1993, 2001).

learning of pragmatics, this means that learners need to attend to the language form and to the relevant factors that affect the form in the given context. This framework posits that merely exposing learners to contextualized input is unlikely to lead to students' learning of pragmatics – that classroom tasks will have more of a payoff to learning if the language forms and relevant contextual features are highlighted and if the relationship between them is explored. Apparently this point has much relevance to how pragmatics is treated in everyday instruction.

To illustrate this point, let us revisit a piece of observational data that an actual language learner collected (see Chapters 3 and 7). Notice in the chart below how the language in the dialogue (quoted as originally spelled) reported by a learner and the contextual factors for the dialogue are juxtaposed to facilitate the analysis of the form–context relationship.

Contextual factors	Social status (S) Relative status (e.g., age, gender, role in conversation)	Distance (D) Level of distance	Intensity (I) Compliment topic
Dialogue	Equals (same age group, females, classmates)	Close	T-shirt (appearance/ possession)
	Jenny: Nice T-shirt! Steph: Well, Jenny, I bought it at a thrift store. Jenny: But it looks new! Steph: Oh, no, it's used, I bought it for $1. Jenny: That's really cheap. Steph: Thanks you.		

Another question about the learning of pragmatics concerns the necessary level of awareness of the linguistic form and contextual factors. This framework distinguishes between at least two levels of awareness, *noticing* and *understanding*. *Noticing* refers to "registering the simple occurrence of some event" – that is, identifying surface linguistic forms. On the other hand, *understanding* entails "recognition of a general principle, rule, or pattern."[9] Noticing includes the noticing of a particular term of address on a certain occasion (e.g., *Jane* or *Professor Doe*). Understanding would imply that learners realize the meaning of the choice of that particular form in the given context. So learners realize, for example, that the term of address, *Jane*, is predictably used by her friends, colleagues, and family members, and that *Professor Doe* would be the term of address most likely used by her students, and understand why different terms are selected and when each term is

[9] Schmidt (1993: 26).

used. When understanding occurs, learners realize why that particular form was used in relation to the contextual factors such as the speaker/writer and listener/readers' relative social status, age, gender, distance, and the level of formality of the occasion. The proponents of this framework would contend that noticing is concerned with the question of "what linguistic and non-verbal material is stored in memory," whereas understanding is related to questions regarding "how that material is organized into the language system".[10] In this framework, learners need to notice the surface features and to understand the principle, rule, or pattern involved for the learning of pragmatics.[11]

In fact, current research in L2 pragmatics generally appears to support the noticing–understanding framework. Experimental studies have found that explicit teaching of pragmatics – that is, instruction which includes metapragmatic information – seems to be more effective by and large than an implicit approach.[12] Such metapragmatic information can include contextual information analyzed in terms of social status, social and psychological distance, and degree of imposition. Mere exposure to pragmatic input (as in *implicit* teaching) may not lead to learners' pragmatic development, or the learning may emerge very slowly.[13] Generally speaking, explicit teaching appears to heighten learners' attention to specific linguistic features and an understanding of how these features relate to contextual factors (both in terms of how the context may shape language and how the use of certain language form can shape the contextual relationship).

Other cognitive frameworks related to L2 pragmatics

Even if learners understand how contextual factors are typically evaluated and how speakers' intent is expressed in L2 forms, we cannot simply assume that learners are able to **produce** these forms themselves in interaction. In addition to noticing and attention, output and interactional opportunities are likely to contribute to learners' acquisition of the L2. During output tasks when learners encounter a difficulty producing language, they may

---

[10] Adapted from Schmidt (2001: 26).

[11] More discussion can be found elsewhere, such as with regard to the control of processing (Bialystok 1993), the levels and types of attention (Kasper and Schmidt 1996), and the varying effectiveness of attention (Rose and Kasper 2001; Schmidt 2001).

[12] See Rose and Kasper (2001) and Rose (2005), for comprehensive reviews of individual studies. See Jeon and Kaya (2006), for quantitative meta-analysis of some of these studies.

[13] However, some implicit teaching techniques (e.g., input enhancement and recasts) have also been found effective to trigger learners' noticing (Alcón 2005; Fukuya and Clark 2001; Rose 2005).

notice gaps in their language system and turn to input for relevant resources in order to articulate their message.[14] Output tasks might facilitate learners' noticing of certain forms that they are lacking while they attempt to communicate their intended meaning in the L2. Although this argument focuses entirely on the development of grammatical ability, various production tasks may be effectively used as a pedagogical tool to elicit learners' noticing of key language features and appropriate modification of the output. Although knowledge of grammar alone does not promise appropriate pragmatic use, learners' grammatical ability is known to relate to their L2 pragmatic competence.[15] In the section below we will discuss various production tasks, as well as tasks for receptive skill development, that may promote learners' pragmatic development.

In addition, the interactional nature of communicative tasks (even some simulations like role-play or multiple-turn discourse completion tasks) also requires learners to attend not only to their own utterances but also to those of their interactional partners and to respond appropriately in context, often in real time. As learners engage in this negotiation of meaning in interaction, they may learn to modify and restructure the immediate interaction in terms of linguistic form, conversational structure, or the content of the message.[16] Interactional opportunities may also promote a learner's retrieval and retention of information, and automaticity in recalling this information could be enhanced, resulting in enhanced fluency.

The role of interaction can also be analyzed through a sociocultural framework, particularly by means of the concept of the Zone of Proximal Development (ZPD). In this framework, interaction is seen more widely as a tool of thinking and learning, as well as a means for communication.[17] The notion of the ZPD tells us that cognitive development occurs in interaction with others who have more advanced cognitive ability (such as a teacher or a more capable peer), rather than in isolation.[18] In the classroom, teachers' (or peers') scaffolding is typically mediated by language or cultural artifacts, and can facilitate learners' cognitive development. Teachers' or peers' scaffolding is woven into dialogic interaction in which learning occurs, and through interaction learners eventually internalize the newly gained knowledge or skills. Then, learners become self-regulated when they no longer need to rely on outside resources to carry out the task or access that

---

[14] See the output hypothesis (e.g., Swain 1998; Swain and Lapkin 1995).
[15] Bardovi-Harlig (1996, 1999, 2001).
[16] See the interaction hypothesis, e.g., Long (1996); Long *et al.* (1998).
[17] Kasper and Rose (2002).
[18] Vygotsky (1978).

awareness, because the new knowledge and skills have now become part of their cognitive repertoire.[19] Viewing learners as social beings, this framework focuses on how learning occurs interactionally, and can provide a rationale for the use of discussion and group work in the classroom that engage learners in interaction with other learners and teachers.[20]

Although theoretical frameworks for cognitive processing certainly help us explain student learning in the L2 pragmatics classroom, it has been pointed out that the learning of pragmatics should not be seen merely in terms of cognitive processing since it most definitely involves the socio-affective domain as well.[21] For instance, learners' motivation, acculturation, social identity, investment, and attitudes are likely to affect the ways in which learners notice pragmatic input, understand the role of contextual factors, negotiate meaning in interaction, and modify their language production across contexts and over time. These factors may also come into play when L2 speakers determine their own optimal level of cultural accommodation in a given setting[22] (e.g., completely emulating the target culture norms, converging partly towards the L2 culture, or resisting L2 norms thoroughly to stay distant as an outsider). We now turn to the interdisciplinary understanding of these social, cultural, psychological, and affective (emotional) aspects in relation to the learning of L2 pragmatics.

Interdisciplinary frameworks relating to L2 pragmatic development

From a cognitive perspective, learners whose language diverges from the expected range of pragmatic norms may be viewed as lacking in pragmatic ability. It may seem that success at L2 pragmatics would mean adhering fully to the local norms. However, if we use the "spotlights on the elephant" metaphor (Figure 6.1), there are other social, cultural, psychological, and emotional lenses through which to view language learning, and some of these have recently been gaining ground in the field of SLA.[23] The basic stance taken is that L2 speakers may have various reasons for not departing so readily from their own values and switching to those in the L2

---

[19] Vygotsky (1978).

[20] See elsewhere for much more on the sociocultural theory, e.g., Lantolf (2000); Lantolf and Thorne (2006). More specific discussion on L2 pragmatics and the sociocultural theory can be found in, e.g., Kasper and Rose (2002); Ohta (2005); Shively (2008).

[21] Kasper and Schmidt (1996); Schmidt (1993).

[22] Yoon (1991).

[23] DuFon (2008).

community.[24] Just as with an L1, the use of an L2 is an expression of one's subjectivity, and so we need to take learners' expressive needs into account in their L2 use and development. Some L2 instructional practices and SLA research reflect native-speaker models, and consequently the role of learner identity is largely neglected in areas like interlanguage pragmatics.[25] Now, as we teach English as an international language, the question of **whose** norms are to be used as the pedagogical model is increasingly being raised since native-speaker norms may not necessarily be relevant in communication in World Englishes. Pragmatically competent expert speakers – regardless of their native or non-native status – have demonstrated their ability to negotiate their social and cultural identity through the use of local norms in each given context.[26] We now turn to a few interdisciplinary frameworks that help us understand learners as social beings and language learning as participation in the L2 community.[27]

Subjectivity and language learning

In a social, cultural, and affective view of language learning, our subjectivity[28] is seen as multi-faceted and in flux. Subjectivity refers to one's views, emotions, and perceptions of the world, as well as one's self-concept in dynamic relation to others[29] (e.g., identity, values, beliefs, morals, feelings, and personal principles). Individuals are likely to have a repertoire of subjectivity (i.e., multiple identities) which is socially and culturally constructed, negotiated, and jointly enacted with others in the interaction.[30] For example, we may possess a range of identities in our various relationships to others such as:

■ national, racial, ethnic, generational, and gender identities (e.g., American, female, middle-aged, Caucasian, Latino);

■ relational identities (e.g., wife, brother, mother);

[24] Byram and Morgan (1994); Dewaele (2005); House and Kasper (2000); Preston (1989).
[25] House (2008).
[26] See for example, DuFon (2008); Horibe (2008); House (2003); Kachru and Nelson (1996); LoCastro (2000); McKay (2002), (in press); and Tarone (2005).
[27] For example, Norton (2000, 2001).
[28] The construct of *subjectivity* is largely synonymous with that of *social identity*, and many researchers seem to equate the two without clear demarcation between them. In this volume, *subjectivity* and *identity* are used interchangeably (see more discussion on these terms in Ishihara 2006).
[29] Weedon (1997: 32).
[30] Norton (2000); Ochs (1993); Weedon (1997).

- socioeconomic, occupational identities (e.g., middle-class, teacher, employee, student); or

- ideological identities (e.g., peace activist, environmentalist).

Certain aspects of our identities may be highlighted or become salient in specific contexts depending on the situational or interactional constraints. That is, we wear different "hats" depending on the relationship and context. In each situational and relational context, our identities are constructed relative to how others position themselves and others. Some aspects of our identities may be more permanent while other aspects shift according to the dynamics of the given social, historical, or political context. Individual subjectivity can be characterized as:

- multiple, dynamic, and non-unitary;

- a site of struggle and sometimes contradiction; and

- changing over time and space.[31]

For example, a person (let us call her Jane for now) may start a day in the family being a wife and mother, but her subjectivity is reconstructed as a teacher when at her workplace her student comes to class. She puts on a collegial hat when another teacher, John, walks into the office. John may exchange a greeting with Jane as a friendly colleague, but then may reposition himself as Jane's former teacher based on their former relationship as they discuss John's area of expertise. However, their subjective positions may overturn when they discuss Jane's area of expertise. Or they may begin to position themselves as equals rather than a former student and a teacher as they work together for a decade. In her attempt to negotiate her subjective position, Jane may have inner conflicts as to how to present herself in each particular context, feeling obliged to conform to assigned positioning on the one hand but wanting to contest the positioning on the other.

In addition, subjectivity is shaped both by individual dispositions and cultural/societal positioning under contextual circumstances. In the example of Jane and John above, when John imposes a less knowledgeable and more powerless positioning on Jane, she may simply accept the lower status, being non-confrontational and respectful in nature. Then, she would tend to use rather polite and proper language with John to index this positioning; in turn, John interprets their relationship as somewhat asymmetrical. Alternatively, Jane may draw on her membership in the progressive school environment and attempt to construct more egalitarian values promoted in

---

[31] Norton (1997, 2000).

the institution. Accordingly, her language would then be generally informal and egalitarian, and presumably John would construct their relationship on roughly equal terms as well. As these examples show, individuals create personal meaning for themselves in the social context where their individual dispositions play a pivotal role in the formation and reformation of identity.

At the same time, subjectivity embodies particular social or cultural norms and conventions created and maintained over time by other group members sharing similar identities. This process contributes to the development of certain linguistic features, social values, beliefs, and norms.[32] Speakers' use of particular linguistic and pragmatic features is symbolic of their group standards, consolidating in-group belongingness as they speak. This connectedness between pragmatics, culture, and subjectivity speaks to the interface between culture and pragmatics discussed in Chapter 1. Within a sociocultural view of subjectivity, language use is viewed as participation in that cultural community. Through participation in particular linguistic, pragmatic, and discourse practices, individuals become socialized into the community and function as competent members of the community.[33]

Another prominent characteristic of identity has been recognized as its agency-giving nature in its relation to power and institution. Agency can be understood as a self-reliant, independent, or self-defining capacity to operate with volition and power to bring about an effect, change, or decision in the particular sociocultural context. Individuals are not always passive, but can sometimes "contest a particular way in which they have been positioned in a social site, seeking to create a new social position for themselves."[34] In asymmetrical power relationships identity may be non-negotiable and simply imposed ("imposed identity").[35] Again, in the example with Jane and John, if John is an extremely overpowering and dominating colleague, lower status may be imposed on Jane, his former student. Or sometimes identities might be comfortably assumed, accepted, and not negotiated ("assumed identities"). On other occasions, individuals may contest and resist their identities in a dynamic interplay ("negotiable identities"). Jane may resist being positioned as a lower-status person, and by exercising her agency she may attempt to negotiate her identity as an equal colleague in the ongoing interaction with John.

In summary, in the negotiation of identity, individuals can exercise active human agency in deciding how to present themselves through their use of

---

[32] Hall (2002).
[33] Schieffelin and Ochs (1986a, 1986b), see also below for a more detailed discussion of second language socialization.
[34] LoCastro (2003: 198).
[35] *Imposed, assumed*, and *negotiable identities* from Pavlenko and Blackledge (2004: 21).

language. The formation of identity is closely related to the surrounding context and is constantly under the influence of power in the relationship, as the examples above show. Yet, individuals can exercise their agency to varying degrees depending on the circumstances as part of their self-assertion. They may be capable of making their own choices as to how they use language, and might choose to contest and resist the positioning imposed upon them as they negotiate in interaction. In L2 development, learners' subjectivity affects the way they learn and use the language. They way they express themselves pragmatically through the use of L2 is also dictated or at least influenced by, for instance, their cultural affiliation and the sense of who they are under the circumstance. In the next section, another theoretical framework is introduced, which further helps to explain this connection between identity, culture, and language/pragmatics.

Speech accommodation theory

Having its origins in social psychology, accommodation theory[36] can be useful in explaining speakers' linguistic variability in social contexts. The speech accommodation theory[37] takes both cognitive and affective variables into account in explicating learners' linguistic behavior in relation to their identity. This framework maintains that learners' social characteristics (e.g., objectively defined social categories such as age, gender, ethnicity, and socioeconomic status) alone would not determine their speech behavior. Rather, learners' "own subjective attitudes, perceptions of situations, cognitive and affective dispositions, and the like may interact to determine their speech outputs."[38] Learners' attitude, motivations, feelings, values, and perceptions (i.e., their subjectivity) influence their social and psychological distance from the target community. As a result, learners' language converges with or diverges from the target.[39] Simply put, when learners are in favor of the target culture or individual members of that culture, they are more likely to take on linguistic features of target-language speakers or characteristics of the language.

---

[36] As the theory has become more interdisciplinary with a wider focus from verbal to non-verbal, and specific linguistic to discourse features, Accommodation Theory is also more broadly termed as the *communication accommodation theory* (Giles *et al.* 1991; see also Weatherall *et al.* 2007 for issues of language and discourse in social psychology).

[37] Beebe and Giles (1984).

[38] Beebe and Giles (1984: 5).

[39] Convergence and divergence are defined as "a speaker's style shifting toward the interlocutor" and "a shift away (to maintain or assert distinctiveness)" respectively (Beebe and Zuengler 1983).

Convergence and divergence can be understood as linguistic strategies for a range of linguistic behavior from, for example, phonological or lexical features (e.g., pronunciation, speech rates, and word choice) to pragmatics and discourse features (e.g., pause, utterance lengths, and turn-taking). Speakers/writers may make an effort to adjust to the perceived speech patterns of the listeners/readers (i.e., convergence or accommodation) to communicate effectively in a timely manner, to attain social approval, or to maintain L2-related social identities. Speakers/writers may choose to accommodate their speech/writing styles when they estimate the cost to be less than the perceived payoff. For example, a speaker from the rural US South may choose to put on an Eastern accent while working professionally in an Eastern city in order to claim membership in what is typically seen as a more sophisticated speech community. On the other hand, speakers/writers may choose to diverge from perceived L2 norms (i.e., divergence or resistance) in order to maintain their distinctive in-group identities, and to accentuate their linguistic differences with an intention to isolate themselves from other language groups. The same Southerner may be proud of his culture and decide to speak with his own accent in a bar to assert his identity among the Easterners. The degree of convergence and divergence may be a function of the speakers' linguistic repertoires, individual differences, and social and contextual factors.

In the following section, another spotlight on the elephant, second language socialization, will be highlighted as a new theoretical framework for understanding the phenomenon of pragmatic language learning. This framework shares an emphasis on social context with accommodation theories. Like accommodation theories, this perspective can also be applied to the analysis of learners' dynamic linguistic variability. However, while accommodation theories emphasize learners' social, psychological and affective factors, language socialization highlights social and cultural dimensions of authentic interactions and views learners' language use as participation in L2 community practices.

Second language socialization theory

The language socialization theory was developed under the influence of anthropology. The framework has been employed by researchers of SLA who attempt to understand L2 learning not only from cognitive but also from social and cultural perspectives.[40] Language socialization theory views

---

[40] Watson-Gegeo and Nielsen (2003).

language learning as socially situated in communities of practice.[41] Novice community members (such as language learners or children) become competent members of the speech community as they acquire the knowledge, orientations, and social practices of the community through activities mediated by language.[42] Novice members learn to use language appropriately through exposure to and participation in the local practices. Knowing linguistic patterns and appropriate language use, in turn, allows the novice community members to become competent communicators and central participants in the community.

International graduate students, for example, gradually socialize into the academic discourse of the host university program as they participate and engage actively in the academic community. With exposure and time in the community, a study found that students increasingly acquired discourse strategies, for instance, for oral academic presentations (e.g., strategies to engage the audience). The students also learned to negotiate with instructors on their expectations and acquired ways to prepare for, perform, and review their presentations.[43] It is when these students were able to follow community norms and practices that they were given central membership in the community.

Much work in language socialization centers on novice members' socialization into community norms, that is, a type of convergence towards community practices. On the other hand, the divergence from those norms can in fact be explained in terms of language socialization theory as well. Novice members are not necessarily passive recipients of the sociocultural practices, but rather may actively and selectively co-construct existing norms in the community and the outcome of the interaction.[44]

Let us take a look at a more specific and authentic example of language socialization in which an L2-speaking community member negotiates and appropriates a community norm. A Japanese Director of Operations for a US university volleyball team, Nobuko, was a long-time community member, a fluent L2 English speaker, and was generally well socialized into the community practices. Her students generally used informal language with her, perhaps in an attempt to construct a relaxed and informal relationship with Nobuko. Or maybe they assumed a casual relationship with Nobuko based on her demeanor or their previous experience with other directors.

[41] Lave and Wenger (1991); Wenger (1998).
[42] Vygotsky (1978).
[43] Morita (2002, 2004).
[44] See, for example, Garrett and Baquedano-López (2002); Ochs (1993); Schieffelin and Ochs (1986a, 1986b); Watson-Gegeo and Nielsen (2003).

However, Nobuko was against a certain informal way that her students spoke to her in athletic contexts. For example, her students often made a casual request to her on a volleyball court, *Do you wanna get the ball?* This language of request struck Nobuko as overly informal and inappropriate, because she herself was so strictly "disciplined" to speak "properly and respectfully" to someone senior and of higher status. This pragmatic norm appeared so deeply ingrained in her subjectivity that she decided to "discipline" her student players on what she thought was a "proper" way of speaking. Sometimes she refused the students' requests in jest, and other times she explicitly pointed out what language students should be using. By doing so, she deliberately flouted the expected norm of more informal and egalitarian behavior. Some students understood her message immediately and began constructing a more formal relationship with Nobuko by promptly altering their L1 behavior. Some needed to hear Nobuko's request for formal language repeatedly in order to understand the intention behind it. Some persisted with their informal language longer, attempting to negotiate a more relaxed rapport. As a result of this negotiation, which often extended over a few years, Nobuko began to see what she felt was a positive change in her students' general language use. Through her accumulated effort over time, she succeeded in resocializing her largely L1-speaking students in the way that they used language pragmatically.[45]

It is notable that language socialization can work bi-directionally, involving negotiation between novice participants and more competent core members of the community. Novice members' socialization into existing practices leads to the maintenance or reproduction of such cultural routines. On the other hand, their creative language use that is divergent from the norms fulfills L2 speakers' expressive needs and can potentially contribute to a minor and temporary change or a greater transformation in the preexisting community practice.[46]

This dynamic interpretation and application of the language socialization theory is particularly valuable in studying linguistically/culturally diverse communities in which social standards themselves may be in flux and negotiable in interaction. In such communities, the process of language socialization can span a lifetime and change over time as bi- or multilingual identity shifts in fluid social contexts and interactional situations.[47]

In summing up, we have so far briefly discussed a cognitive framework of relevance to the learning of L2 pragmatics, the noticing hypothesis, along

[45] See Ishihara (2008c, in press b) for more details.
[46] Garrett and Baquedano-López (2002).
[47] Bayley and Schecter (2003).

with passing mention of a few others. We have also considered the social, cultural, affective, and psychological aspects of pragmatic language learning and use, drawing on identity, accommodation, and second language socialization theories. Now let us think about the role that theoretical understandings could play in the teachers' classroom practice.

Implications for teaching

Explicit and implicit instruction in pragmatics

As in the discussion above, the noticing hypothesis calls for conscious attention to pragmatics-related information in the L2 classroom, rather than learners' mere exposure to pragmatics-rich input. In the language classroom, this would translate into explicit teaching of pragmatics. As discussed above, an explicit approach with a provision of analysis of language and context has been found to be generally more effective than implicit teaching in experimental studies. The explicit teaching of pragmatics is in line with an awareness-raising approach, which has been widely used in the current teaching of L2 pragmatics.

Awareness-raising approach for teaching pragmatics

An awareness-raising approach is grounded in the noticing hypothesis and is designed to facilitate learners' noticing and understanding of the form–context relationship. The following is a listing of possible classroom tasks for receptive or productive skills development, or a combination of both. We include instructional tasks that focus primarily on either the linguistic dimensions or on the social and cultural dimensions.

Tasks with a mainly linguistic (pragmalinguistic) focus:

- analyzing and practicing the use of vocabulary in the particular context;

- identifying and practicing the use of relevant grammatical structures;

- identifying and practicing the use of strategies for a speech act;

- analyzing and practicing the use of discourse organization (e.g., discourse structure of an academic oral, and presentation);[48]

- analyzing and practicing the use of discourse markers and fillers (e.g., *well, um, actually*);

---

[48] See Vellenga and Smith (2008), for a sample activity for teaching components of academic discourse.

- analyzing and practicing the use of *epistemic stance markers* (i.e., words and phrases to show the speaker's stance, such as: *I think, maybe, seem, suppose, tend to, of course*);[49]

- noticing and practicing the use of tone (e.g., verbal and non-verbal cues and nuances).[50]

Tasks with a mainly social and cultural (sociopragmatic) focus:

- analyzing language and context to identify the goal and intention of the speaker, and assessing the speaker's attainment of the goal and the listener's interpretation (see Chapters 14 and 15 for more on this assessment);

- analyzing and practicing the use of directness/politeness/formality in an interaction;[51]

- identifying and using multiple functions of a speech act;

- identifying and using a range of cultural norms in the L2 culture; and

- identifying and using possible cultural reasoning or ideologies behind L2 pragmatic norms.

In reality, these two sets of dimensions focusing on language and culture may actually be intertwined and not clear-cut. For example, in order to communicate effectively, learners need to know the meaning and linguistic form associated with the expressions, *I agree* and *I disagree* (pragmalinguistics). In addition, they need cultural knowledge about the appropriate contexts for using these expressions (sociopragmatics).

The above tasks could be used in conjunction with these classroom exercises:

- collecting L2 data in the L2 community or the media, e.g., films, sit-coms (see Chapters 3 and 7 for data collection procedures, and Chapter 13 for the use of films and sit-coms);

---

[49] See Fordyce (2008) for the effects of instruction on epistemic stance in a foreign language context.

[50] Beebe and Waring (2004) define pragmatic tone as "the affect indirectly conveyed by linguistic and/or nonlinguistic means" and metaphorically characterize it as the "'color' of emotion and attitude on language" (p. 2)." As they point out, pragmatic appropriateness is determined not only through word choice, grammar, and semantic formulas but also by way of tone. The same verbal message can take on different meanings depending on the tone, since affect is encoded in the tone through intonation, certain linguistic structures (e.g., use of adverbials), non-verbal cues (e.g., gesture, facial expressions, posture, and pause) and the like.

[51] For further theoretical discussion and methodological application of linguistic politeness and face (Brown and Levinson 1987; Scollon and Scollon 1995), see Bou-Franch and Garcés-Conejos (2003).

- comparing learners' L1 and L2 pragmatic norms (see Chapters 7 and 11 for examples);

- comparing felicitous and infelicitous L2 pragmatic uses, e.g., comparing successful and awkward interactions (see Chapter 13);

- sharing personal stories about pragmatic failure or similar or different pragmatic norms in another culture (see Activity 10.1 in Chapter 10);

- reconstructing sample dialogues, e.g., recreating dialogues and sequencing of lines from a dialogue (see Chapters 7 and 8);

- role-playing (variation: role-plays with specific intentions, such as where one person attempts to persuade the other to accept an invitation and the other intends to refuse the invitation. The role-play can be recorded for subsequent reflection,[52] see Chapter 8);

- keeping a reflective journal or interaction log (Chapter 11);

- interviewing L2-speaking informants about norms for pragmatic behavior (Chapter 12); and

- experimenting with certain pragmatic behavior in the L2 community (Chapters 7 and 12).

In a **second-language** setting where the target language is commonly spoken outside of the classroom, pragmatics instruction may best capitalize on exercises that encourage learners to study the language as used authentically in the community. This technique is termed *learner as an ethnographer*[53] or *learners as researchers*.[54] In this learner-centered approach with explicit instruction of pragmatics in largely inductive terms, learners act like researchers, collecting naturally occurring linguistic samples from speakers of the L2, or conducting surveys or interviews regarding particular L2 use. Then, learners analyze the linguistic features as well as the non-linguistic contextual factors that influenced the language use in their samples. They might also compare their preexisting assumptions about L2 pragmatic use with their new discoveries. These awareness-raising exercises function as a type of guided simulation for future independent learning of pragmatics. During these exercises, learners observe, analyze, and adopt some features of language they encounter in authentic situations. The learners can be encouraged to create hypotheses about pragmatic L2 use, test them in

---

[52] Bardovi-Harlig *et al.* (1991).
[53] Bardovi-Harlig (1996); Tarone and Yule (1989); Wolfson (1989). See also Roberts *et al.* (2001) for background on this approach and how an ethnographic approach can be incorporated into language and culture learning.
[54] Tanaka (1997).

authentic settings by using the L2 or further observing others, and then revise hypotheses if necessary. A learners-as-researchers approach models this cycle of student-centered learning of L2 pragmatics.

Researchers have suggested several instructional frameworks regarding how pragmatics-focused instructional tasks might be sequentially organized. One instructional model includes the following stages of instruction:[55]

(a) learners' exploration;

(b) learners' production; and

(c) feedback from peers and from the teacher.

Another instructional framework is composed of the following phases:[56]

(a) a feeling (warm-up) phase;

(b) a doing phase;

(c) a thinking phase;

(d) an understanding phase; and

(e) a using phase.

However, the organizational sequence of classroom exercises would largely depend on each instructional context (see below for examples of the learner and language factors), as well as teachers' beliefs (Chapter 2). The instructional organization can best be determined locally, rather than always complying with a particular model. The research-based information presented in the following section can presumably help teachers to make important instructional decisions.

Deductive and inductive instruction for L2 pragmatics

The instructional tasks and techniques listed above can be utilized either with an inductive or deductive orientation, or combination of the two (see Figure 6.2, below). Instruction is *deductive* when outside sources, such as teacher and materials, provide learners with explicit information about pragmatics before learners study examples. In *inductive* teaching, learners analyze pragmatic data to discover L2 pragmatic norms that govern various language uses (see below).[57]

An inductive approach is generally believed to promote higher-order thinking and may be more effective than a deductive approach. However, existing research in L2 pragmatics has shown contradicting results that may

---

[55] Usó-Juan and Martínez-Flor (2008: 352–5).
[56] Kondo (2008: 156–8).
[57] Deductive and inductive instruction here correspond to "actual deduction" (Modality A) and "conscious induction as guided discovery" (Modality B) in Decoo (1996: 97).

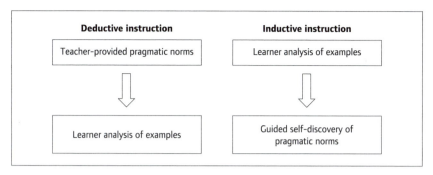

FIGURE 6.2 Deductive and inductive approaches to teaching L2 pragmatics

be inconclusive at this point.[58] It appears that although learners' inductive self-discovery can contribute to pragmatic learning, it may be difficult to "get it right." Even if inductive language learning is an effective means to develop pragmatic control, learners may take differential advantage of it, depending on their learning styles. Effective inductive teaching may also take some practice on the part of the teachers, especially if their professional preparation centered on a more teacher-fronted approach (see Activity 2.2 in Chapter 2 for an example of teacher research on deductive vs inductive teaching). However, a recent study conducted in a **foreign-language** setting has shown promising results for both inductive and deductive instruction.[59] In fact, that study found that pragmatic knowledge gained through induction may even be longer-lasting and more easily accessible in real time than pragmatic knowledge acquired through deduction.

In reality, instruction in the language classroom may often reflect a combination of inductive and deductive approaches. When learners discover pragmatic norms in an inductive approach and share them with their peers, the learning may take a deductive turn for those who have not discovered them yet. If teachers guide learners in the discovery process, then the learning about pragmatic norms can be viewed as being co-constructed, rather than purely inductive or deductive.[60]

Teachers need to give careful consideration to various factors (such as those below) to ensure that learners understand how pragmatic intent is expressed by the L2 and to have sufficient practice time producing such language.

---

[58] Jeon and Kaya (2006); Rose and Ng (2001); Takimoto (2008).

[59] In Takimoto's (2008) study, inductive instruction was found as equally effective as deductive instruction when induction was combined with awareness-raising or structured input tasks.

[60] See Shrum and Glisan (2004) for the teacher and learners' co-construction of grammatical rules.

Learner factors:

- learners' level of linguistic proficiency (How well do they handle the grammar structures and vocabulary in the pragmatic language samples?);
- learning styles (Are learners analytic enough to be able to discover L2 pragmatic norms?); and
- motivation and interest in learning L2 pragmatics (Do learners know why they should learn L2 pragmatics and value positively the development of their pragmatic ability?).

Target language features:

- frequency (Does the target pragmatic feature occur frequently enough for learners to notice?);
- salience (Is the target feature salient enough for learners to notice?); and
- level of complexity of the target structure (How well can learners handle the level of complexity of the target feature?).

An explanatory approach to L2 pragmatics instruction and critical pragmatics

So far, we have discussed the pedagogical implications of drawing on cognitive frameworks for dealing with the cognitive aspects of pragmatics instruction in the classroom. We have also seen above that language learning occurs at social, cultural, psychological, and affective levels in connection to learners' self-concept and in their perceived relation to others. If teacher readers subscribe to this social view of language learning, they may also consider its implications – how this view can shape their teaching practice in the classroom.

Theoretical frameworks and research on language learning from a social and cultural perspective serve to remind language educators of the importance of being sensitive to learners' identities and cultures. Knowing grammatical structures alone does not guarantee understanding of what would constitute generally preferred pragmatic behavior in the L2 and why that would be the case in that culture. If this cultural literacy appears to be lacking, an *explanatory approach* to the teaching of pragmatics (see Chapters 1 and 11)[61] may serve to provide an *emic* view (i.e., insider perspective) of the target culture.

[61] Meier (2003); Richards and Schmidt (1983). Also see Spencer-Oatey (2000) for various explanatory examples relating language and culture.

For example, as was the case with an L2 speaker of Japanese, some Western learners of the language may be uncomfortable emulating what they perceive as Japanese speakers' tendency to reject compliments about their family members given by non-family members (e.g., compliments given by someone about the academic achievements of their daughter). Learners may see a flat-out rejection of this type of compliment (e.g., *no, that's not true at all*). as lacking grace or overly critical of their own family. Consequently, learners may see this particular pragmatic convention (or even Japanese speakers in general) in a negative light. Western learners may prefer to express their love and pride for the family member and accept or upgrade the compliment (e.g., *yes, she is doing really well at school*). However, knowing a common interpretation of this Japanese pragmatic behavior may help L2 speakers to understand why this behavior is sometimes practiced in the culture.

One researcher, who analyzed naturally occurring compliments in Japanese, has observed that Japanese speakers sometimes praise someone's ability not so much in order to build solidarity (as Western speakers might), but rather to widen the gap between the speaker and the listener by placing the listener higher on the interactional scale than the speaker him/herself. So, for Japanese speakers, there is a greater need for the recipient of the compliment to reject it in order to close the gap and reestablish commonality and solidarity in the relationship.[62] Also, the demarcation between in-group and out-group is often clear in the culture; accepting an out-group member's compliment about an in-group family member can be seen as a type of self-praise. In fact, acceptance (let alone, upgrading) of a compliment about one's own family can be interpreted as self-conceited bragging in that culture. An explanatory approach to pragmatics, as in this example, would include classroom discussion of such a cultural point of view, with the intent to enhance the learners' cultural literacy in the L2. Having the background on why the target language uses certain cultural conventions may help learners make a more informed decision as to whether they want to participate in these conventions themselves in speaking the L2 (see another example in Chapter 11).

In fact, in order to assert their subjectivity, learners have various reasons both for choosing to emulate L2 community norms and for deliberately refusing to follow such norms. When culturally sensitive pedagogy is being practiced, these learner choices are respected and not penalized in the language classroom. Knowing the range of L2 community norms and pragmatic

---

[62] Daikuhara (1986).

variability (i.e., having native-like *receptive* skills) can be of benefit to learners, but the pragmatics of language *production* should be each learner's own prerogative. This distinction between learners' receptive and productive pragmatic skills is highly important for everyday practice. Facilitating the negotiation of L2 speakers' voice that reflects their bilingual subjectivity empowers them and assists them in drawing on multiple linguistic, cultural, and pragmatic resources and legitimatizing their voices in their local contexts.[63] Such efforts in *critical pragmatics* can lead to recognizing and working to redress unequal distribution of power that often exists in established hierarchy, such as between so-called native and non-native speakers.[64] This critical/transformative perspective has been called for and already incorporated into the instruction of Japanese pragmatics.[65] For examples of practical classroom approaches and assessment grounded in critical pragmatics, see Chapters 7, 8, 10, 14, and 15.

Discussion

In this chapter, we have briefly discussed some theoretical frameworks for understanding L2 pragmatic use and development. We started with cognitive frameworks related to L2 pragmatics that are prominent in the field. At the cognitive level, research has suggested that explicit teaching – namely, attention to linguistic forms and their relationship to relevant contextual factors – will facilitate the learning of pragmatics more than simply exposing learners to such material.[66] Explicit provision of information regarding pragmatics is likely to facilitate the learning of both norms of social behavior and the language to use in specific situations. We have also looked at interdisciplinary frameworks from social, cultural, psychological, and affective perspectives that have currently been receiving increasing attention in applied linguistics.[67] These frameworks allow us to see how language use and development can be influenced by learners' subjectivity, agency, and participation in the L2 community.

[63] For example, Johnston (2003); Pennycook (2001).
[64] Ishihara (2008b).
[65] For example, Kubota (2008); Ohara et al. (2001); Siegal and Okamoto (1996; 2003). Ohara et al. (2001) have documented learners' critical thinking of the observed pragmatic norms in the target culture and their awareness of sociopolitical positioning and uneven power distribution indexed through the language use (see also Chapter 8 for more details of instructional procedures).
[66] Jeon and Kaya (2006); Kasper and Rose (2002); Rose (2005). However, others, e.g., Alcón (2005); Fukuya and Clark (2001); Rose (2005) do acknowledge the potential of some implicit teaching techniques, such as input enhancement.
[67] DuFon (2008).

With an eye to the practical application of these theoretical frameworks as they relate to explicit L2 pragmatics, various awareness-raising tasks have been suggested for explicit teaching of pragmatics in the second half of this chapter. Explanatory and culturally sensitive approaches to teaching L2 pragmatics have also been discussed in the spirit of *critical pragmatics*. Teachers are invited to become familiar with these tasks and to incorporate some of them into their lesson plans and daily practice. At the same time, the lists of classroom tasks in this chapter are not intended to be exhaustive. Rather, teacher readers are encouraged to adapt them and add their own as they see fit in their own instructional contexts. The information presented in this chapter will hopefully assist language teachers in making more informed instructional decisions – decisions grounded in a current under-standing of L2 pragmatic development (see Chapter 2). Activity 6.1 which follows here is intended to facilitate this connection.

Activity 6.1 Linking theoretical frameworks with your experience of L2 pragmatics

Objectives

1   You will be able to explain theoretical frameworks related to the development of L2 pragmatic ability in your own words.

2   You will be able to connect those frameworks with your experience of learning or teaching L2 pragmatics.

Time: 40 minutes.

Materials: Task sheet: "Theoretical frameworks and key terms for L2 pragmatics".

Directions

1   Get into groups of about three and explain to each other in your own words the second language acquisition theories on the task sheet, "Theoretical frameworks and key terms for L2 pragmatics."

2   List key terms for each framework on the task sheet. Go back to this chapter if desired in this process. (Some terms are already given as examples.)

3   Take a moment to think of your own experiences learning or teaching L2 pragmatics. Which framework(s) might best explain your experiences? Use the space in the task sheet to take notes. Take turns describing your experiences and interpreting them theoretically.

4   Share your discussion with the whole group.

Discussion/wrap up

To conclude, you may wish to discuss the following questions:

- Which theoretical framework(s) are you most familiar with?

- Which framework(s), if any, do you wish to understand better, and what would help you to deepen your understanding?

- Which domain(s), cognitive, social, cultural, or affective, for example, do you focus most on in learning and teaching the L2? In what ways might this activity have helped you understand learning that can occur in other domains?

This activity has been designed to help deepen your learning through dialogue and interaction. You are invited to continue to explore the link between the frameworks presented in this chapter and your students' learning of pragmatics. An awareness of this connection can help you *teach in principle* according to your current knowledge and beliefs (see Chapter 2).

Task sheet: Theoretical frameworks and key terms for L2 pragmatics

Theoretical framework	Key terms	Your experience
Noticing/understanding, awareness, and attention	■ Conscious attention to pragmatics-related information (leading to explicit teaching of L2 pragmatics). ■ Noticing (registering) of form. ■ Understanding of why the form is selected.	
Identity theories		Use of standard L1 at work but local dialect in my home town (related to identity, affiliation, and membership)
Speech accommodation theory		
Second language socialization theory		
(Others of your choice here and below)		

CHAPTER 7

Class observation and teaching demonstrations

Noriko Ishihara

Introduction

In planning, implementing, and assessing pragmatics-focused instruction, teacher readers may find it helpful to observe how their colleagues teach L2 pragmatics. Seeing an actual pragmatics lesson may help teachers expand their repertoire of teaching strategies and ideas about assessment as well. In addition, it is likely to stimulate reflection on effective approaches to teaching and assessing pragmatics. Teachers having colleagues who teach pragmatics at the same or nearby institutions could perhaps make arrangements to observe them teaching. Teacher readers taking a course on instructional pragmatics will most likely have occasion to view their instructor and/or an invited guest speaker demonstrating effective teaching practice. In case any of these resources are unavailable, this chapter provides simulated demonstrations of pragmatics-focused instruction.[1] We first discuss a series of possible observational foci, which could be used in observing others as they teach.

Points of observation for pragmatics-focused instruction

While observing others teaching pragmatics, it is helpful to have one or more points on which to focus. These prompts are intended to help narrow the focus of the observation and to direct attention specifically to the pragmatics aspects being taught.

[1] Also see Chapter 11 for examples of pragmatics-focused curricular materials for teaching Japanese pragmatics in a foreign-language setting.

- What are the overall objectives of this class and what are the objectives that specifically target pragmatics? (E.g., exactly what learners' pragmatic awareness to enhance and what specific productive pragmatic skills to improve)

- How does the teacher trigger learners' noticing and understanding of the target pragmatic function/features? More specifically, what awareness-raising exercises or tasks does the teacher use in this class? How effective do they seem to be in accomplishing the goals of this instruction? (See Chapter 6 for pragmatic awareness-raising.)

- What interactive or output opportunities are provided in this class? How effective do these language production tasks seem to be in accomplishing the goals of instruction?

- How is pragmatic variation demonstrated in the instruction? How might the diversity of pragmatic norms be taken into account in the assessment of learners' pragmatic ability and development?

- How might learners' knowledge of their first language and culture be used as a resource?

- What is the learners' general proficiency level? How much cultural knowledge of the L2 do they seem to have? In what ways does the instruction accommodate learners' levels of proficiency and cultural knowledge?

- How motivated do learners appear to be to learn pragmatics? What factors probably contribute to their level of interest and motivation?

- How does the teacher formally or informally assess learners' pragmatic awareness and production? To what extent is the evaluation of learners' production based on how native-like it is? How much of the assessment is made on the basis of the learners' intentions? (See Chapter 15 for assessment based on learners' goals and intentions.)

- What do I like about this lesson? What can I directly incorporate into my own teaching?

- What modifications, if any, would I need to make in order to accommodate my learners' needs and institutional context?

- Other points of interest:

The remainder of the chapter provides descriptions of two sets of pragmatics-focused instruction in the ESL, EFL, and JFL contexts. Teacher readers are invited to follow along and critically reflect on the instruction with a selected observational focus in mind.

Teaching Demonstration 1: Teaching giving and responding to compliments (ESL)[2]

Learners and the context

The instruction is designed for high-intermediate learners in an oral skills course in a US university ESL context. The target audience are adult international students from various cultures, speaking a range of L1s, who have lived in the L2 community for varying periods of time. Learners' goals include improving English skills to better communicate in their daily lives, as well as to use English more effectively for academic or business purposes in the near future. American English is most relevant to this audience but instruction can be altered to accommodate other varieties of English for other groups of learners.

Objectives

Giving and responding to compliments is culturally bound communicative behavior, largely reflecting the values of the society and the conversational partners. Due to the cultural differences in norms of behavior, ESL learners sometimes experience embarrassment, dismay, and may accidentally offend someone by the way that they give or respond to compliments in English.[3] In the USA, compliments are often used as a "social lubricant," establishing ties of solidarity between conversational partners.[4] In academic setting, compliments from teachers and peers can boost students' confidence, reinforce desirable behavior, and contribute to the development of a cooperative learning environment. How to compliment can be modeled and practiced even at an elementary level and can be used in teacher–student classroom meetings, during peer editing of writing, and when students meet in literature circles.[5] Below are the objectives of instruction for university ESL:

1   Learners will be able to identify differing norms of behavior across cultures with regard to giving and responding to compliments.

2   Learners will be able to assess appropriateness, sincerity, and spontaneity of compliments and responses to compliments, considering the relative social status of the conversation partners, their familiarity with each other, and suitability of the topic of compliments.

[2] This instructional description has been adapted from Ishihara (2003*a*) and Ishihara (2009). Student worksheets can be accessed from a link at: http://www.i.hosei.ac.jp/~ishihara.

[3] Dunham (1992); Holmes and Brown (1987).

[4] Billmyer (1990); Dunham (1992).

[5] See Estrada *et al.*'s (2006) lesson plan for an intermediate fourth-grade ESL course developed in the summer institute on teaching pragmatics at the CARLA. Although pragmatics-focused analysis may need to be rather simple for young learners, an enhanced awareness of context and language can be developed through interactional practice.

3   Learners will be able to express their intentions by producing 1) compliments using various adjectives, topics, and grammatical structures, and 2) a range of responses to compliments according to the context.

Suggested time and materials

▨   Approximately 250 minutes (e.g., five class meetings for 50 minutes each).

▨   Student worksheets.

Classroom instruction/assessment procedures[6]

A Introduction and needs assessment

The introduction is designed to assess learners' initial pragmatic awareness and ability to give and respond to compliments, and to motivate them to learn pragmatic use of language. Initially, learners are asked to discuss some of the most challenging aspects of learning English. This discussion is to introduce the importance of pragmatic aspects (using language appropriately formally, informally, politely, convincingly, aggressively, and the like in the given context). Examples of appropriate (and inappropriate) compliments and responses are modeled, and such concepts and vocabulary as *compliment, response, flatter, brown nose, apple polish,* and *butter up* are taught at this initial stage, using an introductory worksheet.

The discussion prompts on the worksheet can include:

1   How often do you give, receive, or overhear compliments in English compared to in your first language?

2   What do people say in giving and responding to compliments in English? Write a few dialogues illustrating giving and responding to compliments.

3   What do people say in giving and responding to compliments in your first language community? Write a few dialogues in that language and provide a literal translation into English.

4   What do people compliment others on? (What are some topics of compliments?)

5   Who is giving and responding to the following compliments? Pay attention to what they say, and imagine who they are, where they are from, and what their relationship may be.

---

[6] In planning classroom activities, empirical research findings and analysis from Manes and Wolfson (1981) and Wolfson (1989) were utilized. Instructional procedures and materials were adapted from Billmyer (1990), Dunham (1992), and Holmes and Brown (1987) with Tom Fitzgerald's insightful suggestions. See Chapter 4 and http://www.carla.umn.edu/speechacts/compliments/index.html (accessed December 10, 2009) for more information about compliments in English and in other languages.

(a) "Nice shirt!" – "I just dug it out of my closet."

(b) "I like the color of your lipstick." – "Oh, thanks."

(c) "What an unusual necklace. It's beautiful." – "Please take it."

6   Are you comfortable and confident in giving and responding to compliments in English? What issues, if any, do you have? What do you want to know about complimenting and responding in English?

Prompt 1 addresses the issue of frequency of complimenting interactions across cultures. In some cultures, compliments tend to be given much less frequently than in the USA,[7] while in others the tendency might be reversed. Prompts 2 to 6 serve as a diagnosis of learners' current pragmatic awareness and productive skills. The prompts also help teachers to assess their needs at this initial instructional phase. An alternative to Prompt 2 are a few scenarios that elicit learners' compliments or responses to compliments in more controlled settings. From learners with diverse cultural backgrounds, Prompt 3 can elicit various ways to respond to compliments that are usually not common in American English (e.g., *You can have it/It's presented to you* (lit.) (see Figure 7.1, below),[8] and *No, I'm older and uglier*[9]). These cross-cultural examples raise learners' awareness, prompting them to notice that literal translations do not always communicate the same pragmatic meaning in the L2. Prompts 4 and 5 direct learners' attention to contextual factors (such as status and distance between conversation partners, and possible referents of compliments) that influence the language. Some cultural differences may arise in the assessment of these factors, such as Spanish *piropos* (flirtatious remarks) that tend to be more socially accepted[10] in some cultures and sub-cultures (see Activity 5.1 in Chapter 5 for examples of *piropos*). Some research findings on gender differences in giving and responding to compliments are shared with learners.[11] Cross-cultural comparison of pragmatic norms can also be made. For example, the idiomatic expression in response 5(c) may be uncommon in English while it can be acceptable in Samoan and Arabic cultures.[12] After this discussion, the multiple functions of compliments, adjectives commonly appearing in them, and grammatical structures usually associated with them are introduced (see the compliments section in Chapter 4 for

[7] In Barnlund and Araki's (1985) research, American participants reported having given a compliment in the previous 1.6 days, whereas Japanese participants had only done so in the previous 13 days.

[8] An example of Syrian responses to compliments from Nelson *et al.* (1993).

[9] An example of Chinese responses to compliments from Chen (1993). Yu (2008) has a similar example from a Taiwanese learner of English who appeared to adopt her L1 norm in English: *No, I don't* [look great]. *Don't make fun at me. I know I'm just plain-looking* (p. 42).

[10] Campo and Zuluaga (2000).

[11] See the CARLA website http://www.carla.umn.edu/speechacts/compliments/american.html (accessed December 10, 2009) for a summary of gender differences in compliment exchanges in American English.

[12] Holmes and Brown (1987); Nelson *et al.* (1996).

FIGURE 7.1 Compliment about a shirt

this information),[13] along with some interactional practice using these words and structures.

B Student research and analysis of language and contextual factors

In this portion of the instruction, learners observe complimenting behavior of pragmatically competent speakers of English in the community. Using the format on the handout (see the sample material below) learners are to record three or more compliments that they give, receive, or overhear outside of class, and to analyze the overall level of perceived sincerity, spontaneity, and appropriateness of each interaction in consideration of the given contextual factors (e.g., age, gender, social status, role, and distance of the conversation partners, and the language and the topic of complimenting). This process of data collection and analysis can be modeled using a film clip, such as a scene from the film, *Father of the Bride* (see the transcription and analysis to be modeled to learners in the material below). Alternatively, learners can be asked to give compliments and record their own interactions. In offering a compliment, learners are advised to be mindful of appropriate topics in relation to the recipient of the compliment and the context of each interaction.

---

[13] Wolfson and Manes (Manes and Wolfson 1981; Wolfson and Manes 1980) researched 1,200 naturally occurring compliments and found that 97% employed one of the nine grammatical structures identified.

This initial learner involvement in notebook data collection can raise learners' pragmatic awareness, provide authentic linguistic input/output, and create a learner-centered class. Since complimenting could be naturally initiated by learners, they can practice it with other speakers within the course of conversation. Learners review these written interactions repeatedly during the subsequent stages of instruction in order to do the following:

- analyze the grammatical structure and adjectives used in the compliments given;
- assess the level of perceived sincerity, spontaneity, and appropriateness of the interactions; and
- analyze the compliment response strategies used.

C Additional analysis of pragmatic norms related to compliments

A short reading assignment can include excerpts about positive values of mainstream Americans[14] and prompts for critical reflection (e.g., *Does this positive value of being slender apply to both men and women in the US? Why/why not?*; *What possible danger can accompany a compliment on lost weight?*; *What does it mean in mainstream American culture when new appearances or possessions are not complimented on?*). Teacher feedback can be given individually in writing or be provided to the whole class.

D Responses to compliments

At this stage, learners are introduced to and practice a variety of strategies for responding to compliments, such as:[15]

- showing appreciation (*Thank you*);
- agreeing (*Yeah, it's my favorite too*);
- downgrading (*It's really quite old*);
- questioning (*Do you really think so?*);
- commenting on history (*I bought it for the trip to Arizona*);
- shifting credit (*My brother gave it to me*); and
- returning the compliment (*So is yours*).

Short sample exchanges[16] illustrating the strategies listed above are introduced to learners first without the labels in order to stimulate their powers of observation. Then learners come up with other examples for each strategy or look back at their own data to analyze

---

[14] Passages taken from Wolfson (1983: 113–14).
[15] See Chapter 4 or Herbert and Straight (1989: 39) for more complete lists of compliment response strategies.
[16] See Billmyer (1990: 36) and Ishihara (2003*a*) for examples.

the types of response strategies found there. Learners share some of the written inter-actions from their own data, and the class identifies the response strategies used in the interactions.

Finally, the giving and responding to compliments is practiced interactively in a mingling activity. Learners form two concentric circles (see Figure 7.2 for this visualiza-tion and an alternative), each one facing a partner. One compliments the other and the other responds. They then sustain conversation until they are asked to wrap up and change partners. At this point, the outer circle rotates and each takes on a new partner. This procedure is repeated, making sure to switch the roles after learners have practiced a given role sufficiently. In this activity, the learners are advised that they are not always to accept compliments, but to express themselves in the most comfortable manner, using the newly learned expressions for avoiding self-praise avoidance when appropriate.

In case learner production observed in this interactional practice is awkward or not suf-ficiently diversified, it would be helpful to expose learners to additional authentic language data. Learners can role-play authentic interactional samples provided by the teacher, analyze them in terms of the word choice in the compliments and speech act strategies of the responses, and produce similar role-plays to enhance their pragmalinguistic control.[17] Subsequent class discussion can also enhance learners' awareness of the nuances of the interactions (e.g., how sincere or appropriate the compliment sounds, how the conversa-tional partners tend to interpret each other's pragmatic behavior, and what consequences there may be).

E Sustaining conversation using compliments

Using an authentic transcript, a prolonged interaction is modeled in which a conversation opens with a compliment. Learners are guided to notice a function of compliments – to

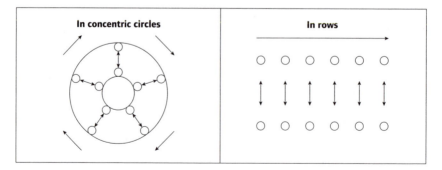

FIGURE 7.2   Interactive practice for giving and responding to compliments

[17] Student worksheets for this additional input are available from a link at: http://www.i.hosei.ac.jp/~ishihara.

open and sustain conversation, and to practice this function interactively using compliments and related topics.

F Closing

The wrap-up stage offers opportunities to assess learners' further needs and development of pragmatic awareness and production with regard to compliments and responses to compliments. Assessment can be conducted not just by teachers but also by learners themselves or by their peers. Informal assessment in particular does not have to wait until the end of instruction but can be incorporated into the regular instructional routine as a way of providing feedback. The teacher can ask learners to role-play what they think typical speakers of the L2 would say to assess their pragmalinguistic control. Learners can also be invited to self-assess their pragmatics with appropriate teachers' guidance. In addition, teachers may choose to elicit and assess learners' awareness of the range of community norms, as well as the match between their intention and listeners' probable interpretations of their pragmatic behavior.[18]

Learners' feedback about the instruction can also be surveyed at this stage. A student worksheet can contain several scenarios to elicit learners' oral and/or written compliments and responses,[19] as well as other prompts such as:

1   Think of a real conversation you recently had with someone in English that included a compliment. Write down the exchange as accurately as possible.

2   What did you learn about: a) giving compliments, b) responding to compliments, and c) social and cultural norms of complimenting and responding to compliments,

3   After studying about complimenting, how comfortable and confident do you feel about giving and responding to compliments in English? What questions do you still have?

4   Which of the following aspects of language and culture are you interested in learning about? What would you like to know about them?

   (a) greetings;

   (b) addressing people;

   (c) opening a conversation;

   (d) closing a conversation;

   (e) making an invitation/accepting and refusing an invitation;

   (f) making a request;

   (g) apologizing;

---

[18] See Chapter 15 and Ishihara (in press, *c*) for more discussion and examples.
[19] Sample scenarios can be found in Rose and Ng (2001: 169–70).

(h) thanking;

(i) complaining;

(j) congratulating;

(k) well-wishing;

(l) understanding and using implied meaning (implicature);

(m) something else (specify).[20]

Sample material: worksheet for learners' data collection (stage B, above)

Giving and responding to compliments: data collection

For the coming week, pay attention to any compliments that you give, receive, or overhear **in English**. Jot them down in a notebook or elsewhere as accurately as poss-ible after the conversation has ended. Observe carefully the **context** in which these compliments were given and received in terms of **age, gender, role, distance/close-ness, and compliment topics**. Fill out the following form and then decide how appropriate the interaction seemed to be.

	Relative status (age, gender, social status)	Distance/ role	Other information (compliment topics)	Appropriate? (sincere/ spontaneous?)
E.g., (from *Father of the Bride*): Dad: *You look all lit up inside.* Annie: *Oh, I feel all lit up inside.* . . . Dad: *You smell pretty good, too.* Annie: *Oh, you like it? It was a present.*	M to F 40s → early 20s L ←—X—→H	Very close C ←—X—→ D Father → daughter	Appearance Perfume	Sincere/ spontaneous/ appropriate
Interaction 1 A: B: (continues)				

---

[20] Tasks similar to those presented in this lesson plan can be used for teaching and researching these speech acts.

	Relative status (age, gender, social status)	Distance/ role	Other information (compliment topics)	Appropriate? (sincere/ spontaneous?)
Interaction 2 A: B:				
Interaction 3 A: B:				

Teaching Demonstration 2: Teaching requesting (EFL)[21]

Learners and the context

The instruction is designed for false beginners in a university EFL context with the learners' scores ranging from 370 to 429 on the paper-based TOEFL® ITP (International Testing Program) Level 2. The target audience are adult Japanese non-English majors, taking a required freshman English course. They have been studying English for at least six years, but most have very little exposure to authentic L2 use and L2-speaking cultures. If learners received traditional English education until high school, they are usually unfamiliar with communicative language teaching, and their oral proficiency is typically extremely limited. Learners' goals include scoring high on a proficiency test like the TOEIC (Test of English for International Communication) or TOEFL (Test of English as a Foreign Language) for better job prospects after university and improving English skills to better communicate in that language.[22] Instruction in the English medium can motivate learners at this level if it is supported with visual materials and made comprehensible. However, because learners share a first (or dominant) language, the instruction may be more effective if selected parts are given bilingually. For example, learners' understanding would most likely be reinforced if imaginary scenarios and reflective prompts are accompanied by written Japanese trans-lations, and learners are allowed to use Japanese in providing reflections if they wish. For this particular **foreign-language** audience, several varieties of English have been incor-porated into the lesson plan as you see below.

[21] The instruction/assessment procedures have been adapted from a research study that has been investigating teacher-based assessment of L2 pragmatics in the class-room: Ishihara (2009).
[22] Learners often lack an authentic need for studying English and have limited opportunities to use the L2; thus, teaching such a population of learners is some-times characterized as *Teaching English for No Apparent Reasons (TENAR)* (Kubota and McKay 2008).

Objectives

In the requesting situation, the speaker/writer is asking the listener/reader to take some action for the benefit of the speaker/writer. Because such an action does not usually profit the listener/reader, the speaker/writer uses various strategies to minimize the imposition involved in the request. These strategies soften the potentially face-threatening requests and can help the speaker/writer get what is needed. Below are the objectives of instruction, which centers on spoken requests:

1   Learners will be able to identify different norms of behavior across different cultures and contexts with regard to requests.

2   Learners will be able to assess the levels of politeness, directness, and formality of various request expressions and pre- and post-request strategies.

3   Learners will be able to use a range of request expressions and pre- and post-request strategies according to different contexts.

4   Learners will be able to analyze interactions in terms of speaker's intention and listener's interpretation in the given context and identify potential consequences of their own pragmatic language choice.

5   Learners will be able to approximate their intention through their pragmatic L2 use.

Suggested time

Approximately 750 minutes (e.g., 15 weeks for 50 minutes each).

Classroom instruction/assessment procedures

A Initial reactions to language use in context

As an introduction to socially and culturally appropriate language use, episodes about the use of Hong Kong English[23] are enhanced with visual materials (e.g., maps and photos) and shared with learners. By responding to the following discussion prompts, learners analyze language of requests in American English, Hong Kong English, and Japanese.

1   What English requests did Rose hear from bank tellers, librarians, and sales clerks in Hong Kong? How are these requests usually phrased in Japanese and in American English?

2   Why do people in Hong Kong tend to make direct requests?

---

[23] Rose (1999: 172–3).

3   What risks are involved in the communication between American English speakers and Cantonese-English speakers?

As further visual support, the request expressions produced in Prompt 1 are placed in a continuum of politeness/directness/formality.[24] The instruction at this stage serves as an informal assessment of learners' awareness of pragmatic variability.

B Production of written request discourse

Four written dialogues are elicited from learners through a situational approach, using multi-turn *discourse completion tasks* (DCTs) (see the sample material below). Writing is used due to learners' weakness in oral skills. Also, because written materials can be analyzed later with relative ease, written dialogues can be used as a projection of their speech. However, alternatively and ideally, learners' online pragmatic competence can be assessed orally and in natural discourse if possible. At this point, learner language is not graded or commented on, but used only for teachers' diagnosis of their pragmatic production.

Learners are then given varied sample responses collected from pragmatically competent speakers of English (see the sample material below), and the request expressions from these data are sequenced on the continuum of formality/directness/formality used at stage A.

C Learners' data collection in authentic L1/L2 discourse

Learners are assigned to collect naturally occurring request dialogues in L1 Japanese or in L2 English. Using a format similar to that for giving and responding to compliments above, learners receive instruction in how to notice and analyze the language of requests in relation to contextual factors (i.e., relative social status, distance, and the level of imposition of the request).

D Learners' reflections on language use in context

Request *softeners* (mitigators) are introduced to learners using material on Australian English.[25] In this activity, learners match examples of short, softened requests with the descriptions of the authentic contexts in which those requests occurred. The linguistic features and the context of the requests that make the match possible are then discussed. Learners' attention is also directed at both the speaker's intention and the listener's interpretation, considering the language form and the context.

[24] At this stage, learners may be shocked to see how low on the continuum the expression, *Please X* is situated. Many Japanese learners seem to believe it is a highly polite expression: Ishihara (2009); Matsuura (1998).
[25] The instructions and materials can be found in Yates (2003). Accessible at: http://exchanges.state.gov/media/oelp/teaching-pragmatics/short.pdf (accessed December 10, 2009).

Finally, learners' reflections on learning the pragmatics of requests thus far and their preference as to how they wish to use English can be elicited though individual written samples (or alternatively, through class discussion). Teachers can give and explain the criteria of assessment for this reflection ahead of time. The assessment criteria may be prepared bilingually and can include the following:

1 awareness of linguistic variations in contexts (e.g., relative status, distance, and imposition);

2 awareness of linguistic variations according to speaker's and listener's age, gender, culture, regional/ethnic affiliation, and educational background;

3 awareness of (newly learned) linguistic details (e.g., grammar and word choice); and

4 awareness of speaker's intention and listener's interpretation.

E Learners' analysis of the language–context relationship

Using the data that learners collected for themselves earlier (at stage C above), learners individually analyze the relationship between contextual factors and the language used in the request, guided by a few prompts (e.g., *Comparing the dialogues you collected, analyze how S [social status, age, gender], D [social/psychological distance], and I [the level of imposition] influence the language used in the request. Explain how S, D, and I influence pre-request strategies and post-request strategies.*)

F Language-focused development and assessment

Instruction at this stage focuses on linguistic aspects of pragmatics. Learners go over a range of request strategies (pre- and post-request supportive moves), such as those below and examples for each category:[26]

1 Checking on availability;

2 Getting a pre-commitment;

3 Giving a reason for the request;

4 Showing consideration for the hearer/Apologizing/Minimizing the imposition;

5 Sweetening;

---

[26] For examples and more information of these categories, see Chapter 4, Blum-Kulka *et al.* (1989), or the summary on the CARLA website, http://www.carla.umn.edu/speechacts/requests/research.html (accessible December 10, 2009).

6   Promising to pay back;

7   Expressing gratitude.

Learners' pragmalinguistic control of these request strategies can be assessed through a quiz.

G Learners' self-revising, role-playing, and refining their request discourse

Learners receive their own responses in multi-turn DCTs which make use of four scenarios (see stage B above) and revise them as an assignment. They are free to review the competent speaker samples provided earlier, and are provided an explanation for a set of assessment criteria at this stage (see below). In class, learners practice their written dialogues orally in pairs, as well as a few other peer dialogues (scaffolded role-plays). Then they are asked to record their best responses to the same prompts once again without looking at any of the written dialogues (unscaffolded written role-plays). These written dialogues can be assessed by the teacher, using a set of assessment criteria that have been provided to learners earlier (see Chapter 15 for other examples of assessment rubrics):

A sample assessment rubric (teacher circles appropriate evaluations on the right)

(a) Overall directness, politeness, and formality; tone (e.g., intonation, use of eye contact, gestures if applicable)	Very appropriate Somewhat appropriate Less appropriate Inappropriate
(b) Choice and use of request strategies (e.g., offering a reason, getting a pre-commitment, checking availability, promising to compensate, showing consideration for the listener, expressing apology/thanks)	Very appropriate Somewhat appropriate Less appropriate Inappropriate
(c) Overall comprehensibility of the speaker's intention (in terms of appropriateness, rather than accuracy) (e.g., pronunciation, word choice, grammar, sequencing)	Highly comprehensible Somewhat comprehensible Less comprehensible Incomprehensible

H Learners' self-evaluation of written-request discourse

While the teacher assesses learner language, learners can also conduct self-evaluation of their own language production (from stage G above) with (bilingual) guiding prompts. Through this self-assessment, learners' pragmatic awareness (*1 below) and language production (*2 below) can both be assessed. Below are some sample prompts based on the scenario c) in the sample material below (see Chapter 15 for authentic example of this self-evaluation):

1   Given the context, how appropriate was Karla's request in terms of overall directness, formality, politeness, and the tone (e.g., intonation, gesture, eye contact)?

(a) What part of Karla's language demonstrates appropriate levels of directness, politeness, and formality? (*1)

(b) What part of her language may need improvement, considering the appropriate level of directness, politeness, and formality called for by this situation? (*1) What should she have said? Write the actual expressions that you think she could have used. (*2)

2   Request strategies:

(a) What requesting strategies did Karla use appropriately? Check the ones that she used on the left column, and write out the expressions that she used in the right. (*1) (Table of strategies here.)

(b) What other strategies could she have used? What might she say? (*2)

3   Listener's interpretation: How do you think Karla's request sounds to Professor Johnson, considering the situation? Check the one that most likely represents Professor Johnson's reaction. Then, explain why you think that is the case. (*1)

(a) Prof. Johnson would be willing to give her an extension because . . .

(b) He would give her an extension, but may not be very happy with Karla's language because . . .

(c) He may not give her an extension because . . .

I Analysis of speaker's intention and listener's interpretation

Because in **foreign-language** contexts learners' authentic L2 input tends to be limited, a feature film is used to demonstrate how speaker's intention is encoded in the language and how it can be interpreted by the listener. One such scene that might be used for this purpose is a short dinner scene from the Hollywood film, *What about Bob?* in which three requests appear. Learners are asked about the message that the speaker intends to convey, how else the message could be phrased, and how the listener interprets the speaker's message. Learners are then invited to discuss the ways that they would like to convey their intention and practice pragmatic L2 use as if they were in the scene.

J Teacher–learner collaborated assessment regarding intention and interpretation

At this final stage of instruction, learners' intentions in making requests are elicited, as well as their language for requesting. Learners and the teacher can collaboratively assess the match between the learners' intent as speakers and the most likely interpretation that listeners would have (see Chapter 15 for how learners' goals and intentions can be elicited).

This assessment is intended to focus the learners' attention on their linguistic skills and awareness of community norms in order to help them to approximate their goal and intention as speakers. The teacher's assessment below is based on the elicited learner input:

Sample teacher's assessment based on learner input

1 Linguistic ability to use community norms	Excellent Good Fair Needs more work
2 Awareness of most probable listener's interpretation	Highly aware Aware Less aware Unaware
3 Match between learner goal/intention and most probable listener's interpretation of learner language	Excellent Good Fair Needs more work
Overall assessment	Excellent Good Needs more work

Sample material

1 Request scenarios for eliciting learner production and sample data[27] (see instruction/assessment procedure B, above).

> (a) Chris and Pat[28] are university students and roommates in an apartment near campus. They are very close friends. Last week, Chris was sick and missed two class sessions. Since the exam is coming up soon, Chris would like to see Pat's class notes. Because Pat is a good student, Chris also wants to ask if they can study together.
>
> Pat: Hey, how's it going?
>
> Chris – 1:
>
> Pat: Sure, no problem, I just need my notes back in a couple of days.
>
> Chris – 2:
>
> Pat: Okay. Let's plan on doing that then.

[27] Sample data collected from pragmatically competent English speakers (Ishihara 2003b). Three different responses were selected to demonstrate pragmatic variation.
[28] Unisex names are used in Scenarios a and c, so that learners are free to choose the gender. In this way, the scenarios become more authentic to learners' needs.

Sample data

Chris – 1:

1   Well, not so well. You know that the exam we have next week? Well, I missed two classes and I don't have any notes. I was wondering if I could borrow your notebook for a while, and see what I missed.

2   You know that class we're taking together, um, well, I was sick like last week. You think I can maybe borrow your notes and see if I can catch up for the exam?

3   Um, not too well. I missed class last weekend and now am not ready for the test. Do you think maybe I could borrow your notes?

Chris – 2:

1   Thank you so much. Um, also, if you're not so busy, would you mind studying together? That way we can make sure that we haven't missed anything and we'll be ready for the test.

2   Okay, no problem, great. And also, if you could help me study, that would be great, too.

3   Can I ask you another favor? Would you mind studying with me a little bit, so I could ask you questions? Thanks a lot, you're a life saver.

(b) John is in a large class taught by Professor Andersen. She shared a very interesting book in class last week. Since she offered to lend it to anyone who might be interested, John decides to go to her after class to borrow it. This is his first time talking to Professor Andersen in private.

John – 1:

Prof. Andersen: Oh, I'm sorry but I've already lent it out to someone else who was interested.

John – 2:

Prof. Andersen: Sure, no problem.

Sample data

John – 1:

1 Um, Professor Andersen, I was wondering if I could borrow that book you showed us last week.

2 Hi Professor Andersen, about the book that you . . . you told us about in class, um, do you think I can borrow it this weekend, and maybe look it over?

3 Professor Andersen, I was wondering if it would be possible to borrow that book you talked about in class last week.

John – 2:

1 Oh, really? That's okay. Um, um, maybe I'll try to borrow it from you later.

2 Oh, okay, ah, that's all right. But if ah, he gives back soon, I, could I borrow that afterwards?

3 Ah, okay. Um, when they give it back, do you think I can look at it, then?

(c) Terry lives with a roommate, Alex, who is a very good friend. However, Alex likes to have his/her TV on loud in the evening, and Terry has difficulty concentrating on the studies. Terry wants to ask that Alex not have the TV on so loud while s/he is trying to study. Alex approaches Terry and says:

Alex: So, have you finished your homework yet?

Terry:

Alex: Why not take a study break for a while and watch some TV with me?

Terry:

Sample data

Terry – 1:

1 No, not yet. Um, it's kind of hard with the TV so loud. Do you think maybe you could turn it down?

2 Yeah, see, no, 'cause the TV is too dumb. Turn it down, Alex. Turn down your TV so I can study, please. That's all I'm asking.

▶

3   No, Alex, because I haven't been able to study, because someone has a TV on so loud.

Terry – 2:

1   Look, I, I can't. I've got tons of work to do, okay? So, so wouldn't you please just turn it down, okay? All right, thanks.

2   Dude, I can't, come on! But would you just turn it down for a little bit. I've got to get this done.

3   Um, okay, let's make a deal. I'll watch some TV, and then, after that, let's turn down the TV so I can study, okay?

(d) Karla takes a large class at a university in Minneapolis. A week before a course paper is due, she notices that she has three more long papers due the same week. She realizes that it is not possible to finish them all by their respective due dates. She decides to go to one of the instructors, Professor Johnson, to ask for an extension on the paper for his course. This is her first time talking to him in private. She approaches him after class is over and says:

Karla:

Prof. Johnson: But you knew the deadline, didn't you?

Karla:

Sample data

Karla – 1:

1   Hi, Professor Johnson, my name is Karla Philips and I'm in one of your classes. Um, I was wondering if it might be possible to get an extension on a paper that's due next week.

2   Um, Professor Johnson, ah, yeah, I was just wondering about the paper. Could I maybe get an extension?

3   Um, Professor Johnson, I was wondering if I could ask you for an extension on the paper that's due next week. Um, do you think that's possible?

Karla – 2:

1   Ah, yeah, I did, but um, I, I, I didn't realize it until I wasn't gonna have enough time to do it. Um, so I was wondering if you could please, please extend the deadline for me. I'd really appreciate it.

2   Um, yeah, I did, I just, I've been really busy with a few of my other classes, and I don't know if I'll be able to get it down on time. Do you think it'll be possible to get an extension?

3   I knew it, but I have three other papers that are due, and I've been working on them, but it doesn't look like I'll be able to finish them all in time. Um, is it possible to have an extension?

Discussion

This chapter started with some guidelines for observing pragmatics-focused lesson plans. Teacher readers are encouraged to observe others' instruction in this area and to do so with a particular focus of observation in mind. Two sequences of speech act instruction, one in **second** and the other in **foreign-language** contexts, were then introduced in which classroom-based assessment was integrated into the instruction. Teacher readers were invited to take a critical look at these examples of instruction and to consider whether they would wish to adapt such materials for use in their own instructional contexts, and if so, how. In conclusion to this chapter, the following activity directs readers to online resources for teaching and researching pragmatics and provides a hands-on opportunity to explore some of them according to their interests and needs.

Activity 7.1 Exploring instructional resources for pragmatics

Objectives

1   You will become familiar with the scope of research-informed online instructional resources for pragmatics.

2   You will be able to locate particular pieces of pedagogical information for teaching pragmatics according to your needs.

Suggested time: 30 minutes.

Materials:

■ computers with an internet connection;

■ Appendix A, "Electronic resources for teaching pragmatics," found on p. 355–6 of the book.

Directions

1   Briefly familiarize yourself with the various resources listed under "Electronic resources for teaching pragmatics."

2   Access resources of interest to you in Section 2, "Lesson plans and pragmatics curriculum for learners." Learn about the aspects of pragmatics that are being focused on and the way that they are taught. Ideally, you have already determined the feature(s) of pragmatics to teach for a particular audience by this time and can focus your research according to your needs.

3   Take notes or store information in your personal file that you wish to come back to later.

4   Share your findings and evaluation of the lesson plans you have read with the rest of the class.

Discussion/wrap-up

If you have identified a lesson plan dealing with a topic relevant to your target for instruction in pragmatics, or an instructional approach you wish to use in your lesson plan, critically examine it and assess how applicable it is for your context. Consider what is likely to work in your own classroom and what aspects need adapting or supplementing. If you are designing instruction without adapting others' lesson plans, start thinking of a set of awareness-raising tasks that would work in your classroom setting. You may wish to refer back to the earlier section of this chapter for examples.

CHAPTER 8

Adapting textbooks for teaching pragmatics

Noriko Ishihara

Introduction

As noted in various other chapters in this volume (e.g., Chapters 3, 4, 6, and 7), current views in the field would underscore the importance of drawing as much as possible on empirically based information in the teaching of L2 pragmatics. However, it takes time and effort for teachers to find empirically based information either in published research studies or elsewhere, and then to create materials. Given the busy lives that teachers lead, this process may not always be realistic. It would be convenient to use textbooks that offer material on pragmatics ready to be taught without the need for modification. While most textbook series are yet to incorporate pragmatics in a robust way, there are publications available which provide sample L2 pragmatics lessons.[1] However, depending on the language being taught, the students' levels of proficiency, and classroom context, it is likely that teachers interested in including pragmatics instruction will need to adapt somewhat the materials they have, or prepare supplementary materials that address pragmatics more effectively. In this chapter, we will look at pragmatics in currently available language teaching materials, compare this pragmatics information with that available from research studies, and consider how we might modify or complement textbook materials in order to highlight appropriate language use in context.

---

[1] See for example, Bardovi-Harlig and Mahan-Taylor (2003: available at http://exchanges. state.gov/englishteaching/resforteach/pragmatics/html, accessed December 10, 2009) and Tatsuki and Houck (in press).

Textbook analysis for pragmatic components

As noted in Chapter 3, in current ESL/EFL commercially marketed materials, empirically based information is rarely used as the source for instructional materials in L2 pragmatics. The majority of published textbooks are written on the basis of the curriculum writers' intuitions. Textbook dialogues may at times sound awkward or stilted. Such dialogues are inauthentic in the sense that they do not represent spontaneous pragmatic language as used in natural conversation. Instead, they may reflect idealized examples of common pragmatic routines. Or in other cases they may not necessarily take issues of pragmatics into account or only give them passing attention.

For instance, while research has demonstrated that the act of closing conversations in American English is fairly elaborate and often realized in multiple turns, these insights have not generally been incorporated into L2 instruction. According to one study,[2] for example, the components of the closing in American English consist of:

- **the shut-down** (i.e., closing the topic) (e.g., *So, let's talk about this next time I see you*);

- **the pre-closing** (i.e., verification of the end of the conversation) (e.g., *OK, thank you very much*); and

- **the terminal exchange** (i.e., the actual good-bye to terminate the conversation) (e.g., *so long. Bye*) (see Figure 8.1, below).

The authors of this study examined the presentation of conversational closures in 20 L2 textbooks and found that only 12 included a complete closing in one or more dialogues and very few consistently included complete closings.[3]

Similarly, another survey of lessons on complaints in seven L2 functional textbooks has demonstrated a mismatch between textbook representations of the speech act and its spontaneous realization.[4] According to the researchers, complaints are often employed as a means for creating solidarity between conversation partners ("commiserating" in *indirect complaints*), but most of the textbooks they studied failed to represent this function completely. For example, a student griping to a fellow student about their badly organized class would be making an *indirect complaint*, while another student going straight to the teacher to discuss the same issue would be making

---

[2] Bardovi-Harlig *et al.* (1991).
[3] Bardovi-Harlig *et al.* (1991).
[4] Boxer and Pickering (1995).

FIGURE 8.1 Saying goodbye

a *direct complaint*. Typical responses to indirect complaints have been researched and the strategies include the following:[5]

1 Agreement/reassurance:

   A: [*In a large class*] God, he's got the most annoying laugh!

   B: *Yeah, and the mic doesn't help matters much.*

2 Advice:

   A: [*At a swimming pool*] Ow, it's cold! You're brave.

   B: Just take the plunge. It feels good once you get in.

3 Joking/teasing:

   A: [*At the service-counter reception*] When we got here there was nobody waiting. Look at it now!

   B: Gray Line drops off a bus load every hour.

4 Questions (showing interest in the complaint):

   A: [*Apartment handyman speaking to a tenant*] I just got back from vacation. Drove in this morning and got a flat tire.

   B: Where'd you go?

   A: Just to the shore.

   B: Good time?

---

[5] Examples from Boxer and Pickering (1995: 52–4).

A: Well . . . and I had just had the thing plugged too.

B: That's too bad.

5   Commiseration:

A: [*Two students talking*] I sat through yesterday's class with total non-comprehension.

B: Oh, yesterday was the worst!

Most textbooks focus only on *direct* complaints as expressions of negative evaluation and dissatisfaction about someone in their presence. The researchers claim that most of these textbook dialogues containing complaints are based on the material developers' intuitions and therefore contrived. In their opinion, this kind of material does a disservice to L2 learners because it fails to teach the positive rapport-building function of complaining.

L2 textbooks can be insufficient both in their sampling of pragmatics, as well as in the quality of the treatment of pragmatics even when it is included. A more recent study of eight L2 textbooks (four integrated skills texts for EFL and four grammar texts for ESL) demonstrated that these textbooks and ancillary materials for teachers contained little explicit information about pragmatics (e.g., how difference in relative social status influences the level of politeness in language).[6] There were few discussions of register, illocutionary force (i.e., the intended meaning as opposed to the literal meaning), politeness, appropriateness, or what would constitute appropriate usage. Also, the range and number of speech acts contained in these texts were fairly limited, and their treatment was largely unsatisfactory, with little contextual information or explicit attention to issues related to pragmatics. In addition, the teachers in this study rarely resorted to outside sources to compensate for the paucity of pragmatic information in these textbooks. Similarly, while implicit messages expressed through conversational implicature are common in our everyday interaction, few examples of these were present in these ESL/EFL textbooks.[7] Even when implicature was included in the textbook dialogues, the textbooks sometimes failed to flag those messages which were conveyed implicitly and often did not point out how the language and the context interacted to convey the message.[8]

If we focus on the teaching of pragmatics in a **foreign-language** setting in particular, we find a similar picture. For example, one study evaluated the

[6] Vellenga (2004).
[7] Bouton (1994*b*).
[8] Bouton (1990).

pragmatics content in the five most commonly used secondary-school EFL textbooks published in Japan.[9] The authors found this content to be limited in terms of the amount of information on pragmatics, the range of situations, and the speech act expressions included. Moreover, the information that was included did not appear to be very learner-friendly, nor did it seem to trigger any noticing of the relationship between the linguistic forms used and the context in which these forms appeared.

Another study focused on the language of requests in five EFL textbooks in tourism published in Spain. The study found a scarcity of contextual information for these requests that would help learners to determine what would be appropriate language use.[10] The author contends, for example, that these textbooks tended to neglect the presentation of modifiers that would normally occur either before or after the requesting utterance. Yet another study, which compared greetings in seven seventh-grade EFL textbooks in Japan and naturally occurring greetings in American English, found that textbook materials tended to misrepresent naturally occurring greetings.[11] The author also analyzed learners' production of greetings and argued that these materials were insufficient for developing learners' pragmatic ability.

Other researchers have focused on how the pragmatics of gendered language is taught in Japanese language textbooks. Japanese norms of behavior and language use are often considered highly gendered. For example, some sentence-final particles, honorific particles, and personal pronouns tend to be associated with femininity or masculinity. Studies of several commonly used Japanese language textbooks found that in many of the textbooks, these features were presented as representing either male or female language, often in contrastive charts.[12] In addition, three of the textbooks stated that females tended to use more polite and formal language. The researchers argued that these descriptions, along with the lack of counter examples, disregard the existence of gender-neutral forms, a wide range of within-gender variability, and cross-gender usage found in natural discourse. This stereotypical depiction of gender in language use is not only inaccurate but can lead to the reinforcement of traditional gender norms in the language, making the target culture seem more exotic and alien.[13]

---

[9] McGroarty and Taguchi (2005).

[10] Usó-Juan (2008).

[11] Kakiuchi (2005*a*).

[12] Five widely used textbooks were surveyed in Siegal and Okamoto (1996), and then seven in their later work (Siegel and Okamoto 2003).

[13] Siegal and Okamoto (1996, 2003).

Using resources informed by research when adapting textbooks

The above analyses of how pragmatics is dealt with in textbooks show that pragmatic language use tends to be underrepresented in these textbooks. It is unfortunate that textbooks do not tend to take advantage of the wealth of information revealed through research with regard to, for example, the appropriate situations in which to use certain forms, the effects of gender on language use, and the common grammatical forms associated with given speech acts, as well as the strategies that have been found to be associated with those speech acts. We are suggesting that teachers of L2 pragmatics should not rely necessarily on the commercially marketed student textbooks alone.

Teachers may first wish to find useful resources informed by research to (re)familiarize themselves with pragmatic norms in the L2 community[14] or by collecting data themselves perhaps with students. Teachers may also be advised to use discretion in their efforts to select materials that mirror a range of L2 pragmatic uses to a reasonable degree, and supplement or replace existing materials with more authentic and varied examples when necessary. In this chapter, we will introduce some of the research-based resources from publications on teaching complaints, requests, and conversational closing.[15] They provide examples of classroom activities that compensate for the gap often found in L2 materials and offer more authentic L2 models. The use of these examples can serve two purposes – both to teach complaints and conversational closings, and to demonstrate how pragmatics can be given a higher profile in the L2 classroom.

Teaching complaints

In contrast to *direct complaints*, which are addressed to the person who is the source of the problem, in *indirect complaints* the expression of dissatisfaction is intended for someone or something not present.[16] As mentioned above, since L2 learners can use them to build solidarity with their peers, indirect complaints can be taught as an effective communication strategy in the L2. Although indirect complaints are often neglected in the L2 curriculum, the following sequence of activities can address this area:

[14] Judd (1999).
[15] Bardovi-Harlig *et al.* (1991); Boxer and Pickering (1995); Griswold (2003).
[16] Boxer and Pickering (1995).

1 presenting examples of authentic indirect complaint discourse and discussing various types of responses (see above for examples);

2 presenting indirect complaints to have learners produce the responses;

3 presenting responses to indirect complaints to have learners produce complaints that precede the responses;

4 discussing the impact of the setting, context, and speaker characteristics in the above exchanges;

5 learners' reconstruction of short sample conversations through the ordering of lines;

6 videotaping of learners' mini-drama role-plays based on the given gender, social status, and distance; and

7 analyzing pragmatic language use in the videotaped role-plays.[17]

The authors of this article provide an abundance of examples of indirect complaints from spontaneous speech, which can provide authentic models for L2 learners. These suggested activities draw learners' attention to interactional issues by constantly presenting speakers' complaints along with their listeners' responses. Some of the sample dialogues consist of multiple turns, and the speech elicited in the tasks could be stretched into extended discourse.

Teaching requests in an academic setting

Requesting is a popular speech function that can often be found in language textbooks. Textbook coverage of the requests is often associated with the grammatical structures and modals (e.g., *could, would,* and *may*). In other cases with textbooks utilizing a functional syllabus, a list of formulaic expressions may be provided, but little information is found in textbooks as to how to use them (e.g., in what situations they are appropriate and to whom the expressions can be addressed). In the teaching of pragmatics, in addition to teaching how to form single-sentence requests (e.g., "Could I please have a glass of water?"), the pragmatics of requests can also be introduced to learners in a more extended discourse. For example, samples of authentic conversation can show learners how the discourse opens up, proceeds, and concludes, how indirect and subtle requests can be used, and in what situations and in what sequences they can be used.

---

[17] The sequence of activities is from Boxer and Pickering (1995: 52–5).

Below is the sequence of activities that was tested with adult learners in a university-level course of English for Academic Purposes in New Zealand:[18]

1 recording learners' role-plays in which a learner attempts to change his/her tutorial schedule with a co-ordinator;

2 discussion about the social factors involved in the context;

3 learners' transcribing and analyzing their own recorded role-plays;

4 analysis of authentic dialogue samples by ordering cut-up strips of possible strategies, studying the strategies in the transcript, and discussing linguistic features of requests (e.g., an explicit request using *want,* softening requests with *just*);

5 comparison of the sample and learner dialogues; and

6 discussion of pragmatic norms of the target culture and learners' own.

The authors of this article ask the question of how realistic and effective it is to have learners analyze authentic conversation. Would it be too distracting or confusing to learners? Would they find it useful? Can they really learn anything from the discourse analysis? The empirical answers to these questions are quite positive in their study, and this seems to point to the value of utilizing authentic pragmatics materials, as well as teaching pragmatics in discourse.

Teaching conversational closing

Another article in the literature focuses on teaching how to close conversations in English and bases the instruction upon naturally occurring data. While some languages and cultures (such as Thai and Nepali) permit exchanges to end rather abruptly with little or no closing, others (such as English and Swahili) tend to require fairly elaborate steps.[19] Learners particularly from those cultures that tend to allow relatively shorter closings may be unaware that a more gradual transition to closing is preferred in other cultures. And even if learners have that awareness, they may not know the language for wrapping up conversations in the L2 in an appropriate manner. Explicit teaching of typical conversational closing routines is likely to help learners to avoid coming across as being hasty, awkward, or abrupt. The following set of activities is geared to high-intermediate adult ESL learners[20] and is readily applicable to EFL students as well:

---

[18] The activities are from Crandall and Basturkmen (2004: 46–8).

[19] Bardovi-Harlig *et al.* (1991).

[20] More details of these suggested activities can be found in Bardovi-Harlig *et al.* (1991: 1–13).

1   guided discussion of the learners' L1 pragmatic norms and ramifications of enacting pragmatic norms appropriately or inappropriately;

2   tape-recording of interaction from an arranged class interruption by a guest, discussion about the interruption, and learners' reconstruction of the interaction through role-play ("the classroom guest" activity);

3   learners' acting out and comparison of appropriate, complete closings and less-than-appropriate ones in textbook dialogues and construction of complete closings;

4   provision of one-sentence closing lines and learners' reconstruction of appropriate closing dialogues; and

5   variations of role-plays, including a situation where one of the speakers tries to end the conversation politely while the other wants to continue.

Another instructional resource draws on the above article, as well as on an earlier one utilizing conversation analysis,[21] and further illustrates how to teach conversational closings in English that are fairly ritualized.[22] The instruction includes a stage where conversation partners indirectly notify each other that no more business needs to be discussed by summarizing their points, restating future arrangements made, or making positive comments about speaking to each other ("shut-down"). The conversation partners also confirm their understanding of each other's intention to conclude the conversation through the use of formulaic expressions (e.g., *well, okay, all right*, and *thank you*) ("pre-closing") in addition to exchanges for actual leave-taking ("terminal exchange"). The steps for classroom instruction include learners' observation of natural conversation. Using transcripts, the following leading questions could be asked in guiding students' discovery of pragmatic norms[23]:

- Where is the conversation happening? What is its purpose?
- What is the relationship between the conversation partners?
- How do the participants in the conversation let each other know that they are about to say "good-bye"?
- What formulas do they use to accomplish this?
- How do they avoid being rude and abrupt in closing the conversation?
- Which utterances are leave-takings?
- How does the relationship between the conversation partners, their roles, the context of the conversation, and its purpose influence the choice of words for these utterances?

[21] Schegloff and Sacks (1973).
[22] Griswold (2003).
[23] Griswold (2003).

Learners' observations can be further reinforced in activities such as group discussion, oral presentation, reflective journaling, skit construction, and role-plays. The entire lesson plan and caveats can be found in *Teaching Pragmatics*.[24]

Teaching conversational implicature

A characteristic of daily language interactions is that messages often have implicit elements which need to be interpreted from the context. For example, if we say, "Do you have any coffee?" in a restaurant, we mean a cup of coffee ready to drink; in the grocery store, the same utterance refers to coffee beans to be roasted[25] (see Chapter 4 for the definition of *conversational implicature*). Research shows that conversational implicature in an L2 is learned only slowly unless it is explicitly taught and that formal instruction can accelerate the learning of most types of conversational implicature. Below is an example of how conversational implicature might be addressed in an advanced ESL/EFL classroom (see Chapter 4 for the classifications and examples):[26]

1   introduction of each type of implicature with the label, definition, and several examples for each;

2   discussion of new examples of implicature:

- identification of the implicature;

- explanation of how literal meaning did not hold and how the implicature was detected;

- identification of what is actually implied in the messages;

- illustration of learners' experiences with implicature;

- identification of similar implicature in learners' L1s;

3   group work creating dialogues containing implicature;

---

[24] *Teaching Pragmatics* (Bardovi-Harlig and Mahan-Taylor 2003, see above for the URL) is a practical and accessible online source that reflects current thinking with regard to the teaching of L2 pragmatics. The other chapters in this teachers' resource guide deal with: general pragmatic awareness and comprehension (e.g., politeness, greetings, terms of address, and pragmatic variation), conversational management (e.g., the use of discourse markers, correcting and contradicting, and contrasting), conversational openings and closings, and other speech acts (requesting, refusing, complimenting and responding to compliments).

[25] Bouton (1994*a*: 88).

[26] Bouton (1994*a*: 102).

4   analysis of new examples of implicature provided by the teacher or by the learners.

The instructional procedure above would take approximately six hours of class time, which can be spread over several weeks. After the bulk of the instruction (steps 1–3) is implemented, step 4 could be used as an occasional warm-up of a regular class meeting. Learners may benefit from a discussion as to who the appropriate recipients of a message with a given implicature would be, such as whether a message with a certain type of implicature tends to be more or less appropriate for higher-status or equal-status conversational partners.

Teaching gendered language

For certain target languages in which language use is more closely linked to gender identity, teachers face the complex issue of how to deal with gender-associated linguistic features in the classroom. Teaching the traditional gendered norms alone could reinforce the stereotypical view of the language use; at the same time, identifying actual diversity of pragmatic norms in the target community would not be a straightforward task. Furthermore, should learners be instructed to use gendered language the way native speakers are seen to use it even if they have doubts about its social implications regarding gender equality? Should learners mimic native-like use even if they may not be expected to behave that way in the target community? Drawing from the field of *critical pedagogy*, teachers could encourage learners to analyze language use and its sociocultural implications critically by means of:

1   discussions about a reading on the social meaning of voice pitch and gender;

2   analysis of selected TV commercials using transcripts where gendered language use and norms of behavior are exhibited;

3   critical discussion and questioning of how the target language and culture are represented;

4   learners' creation and performance of commercials;

5   discussion of frequently used grammar in the commercials; and

6   paired role-play practice and wrap-up reflection as an assignment.[27]

---

[27] Instruction given in Ohara *et al.*'s study (2001).

The study in which the above instruction was given found that learners were able to identify linguistic features that were related to gender, and were also able to critically examine gendered norms of behavior in the target language and culture. In the creation and performance of commercials, learners experimented with gendered language and explored the gender roles played through the use of the language.[28]

Discussion

This chapter has discussed currently available language textbooks for the purpose of teaching pragmatics and has offered a few examples of how we might supplement or adapt these textbooks to teach complaints, requests, conversational closing, and gendered language based on empirically established information concerning pragmatics. Because many language textbooks place minimal emphasis on pragmatics and often teach appropriate language use in an insufficient and inadequate way, teacher readers are invited to be critical appraisers of the material that they use in their classrooms. This would mean making sure that the language samples presented to learners are reasonably natural and authentic. It would also be expected that learners' input would reflect a variety of pragmatic norms used in the target language community.

In the activity below, we will encourage teacher readers to take a more in-depth look at the language textbooks that they actually use in their classrooms, with an eye to examining their suitability for teaching pragmatics. The research-based information about conversational closing will be used as a sample tool with which to investigate textbook materials. This activity is intended to help illustrate how language teachers may evaluate, adapt, or supplement currently available language textbooks in their efforts to incorporate explicit teaching of pragmatics into their L2 curricula. In subsequent chapters, we will continue our exploration of resources for pragmatics instruction that may be used in the classroom or that can provide us with further insights as to how pragmatics can be taught effectively.

[28] Ohara *et al.* (2001).

Activity 8.1 Evaluating textbooks for closing conversations

Objectives

1   You will be able to evaluate language materials utilizing research-based information about closing conversation.

2   You will be able to identify ways to adapt or supplement a textbook for pragmatics instruction.

Suggested time: 40 minutes.

Materials:

- Information: "Closing conversations in American English";[29]

- Task sheet: "Textbook analysis on closing conversations";

- a language textbook of your choice.

Directions

Part I

1   Work individually or in a small group. Use the information, "Closing conversations in American English" and (re)familiarize yourselves with the descriptions of the steps used in conversational closings in English.

2   Look at the authentic examples in the chart and identify steps of conversational closings involved in the dialogues in the right column.

3   Use the sample keys provided and compare your answers.

Part II

1   Work in groups of three or so to examine a chosen language textbook. Ideally, this would be the textbook you routinely use in your classroom. Analyze it in terms of how sample dialogues are closed. Use the chart on the task sheet, "Textbook analysis: closing conversations," to record your analysis. The analysis of the first example is completed for you using Sample dialogue 3 in the information,

[29] Bardovi-Harlig *et al.* (1991: 6–8, 10–13); Griswold (2003).

"Closing conversations in American English." Try another example using Sample dialogue 4 as a whole group before your begin your group work.

2   Evaluate the portion of the book in terms of conversational closings and consider how you would adapt or supplement the material. Use the guiding discussion questions on the task sheet.

3   Share your ideas with the whole group.

Discussion/wrap-up

In reflecting on this activity, consider how authentic are the textbook dialogues that the whole group examined. To what extent are they likely to need to be adapted? What are some strategies the whole group has come up with for obtaining more natural dialogue samples when necessary? In keeping with an awareness-raising approach to L2 pragmatics (see Chapter 6), what activities would be effective in order to highlight the pragmatics of the target language? For example, what features in closing conversation should learners notice? How would you provide learners with an opportunity to compare closings in their L1 and L2?

Information: Closing conversations in American English

In general, conversational closings in English are rather ritualized. Even though there are various ways to say "good-bye," these closings still tend to follow an observable pattern. Below are the major steps in this pattern. Some of these steps can occur in isolation or in combination with the other(s).

- **Shut-down.** Conversation partners indirectly let each other know that they have no more business to discuss. The conversational content here largely reflects the main purpose of the conversation. For example, they can summarize their discussion, confirm the arrangements made, or communicate their pleasure in speaking to the other person.

- **Pre-closing.** The conversation partners confirm their understanding of each other's intentions to end the conversation, usually by saying such things as "well," "okay," "alright," and "thanks."

- **Terminal exchange.** The conversational partners exchange their actual leave-takings.[30]

---

[30] Bardovi-Harlig *et al.* (1991); Griswold (2003). The authentic examples in the table below are taken from Bardovi-Harlig *et al.*'s naturally occurring data (1991: 6–7).

Now look at the authentic examples of conversational closings below in the left column and identify the steps involved in the right.

Examples of conversational closings	Steps in closing conversation

Sample 1

A: All right. See ya.
B: See ya later.

Sample 2

A: All right.

B: OK.

A: So long.

B: See you later.

Sample 3

A: OK. Thank you very much.

B: All right.

A: Now I have to go to French, which is a lot more
complicated than this was. [laugh]

B: All right. Good-bye.

A: Bye-bye.

Sample 4

A: Yeah, well, next time we come up, um . . .
I'll bring our set and . . . you can go through
'em and pick the ones you want.

B: OK. OK.

A: So . . .

B: That'll be fine.

A: OK.

B: Give my love to David.

A: OK. Tell And . . . Uncle Andy I hope he feels better.

B: I will.

A: OK. Thanks a lot for calling.

B: Bye-bye.

A: Bye, dear.

Sample keys: steps in closing conversation[31]

Examples of conversational closings	Steps in closing conversation
Sample 1	
A: All right. See ya.	Pre-closing, terminal exchange
B: See ya later.	Terminal exchange
Sample 2	
A: All right.	Pre-closing
B: OK.	Pre-closing
A: So long.	Terminal exchange
B: See you later.	Terminal exchange
Sample 3	
A: OK. Thank you very much.	Pre-closing
B: All right.	Pre-closing
A: Now I have to go to French, which is a lot more complicated than this was. [laugh]	Shut-down
B: All right. Good-bye.	Pre-closing, terminal exchange
A: Bye-bye.	Terminal exchange
Sample 4	
A: Yeah, well, next time we come up, um . . . I'll bring our set and . . . you can go through 'em and pick the ones you want.	Shut-down
B: OK. OK.	Pre-closing
A: So . . .	Pre-closing
B: That'll be fine.	Pre-closing
A: OK.	Pre-closing
B: Give my love to David.	Pre-closing
A: OK. Tell And . . . Uncle Andy I hope he feels better.	Shut-down
B: I will.	
A: OK. Thanks a lot for calling.	Pre-closing
B: Bye-bye.	Terminal exchange
A: Bye, dear.	Terminal exchange

[31] The interpretation of the steps is adapted from Bardovi-Harlig *et al.* (1991).

Task sheet: textbook analysis on closing conversations

The textbook selected for analysis: _____

Is there a chapter or section that explicitly teaches how target language speakers close conversation? If so, go to the chapter/section and examine the dialogues to answer the following questions. If not, go to any of the chapters and examine the dialogues there to answer the two questions in the table.

Dialogues	Q1. How many turns are there in the dialogue for shut-down, pre-closing, and terminal exchange?			Q2. Given your analysis on the left column, does the dialogue have a complete closing, a partial closing, or no closing?		
	Shut-down	Pre-closing	Terminal exchange	Complete closing	Partial closing	No closing
E.g., Sample 3 in the Information	1	3	2	✓		
E.g., Sample 4 in the Information						
1st dialogue						
2nd dialogue						
3rd dialogue						
4th dialogue						
5th dialogue						

Discussion questions

1   What is your overall evaluation of this portion of the textbook in terms of conversational closing?

2   How would you adapt or supplement this material?

Activity 8.2 Adapting textbooks for the teaching of greetings

Objectives

1   You will be able to identify elements in research-based information that are relevant and useful in teaching your students.

2   You will be able to adapt or supplement a textbook for pragmatics instruction.

Suggested time: 40 minutes.

Materials: Information, "Greetings in English".[32]

Directions

1   Work individually or in a small group. Identify the targeted learner audience and determine their age, level of proficiency, and other relevant characteristics.

2   Study the information, "Greetings in English." The first section provides a dialogue commonly found in EFL textbooks. The second section gives research-based information that can be helpful in adapting the material, with a view to highlighting pragmatics in the EFL instruction.

3   Consider how you would adapt or supplement the material. Design necessary materials and instructional procedures that are appropriate for your students in terms of the age and proficiency in particular.

4   Share your ideas with the whole group.

Discussion/wrap-up

In wrapping up this activity, consider what activities or instruction can precede or follow the material you have just designed if you wish to further the pragmatics-focused instruction. Alternatively, think of how you might formally or informally assess your students' understanding or production of the features of pragmatics being taught in your materials. Note that pragmatics could be incorporated to varying degrees. While the addition of a new curriculum could take up a large portion of your class time, brief pragmatic awareness-raising activities on a much smaller scale may also be effective if implemented on a regular basis (see the possible adaptations for instruction provided as an example).

---

[32] Bardovi-Harlig *et al.* (1991: 6–8, 10–13); Griswold (2003).

Information: Greetings in English

1 Greetings in an EFL textbook

The following is a typical exchange of greetings modeled in English textbooks for junior-high-school students in Japan. In this particular book from which the dialogue is cited,[33] the main characters in the book are introduced in the first page with illustrations. The two participants in the interaction, Kumi Tanaka and Paul Green, would appear to be friends and also similar in age to the targeted students (seventh graders). Kumi Tanaka can be assumed to be Japanese and Paul Green is introduced as an American; however, their actual ages and relationship are unknown.

> Kumi: How are you?
>
> Paul: Fine,* thank you. And you?
>
> Kumi: I'm fine too. Thank you.
>
> *"Very well/Not bad" are also used.
> [note in the teacher's book]

2 Information about English greetings and a sample of naturalistic dialogue

Note: The following information was collected from informants ranging in age from college age to people in their fifties. So the results may be of limited relevance, especially to young learners.

Research-based information about English greetings

> The following data were collected from native speakers of American English. The greetings and questions below were used by the speakers who initiated the greeting:[a]

---

[33] Takahashi *et al.* (2006: 2–3).

Greetings (%)		Questions (%)	
Hi	54	How are you?	45
Hey	24	How (are) you/ya doing?	36
Hello	11	What's up?	9
(Good) morning	9	How's it goin'?	9
Names only	2		

The data below were collected from the recipients of the greetings:[b]

Answer forms (%)		Questions (%)	
(Pretty) good	60	How are you?	53
OK	20	How (are) you/ya doing?	18
Literal answer	20	What's up?	24
		How's it goin'?	6

[a]From Kakiuchi (2005a: 70).
[b]From Kakiuchi (2005a: 72).

Naturalistic sample dialogue

Paul and Erin are college students in the US. They are close friends and equal in social status.[34]

Erin: Hey Paul. How's it going?

Paul: Hey Erin. How are you?

Erin: I'm fantastic!

Paul: I haven't seen you in a long time. Where've you been?

3 Possible adaptations for instruction

Note: The point of this sample adaptation is the addition of Dialogue 2, an informal version intended to integrate pragmatics issues into instruction that may otherwise be largely grammar-focused. Dialogue 1, below, is identical to the original between Kumi and Paul in the textbook. In order to make the dialogues more authentic, you can observe similar exchanges in your instructional setting and edit them based on the language used.

[34] Role-played dialogue from Félix-Brasdefer (2005).

Dialogue 1: At school	*Dialogue 2: On the street*
Kumi: How are you, Ms Anderson? Ms Anderson: I'm fine, thank you. And you? Kumi: I'm fine too. Thank you.	Kumi: Hi, Paul. Paul: Hey, Kumi, how's it goin? Kumi: Pretty good, thanks. How are *you* doing? Paul: I'm OK.

Discussion questions

1   Who is Ms. Anderson? Why do you think so?

2   Who is Paul? Why do you think so?

3   What is the level of formality reflected in Dialogue 1 and Dialogue 2? Mark an X for each dialogue on the line below. What makes you think so?

Informal ←——————————————————————————→ Formal

CHAPTER 9

Discourse, interaction, and language corpora

Andrew D. Cohen and Noriko Ishihara

Introduction

The chapter will consider the role that two sources of authentic language data, *conversation analysis* and *electronic corpora*, play in the teaching of L2 pragmatics. We will investigate how naturally occurring language data can be useful and instructive for the teaching of L2 pragmatics. We will start by describing and illustrating how conversation analysis can be used as a means for better understanding the workings of L2 pragmatics and the organization of L2 discourse. We will also consider how insights from this approach could be applied to instruction on pragmatics. We will then provide a brief coverage of how linguistic corpora have contributed to the field of L2 pragmatics and how such corpora could be used in pragmatics-focused instruction.

The role of conversation analysis in L2 pragmatics

Conversation analysis (CA) is a systematic approach to performing detailed analysis of both the verbal and nonverbal behavior of people engaged in social interaction. Building on an ethnomethodological foundation,[1] CA has demonstrated how what may appear as just ordinary, interactive talk is actually achieved through the application of methodical and complex practices on the part of the participants.[2] Utilizing transcripts of naturally occurring talk, conversation analysts have described this behavior, providing

[1] Garfinkel (1967).
[2] Kasper (2007).

detailed descriptions of how talk is sequentially structured and managed in an interactive fashion.[3] CA has examined, for example, how people take turns in conversation, how these turns overlap, and how conversational repair takes place.[4] Research has demonstrated, for example, how using a CA approach to studying a Japanese foreign-language class can help to elucidate how learners organize their classroom interactions, whether in order to complete a vocabulary exercise with a classmate or to conduct an interview with other Japanese speakers.[5]

As we can see in natural or simulated dialogues transcribed in other chapters (e.g., Chapter 8), speech acts are often realized in multiple turns and a fine-grained analysis of discourse (literally, second-by-second, line-by-line and word-for-word) can reveal how complexly natural conversations are structured and how our intentions can be conveyed in a subtle manner. It has been argued that L2 learners can benefit from the insights CA brings to the learning of pragmatics and discourse.[6]

CA in the study of L2 pragmatics

In recent years, experts have recommended the use of CA in the study of L2 pragmatics, since they would say that pragmatic meanings emerge from participants' efforts at interpreting each others' interactive contributions to a conversation.[7] By adopting a discursive approach, CA experts treat meaning as the understandings that conversational participants display to each other in the sequential organization of their talk. So, for example, speakers indicate through their response how they understand what their conversational partner said, and this then in turn provides an occasion for the first speaker to confirm or repair that understanding. In this way, meaning is constructed socially and interactively.[8]

An advocate of CA has suggested, for example, that this approach to pragmatics can help determine possible reasons for why cross-cultural discourse may diverge from L2 pragmatic norms. Two studies illustrate this: one a study of telephone openings and the other on responses to compliments.[9] In the first study comparing telephone openings by L1 speakers of Farsi vs

---

[3] Firth (1996: 237–8).
[4] Schegloff *et al.* (2002).
[5] Mori (2002, 2004).
[6] Félix-Brasdefer (2006); Liddicoat and Crozet (2001).
[7] Kasper (2007).
[8] Kasper (2006: 294).
[9] Kasper (2007).

those by L1 speakers of German, CA was used to illustrate how Iranian and German telephone openings are different. Whereas Iranian openings predictably include extended inquiries about the other's health and family, German opening exchanges are generally shorter and usually without such ritual inquiries. It is noted that this difference could possibly be a result of negative pragmatic transfer by the L2 speaker.[10]

The second study dealing with compliments illustrated the advantages of CA for comparing responses to compliments in German and in American English.[11] The researcher in this study used CA to illustrate how pragmatic transfer occurs in an episode involving a native speaker of American English – David – and two native speakers of German – Christiane and Annette – at breakfast (see Figure 9.1, below). Whereas CA uses a detailed set of symbols for the purposes of transcription,[12] the episode is presented here in a format intended to be easier for the lay reader to understand:

1 David: That's the best tea– I've – I think I've ever had.

2 Christiane: Great, right?

   (*D gazes at C with puzzled look*)

3 (*Pause*)

4 David: Uh– that lemonny kinda, yeah. It's quite nice.

5 Christiane: (*With a smile*) Yeah, we like it too.

6 (*Pause*)

7 Annette: What was the– exact name of it. It's just called– orange tea?

8 Christiane: Lemon tea. It's *Zitronentee*.

In her explanation of the transcript, the researcher notes that after David pays Christiane a compliment for making great tea (line 1), she responds to the compliment by giving a response strategy that works in German, namely a *same-strength second assessment* ("Great") followed by a *response pursuit marker,* "right?" (line 2). The researcher notes that this is a compliment response atypical of American conversations, and provides several indicators in the transcript that this compliment response is very unusual for David. First, after Christiane has agreed with the compliment and while

[10] Taleghani-Nikazm (2002).
[11] Golato (2002).
[12] For the original transcription of this episode, see Golato (2002: 566).

FIGURE 9.1 Tea at breakfast

she is producing her *response pursuit*, David looks at her with a quizzical expression on his face, since when Americans give second assessments, they usually downgrade.[13] Also, after Christiane's response pursuit marker, there is a brief pause (line 3) after which David continues with a *hesitation marker* ("Uh") followed by a cut-off (line 4). He then continues with an explanation of what he likes, followed by the confirmation "yeah." The researcher sees this as a possible indication that David treated Christiane's response pursuit as a question for clarification (i.e., as "you think this is great?"), or as a confirmation check. David then goes on to produce what an American

[13] Golato (2002: 566–7).

might have expected as Christiane's response, namely a second assessment which is downgraded ("It's quite nice") – a practice that is for compliment **receiving** but not for compliment **giving** in American English. The researcher interprets Christiane's delivery of "Yeah, we like it too" with a smile (line 5) as an indication that she also noticed that there was pragmatic failure in the conversation, prompting her to diverge from the expected German *ja* 'yes' response and instead to give a second assessment ("we like it too"). Next, there is a short pause in which neither David nor Christiane speaks (line 6), after which Annette continues the conversation (line 7).

As well as using CA to better understand pragmatics in discursive behavior, the results from empirical work in CA have been applied to the teaching of L2 pragmatic discourse. For example, differences in a particular discourse – such as patterns of discourse that are likely to follow the question "Did you have a good weekend" in French and Australian English respectively – were explicitly taught to Australian university learners of French. In Australian English, this question is ritualized and generally elicits a short, diplomatic answer, whereas in French it is usually a genuine question followed by extended conversation with details, opinions, and feelings.[14] Learners' role-plays immediately after and one year after the instruction showed learners' accommodation to French discursive norms especially in terms of the content of the talk (rather than the language form).[15] The researchers concluded that interactional norms of the L2 are amenable to instruction. (See below for the instructional procedures used in this study.)

These examples – the telephone opening, the compliment response, and response to a question about the weekend – illustrate how CA can reveal the complex structure of natural conversation and provide an analytic framework with which to closely examine pragmatic and discursive practices of L1 and L2 speakers. The argument made is that CA allows researchers to trace whether L2 speakers come to avoid transfer from L1 pragmatics over time, or whether over the course of repeated interactions, their conversational partners come to view their L1-influenced pragmatic behavior as more or less acceptable.[16] In addition, given its focus on sequential organization and close attention to verbal and non-verbal interactional conduct, CA helps us to see how discourse is structured across multiple turns. The case is made that through the analytical tools of CA and discourse analysis,

[14] Béal (1992), cited in Liddicoat and Crozet (2001).
[15] Liddicoat and Crozet (2001).
[16] Kasper (2007).

researchers can notice, collect, and examine such discursive occurrences. Furthermore, these insights can be applied to the teaching of, for example, conversational openings and closings, turn-taking, interrupting, topic-shift, adjacency pairs (i.e., speaker's utterance and the listener's preferred or dispreferred answer), and conversational repairs.[17] In the following section, we will take a look at some instructional techniques which have adopted a CA approach.

Instructional activities using CA in the teaching of L2 pragmatics

Here, we introduce three sets of instructional activities that detail how conversation analytic insights can be incorporated into the teaching of pragmatic and discursive conventions. (For more activities, see Chapter 8 for teaching the closing of conversation.[18]) Because CA is normally conducted with naturally occurring data,[19] instructional materials incorporating such data provide more authentic L2 models than materials written on the basis of intuition or based on elicited language. The awareness-raising approach (see Chapter 6) used in these procedures facilitates learners' noticing of the typical structure of talk-in-interaction presented through CA.

In the first example, the instructional focus was the conversation that follows the question, *Did you have a good weekend?* in French. As mentioned above, the way Australians would answer this question in their L1, English, differs dramatically from how they might be expected to respond in their L2, French.[20] In cases such as these and others similar to it – where there is a clear disparity across cultures – the instructor could take advantage of university learners' analytical skills and whatever prior knowledge of the target culture they may have. Activities could include the following:

1   Discussion of stereotypes of L1 and L2 cultures and how those stereotypes stem from differences in cultural norms in communication.

2   Comparison of typical L1 and L2 answers to the question, *Did you have a good weekend?* and reading about cross-cultural frustrations experienced by French and Australian English speakers.

---

[17] Dörnyei and Thurrell (1998).
[18] Bardovi-Harlig *et al.* (1991); Griswold (2003); Schegloff and Sacks (1973).
[19] A caveat here is that at times CA is also conducted with elicited data (referred to as "naturalistic data"), as in Félix-Brasdefer (2006).
[20] Liddicoat and Crozet (2001).

3   Discussion of the different features of conversation that the question elicits in French and Australian English using transcribed authentic dialogues.

4   Reconstruction of unscripted videotaped conversation in the L2.

5   Role-plays to practice L2 spoken grammar, vocabulary, and gestures.

6   Peer assessment as to the appropriateness of each other's role-play performance and concluding discussion.

The steps 1 to 3 above are characterized as an awareness-raising phase, step 4 an experimentation phase, step 5 a production phase, and step 6 a feedback phase.[21]

The second example focuses on the negotiation of refusals in Spanish that involves multiple turns and frequent overlaps.[22] As in the first example, university learners' L1 English and L2 Spanish are often compared. In this case, the steps were as follows:

1   Identification of speech acts using short samples.

2   Introduction of the range of politeness and (in)directness in negotiating successful refusals.

3   Listening to naturalistic L1 and L2 refusals and discussion about the politeness, (in)directness, insistence, expressions, and differences observed in the samples.

4   Use of short, written samples from naturalistic data to examine refusal strategies in terms of (in)directness and positive face (e.g., expressions of empathy, positive statement, and agreement), and further small-group discussion about preferred refusal strategies in terms of gender and culture.

5   Analysis of the structure and organization of naturalistic discourse:

   ■   Identification of boundaries of sequences using CA transcripts (opening sequence, refusal responses, and closing sequence).

   ■   Characterization of speech acts in each sequence.

   ■   Discussion about how refusal strategies are constructed across turns and about the nuances that the strategies convey.

---

[21] Liddicoat and Crozet (2001: 135–8).
[22] Félix-Brasdefer (2006).

- Analysis of turn-taking (timing, initiation, and termination of turns).

- Making inferences about the relationships, roles, and identities of the speakers in the conversation.

6 Role-play practice and peer feedback about the refusal strategies used, the appropriateness of the refusal, the distribution of sequences, and the organization of turns.

The instruction involves cross-cultural awareness-raising (steps 1–4), CA (step 5), and production practice (step 6).

Adapting the model indicated in the second example above, the third example applies the discourse analytic perspective to the teaching of Japanese refusals. The following tasks (appearing bilingually in the students' textbook) encourage learners to closely examine two transcripts that they have already listened to: an offer–acceptance sequence and an offer–refusal sequence (see the transcribed Dialogues 1 and 2, below).[23]

Now let us take a closer look at the discourse structure. Examine the transcripts of Dialogues 1 and 2 carefully and discuss the following in a small group:

(a) What are the speakers doing in each turn? For example, is the host mom's first turn signaling an offer, a compliment, an insistence, or a response to either one?

(b) How many turns does it take to realize the acceptance/refusal sequence?

(c) Was the acceptance/refusal sequence realized directly or indirectly in each dialogue? Why do you think so?

(d) Based on the way the offer–acceptance/refusal sequence is realized, how would you characterize the relationship between the speakers? How close/intimate or distant are they? How formal or informal is the situation?

The teachers' guide offers the following sample answers bilingually:

▶

---

[23] Ishihara and Maeda (2010).

Dialogue 1*	Dialogue 2*
(a) Functions of each turn	**(a) Functions of each turn**
Host mother (M)1: How about more rice? (Offer)	M1: How about more rice? (Offer)
Host student (S)1: Oh, I already have a lot. (Refusal/Ritual refusal)	S1: I've had enough. (Refusal)
M2: We have plenty of *nikujaga* too. (Insistence)	M2: We have plenty of *nikujaga* too. (Insistence)
S2: This is really good. (Compliment)	S2: It was really delicious. (Compliment and/or possibly a refusal)
M3: Really? Don't be shy to ask for more then. (Insistence)	M3: Really? Don't be too shy to ask. (Insistence and possibly an acceptance of the refusal)
S3: Really? Could I have just a bit more then? (Acceptance of the offer/request for more food)	S3: Yes, thank you. Thank you for the meal. (Refusal /thanks for the offer)
M4: Sure, of course. I'm glad I made a lot. (Response to the request)	
(b) Six turns of offer and acceptance	**(b) Six turns of offer and refusal**
(c) M1 directly offers more food and S3 also directly accepts the offer.	**(c)** M1 directly offers more food.
M2 and M3 continue indirectly to make the offer.	M2 and M3 represent indirect insistence without pushing too hard.
S1 and S2 indirectly accept the offer (though they may be intended as an indirect refusal).	All turns by S (1–3) constitute indirect refusal of the offer in a thoughtful, subtle manner.

(d) The situation is an everyday family dinner, so not formal. The mother's insistence and the student's polite *desu/masu* language leads me to infer that this is still in the first phase of the visit and that they do know each other very well yet.

* Dialogues 1 and 2 were originally delivered in Japanese and have been translated here as literally as possible.

All sets of activities above are designed to teach pragmatics at the level of discourse and illustrate how a conversation analytic approach can be incorporated into L2 instruction. Needless to say, the use of natural or naturalistic conversations is crucial in the instruction of pragmatics and discourse as demonstrated here. Ideally, collective resources of this kind will expand so that L2 pragmatics instruction will be further based on authentic language use and research-supported insights.

We now turn to the discussion of the role and potentials of language corpora in pragmatics-focused instruction.

The role of language corpora in teaching L2 pragmatics

This section considers the application of language corpora in teaching pragmatics. A language corpus is a large, purposively assembled collection of computerized texts in spoken or written form which is available for analysis using corpus software programs.[24] The appendix to a relatively recent book about electronic text analysis lists over 30 available language corpora, including the British National Corpus (BNC) <http://www.natcorp.ox.ac.uk> and the Michigan Corpus of Academic Spoken English (MICASE) <http://lw. lsa.umich.edu/eli/micase/index.htm>.[25] While it is not a new thing to extol the praises of electronic corpora in the design of instructional materials, their use in the field of applied linguistics is just coming into vogue. The advantages were noted over a decade ago:[26]

1 *Automatic searching, sorting, scoring.* The computer has speed and accuracy in doing certain low-level tasks, and can be valuable in providing data to learners through concordances, frequency lists, and other formats.

2 *Promoting a learner-centered approach.* Learners can access the information when and where they want.

3 *Open-ended source of language data.* A corpus offers a discovery approach to learning.

4 *Enabling the learning process to be individualized.* A corpus approach enables the learning task to accommodate the learner's needs.

Corpora have been valued for a long time because they reflect the way language is actually used. As one leading corpus expert put it, "(l)anguage cannot be invented: it can only be captured" and trying to construct naturally sounding text results in usage that is "often embarrassing and never reliable."[27] The argument is that it is preferable to search through a file of relevant examples for what is required than to think up something that sounds natural, and that while intuition is an important asset, it is not reliable as to how words and sentences are combined in actual communication. For language teaching, many have recommended the use of naturally occurring data obtained through language corpora, as well as through CA.

---

[24] Biber *et al.* (1998: 4).
[25] Adolphs (2006: 141–4). Both BNC and MICASE allow free-of-charge online searches.
[26] Leech (1997: 10–11).
[27] Sinclair (1997: 31).

Since speech acts, for example, have been found to be often realized indirectly, conversation analysts would contend that it is important to look at more extended discourse rather than isolated utterances to "see how particular communicative acts unfold within a conversational sequence."[28]

One way to use a language corpus in pragmatics work would be to take a phrase used in a speech-act-specific strategy, such as in requesting, and to search the database for contextualized examples. The following are sample concordance lines from native and non-native English-speaking students directed to other students in the classroom, making "can you . . . ?" requests, taken from the Limerick–Belfast Corpus of Academic Spoken English (LIBEL CASE):[29]

Can you

20 be . . . modest	can you	eh . . . can you give me . . .
21 don't catch what you say	can you	give a little more detail
22 why? Sunshine	can you	give me some reason
23 . . . your handwriting is . . .	can you	can you mind my take this
24 other sentence you have . . .	can you	show me? . . . eh no just
25 like this song very much . . .	can you	sing a few words for
26 your sentence?	can you	speak out your sentence?
27 agree	can you	speak . . . clearly

We can see how it can be helpful to access examples for how "can you" requests show up in casual conversations in class – specifically, in collaborative work, where students are working independently of the teacher. Advocates of the use of language corpora would see making learners aware of classroom language as a means for facilitating interaction in the classroom in general and task completion in particular.[30]

Along with the benefits of using corpora, corpus experts admit that even large corpora may not have readily accessible examples of what you are looking for, which is why they would recommend using them for language forms where the variety of patterns is more easily revealed through a search of the database. So if you are working with electronic corpora for the analysis of pragmatics, you would ideally search for words or language structures that have been tagged, such as performative verbs (e.g., *compliment, apologize,*

---

[28] Koester (2002: 167).
[29] From Walsh and O'Keeffe (2007: 129), with some of the concordance conventions removed.
[30] Walsh and O'Keeffe (2007: 130).

disagree), discourse markers (*first, but, so*), or conventionally indirect expressions (*why don't you, why not, how about* for suggestions).[31] Say, for example, you go to MICASE (cited above) to find instances of *sorry* as used in a spoken expression of apology. Fortunately after performing a search for a word, you can access the larger context in which *sorry* appeared and check it out.

Here is an example from MICASE. In this corpus, we can narrow the search by specifying speaker and transcript attributes. Let us say we set as speaker attributes: both genders, 17–23 years old, any academic positions/ roles, native and non-native speakers of English, any first language, and for transcript attributes: study group, social sciences and education, all academic disciplines, all participant levels, and highly interactive discourse. The result was 16 matches from two transcripts, with all of the utterances coming from native speakers of American English. The following are slightly edited versions of five of the 10 cases where *sorry* was used in an expression of an apology:

■ Hi, Rachel. I'm *sorry* my alarm didn't go off this morning.

■ I feel bad that I haven't gotten to get my thoughts out because I've had so many thoughts about it but, *sorry*, I just, I had two really full crazy days . . .

■ I know you tried to email it too, so *sorry* you had to do it again . . .

■ I just, I didn't get into like explaining my reasoning in my movies cuz, I just didn't, I'm *sorry*.

■ Yeah it's a little sloppy. I have to leave. I'm *sorry*. Don't worry about it.

The following are slightly edited versions of the six instances where the pragmalinguistic function of *sorry* was not as an expression of apology, but rather one of sympathy or regret:

■ It's a talk show. I'm alarmed, I'm *sorry*.

■ I'm *sorry* that that's she's not cut out for customer service.

■ She doesn't want to go. I'm *sorry*, you'll have a great time together.

■ Like she m– I'm *sorry* but, like you know what I mean like sh– maybe she's like well she couldn't be doing anything else right now.

■ And like I'm *sorry* that like every job has like its pros and cons. She hates her Angell Hall job?

[31] Adolphs (2006).

■ They what? I'm *sorry* it's like, they like don't spend time with their kids or anything on their work.

Similarly, with respect to the function of suggesting, one of the difficulties is that not all the data provided by a corpus are readily available to use in analyzing the distribution of these words or structures. The verb *suggest* may appear in indirect speech (*he suggested that* . . .) rather than in the function of giving suggestions (*I would suggest* . . .); *why not* is used as a straightforward question as well as an expression of suggestion. The lack of direct correspondence between language form and pragmatic meaning makes the pragmatics-focused application of linguistic corpora quite limited at this point. One source acknowledges that "(t)he use of electronic text analysis to support pragmatic investigations of the relationship between speakers, context, and level of directness/indirectness of an utterance is still relatively under-explored. This is mainly because of the difficulty in linking language form to utterance force."[32]

Since finding forms in a corpus that clearly perform a desired function may be a challenge for some speech acts, it is not surprising that corpus studies of L2 pragmatics tend to focus on forms that are easy to locate in language corpora, such as formulaic expressions of gratitude. So, for instance, a study comparing the use of corpus data on thanking from the Cambridge and Nottingham Corpus of Discourse in English (CANCODE) to data from a discourse completion task found that the use of a corpus added some features picked up in interactional data. One example was that in British English, when someone says, "Thanks for that," an acceptable response could be "Cheers!" Also, the corpus data were able to show the use of thanks over several turns:[33]

Speaker 1: Yeah. (*Laughs*) Thank you.

Speaker 2: Thank you.

S1: That's lovely.

S2: All right. And your balance is sixty nine thirty six then.

S1: Right. (*Pause*) Thank you. Sixty-nine?

S2: Er, thirty six.

S1: Thirty six. Right.

S2: Thank you.

---

[32] Adolphs (2006: 124–35).
[33] Schauer and Adolphs (2006: 130).

The researchers in this study concluded that the use of a corpus provided them a broader picture of how gratitude is expressed in British English than they would get just through elicited data. The corpus data also provided them a sense of the collaborative negotiation involved in the expression of gratitude, and revealed the predominance of extended turns.

Various other studies have drawn on language corpora in an effort to examine pragmatic aspects of authentic language use. Such studies include the following:

- the investigation of directness/indirectness of requests and politeness markers used by telephone callers and operators in Britain;[34]

- the use of vague language among native Chinese- and English-speaking adults in Hong Kong;[35]

- complaint–response sequences between family members of equal status in Canada;[36]

- the use of speech acts (e.g., performatives and giving advice/directives) in the workplace;[37]

- the use of discourse markers and backchanneling (e.g., *oh, ah, however, still, sure*).[38]

Thus, with regard to using corpora in the teaching of L2 pragmatics, it helps if the desired material is readily available in a given corpus. However, pragmatic meaning is often not detected automatically, and if that is the case, we would need to start by manually annotating the chosen functional categories.[39] For example, finding apologies may be difficult since, as illustrated above, words such as "sorry" may be used in a non-apologetic context (e.g., "I'm sorry . . . she's not cut out for customer service"), and likewise the speech act of apology can be realized with strategies that do not involve the strategy *expression of apology* at all. For this reason, corpus material representing other strategies in the apology speech act (such as *acknowledging responsibility, offering repair, providing an explanation,* and *promise of non-recurrence*) would need to be tagged in order to have the corpus represent the full range of apology strategies.

[34] McEnery *et al.* (2001).
[35] Juker *et al.* (2003).
[36] Laforest (2002).
[37] Koester (2002).
[38] Brief synopses of these studies can be found in McEnery *et al.* (2001: 105–7).
[39] Adolphs (2006); McEnery *et al.* (2006). A notable exception to manual tagging is the automatic speech act tagging project being piloted by the UCREL (cited in Adolphs 2006, and accessible at: http://www.comp.lancs.ac.uk/computing/research/ucrel/projects.html#spaac).

A user of a corpus therefore needs to do some screening to be sure that the samples are actually samples of the desired pragmatic material. This is why experts would caution corpus users to carefully inspect the verbal environment of words or phrases to make sure that the material is appropriate for the need.[40] In addition, there may be a need to edit data from a corpus before using them for instructional purposes if they have been drawn from actual discourse.[41] The raw data have numerous false starts, corrected misstatements, ellipsis, and other features which could be counterproductive or distracting, particularly for beginning-level learners. However, a possible disadvantage of editing corpus data would be that while target features may be preserved, other features of naturally occurring conversation could be lost, which defeats the purpose of exposing learners to such data.[42]

Despite difficulty in automatically detecting context-dependent pragmatic meaning, the good news is that an increasing amount of corpus data is being used.[43] So, further pedagogical applications of the current and upcoming studies may soon be in order. It has also been suggested that when material is used from a given corpus, the curriculum writers might indicate certain details about the material based on a corpus (such as by way of a footnote).[44] Such information would include:

1   the original context (e.g., such as the conversation about tea, above);

2   the communicative and sociocultural purpose of the text (i.e., what information is being exchanged and who the participants are in terms of age, gender, relative status, role in the conversation, etc.);

3   the place of origin or source (i.e., the place where the data were collected), and the author or proprietor of the corpus material (i.e., who owns or manages the corpus).

Some corpus experts would in fact consider it insufficient to simply supply text material; they would claim that there is a need to indicate the source context in authentic discourse as well.[45] In addition, some of these experts would argue that material elicited through measures such as discourse completion tasks could not be considered authentic. Nonetheless, numerous lesson plans for teaching L2 pragmatics have made use of elicited

[40] Sinclair (1997: 34).
[41] Doug Biber pointed this out in a presentation on using corpus data for generating grammar lessons (Kim *et al.* 2007). See also Carter and McCarthy (2004).
[42] Adolphs (2006).
[43] McEnery *et al.* (2006).
[44] Mishan (2004).
[45] Mishan (2004).

data, often from highly naturalistic role-play situations. Consequently, while we might recommend discretion in the use of elicited data, we would certainly not rule out their use in pedagogy.

By the same token, just because material is authentic does not make it user-friendly. So, for example, simply providing learners with a series of concordance lines may not work very well. Experience has shown that truly authentic material may be difficult to understand, especially without context relevant to the given learners, and that dealing with such material may even be a bit overwhelming.[46] The fact that pragmatics in natural data can show up in ways that are imperceptible to L2 learners[47] justifies editing the natural data when such efforts are likely to make it more efficient for students to learn the material. For instance, go to MICASE and enter *sorry*, as demonstrated above. You will see that a fair number of the cases that emerge call for a certain amount of inference in order to understand them since they are excerpted from a still larger set of data.

By now, various studies have compared real language from corpora with the language appearing in textbooks.[48] One such study described the linguistic forms used to perform the speech act of *suggestions* in both real language and ESL textbooks.[49] Comparisons between suggestions in two authentic settings in a corpus (professor–student interaction during office hours and student–student study groups) and six popular ESL textbooks (three old and three recent) were made to evaluate the extent to which textbook materials reflect real-life language use. Although the new generation textbooks were found to introduce more linguistic structures for suggestions than the old generation textbooks, nonetheless the discrepancies between real language use and ESL textbooks were striking. For example, the formulaic use of *Wh*-questions such as *What about/How about . . . ?* and *Why don't you . . . /Why not . . . ?* was not frequent at all in the corpus data, whereas it was prominent in the textbooks. The corpus research on office hours and study groups showed that *Let's . . .* was the most frequently used structure for suggestions. In addition, the modals *have to* and *need to* for suggestions were more common than was the use of *should*, which could have implications for the forms to promote in class (for more details, see Activity 9.1, below).

---

[46] Möllering (2004).

[47] Belz (2007).

[48] See for example, Pearson (1986) and Scotton and Bernsten (1988) for earlier studies that investigated naturally occurring and textbook language of agreeing and disagreeing (Pearson) and direction-giving and directives in service encounters (Scotton and Bernsten).

[49] Jiang (2006).

The researcher in this study makes various recommendations for instruction.[50] The recommendations include the following:

- That ESL textbooks not simply offer learners lists of decontextualized grammatical structures as in drills and unnatural dialogs, but rather include background information on appropriateness when presenting these grammatical structures, paying attention, as much as possible, to register differences and speaker–listener relationships (e.g., boss–employee, teacher–student, between classmates or friends).

- That teachers provide classroom tasks based as much as possible on naturally occurring conversations.

- That teachers raise learners' awareness of the possible impact of a certain pragmalinguistic choice in delivering a given speech act. For example, in making a suggestion, the use of the form "Why don't you . . . ?" (as opposed to "How about . . . ?" or "You might want to . . .") leaves the listener with few options and so may threaten the listener's face.

Effective use of authentic language material by teachers therefore calls for getting learners to notice how speech acts are actually realized across multiple turns in interactive negotiations, involving overlaps and frequent turn-taking. Some corpus linguists prefer an exploratory student-guided approach to instruction, for example, the instructional sequence of "illustration–interaction–induction," where learners first examine language data (illustration), discuss the data (discussion), and generate rules that will be further refined. Advocates of this approach state that a traditional teacher-fronted approach ("presentation–practice–production") may be a less appropriate option.[51] The discovery-based approach recommended here is compatible with the awareness-raising approach often used for the teaching of L2 pragmatics. Learners who struggle to negotiate their meaning may then realize just how authentic that process actually is in interactive discourse, even among fluent speakers of the target language.

Discussion

This chapter has described what CA is and has illustrated how it can be applied both to learning about discursive pragmatics and to teaching L2 pragmatics. Descriptions of sample instructional activities have also been

---

[50] Jiang (2006: 49–51).
[51] Carter and McCarthy (1995: 155, 2004); McEnery *et al.* (2006).

offered for how to apply these insights to discourse-focused instruction. We then considered ways that language corpora could be used in pragmatics instruction as well. We noted benefits and challenges facing teachers and curriculum writers who would like to use corpus data in the teaching of pragmatics. It is our intention that this chapter will encourage teachers to explore ways to utilize authentic language data through conversation analysis and language corpora in their teaching.

Activity 9.1, below, provides hands-on opportunity to examine the features of spoken and written discourse and to develop instructional tasks or activities based on authentic language data.

Activity 9.1 Designing instructional material using a language corpus

Objectives

1   You will be able to compare characteristics of spoken and written discourse and identify relevant features to teach for a speaking class.

2   You will be able to develop a pragmatics/discourse-focused task or activity by obtaining authentic language samples from an electronic corpus, and by using the research-based information ("Structures used in spoken and written suggestions") provided below.

Suggested time: 1 hour.

Materials:

■   Information: "Suggestions in American English";[52]

■   internet access to the Michigan Corpus of Academic Spoken English (MICASE) for each group.

Directions

1   As a whole group, study the research-based information below, "Suggestions in American English". It has been found that the frequency of these structures is often not reflected in commercially available textbooks.

2   Form into groups of about three participants.

3   On a computer, access MICASE at http://quod.lib.umich.edu/m/micase/. As indicated in this chapter, this is an online corpus of spoken academic discourse

---

[52] Reported in Jiang (2006).

recorded and transcribed at the University of Michigan. Familiarize yourselves with the format of the corpus.

4 If any group members are teaching a speaking class, you could use one of their classroom contexts. If no one teaches speaking, think of an imaginary speaking class and determine the audience.

5 Drawing from MICASE, you are to search for words and phrases that may be used in "suggestions" (i.e., advice, proposals, and recommendations). Note that there is a grey area where suggestions border on requests or commands.

6 Since a corpus is not usually designed so as to provide instances of a given speech act, you will need to search by words and phrases that might be found in that speech act. See the information, "Suggestions in American English" below for specific words and phrases reported in a research study based on a spoken and written academic corpus.[53]

7 Start by searching MICASE for "have to," "let's," "need," and "should." You could also search for "why don't you" and "ought to." Finally, consider other words to include in a search, such as the word "suggestion" itself. If you include all the possible MICASE attributes in your search, you may find yourself with more than 2,000 hits. On the other hand, if you limit your search to certain attributes (e.g., the status and role of the speaker, the native language of the speaker, the type of session that the sample was drawn from, etc.), you may find you get limited or no hits, depending on the attributes you choose.

8 While you are going through the language samples looking for instances of actual suggestions, also keep in mind that MICASE is a corpus exclusively of spoken English. Discuss ways in which this might make the data different from those in the study based on a corpus of both spoken and written language.

9 Compile a set of expressions based on the spoken corpus of American English that you could use for a lesson on making suggestions in a speaking class. You may wish to consider register differences between status-equal talks (as in study groups) and status-differential talks (as in office hours). You could, for example, compile language samples that your students could use in talking to their professors during office hours on the one hand, and in talking to friends in study groups on the other.

10 Report back to the whole class about the task or short activity that you developed.

---

[53] The TOEFL 2000 Spoken and Written Academic Language Corpus (T2K-SWAL Corpus); Biber *et al.* (2002).

Discussion/wrap-up

Discuss what might have been challenging in constructing the classroom task/activity and the strategies that you would recommend for dealing with the challenges that arise. For example, how would you provide contextual information about the original data? Would you modify the authentic data transcribed using a CA convention? If so, how would it be done?

Information: Suggestions in American English

The information below is from the findings of a corpus-based study on spoken and written suggestions in American English.[54]

1   The most frequently used structure for making suggestions in this corpus was *Let's. . . .* This structure can suggest a joint action or in fact be a polite command.

2   The most commonly used modals were *have to* and *need* in either spoken or written discourse. *Should* is a popular modal in textbooks but was much less frequently used in authentic data. The formality of these modals differs and they imply different degrees of speaker authority and urgency of the message.

3   The (phrasal) modals, *ought to* and *must* were hardly used for suggestions.

4   Hedging expressions (e.g., *just*, *probably*, *really*, and *only*) were fairly frequently used along with modals.

5   The formulaic *Wh-* questions (e.g., *How about/What about . . . ?* and *Why not/Why don't you . . . ?*) were not as frequently used as their treatment in textbooks would make it seem.

6   *Why don't you . . . ?* was much more frequently used by non-native speakers than native speakers. This structure may appear less polite, as it implies the speaker's knowledge or judgment is superior to the listener's.

---

[54] Jiang (2006).

CHAPTER 10

Lesson planning and teacher-led reflection

Noriko Ishihara

Introduction

In this section of the book, we have thus far reviewed theories of second language acquisition related to the teaching and learning of pragmatics and have seen various examples of pragmatics-focused instruction and curriculum development. We have also discussed the potential value of making use of naturally occurring data in L2 pragmatics instruction through the use of language corpora and a conversation analytic approach. In addition, we have explored ways to enhance instructional materials through incorporating pragmatics-focused insights and research-based information.

While the book as a whole is largely intended for pre-/in-service teachers and graduate students, this chapter is especially directed at practicing teachers. The chapter is meant to assist you in enhancing your awareness of the issues associated with pragmatics-focused instruction and applying this awareness to your own instruction. We suggest projects and activities that you can engage in individually or preferably in collaboration with others.[1] The first project is the teachers' response journal in which you reflect on selected issues relevant to your own teaching and learning of pragmatics. The second is the design of lesson plans that you utilize in your instructional contexts. Finally, the chapter presents three activities in which you and your colleagues draw on your collective wisdom to explore insights to be

---

[1] If this book is being used as a reference in a course on teaching pragmatics as in a summer institute such as that offered by the University of Minnesota's CARLA, the projects/activities offered here could be used as a part of course assignments.

used for lesson planning and further dialogue for enhancing L2 pragmatics instruction.

Teachers' response journal

Teacher readers are invited to engage in reflective writing as you read about, plan out, and then implement pragmatics-focused instruction in your classroom.[2] You will be asked to contemplate ways that you might increase or enhance your engagement in the teaching and assessment of L2 pragmatics in your classroom. You are to track your learning and thoughts in your journal and further develop them as you write, respond to others, and receive feedback. Journal entries can include (but are not limited to):

- reactions to the recommended readings (see below);
- reactions to the discussions presented in the book (see Chapter 2);
- insights from and reflections on your teaching, learning, and other experiences (see Chapters 2 and 10);
- reflections on cultural, theoretical or philosophical issues (see Chapters 5 and 6);
- reflections on methodological issues (see Chapters 6–11);
- reflections on assessment of pragmatic ability and development (see Chapters 14 and 15);
- reflections on your learners' pragmatic ability, their needs, and strategy repertoire in this area (see Chapters 5 and 12);
- reflections on the educational and institutional contexts in which you are situated in relation to the teaching of pragmatics; and/or
- any other issues associated with the application of pragmatics-focused instruction to your language classroom or other instructional contexts.

If you would like to include in your journal responses to readings beyond this book, the lists of electronic resources (Appendix A) and pedagogically oriented articles (Appendix B) at the end of this book may be of interest to you. The following list of recommended reading may also be useful for this project (for complete citations of these articles and chapters, see the list of references at the end of the book):

---

[2] This response journal can be used as an assignment in a teacher development course, in which case this project may well be started at the outset of the course.

FIGURE 10.1 Journaling

For general topics in L2 pragmatics:

Hinkel, E. (2001) Building awareness and practical skills to facilitate cross-cultural communication.

Judd, E. L. (1999) Some issues in the teaching of pragmatic competence.

For an approach to L2 pragmatics instruction and concrete examples:

Tanaka, K. (1997) Developing pragmatic competence: A learners-as-researchers approach.

Eslami-Rasekh, Z. (2005) Raising the pragmatic awareness of language learners.

For teaching pragmatics in foreign language contexts:

Rose, K. (1994) Pragmatic consciousness-raising in an EFL context.

Rose, K. R. (1999) Teachers and students learning about requests in Hong Kong.

For learners' culture and subjectivity in L2 pragmatics instruction:

Kasper, G., and Rose, K. R. (2002) Chapter 8: Individual differences in L2 pragmatic development.

LoCastro, V. (2003) Chapter 14: Learner subjectivity.

The reflective prompts provided in Activity 2.1 in Chapter 2 may be useful in helping you to frame your reactions to the discussions presented in this book and in recording insights from your own experiences. Part I prompts may help you reflect on your experience of learning and teaching pragmatics; Part II prompts include queries for a range of issues related to L2 pragmatics. If you have already participated in the activity in Chapter 2, it might be beneficial for you to revisit these prompts and your reflections back then. You may find that your knowledge and beliefs about pragmatics instruction have developed or become more refined. You may wish to reflect through writing on any new insights or queries you now have. You are also encouraged to reflect critically on your current practice and to identify an approach that could be applied to your own teaching and/or curriculum writing. You may also wish to discuss issues related to pragmatics instruction that puzzle you or require further consideration.

If possible, make this response journal interactive by working with a teacher colleague, a graduate student, a course instructor, or an administrator who shares an interest in this area. Writing can guide and facilitate your thinking, and engaging in dialogue with someone else (and with yourself) can further your ideas.[3] The process of professional development, such as gaining and internalizing new knowledge, connecting it to already existing knowledge and beliefs, and utilizing it for enhanced practice, requires a sustained and systematic effort, which can be supported through collegial collaboration. One way to support colleagues is by remaining open to their opinions and by facilitating their reflections through questions that you pose. Such questions would serve as a prompt for them to confirm what they had stated or to further develop their views.[4]

Lesson-plan design

This project represents a hands-on opportunity for teacher readers to design a pragmatics-focused lesson plan that can be directly applied to their own classrooms. Teacher participants are first asked to choose some aspect(s) of pragmatics to teach individually or in pairs, and to develop a lesson plan to improve learners' pragmatics. In this project, you are encouraged to tie together various pragmatics-related issues discussed thus far, such as: levels of politeness, directness, formality, and appropriateness, intention and

---

[3] Teacher learning can be viewed as largely influenced by a range of social activities that teachers engage in (Johnson and Golombek 2003; Lee and Smagorinsky 2000; Vygotsky 1978). Teacher learning also is a language-mediated dialogic activity in which language functions as a primary tool for meaning construction (see also Chapter 6 for more on dialogic learning).
[4] In Edge's (2002) model of teachers' cooperative learning, teachers use dialogue to mirror each other's point by probing and asking clarification questions to facilitate articulation of the issue and refrain from giving suggestions.

interpretation, culture, and learners' subjectivity. We strongly recommend that you refer to pragmatics-focused resources such as that offered in Chapter 4 in planning your lesson, or that you collect data yourself or with your students.

What are some components of a lesson plan? The following points require your close attention as you make various instructional decisions in planning a lesson.

- the choice of a pragmatics feature/features to teach (e.g., a speech act, a discourse marker, implicature, or a discourse structure);
- the overall goal for the lesson (e.g., enhancement of a particular receptive or productive pragmatics skill, or both);
- description of learners and instructional context, such as:
  - learners' L1(s) and L2(s);
  - learners' age/grade level;
  - learners' general level of proficiency;
  - learners' educational background;
  - pros and cons of the learning contexts (e.g., second or foreign language);
  - skill focus;
  - integration into the general curriculum;
  - potential coordination with learners' other courses;
- content objectives for the teaching of pragmatics;
  - specific language features (pragmalinguistics) (e.g., communicative functions, grammatical structures, and vocabulary/expressions);
  - the cultural aspects of pragmatics being addressed (sociopragmatics);
- estimated time frame;
- materials needed (including technology);
- sequence of tasks (e.g., preview, activity/follow-up activities, closing);
- procedures for each task;
- assessment (e.g., more formal tests or more informal performance tasks involving rubrics or checklists[5]) (see Chapters 14 and 15 for more details on these examples); and

---

[5] Assessment of learners' pragmatic ability can be through traditional tests (which are often quantified measures for summative assessment) or through performance tasks (often used for formative assessment, involving real-world tasks). The performance tasks are often evaluated with the use of a rubric (indicating the extent to which learners accomplished certain criteria) or a checklist (showing whether or not learners addressed such criteria, Tedick 2002).

■ student materials (e.g., graphic organizers, student worksheets, visual support, and assessment instruments).

If you are doing this project as part of the requirement for a course in teacher preparation or professional development, be sure to cite in your paper the consulted references and resources. In such a context, teacher participants would most likely find it beneficial to give a presentation of each lesson plan. The course papers could be shared among the participants, especially through the use of instructional technology (e.g., online instructional discussion tools, see Chapter 13).

Rubric for self-assessing the pragmatics lesson plan

In designing your lesson plan or after completing it, the following rubric can be used to assess your lesson plan.[6]

Criteria for self-evaluation	Self-evaluation		
The plan provides a specific feature of pragmatics to be taught.	Excellent	Good	Needs more work
Learner characteristics match the choice of the feature of pragmatics to be taught and the overall goal of the lesson.	Excellent	Good	Needs more work
The content objectives for pragmatics are realistic and appropriate for the students' age, educational backgrounds, and needs.	Excellent	Good	Needs more work
The language objectives are meaningful and appropriate in the context of the lesson.	Excellent	Good	Needs more work
The cultural awareness objectives are meaningful and match the overall content objectives for pragmatics.	Excellent	Good	Needs more work
The time frame and choice of materials are appropriate for the lesson objectives and the target audience.	Excellent	Good	Needs more work
The lesson procedures follow a logical and realistic progression.	Excellent	Good	Needs more work
The pragmatics material is largely research-based and the language samples are authentic.	Excellent	Good	Needs more work

[6] For a course project, this self-assessment rubric can be adapted to double as the instructor's evaluative criteria, with an added column further right for instructor assessment.

Criteria for self-evaluation	Self-evaluation		
The tasks trigger learners' awareness of pragmatics in a meaningful context and explicitly facilitate an understanding of the relationship between context and form.	Excellent	Good	Needs more work
The activities provide sufficient and effective language input and/or elicit interactive output to achieve the objectives.	Excellent	Good	Needs more work
The assessment and feedback procedures are well-suited to the lesson and are based on learners' goals and intentions (see Chapter 15 for how this could be done).	Excellent	Good	Needs more work

As in the case of the teachers' response journal, collaborative feedback can help to improve your lesson plans. While teaching pragmatics may include a number of challenges, collegial collaboration can facilitate this process of professional development. Teacher collaborators could be invited to go through each other's lesson plan using this self-assessment list and to comment on the aspects that they perceive to be planned well, along with those that need further development.

Discussion

In this chapter we have put the spotlight on the teacher as we did in Chapter 2 and have suggested projects and activities that are largely teacher-driven. These projects represent hands-on opportunities for teacher readers to apply the information provided in this book to their own instructional context and to prepare classroom-based materials. Teacher readers have been asked to synthesize their various types of knowledge and beliefs, such as their awareness of L2 pragmatics, knowledge of approaches to teaching L2 pragmatics, and knowledge of their learners and teaching contexts, in designing pragmatics-focused instruction and in assessing it themselves through reflection.

The following activities are intended to support efforts to develop L2 pragmatics instruction. The first draws on the teachers' reflections that were initially generated in Chapters 2 and 5 and further facilitates teachers' reflections on their own experiences, which may be incorporated into story-based awareness-raising for teaching L2 pragmatics. The second activity, in a classroom setting, assists in identifying teachers' own area(s) of interest in

L2 pragmatics and in possibly finding a collaborative partner in pursuing the shared interest in the area. In the final activity, teacher colleagues can draw on their collective wisdom to explore immediate issues and inquiries that they may have about pragmatics-focused instruction. Alternatively, this activity can serve as a form of needs analysis for the course instructor, if this is part of a teacher preparation or professional development course.[7]

Activity 10.1 Reflecting on your cross-cultural experiences

Objectives

1   You will be able to identify a personal story that could be shared with your students which communicates the importance of learning about pragmatics.

2   You will be able to write discussion questions that prompt learners' pragmatic awareness.

Suggested time: 40 minutes.

Materials:

▪   Information: "Examples of cross-cultural experiences" (or Rose's examples of pragmatic failure,[8] which could be used as an alternative);

▪   a blank sheet of paper.

Directions

Part I

1   Read the first example of cross-cultural experiences in the Information (or Rose's examples).

2   Work individually to reflect on your cross-cultural experiences. Select a story that your students will find interesting and thought-provoking in terms of learning about pragmatics. It may be a humorous story of your experience of pragmatic failure in another culture, or your observations of similar or different pragmatic norms in another culture. Most importantly, the story should contain some

---

[7] These activities are independent and free-floating in that they can be conducted at any point during a teacher education course.
[8] Two examples can be found in Rose (1999: 172–3).

important message that you can communicate to your students. The examples include:

- instances where pragmatic routines are either identical or dramatically different across cultures;
- instances where pragmatic norms differ even within a culture;
- a case where first language pragmatic norms are not known even to fluent speakers or forgotten by them;
- a case where universal (or at least shared) politeness strategies may apply in a given social context;
- an anecdote that underscores the danger of relying on cultural stereotypes;
- a story that speaks to the value of cultural diversity;
- switching back and forth between first- and second-language norms for pragmatics in a bi-/multicultural context; and
- an illustration of how repair strategies were used in an instance of cross-cultural misunderstanding.

3   Write down the story. Try to describe the relevant details truthfully and concretely.

4   Exchange your sheet with someone else and provide that person with some written feedback.

5   Share your story with the whole class.

Part II

1   Read the sample discussion questions provided for Example 1 in the Information.

2   Get into small groups of two to three participants. Read Examples 1–6 in the Information. Think of how these stories might be useful in the teaching of pragmatics, and what additional details might help to situate the story more effectively in context. What message would each story convey, and how would that be clearly communicated to learners?

3   Consider the discussion questions that would enhance learners' pragmatic awareness.

4   Share your discussion questions with the whole group.

5   Work individually. Go back to your own story you wrote in Part I and rewrite it in language your students can understand.

6   Add some discussion questions that could be used in your class after presenting your story. Direct your students' attention to key features of your story by asking these questions.

7   Share your discussion questions with the whole group and exchange feedback.

Discussion/wrap-up

Teachers' personal narratives can be powerful in attracting learners' attention and making the instruction memorable. Such stories may resonate well in students' minds due to the authenticity and the personal touch they bring. Teachers of L2 pragmatics can collect these stories to share with their learners.

Information: Examples of cross-cultural experiences

Example 1

I was a graduate student and an ESL teacher in the United States at the time of this story. One day, a Chinese friend and colleague teacher of mine invited my husband and me to dinner at her home by saying something like, "We'd like to invite you to our home sometime soon." I answered excitedly, "That'll be great!" as I would when talking normally in English. I was not particularly close to her but we did have so many commonalities in our professional and personal lives that getting together would appear to provide us a chance to get to know each other better. But she frowned slightly after my response.

A similar exchange happened a second time on another social occasion, but this conversation never led to an actual invitation. Around that time, I happened to read an article on Chinese refusals which suggested that I should have probably refused her invitation two or three times before finally accepting it, according to a typical, rather formal Chinese approach ("ritual refusals"[9]). Knowing my Asian origin, my friend probably expected me to respond in a Chinese or what she probably perceived as an East Asian manner. This never occurred to me when I was speaking to her, because we were speaking in English in the US and I was automatically using an American English norm of behavior.

Yet, another chance came by! She mentioned her wish to invite us again when I finally said, "Oh no, don't worry about it. We wouldn't want to put you to so much trouble." Surprisingly, we were soon invited to dinner at a local Chinese restaurant. We expected to share the bill but according to the Chinese tradition they insisted

---

[9] Chen and Zhang (1995). See also Kawate-Mierzejewska (2005) for different prosodic features for acceptance and ritual acceptance in Japanese.

on picking up the bill as they were slightly older in age. At the end of the dinner she said, "I wish we could have invited you over to our humble home, but we have always been very busy."

Sample discussion questions

- Why do Chinese (and some other East Asian language speakers) sometimes refuse some formal invitations a few times before finally accepting it? What values and cultural assumptions underlie that pragmatic convention?

- If you were in the story and noticed that something might be inappropriate in what you said, how could you find out what it might have been?

- Whose speech norms are likely to be used in multicultural situations like this, Chinese/Japanese, English, mixed, or? How might that change over time and across situations?

Example 2[10]

When I was studying Spanish in Mexico, I took a course in figurative speech and idiomatic expressions. One phrase I learned was to say *ni madres* to emphasize negation. Later, when I was in an office at a university, a friend of mine asked me about the course, and for an example of an expression I said *"No entiendo ni madres,"* Everyone in the room looked shocked, then began to laugh hilariously. This expression would have been appropriate for Mexican teenagers to use with each other, but shouldn't have been used in mixed company.

Example 3

Because I have an outgoing personality and Japanese people tend to be polite and forgiving of foreigners, I think it is especially difficult to learn pragmatics when living in Japan, except by observation. I did have a friend, who I called *gyogi keisatsu* or "manners police" who took it upon herself to correct my behavior. I was grateful for her help but often got overwhelmed by the quantity of behavioral norms and resisted changing at some points.

Example 4

Since I originally learned Spanish in Mexico, I do not use the *vosotros* form, even when I travel to Spain. I also have a hard time saying *vale* and instead say *sale* when

---

[10] Examples 2–8 are actual stories as written by anonymous teacher participants in the 2006–8 CARLA summer institute on teaching pragmatics at the University of Minnesota. Slight edits are in brackets.

I'm there for "OK" which is what I'd say in Mexico. *Vale* just feels weird, and kind of snobbish. Spaniards looked at me funny when I'd say *sale* instead of *vale*. Somehow I guess I was retaining my "Mexican identity," Now people tell me I have a Spanish accent.

Example 5

After being in the military for a number of years, I was at a family dinner and said, "Pass the f---ing potatoes," creating a deep shock with the family.

Example 6

Even in English (my native language), I have difficulty. The first time I went to a funeral (I was 48), I had no idea what to say to the widow in English!!

Example 7

[Experience in learning Spanish, translated into English] My sister and I were invited to dinner at the home of Mrs Wilson, the secretary at the Department of Modern Languages. She was my supervisor when I was a student assistant. She served us a wonderful dinner, and at the end of dinner, my sister thanked her by saying, "Mrs Wilson, I thank you for the invitation. The dinner was so terrible," to which Mrs Wilson was startled and exclaimed: "Terrible? Well, you must mean something else!" I elbowed my sister and whispered in her ear and she added: "No, terrific!"

Example 8

We have a great recording in our archives by a French exchange student at XXX University who was completely frustrated and hurt by the "ostensible invitations" [rhetorical invitations] of other American students. "You've got to check this place out! We'll have to go some time on a Friday night!" And he was disappointed and offended when the plans he thought had been made weren't.

[However,] this doesn't just happen to "foreigners." [There are] 3rd culture kids, growing up abroad so that our native instinct is no longer completely trustworthy . . . I worked in a bookstore in Chicago for a year . . . So did another girl, whom I liked but didn't know well. We bumped into each other in the train. I was pleased to see her again and I believe she said something like, "We'll have to get together for lunch." I was delighted and pulled out my agenda. She looked shocked and offered some excuses. Not until years later did I understand better what happened.

Activity 10.2 Identifying interest and finding collaborative partners

Objectives

1   You will be able to identify your interests with regard to L2 pragmatics and determine your future commitment to the teaching of pragmatics.

2   You will identify a collaborative partner in your chosen area of L2 pragmatics.

Suggested time: 20 minutes.

Materials: a blank sheet of paper.

Directions

1   In relation to the lesson planning discussed in this chapter, work individually to reflect on those features of pragmatics that you are most interested in teaching in your classroom – in other words, on those key junctures where language and culture meet.

2   Consider the sort of collaborative relationship you would appreciate in your future efforts to teach L2 pragmatics.

3   Write a "classified ad" as if you were recruiting assistance in a local newspaper or magazine and circulate it among your teacher colleagues.

4   Read others' "classified ads" to see if your area of interest in L2 pragmatics or other skill areas match.

5   If you happen to find a suitable match, sit with this teacher colleague to identify possible future commitments in relation to the teaching of pragmatics. Consider the resources each other can offer and the ways in which they might be useful in your pragmatics-related project.

6   Share with the whole group the highlights of your discussions and the possibility of future collaborative relationships.

Discussion/wrap-up

Articulating your area of interest explicitly can help you identify the area of pragmatics you plan to teach, arrive at a clearer idea of why you have selected it, and advance your future projects. If you have been able to find a collaborative partner with whom you exchange your ideas through this activity, continue to consider the particulars of how you can actually be of benefit to each other for lesson planning and beyond. Having a collaborative partner may also help to keep you committed to the goal(s) you set for yourself.

Activity 10.3 "Dear Abby" – trouble-shooting your burning issues[11]

Objectives

1   You will be able to identify issues that you may have with regard to pragmatics instruction.

2   Through discussion with peer teachers, you will be able to produce clarifications of the issues and their possible solutions.

Suggested time: 30 minutes.

Materials: a blank sheet of paper.

Directions

1   Work individually to write a "Dear Abby" letter addressed to your peer teachers who share the interest in pragmatics instruction. Focus on some particular issue of immediate concern to you with regard to the teaching of pragmatics (e.g., "burning issues" in your classroom). It could be, for example:

   ■   a question you would like a response to or want a second opinion about;

   ■   a point you wish to have clarification on;

   ■   a question that you believe may arise from your students about the learning of pragmatics; or

   ■   a problem you foresee occurring as you teach pragmatics.

2   When you finish writing your letter, pass it on to another participant and take someone else's letter to review. Give whatever feedback you can to that letter and when you are finished, pass it on to another participant to read. Read and respond to as many letters as time allows. Do not return letters to their original writer until the end of the session, so that each letter writer will get a maximum amount of feedback.

3   At the conclusion of the activity, get your letter back and read your peers' responses. If you would like more feedback, share your concern with the rest of the class so that they can talk it out. Or if you see something that you think others would benefit from, you are encouraged to share this as well.

Discussion/wrap-up

Consider what you have learned from this activity. Perhaps it was reassuring to know that some of you share similar concerns and questions about the teaching of

[11] Adapted from Weaver and Cohen (1997).

pragmatics. You may have learned from different perspectives that your colleagues have about your concerns. There may be complex issues that need to be discussed in greater depth. You may have gained ideas from the experiences, insights, and expertise available through your network of teacher colleagues. It is our hope that you will maintain collaborative relationships with your colleagues so that you can share with them your creative insights and concerns with regard to the teaching of pragmatics.

CHAPTER 11

Curriculum writing for L2 pragmatics – principles and practice in the teaching of L2 pragmatics

Noriko Ishihara

Introduction

There may be a misconception among some curriculum writers, teachers, and language learners alike that learners will somehow "pick up" the native-like ability to use language according to context as long as they are immersed in the L2 environment. This false impression may be why pragmatics has had such a low profile in the L2 curriculum. However, if no formal instruction is provided, learners may take an extended period of time – typically over 10 years – to acquire native-like pragmatic ability, even in a **second-language** setting where learners are exposed to the target language on a daily basis.[1] Pragmatic language use is difficult to learn for many reasons, such as differing cultural norms of appropriateness; regional, generational, ethnic, and individual variation; grammatical and lexical complexity; and subtleties of nuances and non-verbal behavior. As we have seen earlier in Chapter 8, existing language textbooks often pay short shrift to pragmatics-related concerns, if they are addressed at all. In the practical world of teaching, textbook materials often dictate the course curriculum, and for these reasons, there is a genuine need for research-based pragmatics instruction that more accurately reflects how language is actually used in context.

---

[1] Olshtain and Blum-Kulka (1985).

This chapter first discusses the use of pragmatics as an organizing principle – the implications of what that means in the development of a pragmatics-focused curriculum. Then, the chapter introduces several principles that readers may find important and applicable in the development of a pragmatics-focused curriculum in their own instructional contexts. In order to provide illustrations of instructional practice, samples of curricular materials are taken from a web-based curriculum for teaching Japanese pragmatics. Other examples are from a classroom-based, teacher-delivered textbook for Japanese pragmatics, an adaptation of the web-based curriculum. The chapter illustrates how these principles can be translated into learner exercises intended to raise learners' pragmatic awareness and improve their productive skills related to pragmatics.

Pragmatics as the organizing principle

In developing a curriculum, the curriculum writer's views, beliefs, and principles in language learning and teaching guide the organizational decisions at multiple levels.[2] When a curriculum is developed with pragmatics as the focus, the issue of appropriateness in the given context becomes a central concern for the curriculum writer, teachers, and learners alike, and will receive prominence in language instruction. In this curriculum, features of pragmatics may become the organizing principle (or at least given substantial attention) with meaningful, challenging, and realistic tasks focused on enhancing pragmatic language use and awareness. The ultimate goal would be for learners to become able to interpret others' messages as originally intended and to use the L2 to successfully communicate their own messages (as discussed in Chapter 1). Learners' tasks and assessment should be informed by a current theoretical and empirical understanding of pragmatics-focused language learning and teaching (e.g., see Chapter 6 for a theoretical discussion).

There are at least two ways in which material on pragmatics can be incorporated into the formal L2 curriculum: as an add-on to an existing curriculum (see Chapter 8 for examples) or as the organizing principle of a newly developed curriculum (as demonstrated in the curriculum below). In the first case, presumably the material would be included in the curriculum to narrow gaps. In this case, curriculum writers would provide extra exercises focusing on pragmatics or incorporate additional pragmatics-related

---

[2] Graves (2000); Tomlinson (2003).

insights into already existing activities.[3] Instruction on pragmatics could involve written as well as spoken discourse (e.g., understanding a nuance of a business letter, or writing a complaint via an e-mail message) and could be part of an integrated skills curriculum.

In the second case, pragmatics content can dictate the organization of the curriculum. Each unit could be composed of one or more of the following:

- a speech act;
- some conversational implicature (see Chapters 4 and 8);
- use of epistemic stance markers (Chapter 6);
- attention to discourse markers and fillers (Chapter 6);
- some discourse structure of interest and relevance (Chapter 9).

Whether pragmatics is an add-on or actually dictates the organization of the curriculum, the message needs to be heard loud and clear that it is not sufficient to teach vocabulary and grammatical structures in a decontextualized manner, but rather that the appropriate use of language in context needs to be accentuated. Consequently, if teachers are to include pragmatics in their instruction, they may well need to reduce the emphasis on other goals to varying degrees in order to keep the cognitive load manageable for learners.

In order to accommodate a possibly substantial change in focus and principles, a pragmatics-oriented curriculum may include supplementary materials that support teachers throughout the curriculum. A teachers' guide could carry information about various teaching techniques for pragmatics in general and specific pointers for each exercise and its assessment. The guide could also provide empirically based information about learners' L1 pragmatic norms. This approach may be particularly well received in **foreign-language** settings, where the majority of learners share the same L1.

Sample pragmatics-focused curricular materials

Let us now take a look at curricular materials for teaching Japanese speech acts to adult intermediate learners in a **foreign-language** setting. In doing so, we draw from a web-based six-unit curriculum,[4] as well as from its

[3] Materials developed by Ishihara and Maeda (2010) constitute a preliminary effort to supplement an already existing Japanese language textbook, *An Integrated Approach to Intermediate Japanese* (Miura and McGloin 1994). The sample of earlier efforts is at: http://www.carla.umn.edu/speechacts/japanese/IntroToSpeechActs/IAIJ.doc (accessed December 10, 2009).
[4] Ishihara and Cohen (2004: available online).

adaptation in a teacher-delivered, classroom-based curriculum.[5] The original web-based, self-access curriculum was developed at the University of Minnesota for third-year intermediate learners of Japanese at the university level to support their learning of five speech acts: apologies, compliments/responses to compliments, requests, refusals, and thanks. While the target level of proficiency was set at novice high to intermediate high according to ACTFL oral proficiency guidelines,[6] its focus on pragmatics and naturalistic speech samples makes it appropriate for some advanced learners as well. The development of this curriculum was financed in large part by the US Department of Education Title VI National Language Resource Center grant to CARLA. The curriculum was designed by Ishihara under the supervision of Cohen during the spring and summer of 2003 and revised repeatedly in 2003–4.[7] All units were pilot-tested with adult learners of Japanese, and their feedback was incorporated into various revisions of the materials.[8]

A web-based, self-access curriculum and a classroom-based, teacher-delivered curriculum both have their advantages. And of course, they need not be mutually exclusive; instruction can combine learners' self-study on the internet and face-to-face class meetings, as in some distance learning courses. Some obvious strengths of a web-based curriculum include its convenience to learners, as well as the independent and learner-centered learning it can promote (see Chapter 13 for the pedagogical use of technology). On the other hand, web-based instruction can benefit from being part of a regular teacher-delivered language course. Teachers can provide systematic attention to learners' contextualized L2 use and give feedback about cultural norms that is tailored to learners' needs. This feedback may more effectively instill in learners a sense of what is commonly considered appropriate language behavior in various cultural and situational contexts. Therefore, it would be valuable to build into the curriculum ample opportunities for individual feedback from the instructor, as well as opportunities for self-reflection and peer assessment. Below we will discuss ways that curriculum writers can structure assessment of pragmatics in the classroom and ways that teachers can provide feedback to learners, drawing examples from the

---

[5] Ishihara and Maeda (2010: to be available as a Japanese language textbook from Routledge).
[6] ACTFL (1999: available online).
[7] There was also input regarding the curriculum from Japanese language instructors at the university, several applied linguists, and Japanese-speaking informants. In addition, Elite Olshtain provided timely insights as curriculum advisor for the project.
[8] Initial versions were funded by the Graduate School and the CLA Infotech Fees Committee and the final revision was funded by a Material Development Mini-Grant from a CARLA Title VI Less Commonly Taught Language (LCTL) project.

teacher-delivered, classroom-based version of the curriculum for intermediate learners of Japanese pragmatics.

Another noteworthy benefit of classroom-based instruction would be that learners are able to engage in interactive practice with their peers and the teacher, promoting the development of productive skills. A pragmatics curriculum for even just occasional classroom use may still benefit from this interactional nature of the classroom. Learners gain opportunities to engage in interactional speaking practice that simulates authentic dialogues. Speaking activities could include role-plays in a series of different situations, followed by discussion of L1 and L2 pragmatic norms and possible cross-cultural misunderstandings. In **second-language** contexts where learners have relatively easy access to pragmatically competent speakers of the L2, it is possible to ask learners to leave the classroom setting in order to observe how model speakers use the target language (as demonstrated in Chapter 7). Learners could also be asked to interview those speakers regarding their preferred language use in certain contexts, and to practice L2 pragmatic use in authentic contexts outside the classroom (*learners-as-ethnographers/ researchers* approach,[9] see Chapter 6). Learners' pragmatic awareness can also be heightened through journal writing tasks, which can be incorporated into the curriculum on a regular basis (see Chapter 15 for a sample task and teacher feedback).

Principles for curriculum development and sample materials[10]

In this section, we will discuss some principles of curriculum development and sample materials that illustrate them. The principles include:

- explicitly stating the primary goal and approach to L2 pragmatics;
- utilizing empirically established information and naturalistic speech samples;
- guiding learners' observations and raising pragmatic awareness;
- providing interactional and language-focused practice;
- facilitating self-evaluation;
- explaining cultural reasoning for L2 pragmatic norms;

[9] Bardovi-Harlig (1996); Tanaka (1997); Tarone and Yule (1989).
[10] For the components of the curriculum and impact on learners' pragmatic awareness, see Ishihara (2007*b*).

- providing communication strategies for pragmatic L2 use; and
- referring teachers and learners to resources on L2 pragmatics.

Now we will take a look at each of these principles, drawing examples from the web-based and classroom-based curricula for intermediate learners of Japanese in a **foreign-language** context.

Explicitly stating the primary goal and approach to L2 pragmatics

The primary importance of a pragmatics-focused curriculum may be to instill in learners a sense of contextualized use of language (rather than to develop grammatical accuracy or fluency in decontextualized discourse). Because there is pragmatic variation across cultures and within cultures, a primary concern for curriculum writers may be to equip learners with a learning tool with which they become able to learn situational language behavior independently, in other words, *teaching them how to fish* in addition to *feeding them some fish*. Consequently, the curricular materials may neither aim to provide comprehensive and detailed coverage of various norms of pragmatic behavior, nor to focus just on linguistic forms without their interactional contexts. Rather, the curricular goal may be to raise learners' awareness of the pragmatic use of language that will enable them to take the initiative in developing their own pragmatic ability over time.

In the development of a pragmatics-focused curriculum, it is important to communicate its primary goals as well as the curriculum writer's approach explicitly to teachers and learners. This may be done first in the preface of the materials written specifically for learners and teachers. For example, in the

FIGURE 11.1 Teaching a fish vs. teaching how to fish

sample curriculum for Japanese pragmatics, the preface to the curriculum states its main goals and the curriculum writers' approach to language learning and teaching, particularly in relation to L2 pragmatics.[11] More specifically, the initial section of the curriculum includes information about:

- the importance of learning language in sociocultural context, a definition of speech acts, and the reason why they are focused on in the curriculum;
- the nature of pragmatic variation and diversity of pragmatic norms and curricular efforts to illustrate the variety;
- the pedagogical approach to learning and teaching pragmatics;
- the variety of the L2 being dealt with in the curriculum;
- the scope of situations (e.g. academic situations that college-age speakers might find themselves in);
- the structure and the content of the curriculum;
- information about supplementary materials; and
- the curriculum writers' consideration of learner *agency*, that is, the capacity of learners to decide whether or not to follow native-speaker norms.

Because the focus of this curriculum may be different from what teachers are accustomed to, it can be beneficial to support the teachers by inserting into the curriculum occasional illustrations as to how to include elements of a pragmatics curriculum in everyday classroom practice. Examples of this teacher support will be shown in the following sections.

Utilizing empirically established information and naturalistic speech samples

Following the current argument that instruction in pragmatics should be research-based,[12] curriculum writers may choose to rely largely on empirical findings from research reports (see Chapters 3 and 4). Since language often operates automatically below the level of the speakers' consciousness, it is important to ensure the authenticity of the language material, rather than

---

[11] See Ishihara and Maeda (2010), for an example. The preliminary attempts can also be viewed at http://www.carla.umn.edu/speechacts/japanese/introtospeechacts/forstudents.htm and http://www.carla.umn.edu/speechacts/japanese/introtospeechacts/forteachers.htm (accessed December 10, 2009).

[12] For instance, Kasper and Rose (2002).

relying exclusively on the curriculum writers' or teachers' intuitions (Chapters 3 and 8). Therefore, if curriculum writers are not yet familiar with the research-informed insights, they may first turn to available resources (see Chapter 4 and the section on providing resources below) to learn the pragmatics of the L2. It would be useful to identify commonly used language-focused strategies and the cultural norms that tended to prompt this behavior. Whereas curriculum writers would certainly want to cross-check this information with their own intuition and knowledge of the L2, it may also be valuable to turn to other competent speakers of the target language. These L2-speaking informants can be asked to provide linguistic samples for the materials through extended role-play, and their tone of voice, pauses (both filled and unfilled), language-focused strategies, discourse organization, and non-verbal behavior (e.g., eye-contact and bows) can be observed and incorporated into the curricular materials. More than one pair of speakers could be recorded so that some pragmatic variation would be modeled to learners.

In addition, in order to ensure authenticity of language material, linguistic samples need to be naturalistic. Model speakers can be asked to speak as naturally and spontaneously as possible. Their role-play performance can be compared with the research-based information, and can be checked by the curriculum writers and the model speakers themselves to verify the authenticity. From the learners' perspectives, however, natural language can be overwhelmingly complex and loaded. If this is presumed to be the case, curriculum writers may consider including language-related scaffolding. For example, audio- or video-recorded speech samples can be accompanied by vocabulary notes, transcripts, and translations.

Guiding learners' observations and raising pragmatic awareness

In the teaching of pragmatics, a situational approach – simulated practice with imagined scenarios and characters – may be used for facilitating learners' analysis of language use in context. Because L2 pragmatics is at the intersection of language and culture, learners could first be exposed to some cultural differences in order to enhance their awareness of pragmatic variation (see Chapters 1 and 7). As an introduction to the learning of pragmatics, a simulated format could be used, which asks learners to imagine a situation in which an exchange student is likely to encounter in Japan, and elicits their interpretation of the pragmatics of the situation and the language that they would use. This introductory exercise would direct learners' attention to various contextual factors embedded in the social context, and communicate to them that it is not sufficient to know the language forms, but rather that it is also crucial to know when and how to use them.

The following is a sample of introductory materials for learners' pragmatic awareness-raising.

Example 1[13]

Introduction to speech acts

This introduction will walk you through several little incidents you are likely to encounter in your daily life in Japan as an exchange student. Use your imagination and see if you can determine for each situation what a culturally appropriate interpretation might be and how best to respond in that situation.

Let us assume that you have been studying abroad at a Japanese university in Tokyo for the last few months. This is your first time in Japan. You have taken a few years of Japanese at a university level in the US, and you have always been a pretty good student. You are living in an apartment with a Japanese roommate, Jun. You love Japanese animation; in fact that is how you initially became interested in the language and culture. You are also a music lover. Aside from classes in Japanese language, you are studying Japanese history and international relations. You are sociable by nature, which is why you wanted to have a roommate.

In the sample curriculum, the introductory unit commences with a set of imaginary (and presumably realistic) situations for learners. One of the situations reads as follows:[14]

You are waiting in line at a department store to return an iPod that you had bought a few days earlier. The person in front of you in line is returning a defective digital voice recorder that she apparently bought the previous week. And then, much to your surprise, instead of complaining, she apologizes with すみませんが sumimasenga! You ask

▶

---

[13] From http://www.carla.umn.edu/speechacts/japanese/introtospeechacts/introductiontospeechacts1.html, accessed December 10, 2009.

[14] The situation and feedback adapted from http://www.carla.umn.edu/speechacts/japanese/introtospeechacts/introductiontospeechacts7.html, and http://www.carla.umn.edu/speechacts/japanese/introtospeechacts/feedback7.htm, accessed December 10, 2009.

yourself why she needs to apologize. After all, she received faulty goods and has had to go to the trouble of returning the product to the store. She also says お手数ですが otesuudesuga. What does that mean? If she is apologizing for returning what is clearly a defective item, what would be culturally appropriate behavior for you, wanting to return an item you just do not like? What language would you use in attempting to return an item that works perfectly well?

In a web-based program, the learners' observation of the situation is elicited in writing. When the learners electronically submit their responses to the curriculum writers (and/or their instructor) through the web system, pre-programmed feedback can be presented instantly:

In this situation, the person ahead of you in line is probably using the expression すみません(が) sumimasen(ga) as a conversation opener and also as a way of signaling the upcoming request/complaint. She may also be a bit apologetic for causing the store clerk some trouble in having to deal with this defective item. お手数ですが otesuu desuga "(literally) (I realize) I am causing trouble for you" is another commonly used apologetic phrase in this type of situation that softens the force of the request/complaint.

Returning the item that works perfectly well is not acceptable in many cases in Japan. It is best to check the store policy in advance, but generally, you are often held accountable for the item when you decide to buy it. You could try being as apologetic as you can in attempting to return it, and see what happens. In cases where you are not sure of whether to go ahead and purchase a certain product, you can always ask about the store policy (although small retail stores may not even have a policy). If you ask, they may make you an exception, allowing you to exchange it later.

In classroom-based instruction, teachers may ask learners to describe some social contexts in which they had problems responding appropriately.[15] These learner-generated scenarios would have an advantage of being truly authentic to learners' needs. Since the emphasis of this awareness-raising unit is on the cultural aspects of language use and not on grammatical fine-tuning, discussions may center on the cultural interpretation of the situation, if this exercise is to serve as an introduction.

[15] McLean (2005).

In further teaching of pragmatics, curriculum writers may choose to directly provide information concerning appropriate pragmatic behavior, as opposed to simply presenting it and assuming or hoping that students will learn it (see Chapter 6). Depending on the learner characteristics and instructional contexts, the choice may be: 1) to start by providing the pragmatic norms at the outset so that learners can study them and then practice applying them to interactional situations (a deductive approach), or 2) to expose learners to the situations straightaway and encourage them to use their own powers of self-discovery to determine the pragmatic norms (an inductive approach[16]).

In another approach, learners can be exposed to language samples and asked to guess the identities of the speakers and the relationship between the conversation partners by attending to the linguistic features in the samples. For example, by focusing on certain verb forms or sentence-final particles, learners may be able to determine the recipient of a request or a compliment, or guess the relationship between the speakers and the topic of conversation.[17]

The sample curriculum adopts the latter approach wherever possible so as to provide ample opportunities for self-guided learning. A unit typically starts with exercises in which learners are asked to compare their L1 and L2 use or contrast examples of L2 use for different purposes. In a unit on apologizing in Japanese, for example, learners can be given a situation where they respond in their L1 and then compare this L1 response with an L2 sample provided with some guiding prompts.[18] Learners could also compare the language of apology according to the relative social status and distance in the given exchanges, or analyze the use of intensifiers (e.g., *really, very, terribly*) used for different levels of offense. Learners could then read the transcript of the sample L2 dialogue to facilitate analysis. They may be able to generate their hypotheses (or questions) about Japanese apologies, which could lead to a lively class discussion, especially if learners have insights from similar authentic situations. In the case of a web-based program, learners' analysis can be guided through a pre-programmed feedback such as the following:[19]

---

[16] Also termed as "a guided discovery approach," Crandall and Basturkmen (2004).

[17] Sample exercises are available at: http://www.carla.umn.edu/speechacts/japanese/Requests/Ex4-3.htm; http://www.carla.umn.edu/speechacts/japanese/Compliments/Ex3-1.html and http://www.carla.umn.edu/speechacts/japanese/Thanks/Ex9.html, accessed December 10, 2009.

[18] See http://www.carla.umn.edu/speechacts/japanese/apologies/ex1.html (accessed December 10, 2009) for an example.

[19] Sample of feedback to be given to learners at the end of an exercise in a unit on thanking in Japanese (available at: http://www.carla.umn.edu/speechacts/japanese/thanks/feedbackex2.htm accessed December 10, 2009).

Example 2

Let's review the contextual factors in the two scenarios.

	Scenario 1	Scenario 2
Age difference between the two speakers:	Equal	You are much younger
Role/status difference between the two:	Equal	You are of lower status
Closeness or distance between the two:	Close in both scenarios	
Magnitude of your request/thanks:	Somewhat similar in both scenarios	

- Notice the clear difference in the language used when talking to an equal-status/age friend (Scenario 1) and when speaking to someone who is older or of higher status (Scenario 2).

  arigatou + gomen – for equal status

  arigatou gozaimasu – for higher status (the polite *desu/masu keigo*)

- The language of thanks (just like other aspects of Japanese) is often more influenced by age and status than the magnitude of the thanks/indebtedness. So, the key strategy is using appropriate thanking expressions according to the interlocutor and the situation (Kim 1994).

- Notice how many times expressions of apology and thanks are used in the dialogues. The number may generally be higher in Japanese than in English. In interacting with fluent Japanese speakers, listen to them carefully and observe their use of thanking strategies. Arrive at your own hypotheses regarding appropriate use in Japanese and be willing to revise these hypotheses as necessary.

Because this immediate input is pre-packaged and of a general nature, learners may need more individual feedback specifically about the appropriateness of their own language use (see the section on evaluation below). The curriculum could be written in a way that teachers are to provide individualized feedback to learners and answer the questions they may have while doing the exercises. (See also Chapters 7 and 15 for other awareness-raising exercises.) While a downside of providing individual feedback is its time-consuming nature especially for large **foreign-language** classrooms, the systematic use of rubrics may alleviate the issue (see Chapter 15).

Providing interactional and language-focused practice

Although pragmatic awareness-raising is vital and may be an ultimate goal in the instruction on pragmatics, learners also generally need to acquire the linguistic forms that will enable them to produce the L2 in a culturally and contextually appropriate way. With this aim in mind, some of the exercises may focus specifically on producing commonly used words or expressions. Other exercises may center on having the learners use pragmatic judgment regarding alternate forms so that they come to fine-tune their language or interpretation of language forms (see more examples in Chapter 6). In exercises where the focus is on language, a strategic approach may be to limit the amount of contextual information and to provide clear-cut answers regarding acceptable language forms (see Example 3, below).

In an exercise from the sample curriculum, learners focus on appropriate adjectives or phrases that they could use for complimenting the particular speaker in the given situation. As is the case with other exercises in the web-delivered curriculum, learners can listen to samples and view vocabulary assistance and clues to exercises whenever they want (see Chapter 13 for the technology). A disadvantage of this technology is that although an unlimited number of appropriate expressions are possible, only typical word choices are provided in this exercise. Classroom-based instruction would be able to follow up on other expressions that are not pre-programmed in this web-based exercise.

Example 3[20]

Another exercise encourages learners to attend to the various linguistic forms and determine the degree of appropriateness of each form using a multiple-choice format (see Chapter 13 for an example of this online exercise). This type of exercise could be developed based on research findings about respondents' judgments.[21] Another type of language-focused exercise

---

[20] Available at: http://www.carla.umn.edu/speechacts/japanese/compliments/ex4-2.htm (accessed December 10, 2009).
[21] A sample exercise available at: http://www.carla.umn.edu/speechacts/japanese/requests/ex5-2.htm (accessed November 14, 2008). In this exercise, answers are based largely on the responses that 100 native-speaking research informants provided to the same prompts (Rinnert and Kobayashi 1999).

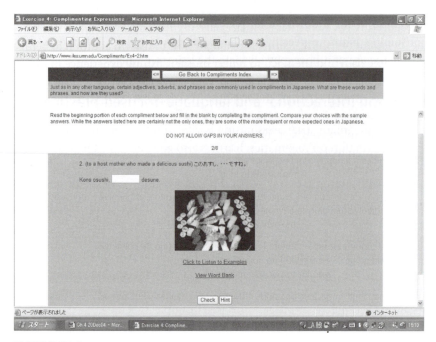

FIGURE 11.2

can be a matching activity where learners physically move electronic panels to match the descriptions of the speech-act strategies of a speech act with their examples (see a sample electronic item in Chapter 13).

Along with these language-focused exercises, learners would also benefit from interactional practice for using contextualized language. In a web-based program, multi-turn spoken discourse can be simulated in writing, while in classroom-based instruction, learners can practice more extended oral interaction through role-plays. The following section provides examples of interactional exercises in both web-based and classroom-based curricula.

Facilitating (self-) evaluation

If an inductive approach is used in the curriculum, learners may not necessarily be told whether their response is right or wrong immediately. Rather, they may first be asked to self-assess their responses (with some guidance built into the curriculum) in terms of how they think they are likely to be interpreted by most L2 speakers (Chapter 6). This self-reflective procedure may be promoted throughout the curriculum, so that learners form the habit and gain the skill of independent learning – that is, observing others and reflecting back on their own language use for improvement. That is, in the metaphor of fishing, learners are taught how to fish (in addition to being given some fish) and then, led to reflect on their fishing experience in order to improve their future experience. Self-evaluation prompts can encourage the learners to compare various examples of speech behavior in order to arrive at an understanding of a range of preferred norms of pragmatic behavior.

In the sample web-based curriculum, learners perform a simulated written dialogue, listen to a sample dialogue provided online, and compare strategies used by the model speaker and themselves (see below). Learners have a choice of viewing the transcript and the translation, along with another dialogue for showing pragmatic variation, which is also accompanied by the transcript and the translation online. After they complete and send their dialogue response and analysis electronically to curriculum writers and/or their teachers, they are given pre-programmed feedback that provides sample answers and discussion of the key pragmatic features in the language and context.

Example 4[22]

Exercise 9: Simulation exercises for making a refusal

A good friend of yours, Kunie, approaches you after class and asks if you could meet with her and edit her English paper that evening. You want to help her, but you have to study for your Japanese final exam the following morning. You remember that when you helped her last time, it took a good two hours. Her paper this time seems even longer, so you really don't have time for it this particular evening.

Kunie: ねえ、明日までの学期末の英語のレポート、見てくれない？ *Nee, ashita madeno gakkimatsuno eigono repooto, mite kurenai?* "Hey, can you check my English final paper due tomorrow?"

You – 1: (You refuse the request by telling her you have an exam yourself tomorrow.)

---

[22] Available at http://www.carla.umn.edu/speechacts/japanese/refusals/ex9.html (accessed December 10, 2009).

Kunie: そこをなんとかお願い！ *Sokowo nantoka onegai!* "I know that, but please, work something out for me."

You – 2: (You apologize and refuse again.)

Kunie: そうか、無理かあ。*Souka, murikaa.* 'Oh well, I guess you can't."

You – 3: (You give an alternative or two to help her.)

Kunie: そうか、じゃあ、悪いけどそうしてもらえる？ほんとにありがとう。*Souka, jaa, waruikedo soushite moraeru? Hontoni arigatou.* "Oh, then, sorry for bothering you but would you do that? Thanks so much."

Self-evaluation

Listen to a sample dialogue and evaluate your responses by filling in the chart below. Read the instructions in each column and write down an appropriate response in the box.

<u>Click to Listen</u>

Below is the self-assessment chart (offered bilingually) that follows the above webpage.

Sample dialogue	*Your response*
Fill in this column below as you listen to the sample dialogue. Write down what the second speaker says in response to Kunie.	Compare your responses to those in the left column. Self-evaluate the appropriateness of the choice and use of your refusal strategies.

Response 1

[Learners' dictation here]	[Learners' self-evaluation here]

Strategies used:

- Making a direct/indirect refusal
- Giving a reason
- Using an appropriate level of politeness

Sample dialogue	Your response

Response 2

[Learners' dictation here]	[Learners' self-evaluation here]

Strategies used:
- Making a direct/indirect refusal
- Apologizing
- Speaking hesitantly

Response 3

[Learners' dictation here]	[Learners' self-evaluation here]

Strategies used:
- Giving an alternative

Some learners may not be quite as reflective as others and may need more fine-tuned scaffolding to make their self-assessment effective. In that case, teachers, especially in the classroom setting, can ask further guiding questions such as:[23]

- Did you use the strategies of refusals given on the left of the table?

- If you did, what features do your strategies share with those in the sample dialogue? How are your strategies likely to be interpreted by the listener?

- If you didn't use any of those strategies, consider your reason why not. Was it because you weren't that familiar with the possible strategies or lacked vocabulary? Was it because you felt resistant to using Japanese pragmatic norms? If so, why did you feel that way?

- If you didn't use the strategies listed above, what other strategies did you use? How is your use of strategies most likely to be interpreted by your listener?

In a classroom-based curriculum, teachers can encourage peer assessment of each other's role-play performance, using the prompts as in the example below:

[23] From Ishihara and Maeda (2010).

Find a partner and exchange your written (or orally recorded) role-play. Read (or listen to) your partner's work carefully and answer the following questions. Remember to be supportive and respectful – rather than critical and evaluative – in your review. (Your review will be part of your grade.)

- ■ What makes your partner's language appropriate for the context?
- ■ What makes it less appropriate, and why do you think so?
- ■ What questions or suggestions do you have for your partner?
- ■ What did you learn from this peer review process?

More formal teachers' evaluation of learners' L2 pragmatic uses would also give recognition to pragmatics elements. Curriculum writers and teachers can choose from various forms of assessment, each focusing on different aspects of L2 pragmatics. For example, teachers can evaluate learners' choice and use of strategies, or culture-focused (sociopragmatic) skills. Alternatively, teachers may collaborate with learners to assess the match between the speaker's intention and the listener's interpretation.[24] (See Chapters 14 and 15 for more on assessment.)

Explaining cultural reasoning for L2 pragmatic norms

Just because learners encounter pragmatic norms that are different in their L1 and L2 does not mean that there will inevitably be a problem in learning them. Sometimes differences may actually enhance learning due to their salience. However, when learners' L1 norms or personal values directly conflict with certain L2 norms,[25] the learners may make a negative value judgment about the target culture, which could lead to negative stereotypes of that culture and the community members.[26] Consequently, learners may have difficulty deciding whether (and/or to what extent) to emulate the L2 norms, or to resist them altogether. It is at these times that it may be helpful for the learner to be well-informed as to **why** target language speakers speak as they do. Knowing the cultural reasoning behind language use can provide learners with an insider view of the culture, whether they like it or not. This would allow them to make informed pragmatic choices (see also Chapters 1 and 6).

[24] See Ishihara and Maeda (2010) for sample rubrics and teacher support.
[25] Di Vito (1993); Ishihara (2006).
[26] Wolfson (1989).

For this reason, the sample curriculum attempts to provide as much cultural interpretation as possible,[27] drawing from the research literature on sociolinguistics and intercultural communication. For example, in the unit on making refusals in Japanese in the sample curriculum, some explanatory information about Japanese speakers' use of a white lie is provided. In speaking diplomatically, it may be socially and ethically acceptable for Japanese speakers to use innocent, untruthful remarks as a way of face-saving both for themselves and for their conversational partners.[28] While some American learners of Japanese see this practice as dishonest,[29] they may appreciate knowing the cultural value behind this particular pragmatic convention, which may be constructed differently in their L1.[30] With this knowledge, learners would be familiar with generalized values in the target culture and able to make a more informed decision as to their own language use. In the sample curriculum, the following feedback is given to learners after they have performed an interactional role-play where model speakers do in fact use white lies as a way of declining an invitation.[31]

A white lie is used also as a face-saving strategy when the speaker does not want to comply with the listener's request or invitation. It is normally considered polite and desirable to give a reason the speaker has no control over, rather than saying that the speaker simply does not want to comply (Moriyama 1990).

In talking with a close friend, however, speaking honestly may be more appreciated, depending on the personality and relationship (Moriyama 1990). So the strategy here is choosing an appropriate reason for the refusal according to the situation.

As you see, cultural norms for interpreting and performing speech acts are very complex. We recommend that you listen to other Japanese speakers carefully to observe their use of speech act strategies along with the situation. Arrive at your own hypotheses regarding appropriate use of the target language and be willing to renew them as necessary.

---

[27] This approach is referred to as "explanatory pragmatics" (Meier 2003; Richards and Schmidt 1983; see also Chapters 1 and 6).
[28] Moriyama (1990).
[29] Ishihara (2007b); Kubota (1996).
[30] See Hancock (2008) for discussion on white lies in American English.
[31] Available at: http://www.carla.umn.edu/speechacts/japanese/refusals/feedbackex2.htm, accessed December 10, 2009.

Cultural differences like the social acceptability of white lies can be an effective springboard for discussion in pragmatics-focused instruction in the classroom. Some learners appear to find this type of discussion memorable and value the explanatory information about L2 pragmatic norms.

Providing communication strategies for pragmatic L2 use

Let us now shift the focus from teachers and teaching to learners and learning, and look at the possible place for learner subjectivity in the pragmatics curriculum. Learners may be in a particular place in the L2 community where community members at times expect learners to behave "foreign."[32] At other times, even if learners are generally able to interact successfully with L2 speakers and to participate in local cultural practices, they may on occasion prefer to distance themselves from the community as a way of asserting their own identity. For this reason, curriculum writers who wish to be culturally sensitive may avoid imposing native-speaker norms on learners. (See Chapter 15 for this issue related to assessment.) So, curriculum writers and teachers alike are in a position "to equip the student to express her/himself in exactly the way s/he chooses to do so – rudely, tactfully, or in an elaborately polite manner. What we want to prevent is her/his being *unintentionally* rude or subservient."[33]

The main idea is for teachers and curriculum writers to support learners in making truly informed decisions, whether they choose to emulate L2 pragmatic norms or not. If in fact learners wish to diverge from L2 norms, they ought to be well informed as to the rationale behind those norms, the listener's likely interpretations for different kinds of behavior, and the potentially negative consequence of resisting the norms.[34] In order to support learners' well-informed expression of subjectivity, curriculum writers may promote the use of *communication strategies* which let learners take advantage of their "special" status as bi-/multilingual speakers.[35] In other words, there may be some strategies that allow learners either to enhance the way they communicate their intentions, or to help them compensate for their gap in pragmatic ability. These strategies may include:

---

[32] For example, Barron (2003); House and Kasper (2002); Iino (1996); Ishihara (2008b); (in press, b).
[33] Thomas (1983: 96).
[34] For instance, Kasper and Rose (2002); Thomas (1983).
[35] Aston (1993).

- providing metapragmatic comments (comments and explanation about their own language use) as a reinforcement of the real intent;

- alerting their conversational partner as to their unfamiliarity with L2 norms;

- looking for relatively appropriate L2 expressions that better communicate the L1 feel; and

- resorting to a third language that approximates their intention, rather than just relying on the L1 or L2.

These communication strategies are more fully discussed in Chapters 6 and 12. Some examples are also available in the sample curriculum.[36]

Referring teachers and learners to resources on L2 pragmatics

The last principle concerns informing teachers and learners about research-based information related to the pragmatics of the target features being taught in the curriculum. Even when teachers are fluent speakers of the language they teach, they may need additional awareness-raising in order to gain an explicit knowledge of the L2 pragmatics. The information can be included in the teachers' guide if the curriculum is teacher-delivered, or could be placed online for teachers and learners to view. Depending on the target language, the relevant information may already be found in Chapter 4 or posted in the CARLA database.[37] Additional information can also be provided to avid teachers, teacher researchers, and learners alike who wish to further follow up on the pragmatics discussed in the curriculum.[38]

Discussion

In this chapter, we have discussed the nature of a curriculum that has pragmatics as its organizing principle or as its main focus, and have considered some principles that may be used in such a curriculum. There is value in systematically incorporating pragmatics into the L2 curriculum expressly

[36] See http://www.carla.umn.edu/speechacts/japanese/introtospeechacts/communicationstrategies.htm for preliminary examples (accessed December 10, 2009).
[37] Available at: http://www.carla.umn.edu/speechacts/descriptions.html, accessed December 10, 2009.
[38] An annotated bibliography in the area of L2 pragmatics may also be useful for a broader range of interest (available at: http://www.carla.umn.edu/speechacts/bibliography/index.html, accessed December 10, 2009).

because it has been a relatively neglected area in language learning. With the curricular focus placed on pragmatics, it would be vital for curriculum writers to communicate its principles clearly to the users of the curriculum, and to support teachers throughout with supplementary materials.

As recommended in this teachers' guide, curriculum writers may decide to present pragmatics information explicitly and draw on research-based insights, rather than solely relying on their own intuitions as fluent speakers of the L2. To illustrate how principles can be manifested in a pragmatics curriculum, examples have been taken from a web-based curriculum and its adapted classroom-based curriculum for learners of Japanese as a foreign language. The sample exercises from the curriculum have demonstrated the way learners' pragmatic awareness can be heightened through the inclusion of naturalistic language samples, language-focused exercises, and interactional practice. In order to facilitate learners' observation of pragmatic language use, the sample curriculum has taken an inductive, self-guided approach, encouraging the learners to analyze others' pragmatic behavior. Learners are also guided to self-assess their own pragmatic awareness and language use through the pre-programmed prompts and individualized, teacher-generated feedback. A pragmatics-focused curriculum could also include cultural reasoning behind certain pragmatic norms that would enhance learners' cultural literacy and provide insider perspectives regarding the L2 culture. Additional resources in the curriculum may include communication strategies for pragmatics and information for further learning of pragmatics.

We are now fortunate to have some research-based resources for teaching pragmatics. It would be helpful to further develop curricula that cover many more pragmatic features,[39] whether through a classroom-based, teacher-delivered curriculum, a web-based, self-access curriculum, or a combination of the two. In fact, L2 learners tend to respond favorably to pragmatics-focused instruction,[40] especially if they perceive pragmatics as essential to their communicative needs. The following activity is designed to facilitate curricular efforts in this area. Curriculum writers are encouraged to develop materials, field-test them, and share their results with the community of interested teachers.

---

[39] Features of pragmatics other than speech acts would be especially welcome in future language materials.

[40] For example, Crandall and Basturkmen (2004); Ishihara (2004).

Activity 11.1 Designing a pragmatics-focused curriculum

Objectives

1   You will be able to identify your own principles in learning and teaching L2 pragmatics.

2   You will be able to initiate an effort to develop a pragmatics-focused curriculum according to your own principles.

Suggested time: 40 minutes, and then more as needed.

Materials: a language textbook that you wish to adapt (if you plan to incorporate pragmatics into an existing curriculum).

Directions

1   In a small group of approximately three, brainstorm your beliefs related to the learning and teaching of pragmatics. You may also wish to look back at your own reflections in the Chapter 2 activity.

2   Independently or in a small group of curriculum writers sharing the same interest, decide how you would like to construct a pragmatics-focused curriculum. Would you choose to design a brand new curriculum, or to supplement one that already exists by adding pragmatics-focused components?

3   If you are to design a new curriculum, sketch out the structure of the curriculum by selecting features of pragmatics to be included as instructional foci, and by sequencing them logically. Then, consider the components and structure of each unit. If you are supplementing a textbook, look through it carefully with an eye to identifying the pragmatics components that appear to be missing from the instruction.

4   Report back these initial efforts to the whole class by discussing what features of pragmatics you plan to teach, in what ways, and why.

Discussion/wrap-up

An advantage of collaboratively discussing curricular efforts is that you may become more aware of your beliefs and principles as you articulate them in interaction with other teachers. It would be best if these principles permeate your curriculum and inform your curricular decisions;[41] then, a consistent message could be sent to the users of the curriculum as to how L2 pragmatics can be learned effectively. You are invited to continue your efforts at developing a pragmatics-focused curriculum beyond this activity and share them with other like-minded curriculum developers and teachers.

---

[41] Graves (2000).

PART THREE

Further issues in the learning, teaching, and assessment of pragmatics

CHAPTER 12

Strategies for learning and performing speech acts

Andrew D. Cohen

Introduction

Why discuss language learner strategies in a book on pragmatics for teachers? The main reason is that our ultimate goal is to have learners be more effective pragmatically in the L2. Research has demonstrated the benefits of explicit strategy instruction in the classroom.[1] Given the challenges associated with learning L2 pragmatics, it makes sense for learners to develop their own repertoire of strategies for both learning and performing pragmatics.[2] While other chapters in the book have looked at what learners do with pragmatics (such as Chapters 5 and 9), this chapter looks specifically at the role of the actual strategizing that they may do, both in learning L2 speech acts and also in performing what has been learned.

The chapter focuses on factors that contribute to whether strategy use is successful, and introduces a proposed taxonomy of learner strategies for acquiring pragmatics, with an emphasis on speech acts. The chapter ends with two activities. Activity 12.1 gives you a firsthand opportunity to experience using strategies to collect information about an L2 speech act. Activity 12.2 provides an opportunity to observe the strategies that you use in performing a speech act and to learn from others about the strategies that they use for the same speech act.

---

[1] Cohen *et al.* (1998); Chamot (2008); Rubin *et al.* (2007).
[2] While this chapter focuses on speech acts, pragmatics also deals with matters of reference, presupposition, discourse structure, and conversational principles involving implicature and hedging; see LoCastro (2003) for more on these areas.

Strategies in language learning and language use

While definitions have varied over the years, there is some agreement among experts that *language learner strategies* are conscious or semi-conscious thoughts and actions deployed by learners, often with the intention of enhancing their knowledge of, and facility with an L2.[3] From the initial focus some 30 years ago on the strategies that good language learners use,[4] there has been a growing consensus that language learner strategies can play a role in L2 learning. This view led to the introduction of *strategy instruction* into the curriculum.[5] The basic premise was that if learners have a well-functioning strategy repertoire, then these strategies will enhance the learning of an L2, whether in teacher-led, instructional settings or in one of the alternative options, such as self-access, web-based instructional settings, and other forms of independent language learning. In recent years, this position has been increasingly supported both by descriptive studies[6] and by studies involving some form of strategy instruction treatment.[7] Such studies have demonstrated that learners who use strategies produce better results in their language learning than students who are less strategic. Let us now take a closer look at language learner strategies.

The act of planning and making a request involves a sequence or cluster of different strategies. You need what was referred to in Chapter 1 as speech act strategies, namely, strategies for dealing with specific speech acts (e.g. acknowledging responsibility or offering repair in an apology). But you also need strategies for **learning** the speech acts in the first place and for **performing** the speech acts. For instance, at the moment that you as an L2 speaker are planning your request for directions to the airport, you would presumably use *planning*, one of the *metacognitive* strategies (along with *monitoring* and *evaluating*). The moment that you shift the focus so that it is on the language material to use in the request (e.g., appropriate vocabulary, verb forms, or sentence structure), the need would now be for *cognitive* strategies to help you retrieve and produce these words and forms. The speaker may, of course, return to the use of metacognitive strategies this time using the strategy of *monitoring*, in order to check for how the selection of material is going. The request would involve social strategies when your focus shifts to whom you will choose to ask for directions and how you will

---

[3] Cohen (2007*b*).
[4] Rubin (1975); see also Griffiths (2008).
[5] For example, Cohen and Weaver (2006).
[6] For example, Vandergrift (2003).
[7] For example, Cohen *et al.* (1998); Grenfell and Harris (1999); Harris and Grenfell (2008); Macaro (2001).

go about asking this person (depending on the age, gender, and presumed social status of the listener). Then, if you chose to avoid the possible anxiety associated with asking directions from a stranger in your L2, but rather follow a map exclusively, this would constitute an *affective* strategy.

Now that we have looked at language learner strategies in general, let us take a look at a suggested taxonomy of strategies intended specifically for the learning and performance of L2 speech acts.

A taxonomy of learner strategies for acquiring speech acts

The strategies in this taxonomy are drawn from a larger and more detailed taxonomy appearing in the literature.[8] Sources for strategies in this taxonomy include the general learner strategy literature, the speech act literature (as illustrated in Chapter 4), and insights from recent strategy research conducted to enhance college students' learning of Japanese L2 speech acts through a strategies-based online curriculum[9] (see also Chapter 11) and from a language and culture study abroad project.[10] While explicit strategy instruction has been found to benefit language development in general,[11] its application to the learning and use of speech acts at present is still limited. One recent application was in an investigation of speech acts strategy intervention for study-abroad students in Spanish- and French-speaking countries.[12]

This taxonomy constitutes a hypothesized list. While there is a good likelihood that these strategies contribute to enhancing learners' pragmatic ability, there is as yet no certainty based on empirical evidence. The taxonomy includes (1) strategies for the initial learning of speech acts, (2) strategies for using the speech act material that has already been learned to some extent, and (3) learners' strategies for planning, monitoring, and evaluating their pragmatic strategy choices (the metacognitive strategies mentioned above).

Note that some of these strategies, if phrased in an age-appropriate manner, could be performed effectively by young learners. For example, they could perform a simple survey with competent speakers of the language and report their findings back to class. This could really help to bring the language alive for these young learners.

---

[8] Cohen (2005).
[9] Cohen and Ishihara (2005).
[10] Cohen *et al.* (2005); Paige *et al.* (2004).
[11] See, for example, Cohen *et al.* (1998); Dörnyei (1995); Nakatani (2005).
[12] Cohen and Shively (2007).

Strategies for the initial learning of speech acts

Here, then, is a set of strategies for learning about speech acts in the first place.

- Gathering information (through observation and interview) on how speech acts are actually performed in a given speech community (e.g., at the workplace: making requests to colleagues, refusing requests made by people of higher status, and thanking people in service such as cafeteria workers or custodians) – noting the following:

  1 what they say;

  2 how they say it (speed of delivery and tone of voice); and

  3 their non-verbal behavior as they say it (e.g., facial expressions, body posture, and gestures).

- Conducting a "lay" cross-cultural analysis by:

  1 thinking through and even writing out what the appropriate things to say would be for that speech act in the L1 speech community, depending on the situation;

  2 identifying the cultural norms for performing these speech acts in the L2 speech community;

  3 identifying strategies that tend to be used with a given speech act (drawing on descriptions of strategies specific to individual speech acts, such as those listed in Chapter 4), and then checking to see if a particular strategy works in a given situation (e.g., whether an *offer of repair* is an appropriate strategy for a given apology situation);

  4 identifying the words and phrases to use, consistent with the local norms (e.g., whether to use the word "apologize" in the expression of apology or just "sorry"; whether to repeat "sorry" more than once, and whether to intensify with words like "really," "awfully," or "so");

  5 determining the similarities and differences between the two cultures, and then making a mental note or a notebook entry regarding the difference(s);

  6 obtaining a viable interpretation for the cross-cultural differences (e.g., by asking members of the L2 speech community, such as friends or colleagues).

- Asking competent speakers of the L2 (instructors and non-instructors) to model performance of the speech acts as performed under differing conditions to see if there is variation according to:

    1   the magnitude or seriousness of the issue prompting the speech act (e.g., apologizing for missing a meeting vs spilling hot coffee on a friend);

    2   the relative age or status of the speaker and the listener (e.g. of age: a request to an elderly supervisor at work or to a young child; e.g. of status: a request to the CEO of a company or to a custodian);

    3   the relative roles of the speaker and the listener in the relationship (e.g., making a request to a state senator colleague at a public meeting vs to a server at a local bar);

    4   the distance between the speaker and the listener (e.g., making a request to a stranger about switching seats on an airplane vs making an appeal for assistance to a friend at a coffee shop).

- Accessing published materials dealing with speech acts:

    1   websites with instructional materials on speech acts (e.g., websites for self-access learning of key speech acts in a given language);[13]

    2   L2 textbooks which have coverage of the speech acts of interest while keeping in mind the issues raised about textbooks in Chapter 8 and elaborated on in Chapter 11; and

    3   research articles providing insights on speech acts not available from other sources.[14]

Strategies for performing speech acts

Here are strategies for taking what has been learned, however partially, and putting it to use. So, in other words, we assume that students have learned about speech acts, either through previous exposure to the L2 culture, through reading about how speech acts are performed, through attending to what a teacher has taught them, or through collecting data on their own. The challenge is to take this learned material and use it in pragmatic performance.

[13] See Cohen (2007*a*); Cohen and Ishihara (2005); Ishihara (2007*b*); Sykes and Cohen (in press).

[14] For instance, the study by Daly *et al.* (2004) on the *f*-word expletive being used in requests and refusals on the factory floor in New Zealand as a signal of solidarity.

- Using some mnemonic for retrieving for performance purposes the speech act material that has already been at least partially learned (e.g., visualizing a list of the strategies specific to the performance of a given speech acts set and then selecting the ones that seem appropriate for the given situation).

- Practicing those aspects of speech acts performance that have been learned:

  1 Engaging in imaginary interactions, perhaps focusing on certain language structures in the speech acts.

  2 Engaging in speech acts role-play with fellow learners of the L2 or with competent speakers of the L2 playing the other role.

  3 Engaging in "real play" with competent speakers of the L2 in the speech community who have agreed to perform their usual roles (e.g., sales clerk, cashier, or receptionist) for the sake of you, the learner, whose purpose is exclusively to practice speech acts. In actual service encounters, the interactions are usually limited to a few brief exchanges. In real play, they may purposely be lengthier since the goal is to create language, not to buy a product, for example.

  4 A variation on #3, namely, engaging in interactions with pragmatically competent speakers of the L2 without them being aware that your purpose is actually to practice speech acts.

- Asking pragmatically competent speakers of the L2 for feedback as to what was and was not appropriate in the speech act performance.

- Taking a style preference inventory and then trying an approach to speech act delivery that is consistent with the results (e.g., if you find yourself to be more *reflective*, then thinking through the elements in the speech act before performing it; if more impulsive, then just doing it online and seeing what the response is).

- Using communication strategies to get the message across:

  1 Using an alerter as a social (interactive) strategy to signal to the addressee before the delivery of the speech act that it may not come out right (e.g., "I want to make a request here, but I'm not sure it will come out right . . .") (Figure 12.1, below).

  2 After performing the speech act, making comments about it in order to repair the situation in the case of pragmatic divergence which could possibly lead to pragmatic failure (see Chapter 5 for more on divergence).

FIGURE 12.1 Learner at work

3   Attempting to approximate what competent speakers of the L2 might do in that speech act situation:

(a) weighing the assumed force and impact of several different approaches, and then on that basis selecting one;

(b) going on the basis of "feel" as to what competent speakers would do based on L2 knowledge that has accrued;

(c) basing speech act performance on a sense of what seems reasonable to expect competent speakers of the language to do in that speech act situation based on the learners' perception as to how similar the L2 is to their language.[15]

4   Compensating for a gap in knowledge by translating from the L1 or from another language what would be said in that language in order to perform the speech act (i.e., without any preconception that the words and phrases will be acceptable).

■   Having the knowledge to perform the speech act appropriately but, as an expression of self-agency or subjectivity, remaining true to your own inclinations in your speech act delivery and trying not to be overly native-like (referred to in Chapter 5 as "resistance to using perceived L2 pragmatic norms").[16]

While the taxonomy distinguishes strategies for learning speech acts for the first time from those for using the speech act material once it is learned,

[15] Kellerman (1983).
[16] See LoCastro's 1998 paper and a chapter in her 2003 book for a description of learner subjectivity, and Ishihara (2006) for research on the topic.

there actually is some overlap. In fact, it is possible that the same strategy used to learn new speech act behavior could also be used to perform the speech act once learned. For example, an entry under "Strategies for Performing Speech Acts", below; "Asking competent speakers of the L2 for feedback as to what was and was not appropriate in the speech acts performance" could also be seen as a strategy for learning new things about that speech act.

Metacognitive strategies for the learning and performing of speech acts

We now come to the strategies for a) planning which pragmatic strategies to use and when to use them, b) checking how their use is going, and c) evaluating afterwards how effective it was to use them. These are the metacognitive strategies for supervising the use of strategies. Here are some examples:

- Determining the extent to which the focus is on comprehension of the speech act, on the production of.it, or on both.

- Focusing attention on tone of voice, facial expressions, and gestures in speech act delivery. (Whereas an actor usually gets coached in such matters, language learners are invariably left to figure it out by themselves.)

- Determining the amount of pre-planning of the speech act to do beforehand, the nature of the monitoring that will go on during its delivery, and the evaluation that will go on afterwards.

- In an effort to avoid pragmatic failure, monitoring for:

  1 the appropriateness of the chosen level of directness or indirectness in the delivery of the speech act (e.g., finding the right level of directness with an L2-speaking stranger on an airplane);

  2 the appropriateness of the selected term of address (e.g., referring in the L2 to Dr Felicia Bloom as "Doc," "Felicia," or "you");

  3 the appropriateness of the timing for a speech act in the given situation (e.g., whether to attempt to apologize to a colleague for a work-related incident during a social encounter);

  4 the acceptability of how the discourse is organized (e.g., conveying the bottom-line message right from the start of the communication, gradually building up to it, or saving it for the last possible moment); and

  5 the cultural appropriateness of the selected strategies and the appropriateness of the language structures used to represent them

(e.g., whether it is appropriate for a college student to give an outright refusal to the department chair's invitation to dinner and whether the refusal could include – even in jest – an informal phrase such as "No way!").

As indicated above, this constitutes a preliminary effort to provide a taxonomy of strategies that might play a role in the learning of speech acts, as well as in the subsequent comprehension and production of the speech acts afterwards.

Now that we have looked at a taxonomy of strategies for L2 speech acts, let us consider how learner, task, and contextual factors can influence strategic performance of speech acts.

Factors influencing successful use of speech act strategies

The relative success that L2 users have in deploying a given strategy for learning or performing speech acts may depend on various factors, such as the characteristics of the learners, the nature of the task, and the context for language use.

Learner characteristics

The following are learner characteristics that may have an impact on the use of strategies for learning and performance of L2 pragmatics:

- Age: a 25-year-old learner may have an easier time remembering the set of strategies specific to apologizing in the L2 than a 55-year-old learner. Also, young learners can strategize effectively. Some learners can do so as of second grade. Others gain this awareness a bit later. The point is that a teacher could talk up pragmatics strategies with young learners, and these learners may find it fun to strategize in this area, especially if silly visuals are included in the effort – created, if possible, by the learners themselves.

- Gender: women may be expected to use a different set of politeness strategies from those that men use in a given society or subgroup of that society.

- Language aptitude: learners with a predisposition to noticing and dealing with inflections for, say, gender could have an easier time with Romance languages than learners who have difficulty making such distinctions.

- Style preferences: using certain strategies may be easier for those with a style preference that caters to those strategies (e.g., a more intuitive learner being willing and able to make inferences about an implicit complaint in an email message at work, as opposed to a more concrete learner who prefers having things spelled out explicitly and misses the indirect complaint in the message entirely).[17]
- Personality: introverts who do more listening in the L2 classroom than talking may have an easier time perceiving a sarcastic tone in a presumed compliment than extroverts who do more talking than listening.

The nature of the task

Not all tasks involving pragmatics are created equal. Some are more demanding than others, depending on factors such as similarities and differences between the L1 and the L2. And at times knowing the meaning of key words in a message can have a major impact on the pragmatics of the situation. For example, let us say that an Israeli speaker of English receives the following e-mail message from his native-speaking colleague, Brian:

Hi, Avi. I wanted to say something about your talk last evening, I think you did an impeccable job of presenting the issues. What really came across was your integrity. We can discuss it in person next week when I'm back from my trip.

Best,

Brian

But supposing that Avi does not really know what two key words in the message, "impeccable" and "integrity," mean. In this case, his first task is to look up the word "impeccable," which he finds a Hebrew translation for without difficulty. His second task, looking up "integrity," is more problematic since there is no direct equivalent in Hebrew. Consequently, Avi is a bit confused as to just what trait of his is being identified, and is not sure as to what his response should be.

Likewise, if the task is a complex one, such as submitting a request to your employer at the workplace regarding a work-load issue, then it may call for a high level of tact and discretion. Strategies need to be fine-tuned in

---

[17] For more on style preferences and strategy repertoire, see Cohen and Weaver (2006).

order to deliver the communication responsibly, without alienating an employer and risking being let go. So the employee would probably need to be obsequious enough so as not to anger the boss, but at the same time forceful enough so that the person is clear what the request is. In English this means that the employee needs to be gracious, as in the following simulated interaction:

> Steve (*the employee*): How are you, Bethany? How's the family?
>
> Bethany (*the boss*): Well, I'm OK. Still fighting that cold from last week. What can I do for you, Steve?
>
> Steve: I just wanted a few minutes of your time to go over some work-related issues. Uh, you know, uh, that . . . well, I have been doing the best I can to meet your deadlines and all. I know how important this is to you. And you've said to me more than once that, uh, you're pleased with how I've been doing it.
>
> Bethany: That's true, Steve . . .
>
> Steve: Well, I wonder if we could take a look at my work load and, uh, see whether it might be possible to make, uh, some adjustments here because there are just so many hours in a day and . . .

In this example, Steve had a difficult message to deliver to his boss – namely, that he felt he was overworked. He starts his complaint with the strategy of providing a personal greeting, and then as his next request strategy, he uses an indirect means for broaching a touchy issue: "I just wanted a few minutes of your time . . ." This strategy is referred to as one of *negative politeness* or a desire to give deference and minimize the imposition.[18] He then uses the strategy of calling attention to his high level of performance on the job in order to justify requesting a raise. When he gets his boss's confirmation of this, he makes the request to have his work load lightened somewhat.

As a third example, let us take the case of a teenage daughter asking to borrow a car from her parents over the weekend. She could make the request as follows:

> Hey, dad, can I take your old car this weekend?

---

[18] Brown and Levinson (1987).

or in a more indirect manner:

> Hey, dad. I was wondering whether you were planning on using the Mazda this weekend. I promised Caitlin and Megan I'd take them out to the country arts fair in Lanesboro . . .

Depending on the language and culture, it may be strategic for the speaker to adjust the delivery of the speech act according to the age, relative status, or gender of the listener. The speaker would also need to know what it means to borrow a car in that particular context – that is, how big an imposition it is considered to be in that culture (e.g., whether a car is a daily necessity or a luxury) and in that specific context (e.g., borrowing a new and relatively valuable car vs an older "spare" car). In some cases, it may be important to refrain from mentioning the borrowing of the car altogether, but rather just to call attention to the need for transportation and to leave it to the listener to determine whether to offer a car or not. In this example, there may also be some family history involved, such as whether the father feels that his daughter will drive the car safely. Issues of family personalities and relationships are also likely to play a part in the phrasing of the daughter's request and in the father's response to this request. And natural discourse retrieved through corpus data reveals that it could take a number of turns for the interaction to resolve itself, one way or the other.

As was demonstrated in Chapter 1, effective speech acts performance entails not only having the cultural knowledge about whether it is appropriate to ask to borrow the car and if so when to ask, but also the language knowledge in order to do it appropriately in the given speech community ("Can I take . . . ?" vs "I was wondering if . . ."). Pragmatically competent speakers of English and in this case, a daughter, might either make a direct request or soften it through the use of the past progressive tense (e.g., "I was wondering if . . ."). While many learners of English may well have studied this tense of the verb, they would not necessarily have sufficient control over its use in their requests to know whether or when to use it.[19] There are other ways to make a request seem less imposing, such as by using mitigators to downplay the demands: "Professor Cohen – would it be possible for you

[19] Bardovi-Harlig (2003).

to take *just a few minutes* of your time to read through my thesis and *perhaps* give me *an idea or two* about how I might prepare it as a journal article?"[20]

The context for language use

With regard to the context, learners may have such limited access to a particular speech acts situation that they find themselves unsure of just how to behave when confronted with the situation. For example, an L2 user may not know what to do or say at a funeral, and the textbooks are unlikely to have a unit on this. Saying or doing the wrong thing can be particularly upsetting both to those in mourning and to the learner! The learner may in such situations draw from cultural patterns of behavior associated with the L1 (where, for example, it might be appropriate to share how one of their own loved ones died), but may well find that they are being inappropriate in this L2 culture.

It is likely that learners will acquire the speech acts that they come in contact with the most, that they notice, or for which they have the most need. So, for example, they need to deal with forms of greetings and leave-takings, and with requests immediately. Depending on the tasks they encounter, other less mainstream situations will emerge as important. For example, if L2 learners are backpacking across a country, then they may need to learn the strategies that are appropriate for hitchhiking in that culture. When hitchhiking in the US, for instance, the hitchhikers may consider it their role to entertain the driver, particularly at night where talk may help to keep him/her awake. In other cultures, such as in Israel, hitchhikers may, depending on the driver, be expected to keep silent and only speak in response to a question posed to them.

Discussion

This chapter has focused on the need for supporting learners in their efforts to acquire pragmatic ability through calling their attention to strategies for enhancing how they learn and perform speech acts. The speech acts strategy taxonomy provided here is seen as a preliminary step in this direction.

Ideally, you will take away from this chapter some ideas for how to support your students in their efforts to learn and to perform speech acts both in and outside of the classroom.

---

[20] Italics are used here to identify the mitigators.

In order to make the taxonomy more "real" for you, we would like you now to undertake Activities 12.1 and 12.2 (below). Activity 12.1 will give you an opportunity to do some actual gathering of L2 speech acts data from a competent speaker of an L2, drawing as necessary from the "Strategies for the Initial Learning of Speech Acts" section of the above taxonomy of learner strategies for acquiring speech acts. Activity 12.2 will give you a chance to perform a speech acts interaction and to observe the strategies that you and your partner use.

Activity 12.1 Collecting information on L2 speech acts

Objectives

1   You will be able to use strategies to collect information about an L2 speech act.

2   You will be able to identify the strategies that other participants have used to gather data for learning and performing speech acts.

Suggested time: 45 minutes.

Materials:

■   Task sheet, "Speech acts data-gathering tasks," with several speech acts situations for which to collect data;

■   the "Strategies for the Initial Learning of Speech Acts" section from the *Taxonomy of Learner Strategies for Acquiring Speech Acts* in this chapter.

Directions

1   Select one of the two speech act situations provided in the task sheet and think through the issues on your own.

2   Find a competent speaker of the L2 you identify as a "consultant" for an L2 speech community that you are **not** familiar with, and gather information from that person as to how to perform the speech act tactfully. (More guidance is provided under point 1 in the task sheet below.)

3   If possible, make the session two-way by having your partner collect data from **you** on how to perform a speech act tactfully in **your** L1 (say, if the person is a native speaker of Italian and you a native speaker of English). If you cannot find a competent speaker of the L2 which you are learning, you could serve as "advisors" in this data-gathering process, making suggestions to both the data gatherer and the consultant who is providing the information.

4   While in the data collection phase, have "Strategies for the Initial Learning of Speech Acts" from the *Taxonomy of Learner Strategies* handy and select strategies from it to assist you in completing the task. Bullets 2 to 4 include strategies that could be particularly relevant to your probing for information.

5   When the data collection phase is over, each group is to report back to the whole group as to insights gained from the task.

Discussion/wrap-up

Looking back over the processes that you went through in this activity, consider the extent to which the exercise helped you to identify the strategies involved in performing a speech act effectively. What were the challenges associated with this type of data gathering? How might you encourage your students to use these strategies in their future language learning?

Task sheet: Speech acts data-gathering tasks

1 Gathering information about complimenting

You are by nature a friendly person and like to compliment people on how they look and on the things they do well. The following are two kinds of compliments you are likely to give to your colleagues:

(a) Hey, _____ , that _____ looks really good on you! Where did you get it?

(b) Hey, _____ , your talk was really good. You had a lot of interesting things to say.

Notwithstanding your desire to pass on well-deserved compliments, you have been advised that in the L2 speech community in which you are now living, it is possible to offend people unintentionally when you mean well. You have heard, for example, that depending on your age, your status, or your gender, an intended compliment, at worst, may be taken as an insult and, at best, may be considered inappropriate coming from you to that person.

2 Gathering information about refusing

You are living in an L2 speech community where you find people making requests of you that you want to refuse. The problem is that your L2 textbook did not teach you how to refuse tactfully, and your teacher did not cover it either. The following are two of the typical situations:

(a) You are invited to a friend's party, but you don't want to attend because there is usually a lot of smoke, noise, and drinking. In addition, such parties usually go on too long for you (since you start working early in the morning), and you know from experience that it is difficult to cut out early. How do you decline the invitation?

(b) Your colleague asks you to edit an article for him/her in English for publication in your school's electronic bulletin. Not only is your time very limited, but also you know s/he is a weak writer both conceptually and in terms of language proficiency. You absolutely need to turn this one down without offending him/her. How do you do it?

Find someone who is a competent speaker of the language in that speech community and gather information from this person about refusals. Check with this informant as to some acceptable ways to perform each of the two refusals above, depending on who you are (age, status, gender, role in the relationship, and personal consequences of refusing) and who the recipient is.

Activity 12.2 Strategies for performing speech acts

Objectives

1   You will be able to identify the strategies that you use in performing a speech act.

2   You will be able to identify the strategies that others use for learning and performing speech acts.

Suggested time: 45 minutes.

Materials:

■   Task sheet, "Performing speech acts," with speech acts vignettes;

■   the "Strategies for Performing Speech Acts" section from the *Taxonomy of Learner Strategies for Acquiring Speech Acts* in this chapter.

Directions

1   Select one of the compliment or refusal vignettes provided on the Task sheet and perform it in the L2 with a competent L2 speaking partner.

2   While in the data collection phase, have the "Strategies for Performing Speech Acts" section of the *Taxonomy of Learner Strategies* handy and select strategies from it to assist you in completing the task. For example, see if you are able to use one or more monitoring strategies to determine how well you performed the speech act.

3   As you perform the speech act, pay attention to the strategies that you use to select and perform the act appropriately.

4   Also pay attention to the strategies that your partner uses.

5   When the speech acts interaction comes to a natural conclusion, share insights with each other regarding the interaction. Pay attention to what you might have learned about the interaction which you could pass on to your students regarding their efforts to use speech act material.

Discussion/wrap-up

Review the processes you went through in this activity. Consider the extent to which this exercise helped you to sharpen your understanding of the strategies involved in performing a speech act effectively. Also identify any challenges you encountered. How might you encourage your students to use these strategies in their future language learning?

Task sheet: Performing speech acts

Apologizing in an L2

(a) You need to report back to a friend about a limited edition of a book on the history of jazz in New Orleans that he lent you last week. It accidentally slipped out of your bag on the bus, and when you called the Lost and Found, they said no one had turned it in.

(b) You really enjoyed the meal that your colleague cooked for you and your spouse on Saturday night. It wasn't until the end of the next week that you remembered you hadn't thanked her properly for the evening. You come to her office to apologize for that oversight.

Complaining in an L2

(a) You go to a friend's party but are having difficulty staying there because there is so much smoking. The music is also a problem for you since you are sensitive to loud noise. You could just cut out but decide instead to stay because you like this friend, but you feel the need to complain to her about the excessive smoking and the decibel level of the music.

(b) You and your date have been waiting over 45 minutes for your meal to be served at a fancy downtown restaurant. You usually enjoy a leisurely meal, but this evening you have theater tickets and the show is going to start in less than an hour. You specifically chose this restaurant because the last time that you ate there, your meal came promptly. You feel the need to complain to the waiter about the excessive delay.

CHAPTER 13

Incorporating technology into pragmatics-focused instruction

Noriko Ishihara

Introduction

The use of technology can help teachers diversify their instruction in ways that greatly benefit their learners. There is a growing body of research which underscores the role of technology-assisted learning and teaching of L2 pragmatics, especially computer-mediated language learning.[1] Drawing on that research as a basis, this chapter reports on how various forms of technology can be applied to teachers' daily practices. We will also discuss application of different instructional technologies in terms of the levels of cognitive learning that these technologies are likely to promote. Teachers are encouraged to assess the availability of these technologies in their respective contexts, as well as the potential benefits for their learners considering, for example, their level of proficiency and learning style preferences. It is also important that when certain forms of technologies are applied to the classroom, both teachers and learners are comfortable with them and that there is sufficient technological support.

Viewing technology broadly, we will discuss the application of the following forms of technology to the teaching and learning of pragmatics:

- feature films and situational comedies;

- audio/video materials and other forms of visual support;

---

[1] See, for example, Belz (2007).

- online tools for creating language exercises; and
- computer-mediated communication (CMC) tools.

We now start by giving examples of how the above forms of technologies can be applied to formal instruction of L2 pragmatics.

The use of feature films and situational comedies

As many language teachers can attest, learners' level of motivation often rises when feature films, situational comedies, or other authentic media-based materials are introduced. The situational context, the high-interest content, and the rich visual imagery combine to provide learners with multi-sensory input that tends to be reasonably close to what we find in authentic interaction.[2] Although the language in these materials is scripted and often delivered with exaggerated gestures and actions, the dialogues in these sources are not written for instructional purposes (not written to match the grammar-focused syllabus, for example) and thus can provide a relatively authentic model for pragmatic language use in a particular subculture(s) of the L2 community. If selected carefully, video clips or full-length materials can be a suitable source of pragmatic models especially in foreign-language contexts where learners' authentic input might be limited.[3]

As the teaching of pragmatics is gaining greater popularity, it is now possible to find innovative ideas for using media-based materials at professional conferences and in practically oriented publications. Some of them are introduced in the following table, and those of you who are teacher readers are invited to add on to this list of sources for the language that you teach and for features of pragmatics beyond speech acts.

Areas of pragmatics taught	Materials used	Brief description
Apologies and requests in English[a]	*Annie Hall* (film)	Analysis of language forms and strategies of requests; discussion on the appropriateness of forms in relation to context
Requests in English[b]	*Few Good Men* (film)	Analysis of the forms of polite and impolite requests; follow-up discussion on style-shifting

[2] Arcario (1993); Martínez-Flor (2008).
[3] Eslami and Eslami-Resekh (2008); Rose (1994b); Martínez-Flor (2008).

Areas of pragmatics taught	Materials used	Brief description
Requests in Spanish[c]	La flor de mi secreto (The Flower of My Secret), La ardilla roja (The Red Squirrel) (films)	Analysis of a range of requests in Spanish in relation to various social contexts
Terms of address in English[d]	Tootsie (film)	Identification of terms of address; discussion on the social and interactional meaning behind those terms
Self-introduction routine in English[e]	Seinfeld (sitcom)	Analysis of limits and boundaries of speech routines; analysis of pragmatic violations and reactions invoked
Requests in English[f]	Seinfeld (sitcom)	Analysis of indirect requests (hints); follow-up discussion on how requests can be made differently across cultures
Requests in English[g]	Stargate (TV series)	Identification and analysis of direct and indirect requests; dialogue-writing; analysis of excerpts and awareness-raising; discourse completion tasks
Implicature in English[h]	Desperate Housewives (TV series)	Identification of implied meanings through facial expressions and the contexts

[a] Rose (1999: 178–80).
[b] Fujioka (2003: 13–14).
[c] Mir (2001) (written in Spanish). This article offers a specific technique for teaching pragmatics with film in Spanish and may be of particular interest to teachers of Spanish.
[d] Fujioka (2004: 17–19). For teaching terms of address, see also Takenoya (2003) and Howard (2008).
[e] Washburn (2001: 22–4).
[f] Rose (1997a: 9–10).
[g] Alcón (2005: 422–3).
[h] Armstrong (2008: 4–7).

Although experts generally approve the use of feature films in L2 pragmatics instruction, we should bear in mind that natural pragmatic uses are not always reflected in these materials. For example, studies comparing naturally occurring compliments with those in films and TV interviews have found both similarities and differences. While, for instance, the grammatical structures of compliments were similar in films and natural data, compliments in the media tended to more noticeably employ "inflated" adjectives (e.g., *stunning* or *fabulous* instead of *beautiful* or *nice*).[4] This seems to suggest that teachers should use their best judgment in selecting material to introduce to learners in terms of pragmatic representativeness and appropriateness. It would be best to ensure that learners' input is reasonably

[4] Rose (1997b, 2001); Tatsuki and Nishizawa (2005).

authentic; pragmatic behavior that is exaggerated or odd just to be entertaining is less likely to mirror authentic language use.

On the other hand, another strategy is to demonstrate pragmatic failure through media-based materials such as in situational comedies. Even though pragmatic violations may be exaggerated and do not necessarily reflect naturally occurring conversation, obvious pragmatic blunders and the reactions of studio audiences help learners to identify the limits of pragmatic norms in the L2 and provide them an opportunity to analyze the consequences of pragmatic violations.[5] In addition, teachers and learners can engage in critical reflection on how media-based materials may differ from real life, why that might be the case, and how potential disadvantages of media-based input might be compensated for in the learning of pragmatics.

Audio/video materials and other forms of visual support

Technology can be applied with relative ease to pragmatics-focused instruction in order to enhance the input and metapragmatic information (i.e., information about pragmatics, see Chapter 6) provided to learners. Audio- and video-recordings of sample dialogues, for example, are often used for the purpose of input enhancement. Auditory and visual features in recordings (as in audio and video podcasts and streaming videos) offer verbal and non-verbal information, which both affect the pragmatics of communication (e.g., intonation, pauses, hedges, gestures, facial expressions, and space). Many of the currently available materials focusing on pragmatics include either or both types of materials.[6] Depending on the learners' levels of proficiency, supplementing these audio/video materials (along with other media-based materials) with transcripts can be beneficial for learners. Teachers and learners themselves can also audio- or video-record pragmatic language use in order to provide models or facilitate evaluation of learners' pragmatic language use and self-reflection (see Chapters 3, 7, and 15 for examples of what to collect and how the collected data could be analyzed).

In addition, pragmatics instruction can also be enhanced through certain electronic functions that technology allows us to apply readily. Earlier in this book, we discussed the importance of "noticing" language form and "understanding" the form–context relationship – the role that relevant

---

[5] Washburn (2001).

[6] For example, see the lesson plans presented in *Teaching Pragmatics*, 2003, and *Pragmatics from Research to Practice: Teaching Speech Acts*, in press; and pragmatics-focused curricular materials in Japanese and Spanish (Ishihara and Cohen 2004; Sykes and Cohen 2006).

contextual features play in determining the form that the message actually takes (see Chapter 6).[7] For example, key features to learn in order to make a request in discourse include:

- the grammatical structures and word choice used to formulate the request;
- the pauses and hedging devices for mitigating the force of the request;
- the pre- and post-request strategies (such as *giving a reason for the request* and *thanking*); and
- adjusting for the relative social status of the speaker/writer and the listener/reader, the level of distance/closeness, and the severity of imposition of the request.

The first three constitute language, or the *form* of the request, and the last represents crucial contextual factors involved in the situation. In the learning of pragmatics, students are expected to notice how the context influences the choice of language forms (form–context relationship), as well as how the choice of language shapes the context at the same time. In fact, technology can be used to trigger learners' noticing by clearly differentiating important information from optional or extra resources. Various forms of input enhancement can be devised with relative ease, for example, through the use of **bold text**, *italics*, <u>underlining</u>, or the highlighting of key language features or contextual factors.[8] These crucial features can also be presented, for instance, in noticeable colors, with pictures (as in picture-enhanced DCT[9]), or in perceptible designs (such as captions on the screen[10]) to attract learners' attention. Although much research seems to indicate that the explicit teaching of pragmatics is more effective than an implicit approach, implicit techniques of input enhancement may also be successful.[11]

Online tools for creating language exercises

The use of instructional technology often gives a greater degree of independence to learners than conventional modes of instruction. The use of available technologies allows learners to progress at their own pace and may give more choices, for example, as to what materials they can study, the sequence that they study them in, how they practice language, and the sections that they decide to review. When they have independent learning options, learners

---

[7] Schmidt (2001).
[8] Derewianka (2003).
[9] As in Yamashita (2002).
[10] As used in Fukuya and Clark's (2001) intervention on request mitigators.
[11] Fukuya and Clark (2001); Martínez-Flor and Fukuya (2005); Rose (2005).

may be more likely to link to what attracts their attention and interest, rather than proceeding linearly through material in the order that it is presented. Currently available web-based instructional tools enable teachers to quite easily provide self-study exercises, learner-directed feedback, optional tasks, and linguistic and cultural scaffolding built into the material. Learners are free to use or ignore such scaffolding and extra information available.

Let us start by taking some rather simple but teacher-friendly web-based exercises as examples. What can awareness-raising exercises for pragmatics look like? Here are some types of exercises that can be prepared through the use of instructional software programs. The first six use templates available by downloading the free software, *Hot Potatoes*,[12] the seventh utilizes other online tools,[13] and the last a webpage editor, *Dreamweaver*:[14]

1 multiple-choice exercises;

2 cloze (fill-in-the-gap) exercises;

3 close exercises with drop-down descriptors;

4 jumble-sentence exercises;

5 matching exercises;

6 ordering exercises with drop-down descriptors;

7 mind-mapping exercises;

8 "Form Mail" exercises.

Figures 13.1 to 13.3 contain a few examples of actual learner exercises available online.[15]

Multiple-choice exercises

This multiple-choice item is intended to enhance learners' pragmatic awareness by addressing comprehension of several request expressions. On the page in Figure 13.1, the imagined situation takes place in a convenience store, where a male stranger about 10 years your senior puts his bag on top of your document file (as in the webpage photo). So, you ask him to move

[12] Examples of the first six exercises can be viewed from the *Hot Potatoes* Tutorial link: http://hotpot.uvic.ca/wintutor6/index.htm, accessed on December 10, 2009.
[13] Mind-mapping tools allow electronic visualization of concept mapping, which may be useful for organizing word choice or pragmatic strategies (see Activity 13.2, below, for links of some of these programs).
[14] While the "form mail" exercises introduced here were developed through *Dreamweaver*, other less expensive and perhaps more user-friendly webpage editors are now available, such as *SeaMonkey* and *Adobe Contribute*.
[15] See Chapter 11 or Ishihara and Cohen (2004: available online) for more examples.

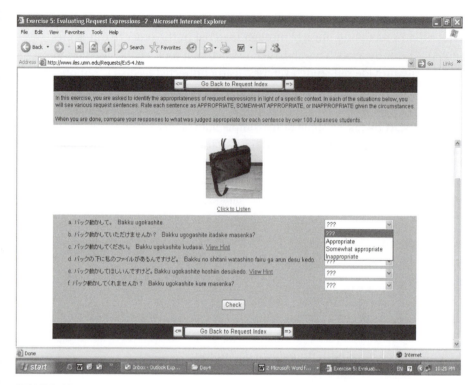

FIGURE 13.1

it so you can get at your file. Learners are to judge the level of appropriateness of six request expressions (i.e., *appropriate, somewhat appropriate,* or *inappropriate*), using the pull-down descriptors. The situation and the answer are based on a research study with 100 Japanese university students.[16] With the use of the technology that the program *Hot Potatoes* allows, learners are able to listen to audio samples representing each request and to view hints if they wish. The visual image facilitates the learners' ability to envision the situation. Learners can also check their responses on the spot by clicking on the "check" button and come back to this item later as they wish.

Matching exercises

This sample item (Figure 13.2) is from a unit on learning refusals in Japanese. The exercise functions as a review of various refusal strategies that have been identified through empirical research.[17] Learners read and/or listen to refusal expressions given in the left column and match them with the semantic

[16] Rinnert and Kobayashi (1999).
[17] For example, Beebe *et al.* (1990).

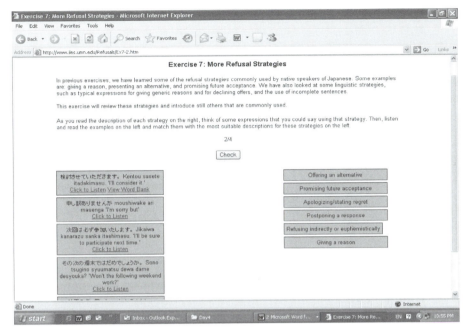

FIGURE 13.2

descriptions in the right column by physically moving them. This particular exercise consists of four items with increasing difficulty, with more strategies added as the exercise progresses. Technology makes this exercise highly kinesthetic and interactive, allowing immediate feedback – when learners click on the "check" button, inaccurate matches move back to their original places and learners are shown their score. As in the multiple-choice item introduced above, learners are able to get help with the vocabulary if desired. The last item in this exercise has a link to a summary of possible strategies, with multiple examples for each category. Web-based exercises like these (1–6 above) can be developed by the software program *Hot Potatoes*, which is downloadable free of charge from http://hotpot.uvic.ca/index.htm.

"Form Mail" exercises

"Form Mail" is another type of program that sends learner responses to e-mail addresses that have been pre-programmed, such as those of the instructor or of the curriculum writer. This program allows for the generation and assessment of a textual response as shown above. Learners can be asked to analyze a sample dialogue (just like in the example in Figure 13.3), produce the target language in imagined dialogues, or compare and contrast

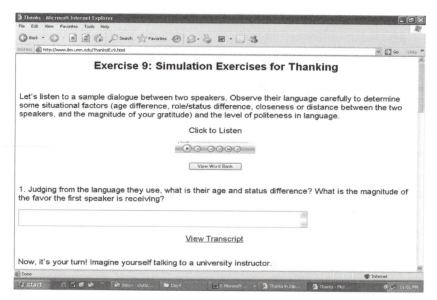

FIGURE 13.3

their own language production with language use in sample dialogues. Again, technology allows learners to access multiple forms of scaffolding along the way, such as vocabulary help, transcripts of audio dialogues, and hints providing learners with some clues. When learners complete their responses, they click on the "submit" button, which sends them to a new page with immediate pre-programmed feedback. Although this feedback is not individualized, research-based information about relevant pragmatic features is summarized on these web pages.

Computer-mediated communication (CMC) tools

As we have seen, pragmatic aspects of language can be underscored and practiced through the use of computer mediation. *Computer-mediated communication* (CMC) as it relates to pragmatic use of language and development has been gaining increased attention in the research literature.[18] Learners' pragmatic language use can be observed or practiced through various forms of CMC such as:

- e-mail;
- blogs;

---

[18] See, for example, Belz (2007) for a summary of research on the role of technology-assisted learning and teaching of L2 pragmatics.

- educational discussion forums or collaboration tools (e.g., as in *Blackboard, Moodle,* or *Wikis*);
- written and voice chat (e.g., *Wimba*);
- video-conferencing (e.g., *Skype*); and
- gaming and virtual interaction (e.g., *Second Life*).

E-mail, blogs, and educational discussion forums provide asynchronous (i.e., non-concurrent) internet communication tools. Users of these tools can create or edit content at their convenience. Continued discussion about different topics can be organized under different "threads" or under e-mail subject lines and develop over multiple turns in the form of messages or online postings. Because the record of interaction can be readily saved in personal in-boxes or online, one way of using these technologies is for learners to utilize the data as language input to analyze or employ as models. Language data in blogs or threaded discussion may contain a wealth of language samples (for example, the use of the discourse marker, *actually,* and learners can analyze ways to correct or contradict others' contributions[19]). In another case, these communication tools can be used between learners and the teacher where learners generate data for teachers, themselves, and peers to assess later. For example, learners can be asked to send an e-mail inquiry to the teacher (preferably a genuine one), which the teacher compiles for group assessment and improvement.[20] In another case, the teacher can collect authentic e-mail models, such as those from students asking for a letter of recommendation, for use as the basis of instruction.[21]

Even more interactive are synchronous (i.e., real time) written and voice chat and video-conferencing programs that can engage learners in more extended and concurrent interaction. In these types of prolonged interactive sessions, learners are able to negotiate meaning real-time on the internet. If they are using a video-conferencing program, they are also involved in the use of nonverbal communication, such as gestures. Although it may be possible to integrate some specific pragmatics-oriented tasks (e.g., observe and practice backchannelling in the target language), much of this type of interaction may go beyond the control of the teacher and the learners themselves. There may not even be a preestablished curriculum in authentic synchronous interactions, such as those using chat programs, where learners freely and independently interact with other speakers of the target language.

[19] See Barsony (2003) for a classroom-based lesson on this topic.
[20] See Mach and Ridder (2003) for more instructional details, rationale, and caveats.
[21] See Akikawa and Ishihara (in press) for a classroom-based lesson on this topic.

One way to structure the learning of pragmatics mediated by e-mail, blogs, discussion forums, chat, or video-conferencing programs may be to give learners metapragmatic tasks (i.e., tasks explicitly about pragmatics) such as the following:

- collecting samples of pragmatic language use from competent speakers of the target language by going through the record of the interaction (e.g., the use of the discourse marker *actually* in online chat interaction);

- observing authentic pragmatic language use in communication (e.g., openings and closings in e-mail messages, agreement and disagreement in blogs, or video-conferencing, or humor employed by the conversation partner in voice chat);

- interviewing competent speakers of the target language regarding their use or perception of a speech act (e.g., occasions at which compliments are given or avoided, the appropriateness of complimenting on the given topic, and the choice of recipient for the compliment – whether by e-mail, chat, or video-conferencing); and

- exchanging analyses with others of pragmatics-focused observations or interviews (e.g., reporting on the examples of cynicism and the implications, or exchanging analysis of how humor might be different in L1 and L2 in educational discussion forums).

These tasks could also be pursued in face-to-face communication alone or in combination with computer-mediated technologies especially in the **second-language** settings where learners generally have relatively frequent access to other target-language speakers (see Chapter 7 for examples). It should be noted that in CMC, there may be media-specific norms, and certain pragmatic uses may be different in face-to-face interactions.[22]

Telecollaboration utilizing chat and video-conferencing programs, for example, offers language learners real-time opportunities to interact with other target language speakers for both educational and entertainment purposes over the internet. Not only does it provide increased opportunities for input, output, and interaction for language learning in extended meaningful discourse, but it can also be an authentic vehicle for intercultural communication.[23] Synchronous tools can be used in conjunction with asynchronous technologies (such as e-mail) and can enable learners to engage in extended dialogues with other target language speakers, such as

[22] See for example, Zitzen and Stein (2004) for similarities and differences between chat and oral language.
[23] Belz (2007).

pragmatically competent speakers or learners of the same target language in another culture. Language instruction utilizing telecollaborative tools often involves engaging cross-cultural discussion about current topics and explicit pragmatics instruction such as the following:

- the use of formal and informal personal pronouns (e.g., T/V forms in French and German[24] and T/S forms in Spanish[25]);
- other terms of address (e.g., Jane, Ms Doe, Professor Doe, Dr Doe);[26]
- active listening and backchannelling;[27] and
- use of discourse markers (e.g., *oh* and *well*).[28]

Because telecollaboration can offer authentic intercultural opportunities and engaging interaction over an extended period of time, participants may be better prepared if they have, ahead of time, some intercultural skills training or awareness-raising, for example, about cross-cultural perspective taking or critical evaluation of one's culture.[29]

In another form of CMC, gaming and virtual interaction, learners assume an imagined identity represented visually in the form of an *avatar* in electronic three-dimensional space, where they interact with other virtual characters verbally and non-verbally (e.g., through hand gestures and body language). Possible advantages in this electronic interaction include that learners can participate individually at their own pace, enact multiple roles and identities if they wish, and enjoy multimodal processing.[30] Due to the lower risk of real-life consequences of their pragmatic language use in this virtual environment, learners can practice and experiment L2 pragmatics without running a high risk. Learners may enjoy such virtual interactions, participate actively, and report perceived development of their L2 pragmatic ability, although the pedagogical role of this type of instruction still needs to be further examined.[31]

Thus far, we have discussed the potentials of various technologies that can mediate the learning and teaching of pragmatics, along with some

[24] See Belz and Kinginger (2002) for a learner's use of these personal pronouns in telecollaborative interactions extended over 50 days.

[25] See González-Lloret (2008) for Spanish learners' development of the use of T/S pronouns in synchronous telecollaborative interactions over 10 weeks.

[26] See Takenoya (2003) for an EFL lesson on the terms of address, which may be integrated into language instruction involving telecollaboration.

[27] See Berry (2003) and Gallow (2003) for lessons on active listening.

[28] See Lee (2003) for lessons for teaching these discourse markers.

[29] Also see Schneider and von der Emde (2006) for dialogic conflict management.

[30] Sykes (2008).

[31] Beltz (2007). See also Sykes (2008) for empirical investigation of pragmatics-focused intervention in the synthetic immersion environment.

possible ways to apply them to pragmatics-focused instruction. These technologies can be employed alone or in combination to maximize their benefits and compensate for shortcomings. In the following section, we will examine how these technologies can help activate different levels of cognitive learning in order to stimulate learners' higher-order thinking.

Instructional technologies and learner cognition

Let us now consider a range of task types that may be more or less appropriate for CMC or other forms of technology-assisted language learning. Although technology may facilitate the learning of pragmatics, not all tasks are equally amenable to delivery with a certain form of technology. In order to analyze task characteristics in terms of the levels of cognitive demand, the well-known Bloom's taxonomy may be useful (Figure 13.4).

Bloom classifies levels of intellectual behavior in the cognitive domain into six categories: *knowledge, comprehension, application, analysis, synthesis,* and *evaluation.*[32] The lowest cognitive domain, *knowledge,* can be exemplified by simple recall or recognition of facts. The second level, *comprehension,* is still considered a lower-level cognitive activity requiring learners to understand the material and able to interpret it on their own, as demonstrated, for example, through translation, restatement, and exemplification. The other categories, *application, analysis, synthesis,* and *evaluation,* represent higher levels of cognitive learning, requiring greater cognitive demands. *Application* involves using newly acquired information or skills in a new situation, while *analysis* constitutes an investigation of the components and the organizational structure. *Synthesis* and *evaluation*

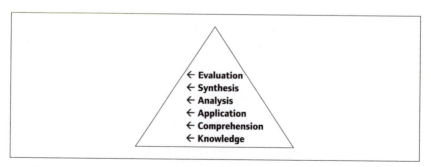

FIGURE 13.4 Bloom's taxonomy of cognitive learning

---

[32] Bloom (1956).

call for higher-order thinking at abstract levels. At the cognitive level of *synthesis*, learners put various components of language or ideas together to construct a new sentence or stretch of discourse. At the level of *evaluation*, learners assess the value or quality of the material (see the "information" at the end of Activity 13.1, below, for explanations, sample tasks for pragmatics instruction, and key words to prompt such tasks in those categories). As with any area of learning, it is important to diversify our task demands in pragmatics-focused instruction in order to activate various levels of cognition on the part of our learners.

What tasks and cognitive levels can best be developed through technology-mediated learning? The answer depends largely on what teachers want learners to become able to do and which technology is selected for use. For example, simple retention of vocabulary words and their meanings may be accomplished effectively through electronic exercises where there is one-to-one correspondence between a question and a "correct" answer. Learners can effectively use computerized exercises to acquire certain bits of knowledge and check comprehension or retention of that knowledge at lower cognitive levels. For instruction about pragmatics, this level of learning may involve the learning of formulaic expressions and developing automaticity in producing them. If available technology allows for communication among learners (as chat, video-conferencing programs, and instructional discussion tools do), then learners can engage in more meaningful discussion, for example, as to the observed norms of the target culture. This would require higher-order cognitive skills, such as *analysis, synthesis* and *evaluation* in Bloom's taxonomy mentioned above.

Discussion

In this chapter, we have viewed technology broadly and have discussed potential application of various forms of technology to pragmatics-focused learning and teaching. We have first looked at potentials of feature film, situational comedies, and other media-based material conducive to the learning of pragmatics. We have also discussed the use of audio and video materials, as well as other forms of visual support that computers make it possible to include with relative ease. We have also discussed online exercise makers and CMC tools, their pedagogical advantages, and sample tasks or areas of L2 pragmatics that may be amenable to teaching through those media. Finally, using Bloom's taxonomy of cognitive learning, we have considered different levels of cognitive demands. Learners can take advantage of online exercises not only to practice and acquire lower-level skills while working individually, but also to obtain feedback from the teacher or curriculum writer and use higher-order thinking to engage in discussion, self-reflection, and evaluation. Authentic interaction through telecollaboration can activate learners' critical thinking when they are given tasks that require higher cognitive levels of *application, analysis, synthesis, and evaluation.*

The first activity below provides teacher readers an opportunity to brainstorm about the various forms of technology that may best facilitate tasks at different levels of cognition. This activity is designed to help teachers when they have certain pragmatics-oriented tasks in mind and wish to identify suitable forms of technology for them. The second activity offers a hands-on experience where teachers are encouraged to explore possible technologies for creating instructional tasks suitable for the given classroom situation.

Fortunately, a variety of technologies are becoming more reliably available primarily through computer mediation so that learners have multi-sensory input and authentic interaction in extended discourse. On the flip side, technological glitches may crop up and hinder effective operation of the program, or may even deny access to what is otherwise conveniently available. Technological failure can frustrate or completely demotivate learners. Teachers need to ensure on an ongoing basis that learners have access to appropriate equipment and that there is an adequate technological support system.

Activity 13.1 Levels of cognitive demand and computer-mediated learning of pragmatics

Objectives

1   You will be able to analyze pragmatics-focused tasks in terms of their levels of cognitive demand.

2   You will be able to identify suitable form(s) of technology for pragmatics-focused tasks at different cognitive levels.

Suggested time: 20 minutes.

Materials:

1   Information: "Bloom's taxonomy of cognitive learning";

2   Task sheet: "Different tasks, different technologies".

Directions

1   In groups of approximately four, (re)familiarize yourselves with Bloom's taxonomy using the given information.

2   Go to the task sheet. For each cognitive level, there is an example of pragmatics-focused tasks representing that level of cognitive demand. In your group, determine the forms of technology that appear to be most compatible with each task and discuss why they seem most suitable.

3   Share your ideas with the whole group.

Discussion/wrap-up

While some tasks are perfectly appropriate for CMC tools, others may be better delivered through other types of technology even though they are not "cutting-edge." This activity is designed to help diversify your classroom tasks in terms of their cognitive demands and to develop a repertoire of technologies conducive to your students' learning. You would then choose the best media in light of the characteristics and availability of those technologies.

Information: Bloom's taxonomy of cognitive learning[33]

Cognitive levels	Sample tasks for L2 pragmatics and key words
Knowledge Identification or recall of certain information.	**Sample tasks**: identify three examples of discourse markers in the dialogue. **Key words**: define, describe, identify, know, label, list, match, name.
Comprehension Understand the meaning, translation, and interpretation of the material.	**Sample task**: explain in your own words what Speaker A really means when he says X. **Key words**: explain, give examples, infer, interpret, paraphrase, rewrite, translate.
Application Use a newly learned concept in a novel situation.	**Sample task**: review the softening strategies used in making requests, and predict how they apply when you refuse a friend's invitation to her birthday party. **Key words**: apply, demonstrate, relate, predict, modify, prepare.

---

[33] Adapted from Clark (2001: available online).

Cognitive levels	Sample tasks for L2 pragmatics and key words
Analysis Separate the whole into component parts so that its structure or the relationship of cause and effect may be understood.	**Sample task**: analyze the reason why you think Speaker A used language X rather than language Y. (In doing this, consider the relationship between Speakers A and B and the situation they were in.) **Key words**: analyze, break down, compare, contrast, diagram, distinguish, outline, relate, select, separate.
Synthesis Build a new structure from multiple elements. Put parts together to form a new whole.	**Sample task**: imagine two people speaking to each other on the phone and construct a skit. Make sure that what you have learned about opening and closing conversation is reflected in your dialogue. **Key words**: combine, compile, compose, design, organize, plan, summarize.
Evaluation Make value judgments about the material.	**Sample task**: using the rubric below, evaluate your own language of apologies. **Key words**: appraise, critique, conclude, evaluate, assess.

Task Sheet: Different tasks, different technologies

Cognitive levels	Examples of pragmatic tasks	Form(s) of technology
Knowledge	From the word bank given below, choose five most appropriate adjectives for praising your friend's new car.	
Comprehension	In this video clip, in response to his friend's question, Bob says, "Is the Pope Catholic?" What does he actually mean? Choose the one that is closest in meaning.	
Application	So far we have observed how English speakers use hesitation in conversation and what hedging expressions they use. Now let's practice using them in dialogue.	
Analysis	Listen to a dialogue and guess who is speaking. What is their relationship? What is the level of formality of the situation? Why do you think so?	
Synthesis	In a small group, choose a social topic of your interest from below and discuss it. Try to use appropriately the discourse markers that we have been studying.	
Evaluation	Look at your classmate's work and give feedback using the given rubric. How would the listener most likely understand your classmate's intention?	

Activity 13.2 Experimenting with technology-assisted material

Objectives

1   You will be able to identify a form of technology that is suitable for your chosen pragmatics-focused task.

2   You will be able to develop technology-assisted material for pragmatics-focused learning, test them, and reflect on its effectiveness.

Suggested time: initially 30 minutes and then more as needed.

Materials:

■   Information, "List of technological resources";

■   a pragmatics-focused task of the participants' choice;

■   internet access.

Directions:

1   Individually or in a small group, identify a form of technology that is suitable for your chosen pragmatics-focused task.

2   Use the information, "List of technological resources" and create a technology-assisted task for your selected group of students.

3   Get together with another group and exchange the exercise you have just developed. Test the other group's web exercises and share your observations with them.

4   Share the descriptions of the exercise you created and the ensuing discussion with the whole group.

5   Test the material out with your own students and reflect on their learning and reactions.

Discussion/wrap-up

The challenge is to select media of instruction that are realistic and appropriate in terms of the task demand, instructional context, and your students' readiness for technology. In developing the materials, try to envision the problems that your students might face. What are some possible solutions for those problems? What are some advantages of delivering your task through the medium that you select?

Information: List of technological resources

This is a starting list of technologies potentially useful for your classroom. You are invited to update and add more entries.[34]

1   Feature films and sit-coms:

- http://www.simplyscripts.com/ (over 1,000 downloadable film scripts);

- http://www.seinfeldscripts.com/ (*Seinfeld* scripts for 180 episodes from nine seasons).

2   Audio- and video-recording of sample dialogues, class instructions, and students' interactions:

- http://www.youtube.com/;

- http://audacity.sourceforge.net/;

- http://www.wimba.com/products/wimbavoice/[35].

3   Online exercise-making tools:

- http://hotpot.uvic.ca/ (*Hot Potatoes*, see above for examples);

- http://trackstar.4teachers.org/trackstar/;

- http://languagecenter.cla.umn.edu/index.php?page=makers;

- http://www.seamonkey-project.org/ (web-editor);

- http://www.thebrain.com/; http://www.visual-mind.com/index.php (mind-mapping tools).

4   Online classroom tools and wikis:

- www.moodle.org;

- www.blackboard.com/us/index.bbb;

- *tappedin.org/tappedin* (K-12-oriented discussion tools and private text chatrooms);

- http://pbwiki.com/;

- http://calper.la.psu.edu/tools.php (chat, blog, and wiki hosting for educators).

---

[34] All the web links listed here were accessed on December 10, 2009.

[35] Although *Wimba* has been gaining popularity in US higher education, it is at present a rather expensive software program and must be licensed by an institution.

5 Blogs:

- https://www.blogger.com/start;
- http://www.typepad.com/;
- http://edublogs.org/ (blogging for teachers and students).

6 Chat and video-conferencing programs:

- http://messenger.yahoo.com/features/chatrooms;
- http://www.skype.com/;
- http://flashmeeting.e2bn.net/index.html (video-conferencing for use in schools).

7 Gaming and virtual interaction:

- http://secondlife.com/;
- http://www.worldofwarcraft.com;
- http://www.activeworlds.com/.

CHAPTER 14

Approaches to assessing pragmatic ability

Andrew D. Cohen

Why assess pragmatics in the classroom?

Tests of pragmatic ability have not tended to find their way into the classroom. Even recently, the view has been expressed that before classroom assessment of pragmatics can be implemented, there is first a need to further develop theories of communicative competence and communicative language teaching and a commensurate need to conduct more empirical investigations.[1] In our view, the need for more theoretical development and empirical investigation is not a reason for avoiding classroom assessment of pragmatics, especially given its demonstrable value. So let us consider why:

1   Classroom assessment of pragmatics sends a message to the students that their ability to be pragmatically appropriate in the comprehension and production of language in different sociocultural situations is valued or even advantageous.

2   The very act of putting such items on a test gives the students an incentive to study L2 pragmatics.

3   Assessment gives teachers an opportunity to see the relative control their students have in what may at times be a high-stakes area for L2 performance (e.g., getting or holding a job).

4   It gives teachers an opportunity to check on whether learners have learned what they explicitly taught them.

While there should be a good fit between what is taught and what is assessed, in practice it does not always work that way since some of the most

[1] Yamashita (2008: 209).

interesting things that are taught do not lend themselves to easy assessment. To make this more concrete, take the speech act of apologizing. How do we determine a standard for appropriateness? Is it what natives do or are supposed to do? Is it not possible that natives will not necessarily get it right, as in the case, say, of a husband's half-hearted apology to his wife that fails to appease her? For example, supposing the husband performs the act in a slightly facetious tone of voice (Figure 14.1), his wife may not feel appeased, as in the following:

> Husband (*facetiously*): Sorry about that, dear.
>
> Wife: Well, I'm still upset!

But if the husband were to apologize with a sincere tone, and with the strategy of accepting responsibility as well, it might well be better received:

> Husband: I'm really sorry about that, darling. That was really insensitive of me.
>
> Wife: Thanks. I accept your apology, dear.

What could be difficult to assess is the sincerity of the apology, especially if the speaker uses a facetious tone in its delivery. If the apology is delivered in a straightforward way, as in the last example, then the assessment would presumably be easier to perform.

So, pragmatic ability is challenging to measure. For one thing, there is a need to provide students with adequate context since an appropriate answer

FIGURE 14.1 Apology that fails

is likely to be dependent on the situation. And on what basis are scores assigned to performance? Depending on the situation, even highly competent speakers of the given language may vary enough in their responses so that it is not clear what an acceptable or unacceptable answer would be.[2] Consequently, keeping the test practical in administration and scoring may not be easy. For example, role-plays take time to conduct and may require multiple ratings. In addition, they are difficult to standardize if every conversation is truly co-constructed by the given participants. Also, constructing a discourse completion test (DCT) can be a challenge.[3] Thus, it can take creativity to design instruments that test pragmatics reliably and without expending an excess of time and effort.[4]

Despite the challenges posed by attempting to assess complex L2 pragmatic behavior, there are enough tendencies or preferred approaches among native or near-native speakers of the language to warrant both teaching these to learners and assessing their performance. There are, in fact, benefits to including pragmatics among those language features that are assessed, especially if we focus on areas of pragmatics that bring into contrast key differences between two language communities. The emphasis in teaching would be on situations where divergence from the native-like norm in performance may lead to *pragmatic failure* – namely, when the uptake from the speech act interaction is not what the speaker desired (usually because the speech act somehow violated the norms of the community; see Chapter 5).

If you as teacher readers accept that pragmatics has an important role to play, then we can underscore that position by being sure to include its assessment in both short quizzes and longer tests. As indicated above, learners tend to pay extra attention to what they are going to be tested on. So let us say, for example, that a teacher of Japanese provides instruction on how to complain effectively in Japanese (e.g., a customer to a sales clerk about the slow service in the store). It would then be useful to test for the students' ability to perceive and produce such complaints. In this chapter, we will explore some principles for constructing tasks that elicit and, to some extent, assess learners' pragmatic comprehension and production.[5] Chapter 15 will provide practical examples of classroom-based instruments, with more in-depth attention to how classroom teachers might evaluate learners' pragmatic receptive and productive skills and give feedback to learners.

[2] See McNamara and Roever (2006).
[3] See McNamara and Roever (2006: 54–75).
[4] Roever (2004).
[5] For more on assessment of pragmatics as a research tool, see Cohen (2004); Roever (2004).

Approaches to assessing performance of L2 speech acts

In this section we will look both at how to elicit speech act performance and also how to evaluate the students' responses once they have been elicited. A prime concern is making sure, if you are teacher readers, that your students understand the situations in which pragmatic performance is being assessed. It may be appropriate, for example, to describe the situation in your students' L1 or dominant language, in order to make sure that they fully understand the contextual factors involved, especially if they are in a **foreign-** rather than a **second-language** context. Such factors might include among other things:

1 the degree of imposition in a request or the severity of the infraction in an apology situation;

2 the level of acquaintance between the speaker and listener; and

3 their relative social status.

Measuring comprehension of speech acts

Assessment of pragmatics looks both at comprehension and production. Measuring *comprehension* of the pragmatics in language behavior often takes an indirect, metapragmatic approach. Learners are asked to assess how well they **think** someone else has performed pragmatically. So, for example, assessment could entail looking at learners' reactions to videotaped role-play, screen plays (from a TV series), or written descriptions of speech acts situations. The learners indicate their reactions by completing rating scales or multiple-choice items. Returning to the issue of marital relations, let us suppose that the students viewed a video clip which had the following exchange between a husband and wife:

> Wife: Darling, I don't like it when you criticize our children in front of other people. I was really annoyed last evening when you made cracks about them at the dinner party. I realize it was your effort to be amusing, but people can take it the wrong way, and . . .
>
> Husband: Really? I don't think so. In fact, I think you're overreacting – it's not such a big deal. But if you insist, I'm willing to watch what I say. . . .

A sample item could include the following:

> Indicate with an X how you would rate the level of the husband's apology:
>
> 1 High ____
>
> 2 Moderate ____
>
> 3 Low _X_
>
> 4 Non-existent ____

In addition, learners of the particular target language (in this case, English) could be asked to add their rationale for giving a certain rating. So in the above example, a given learner might add, "It isn't apologetic enough. The tone is sarcastic and like criticizing his wife. It isn't clear that he will actually change his behavior." This would serve as a good response.

Learners may have differing reactions, many of which could prompt interesting class discussion. If the focus is on the likely effect of the speaker's/writer's delivery of a speech act on the listener/reader (i.e., the *uptake*), then we could start by assessing how the speech act is perceived by the learner. The following is a sample vignette where the students are to respond both in a multiple-choice format and by also providing an open-ended comment as well:

> Amir is doing his holiday shopping in Manhattan and has only about 15 minutes before the department store closes. He needs to get across the entire store to the opposite corner to check out the gift specials at the women's perfume counter, but in front of him is a stout lady with bags in hand. She is in the midst of a heated conversation on her cell phone and is blatantly blocking the aisle. Amir tries desperately to get around her, but in the process inadvertently knocks over some of her bags, tangles up her cell-phone arm, and causes the lady to drop her phone as well.
>
> Lady: My goodness! What are you doing, young man?!
>
> Amir: Very sorry, lady, but you were in my way!
>
> How likely is the stout lady to consider Amir's response an apology?

(a) Very likely.

(b) Somewhat likely.

(c) Not very likely.

What is your rationale for your choice?_____

_____

Some students may have learned that the intensifier "really" in an apology signals regret and that "very" is more a marker of etiquette. If so, this would help signal to them that (c) is the correct multiple-choice response. But actually, in this case, the speech act-specific strategy, "acknowledgement of responsibility," is the key concern here. A preferred rationale statement would be as follows:

Amir isn't really taking responsibility for knocking into the lady. He's putting the blame back on her.

In cases where the students all share the same L1 and the teacher knows that language, then students could make their rationale statements in that L1 if it allowed them more thoughtful analysis.

Tasks like this one would be intended to tap learners' understanding of speech act performance by others, and in this case, the added ingredient of annoyance or sarcasm. Sometimes the identification of the speech act is not so challenging, but its function in the interaction can depend on the tone or attitude of the person who delivers it.

Assessment of the ability to comprehend pragmatics could also entail measuring it directly. For example, teachers could construct some items for their learners which have pragmatic input that is perhaps subtle in nature (e.g., veiled criticism about a talk the person just gave or a complaint about the person's working style). The intent would be to see if the learners understand the intention of the message and are able to comprehend it in an appropriate way pragmatically.

It would also be possible for learners to be asked to do self-assessment, much as they would assess someone else's pragmatics (see Chapters 7 and 15 for more on self-assessment). The problem with this is that learners may not be as good at rating how well they comprehend their own pragmatic performance as they are at rating how someone else comprehends their performance. They may find in rating their own comprehension that it is perhaps too familiar to them to analyze properly. In other words, they would have an insider's angle on what they intended by what they said, which is not the case when they are assessing their comprehension of someone else's pragmatic performance.

Measuring speech acts production

Oral role-play

Under ideal circumstances, it would be nice to have samples of students' pragmatic performance in non-elicited situations, both in and out of the classroom. In terms of out-of-class data, it might be possible to have students record themselves, perhaps as part of a speaking portfolio that they establish and add to over a period of time (e.g., a semester, in the case of college students). One problem with collecting impromptu data in class is that some students say more than others. In addition, they may not use the pragmatic structures that are the focus of assessment. So teachers may have little alternative but to elicit the L2 pragmatics performance that is the target of the assessment.

In order to "bias for best" in the elicitation process,[6] you may wish to give your students some warm-up time, rather than to assume that they are ready to perform pragmatically on demand. Their minds may need to get going in the target language first. Warm-up can be done in several ways. One way is for you to give students a chance to rehearse what it is they will need to say or write. If it is to be oral, they could even be given time to rehearse it with a partner. You may wish to set up role-play situations, such as the following:

> You completely forget a crucial meeting at the office with the boss at your new job. An hour later you show up at his office to apologize. The problem is that this is the second time you've forgotten such a meeting in the short time you have been working at this job. Your boss is clearly annoyed when he asks, "What happened to you this time?" Do your best to smooth over the situation.

[6] Swain (1984).

The sociocultural factors of interest in measuring pragmatic ability, such as in a role-play like this, often include the following:

- the relative status of the speaker and listener;
- the level of acquaintance of the speaker and listener;
- the degree of severity, imposition, or other impact caused by the situation.

In this case, the speaker is clearly of lower status in being an employee. Since it is a relatively new job, the speaker is probably not that acquainted with the boss. The meeting was crucial so the severity level is high. The responses in such role-play situations could be rated for:

- the ability to use an appropriate speech act;
- the typicality of the expressions used;
- the appropriateness of the amount of speech and information given; and
- the appropriateness of the level of formality, the directness, and the level of politeness.

So let us say the response from a learner of English looks like this:

> Very sorry, Mr Peterson. You see . . . uh . . . I have sleeping problems and . . . uh . . . then I missed the bus. But I can make it up to you.

In this instance, the speaker has apologized using the strategies of expressing an apology, giving an explanation, and offering repair. So three of the key apology strategies were used. Nonetheless, it is likely that pragmatically-competent speakers of American English would not state the explanation and the offer of repair in such a cursory way. They would probably say something more like the following:

> Oh, I'm really sorry about that, Mr Peterson. I've been suffering from chronic sleep disorder and as a result I have trouble getting going in the morning. I can get you a doctor's note about it. And to make matters worse this morning, I got to the bus stop just as the bus was pulling away. I'm really sorry about that. What can I do to make it up to you? I'll work overtime, whatever.

Let us assume that the excuse here is legitimate, both with regard to the sleeping disorder and the missed bus. A sympathetic boss in a US company would probably accept it, especially with a doctor's note. Notice that the more pragmatically preferred performance in this speech community would probably entail including some details about the actual health problem (e.g., giving it a label) and of what happened with the bus. In addition, such performance would also probably include suggested ways to make it up to the boss, such as by working overtime. (See Chapter 15 for a sample rubric that can be directly used for classroom assessment.)

Here is another possible response from an L2-speaking office worker:

> So sorry I missed the meeting. I had problem at home and then I forgot the meeting and when I remembered it was too late.

In this instance, the worker expresses an apology, gives an explanation, and acknowledges responsibility. As in the previous response by a learner, the speaker used three apology strategies. Is the response apologetic enough? Would most highly fluent English speakers express the apology that way? Would the boss accept it? In this instance, a boss might respond as follows:

> Oh, sorry to hear that there was a problem at home. I hope you were able to resolve it. And you know, Wu, this has happened before. I get that you mean well, but you need a better system for keeping track of your meetings.

The number of strategies called for in performing a given speech act will vary according to the situation and speech community. For example, the strategy of "expressing an apology" may be sufficient for setting things right in an e-mail exchange with a colleague in a US academic institution: "I'm really sorry for that inappropriate e-mail I sent you." Likewise, the strategy of offering an explanation or an excuse, "The bus was late," when an employee arrives late for a meeting in Israel, may be accepted by the boss as sufficiently apologetic, since busses can be late there and consequently employees are only partially responsible for getting to meetings on time.

APPROACHES TO ASSESSING PRAGMATIC ABILITY   273

The following are two further examples of oral role-play prompts. Here is the first:

> Your next-door neighbor keeps his dog out on his porch well into the evening and the barking is driving you crazy. Role-play the part of the irate tenant who knocks on the neighbor's door and requests that the dog be kept inside at night. Your partner will play the role of the partially deaf, elderly neighbor, who wants to keep this dog happy since it was the pride and joy of her deceased husband.
>
> Elderly neighbor: Well, hello, _____. What can I do for you?
> You:
>
> The neighbor:
>
> You:

Here is the second:

> You promised your friend that you'd get tickets in advance for a special showing of a movie but forgot, and now the show is sold out.
>
> Classmate: What a bummer! I really wanted to see that movie this evening. I was supposed to report on it in film class tomorrow.
> You:

The first situation calls for being tactful and understanding, while making the need for quiet very clear. Presumably the L2 course has introduced tactful requests, and the rating here would be for the ability to make a polite request (assuming the learners want to present themselves as polite). The second situation calls for a profuse apology, and a convincing one. The offer of repair here may be crucial (e.g., offering to drive the classmate to a more distant theater where tickets are still available). Open-ended speech production in situations like these requires that the learners perform a sometimes challenging search of their memory and then select the appropriate forms from a wide array of possible solutions.[7] Also, open role-plays approximate authentic interactions in that there is the full operation of turn-taking, sequencing of moves, and negotiation of meaning.[8] More examples of classroom-based assessment are provided in Chapter 15.

Written discourse as if spoken

An alternative to assessing oral language production would be to have your students produce written responses, intended to reflect what they would say in the situation. Even though it is a written test, it could still elicit learners' projected oral language efficiently. Learners may be able to provide more thoughtful or socially desirable responses in such written tests, possibly even more indicative of their knowledge of what a speaker might say than when put on the spot orally.[9]

The DCT, mentioned above, is a popular approach to the assessment of speech acts in written discourse. The format often calls for two or more turns by both the speaker and the listener that the student needs to take into consideration in responding:

> You arranged to meet a friend in order to study together for an exam. You arrive half an hour late for the meeting, and your cell phone battery was dead so you couldn't call to alert your friend.
>
> Friend (*annoyed*): I've been waiting at least half an hour for you!
>
> You – 1:
>
> Friend: Well, I was standing here waiting. I could have been doing something else.
>
> You – 2:
>
> Friend: Well, it's pretty annoying. Try to come on time next time.

Here are responses to You – 1 and You – 2, provided by a native speaker of Hebrew:

[7] Kasper (1999).
[8] Kasper and Dahl (1991).
[9] Beebe and Cummings (1996); Kasper and Dahl (1991).

> You – 1: So what! It's only an – a meeting for – to study.
>
> You – 2: Yeah, I'm sorry. But don't make such a big deal of it.

If you were rating for the ability to be properly informal with a friend, then this respondent would come out high on that scale. The responses are informal. On the other hand, this reply is likely to be seen by the friend as not very apologetic and might get rated down on that basis.

Here is another apology DCT, in which the severity of the infraction is major, the learner respondent as listener in this situation is highly acquainted with the speaker (being the professor's intern), but the learner's relative status as student is considered lower:

> You are a graduate assistant for a professor who requested that you pick up a library book to help him finish the review of literature for a research proposal which is actually due tomorrow. You arrive at the meeting without the book. The problem is that you were supposed to get the book to him at your meeting last week and it slipped your mind then.
>
> Professor: Do you have that book we need in order to finish up the review of literature?
>
> You – 1:
>
> Professor: Yeah, but you actually said you were going to get it for our meeting last week, and you didn't bring it then either.
>
> You – 2:
>
> Professor: Still, I think you might need a better system of tracking your tasks as my RA. You know . . . uh . . . we need to finish this today so we can submit it tomorrow.
>
> You – 3:

▶

> Professor: OK. I guess that'll help, but I'll be teaching when you get back, so you'll have to work through that section on your own and leave your suggestions in my mail box.
>
> You – 4:

The query by the professor would presumably be answered by some explanation or excuse and then by an expression of apology with the appropriate intensity attached (Y – 1: "Whoops! I forgot it. You can't imagine how many things I've had on my mind lately . . . I'm really sorry about that."). The professor's reply might be met by a further expression of apology (Y – 2: "Oh, well, I'm terribly sorry about that . . ."). The next turn calls for an offer of repair (Y – 3: "I'll go and get the book right now."). But as often happens in life, the professor is no longer available at that point to work on the task. The graduate assistant would then need to apologize again and perhaps offer a promise of non-recurrence (Y – 4: "I'll make sure nothing like this happens again.").

As indicated above, if the person doing the scoring of the responses knows which apology strategies are likely to be used by competent speakers in the given situation, then scoring the learners' responses becomes easier. The use of multiple turns in a DCT task is intended to reflect an actual interaction more than would a single prompt, a space for a reply, and no subsequent turns by the other person. A way to score the above interaction could be to give a "3" if the response seems fine (which is probably the case for the responses offered in the preceding paragraph), "2" if it is fair, and "1" if it is weak for each of the four slots. So, 12 points would be the highest possible score on the item. The score could take into account the following six elements in a holistic fashion:

- the selection and use of strategies for realizing a given speech act,
- the typicality of the expressions used,
- the appropriateness of the amount of speech and information given,
- the appropriateness of the level of formality,
- the directness, and
- the level of politeness.

The development of tasks such as these allows us to manipulate the social factors (such as status, as in student–professor interactions) and situational factors (such as the level of imposition or of severity in an apology situation). The use of multiple turns represents an effort to make the DCTs more reflective of the conversational turn-taking that takes place in actual speech, the lack of which has been a criticism of written DCTs.[10] This approach constrains your students to shape their L2 pragmatics behavior to conform to a given situation. It is probably best to indicate in the instructions that they are to respond according to what people would typically say, which may not be consistent with their own preferred way of self-expression. This then would give you a sense of their awareness of generally preferred or commonly used target-language behavior, regardless of what their personal preferences are. (See Chapter 15 for suggested ways to assess preferred self-expression in pragmatics.)

Multiple-choice and short-answer completion items

There is a way to assess oral production indirectly, such as by using multiple-choice items since they are easier to score than are open-ended items. Such items may seem like measures of how well they comprehend the pragmatics of the situation, but they are intended to tap the ability to produce the correct responses through what is referred to as "projected ability." For example:

Indicate which of the following is most likely Brad's response to Tom in leave taking.

Tom: Hey, Brad. It's been nice talking with you. Let's get together some time.

Brad: (a) Good idea – when would you like to do it?

(b) You always say that but don't mean it.

(c) Sounds good. Take care.

(d) I won't hold my breath.

[10] Bardovi-Harlig and Hartford (1993*b*).

It is likely that for competent speakers of American English, (c) would be the expected choice in that this is what people usually say. The other three response choices are possible, especially (a), but selecting them would mean departing from the expected speaking routines for this speech community. The vague statement "Let's get together some time" does not usually constitute an actual invitation.

Another approach to assessing production of pragmatically appropriate forms would be to use a sentence completion format. The following would be an example of a "guided" response situation if the learner were provided, say, with the base form of the lexical item to use:

Brad is requesting a raise from his boss. Complete his request so that it sounds tactful:

I was _____ if you _____ consider increasing my pay a bit.

    (to wonder)   (will)

A more difficult format, for more advanced students, would be the same but without a base form as a clue to the intended response for the given blank:

I was _____ if you _____ consider increasing my pay.

By means of this sentence completion format, it is possible for you to see if your students have control over certain grammatical and lexical forms that are routinely used in order, for example, to mitigate or soften their requests.

Suggested strategies for assessing L2 speech acts

We conclude this chapter by considering six strategies for assessing pragmatics.

Realistic situations

Keep the speech act situations realistic (for the learner group) and engaging. So if your students are learning Japanese, you would avoid a vignette about babysitting since this is not likely to be a culturally prevalent activity in

Japan since family members tend to do the babysitting. In terms of finding vignettes that are engaging, the logical approach would be to check with locals of the given speech community. But another source can be the learners themselves since they are the ones who may be acutely aware of just those situations for which they would like guidance in pragmatics.[11] Here is one such situation supplied by a Japanese EFL student:

> You are at a restaurant and someone at your table says something funny. You laugh and spray a little food. You are embarrassed and think you should apologize. What do you say?[12]

In reality, students may be excellent at furnishing situations, regardless of whether they have any idea as to how to deal with them in a pragmatically appropriate way. So, teachers could actually prevail on learners to supply situations for pragmatics items, by making the following request:

> Think of a social situation where you had problems communicating (e.g., making a request or refusal, apologizing for something you did, complaining about something). Describe the situation briefly, and end it with "What do you say?"[13]

Rating for key aspects of performance

You could start by checking the cultural appropriateness of the strategies in the given situation. For example, the students need to rate the following two questions addressed to co-workers at a lunch break in terms of their cultural appropriateness:

> "I see you got a new car. How much did you pay for it?"
>
> "How much do you make a month?"

[11] From McLean (2005).
[12] From McLean (2005: 156).
[13] Based on the ideas in McLean (2005).

You could score performance on, say, a broad four-point scale: "very appro- priate culturally," "somewhat culturally appropriate," "somewhat culturally inappropriate," "culturally inappropriate." Under most circumstances in the US, asking these two questions would be rated as "culturally inappropriate."

You could also check for the appropriateness of the language forms used with regard to the level of formality (e.g., "too informal," "just right," or "too formal"), the degree of politeness (e.g., to what extent it is appropriate for that situation in that language and culture; 4 – appropriate, 3 – somewhat appropriate, 2 – somewhat inappropriate, 1 – inappropriate), and the amount of language used (e.g., "too much," "just right," or "too little"). The best rule of thumb is to be generous in your ratings since there is variation among competent speakers.

Debriefing student interpretations of the context

You could have a discussion with your students after they have performed L2 pragmatics tasks as to how they understood the contextual factors, having them identify the factors that most contributed to their responses. Refer to Chapter 15 for how this could be done.

Checking for the role of subjectivity in L2 pragmatics performance

You could have your students write or say both what they think a native-like response would be, as well as how their own L2 pragmatic performance might depart from the perceived native norms if they are unwilling to do it the way natives would. This allows for a discussion of how the students relate to the pragmatics of the L2 speech community.[14]

So in the situation of forgetting a meeting with their boss for the second time in Israel, students in an L2 Hebrew class would be alerted by their teacher to the likelihood that native Hebrew speakers might well express an apology **without** offering a repair. Then if the students were expressing their own subjectivity as, say, an American speaking Hebrew, they might indicate that they would offer repair (e.g., "I can be there in five minutes and deal with the matter"). While the score in this situation would be based on the awareness of the community norms, students would not be penalized for departing from those norms if they are able to state it as a conscious preference.

[14] For more on this, see Ishihara (2006).

In this case, students could be rated **both** for their awareness of the norms (e.g., 3 – high awareness, 2 – moderate awareness, 1 – low awareness) **and** for their explanation for why they depart from or resist that norm (e.g., 3 – clear statement of reasons for resistance, 2 – some statement of reasons for resistance, 1 – no statement of reasons for resistance). If the students write that native speakers would not offer repair (because it would be viewed as yet another infraction given their status as employee), they would get a "3" for being highly aware of the cross-cultural difference. If they go on to note that for them it would be imperative to indicate to the boss what they were willing to do to make it up, they would get a "3" for noticing the gap between what was expected and their own preferred behavior. See Chapter 15 for other examples of how to elicit from learners a sense of their awareness and pragmatic choice.

Checking your learners' rationale for their speech acts responses

You can have your students provide a rationale for why they responded as they did in the given social situation. If the group is not too large, you could have them audio-tape or write their reactions at the time they are responding or just afterwards. Otherwise, you could have them provide a brief written rationale. You are better able to evaluate their understanding of the pragmatics this way. The request for providing a rationale could look like this:

> Please give an explanation for why you responded in this situation the way that you did. What were the factors that influenced your response?

Determining when to assess for speech acts performance

You need to be strategic about when to assess what. For instance, at the beginning of your course and with less proficient learners, you would probably assess less complex or limited interaction involving speech acts such as complimenting, thanking, leave-taking, and basic service encounters (e.g., simple requests). While there is a need to teach (and assess) some aspects of requesting, making invitations, refusing, apologizing, and complaining early on, the more complex aspects of pragmatic behavior could be reserved for assessment later in the course or in courses for more advanced levels of instruction.

Discussion

This first of two chapters on assessing L2 pragmatics in the classroom made the case for why to do it in the first place. It then looked at both the assessment of comprehension and production, with the former involving how learners think either they or others have performed pragmatically, and the latter involving assessment of how well learners produce L2 pragmatics. This could entail both oral role-play, written discourse as if spoken, and multiple-choice and short-answer completion items. The chapter ended with a listing of strategies for constructing and implementing the assessments.

Activities 14.1 and 14.2 (below) are intended to provide an opportunity for constructing at least one task involving comprehension of a speech act and one task involving production of a speech act. The activities include both suggested situations and possible formats for the tasks, with the instructions either in the target language exclusively or bilingually. In the next chapter you will be asked to construct classroom-based assessments and to practice rating students' samples.

Activity 14.1 Writing a task to assess comprehension of speech acts

Objectives

1 You will be able to construct a task that checks for learners' ability to appraise a speech-act situation.

2 You will be able to construct speech-act comprehension tasks.

Suggested time: 45 minutes.

Materials: Task Sheet: "Situations and formats for writing a speech acts comprehension task" with four situations and two formats for the task construction.

Directions

1 Select a partner for this activity.

2 With your partner, start by reviewing the two speech-act comprehension tasks presented above (the one between the husband and wife, p. 267–8 above, and the bumping accident in the department store, pp. 268–9) with regard to how comprehension of speech act performance is assessed.

3 Jointly select your item formats for assessing comprehension of pragmatic ability.

4 Select a situation (four are provided in the task sheet, but you could use your own if you prefer).

5   Determine the criteria that you wish to use in your assessment (e.g., degree of regret in keeping with the nature of the infraction, sincerity of apology).

6   After you have blocked out your task, take turns responding to it, whether in English or in an L2 that you both know. This will serve as a form of a "pilot" for your task. If possible, audio-record your responses so that you can re-listen to them to facilitate analysis.

7   Each pair is to report back to the whole group as to what the task is intended to measure, how learners' responses are to be scored, the relative ease in constructing such a task, and potential challenges associated with it.

Discussion/wrap-up

Look at ways that this exercise has helped sharpen your understanding of how pragmatic tasks can be constructed.

Task sheet: Situations and formats for writing a speech acts comprehension task

1 Situations

(a) Forgetting to get the medicine you promised to pick up at the pharmacy for the sick child of a single-parent neighbor.

(b) Apologizing to your spouse for accidentally revealing personal information about her at a dinner party – information that she didn't want revealed.

(c) Apologizing to a college student for causing him to have to make an abrupt turn on his bike due to your jaywalking.

(d) Apologizing to your mother for forgetting to send her a birthday card.

2 Formats

(a) *Multiple-choice.* You could make up a multiple-choice response to a situation where learners have to choose the most appropriate response for a given situation.

(b) *Rank order.* You could have your students rank the order of responses (e.g., in terms of level of directness). You give a series of apologies which are on a continuum from more casual and detached to more regretful and engaged (e.g., "Oh, sorry about that . . ." to "Oh, my goodness, I am really very sorry about that . . .").

(c) *Open-ended questions*. In this case, since it is for comprehension and not production, the use of open-ended questions would be, say, to probe students' rationale for their choice of multiple-choice response, as in the example on p. 281, above. Note that this is not a format for assessing comprehension directly, but rather as a means for probing cognition – to better understand the response process.

Activity 14.2 Writing a task to assess production of speech acts

Objectives

1   You will be able to construct tasks that have learners perform orally or in writing their ability to engage in a speech acts interaction.

2   You will be able to identify criteria for judging the effectiveness of the given speech acts performance.

Suggested time: 45 minutes.

Materials: Task sheet: "Situations and Formats for Writing a Speech Acts Production Task," with three situations and three formats for constructing a task.

Directions

1   Start by reviewing the speech act production tasks in this chapter (four apologies: forgetting to meet with the boss, p. 270; forgetting to buy movie tickets, p. 273; forgetting a study date with a friend, p. 274; and forgetting to get a library book for a session with a professor, p. 275; one complaint: about the neighbor's dog, p. 273).

2   Select a format for assessing production of pragmatic ability from Section 2 of the task sheet below.

3   Select a situation, either from the list of suggestions or from your own experience.

4   Determine the criteria that you wish to use in your assessment (e.g., appropriateness of directness or politeness given the seriousness or severity of the situation with regard to a complaint, request, or apology).

5   After you have constructed a draft version of your assessment task, find a partner and have that person respond to it, whether in English or in an L2 that you know. This will serve as a form of a "pilot" for your task. Pay attention to similarities and differences in the written answers that you produced, in an effort to be mindful of variation in responses.

6   Each pair is to report back to the whole group as to what the task is intended to measure.

Discussion/wrap-up

Look at ways that this exercise has helped sharpen your understanding of how pragmatic tasks can be constructed. The discussion could include your participants' comments about the relative ease involved in constructing such a task, potential challenges associated with it, and ways to address these challenges.

Task sheet: Situations and formats for writing a speech acts production task

1 Situations

Use either the example provided or create your own for:

(a) *Requesting a second opinion* (e.g., from another doctor at the hospital when the diagnosis for your loved one's situation is unacceptable to you).

(b) *Complaining* (e.g., to the manager of a pricey restaurant about slow service and mediocre food).

(c) *Complimenting* (e.g., a very modest friend in front of others on the good advice that friend gave you).

(d) *Apologizing* (e.g., to a female colleague for your unpleasant behavior towards her at a meeting the previous day: you weren't feeling well and took it out on her).

2 Formats

(a) *Guided response: multiple-rejoinder response*. You could use this format of providing three or four responses that the hearer provides in the interaction and leaving the answers open for the learner to complete (as in the apology to the professor for forgetting the library book).

(b) *Open-ended response: oral role-play response*. You design a situation with a description such as in forgetting the meeting with the boss for the second time (see above). Possibly you provide an initial utterance from the speaker (in this case, the boss) in the interaction, as in "What happened to you this time?"

(c) *Open-ended response: written*. The format is like in (b) above, but in this case the learner writes a response. It would most likely be in the form of a single answer.

CHAPTER 15

Assessment of pragmatics in the classroom

Noriko Ishihara

Introduction

Formal or informal assessment of learners' pragmatic ability, both receptive and productive, is an indispensable component in the teaching of pragmatics. Assessment of learners' ability gives insights as to what the students have and have not learned. Assessment also gives teachers feedback as to how effective their instruction has been, and how well the assessment itself has been planned out and conducted. It is a relatively recent phenomenon that pragmatics has been incorporated into the curriculum in a rigorous manner. Since efforts to assess learners' pragmatic ability in the classroom setting have appeared to lag behind these instructional efforts, it is our intention in this book to give greater attention to this issue.

Chapter 14 focused primarily on principles for constructing tasks that elicit learner language and possible ways of rating that performance in formal and informal settings. In this chapter, we will zero in on means for classroom-based assessment of learners' pragmatic ability, and consider practical applications of classroom assessment tools, as well as sample learner language in those assessments and teacher feedback. As the label suggests, classroom-based assessment (also termed *teacher assessment, teacher-based assessment, alternative assessment, alternative in assessment*[1]) is conducted by the actual instructor of the classroom, not by an outside researcher or trained rater. Classroom-based assessment is intended to facilitate learners' development within the everyday classroom context.

---

[1] Brown and Hudson (1998); Norris *et al.* (1998); Rea-Dickins (2008); Shohamy (1996).

Teacher-based assessment contrasts with the type of traditional assessment which sometimes takes the form of standardized multiple-choice items and measures learners' knowledge of language in numerical terms for the purpose of rank-ordering them.[2]

In this chapter, we first discuss the value of using research-based information as the basis for assessing pragmatics. Examples of classroom-based assessment instruments, samples of learner responses, and teacher assessment/feedback will be provided with a focus on linguistic, cultural, or analytic (metapragmatic) aspects of L2 pragmatics. These assessments give teachers an opportunity to evaluate learners' pragmatic ability and at the same time function as a way of providing learners feedback about their pragmatic use of language. Additionally, we underscore the importance of learners' self- and peer-assessments, which are inseparable from classroom instruction. Also, if we aim to provide culturally sensitive teaching of pragmatics (see Chapter 6), then it is necessary to take **learner intention** into consideration in assessing how effective learners are in their use of L2 pragmatics.

The examples of different kinds of assessment provided in this chapter have been piloted with ESL/EFL and JFL learners, and the effectiveness of these assessments has been researched in an EFL context[3] and in a Japanese-as-a-foreign-language context.[4] The examples are only preliminary, and teacher readers are invited to share their ideas and experiences to further refine classroom-based assessment of pragmatic ability.

Research–based assessment of pragmatic ability

Throughout this book, teacher readers have often been reminded that the teaching of pragmatics should include material that is informed as much as possible by research studies, even if teachers are native or fluent speakers of the target language. While teacher intuition has an important role to play, language samples collected by researchers, teachers, and students add key insights to the L2 pragmatics curriculum. Likewise, the assessment of pragmatics will reflect authentic use of language more closely if there are other dependable points of reference than a single teacher's intuition alone. Teachers (and learners, in the case of self-assessment) can turn to the data which show how pragmatically competent speakers would respond in the

---

[2] McNamara (2001).
[3] Ishihara (2009).
[4] Ishihara *et al.* (2008).

same situation, and use the data as a baseline in assessment. What would such an assessment instrument look like? Below is an example of an exercise in which research-based information about apologizing in Japanese is utilized by learners (and possibly by teachers as well) as a point of comparison in assessment (which in this case is a form of self-assessment).

Example 1[5]

Situation: Yuta is a college student. He has an appointment with a senior professor, Professor Ito in another department to discuss your project. She is in her late fifties and although Yuta has communicated with her by e-mail, he has not met her yet. The appointment is at 3 today. However, for some reason, Yuta finds that he will not be able to make it. He calls the professor and asks if he could change the appointment. The professor sounds reluctant.

Prof. Ito (*on the telephone*): はい、伊藤ですが。 "Hello. This is Ito."

Yuta – 1: (*identify yourself*)

Prof. Ito: あ、・・・さんね。どうしました？ "Oh, . . . san. What's up with you?"

Yuta – 2: (*tell him that you won't be able to come today*)

Prof. Ito: そうですか、どうにもならないの？ "Is that really so? Can't you make it at all?"

Yuta – 3: (*present your reasons*)

Prof. Ito: ああ、そう、大丈夫なの？ "Oh, really? Are you all right?"

Yuta – 4: (*ask if you can meet with him on another day.*)

Prof. Ito: じゃあ、今回はなんとかしましょう。来週の同じ時間はどうですか？ "All right, let's make it work this time. How about the same time next week?"

Yuta – 5: (*accept and apologize again*)

Prof. Ito: はい。 "That's okay."

Yuta – 6: (*close the conversation*)

[5] Adapted from Ishihara and Cohen (2004) and Ishihara and Maeda (2010).

Prof. Ito: はいどうも。 *"OK."*

Yuta – 7: (*say good-bye*)

Self-assessment. Now look back on what you have written in Yuta's role and answer the following questions.[6]

1   (a)   What reasons did you give to the professor for the cancellation?

    (b)   Now compare your reason(s) with the reasons Japanese university students gave in this task. How appropriate are your reasons?

Below are the reasons for cancellation given by Japanese university students:

1   family illness (23%)

2   your own physical condition (19%)

3   conflict with your school business (19%)

4   trouble with transportation (10%)

Common characteristics among these reasons are their realistic nature and the fact that they are beyond your control.

---

2   (a)   Where and in what way was your reason presented in your dialogue?

    (b)   Now view common strategies used by Japanese university students in this task. How does your use of strategies compare to theirs?

■   Japanese university students first tended to give a generic reason using a formulaic expression. Then as the professor asks for more detail, they gave more specifics. Note that a lengthy presentation of a reason/reasons may give the listener the impression that the speaker is self-centered or justifying the cancellation (which the student is not really entitled to).

▶

[6] The data presented in boxes below in this exercise are from a study by Hayashi (1999).

■ Japanese students also used certain strategies to communicate their lack of intention to cause the infraction.

   ■ They often use *jitsuwa* "actually" before introducing the specific reason to prepare the professor for the upcoming reason. [sample exchange here]

   ■ The use of . . . *shimatta* implies that they had no control over what happened or that something came up despite their intentions.

      Student: すみません。今日になって突然都合がつかなくなってしまいました。 "I'm sorry but some inconvenience occurred today."

3 (a) Which apology expression(s) did you use?

   (b) Compare your apology expressions with those of Japanese students and evaluate the level of politeness in your apologizing expressions.

Apology expressions used by Japanese students (in the order of frequency):

1 申し訳ありません *moushiwake arimasen* type;

2 すみません *sumimasen* type;

3 失礼しました *shitsurei shimashita* type;

4 許してください *yurushite kudasai* type;

5 恐れ入ります *osore irimasu* type;

6 ご迷惑をお掛けします *gomeiwakuwo okake shimasu* type.

These apologizing expressions may be intensified with the use of, for example, *hontouni*, *doumo*, *taihen*, and *makotoni*. Usually these intensifiers are pronounced emphatically to communicate a sincere tone of voice.

---

4 (a) How many apologizing expressions did you provide?

   (b) Notice the number of times Japanese students used apologizing expressions and evaluate the sincerity of your apology.

The number of apology expressions offered by Japanese students (all apology expressions combined):

Two times (40%)

Three times (25%)

Four times (21%)

Note. In Hayashi's study, Japanese students wrote down imagined interactions. When they were to speak, they might actually use more apology expressions than shown above.

5   (a) What was the level of politeness in your language in general?

    (b) What levels of politeness did Japanese students use?
         Compare the levels used in the sample dialogue with yours.

The speaker in the sample dialogue uses polite to very polite language. She uses the *desu/masu* style all the way, sprinkled with some very polite usage – the humble form of some verbs.

Examples of the humble forms in the dialogue:

- 加藤と申しますが "This is Kato".

- 伺うことができなくなってしまったんです *ukagau kotoga dekinaku natte shimattan desu* "it so happened that I was made unable to come (lit.)"

The data presented in the boxes above can be given to learners either by the teacher or through web-links. The assessment becomes highly authentic when teachers use actual language of a group of college-age research participants. While such naturally occurring data are usually difficult to obtain, elicited data, such as target speakers' collective judgment of normative pragmatic behavior (as in the above example), would help make for more authentic assessment. When the speakers providing data may be closer in age to learners than the teachers themselves are, the assessment can more closely reflect pragmatic use and awareness of a sub-group of target language speakers that learners may be most likely to want to emulate.

Assessment rubrics

One form of teacher-based assessment is the evaluative rubric (or checklist[7]) that teacher readers may find useful for evaluating learners' receptive and productive pragmatic ability. The use of rubrics highlights important pragmatic aspects being focused on, and enables students and teachers alike to pay attention to those crucial aspects during instruction and assessment. In fact, assessment – especially formative assessment – could be seamlessly integrated into the instruction. For example, with the teacher's guidance, learners can engage in self-assessment or peer assessment of their own or others' pragmatic use, where the evaluative process itself can feed into the learning of pragmatics (see the section on self-assessment below). Learners' pragmatic awareness could also be informally assessed during class discussion while learners contribute their observation of L2 pragmatic norms.

A principle of teacher-based assessment is that the choice of criteria in the evaluation rubric aligns with the instructional goals in a consistent manner.[8] In other words, the focus of instruction also receives major emphasis in the assessment. In addition, it is important that learners be informed as to the assessment criteria **before** teachers assess their pragmatic ability. What might such assessment criteria look like, then? The next section presents areas of focus for assessing pragmatic ability:

- linguistic aspects (pragmalinguistic ability);
- cultural aspects (sociopragmatic ability); and
- analytic aspects (ability to analyze and evaluate pragmatic use – referred to as *metapragmatic ability*).

Classroom-based assessment of pragmatics might include a focus on one or more of these aspects of L2 pragmatics.

Focus on linguistic aspects (assessing pragmalinguistic ability)

Teachers assessing learners' receptive and productive pragmatic ability with a focus on the language forms would be answering questions such as:

---

[7] While evaluation using rubrics shows the degree to which the criteria are achieved, checklists consist of a simpler dichotomy just indicating whether those criteria are achieved or not (Tedick 2002). An example of a checklist for assessing the structure of discourse can be found in Akikawa and Ishihara (in press).

[8] Brown (2004); O'Malley and Valdez Pierce (1996).

- To what extent do learners understand the language as intended by the speaker?
- How is the learner's language most likely interpreted by L2 community members in terms of the dimension(s) below?
- To what extent is the language effective in conveying the speaker's intention?

The specific dimensions of language include the choice and use of:

- vocabulary/phrases (e.g., a *big* favor, I *just* need . . .);
- grammatical structures (e.g. *Can you . . . / Would you . . . / I was wondering if . . . / Would it be possible . . . ?*);
- strategies for a speech act (i.e., the selection of formulas and the way they are used) (e.g., *giving a reason for a request, apologizing for the trouble, thanking for complying with the request*);
- choice and use of pragmatic tone (e.g., how sincere the speaker appears with verbal and non-verbal cues, see Chapter 6);
- choice and use of organization (rhetorical structure) of the written/spoken discourse (e.g., introduction, body, conclusion);
- choice and use of discourse markers and fillers (e.g., *by the way, speaking of . . . , well, um*); and
- choice and use of *epistemic stance markers* (i.e., words and phrases to show the speaker's stance, such as: *I think, maybe, seem, suppose, tend to,* and *of course*).

This list represents a scope of potential evaluative criteria, so teachers would need to select, add, or adapt the ones that suit their instructional contexts. Again, it would be best to have the choice of instructional focus directly correspond to the evaluative focus. It would be ideal if the teachers have baseline data (through either formal or informal research) of (ideally naturally occurring) pragmatic behavior sampled from the target language speakers and use these data as a reference in evaluating learners' pragmatic receptive and productive skills. Below is an example of analytic scoring[9] focusing on linguistic aspects.

Example 2

This is adapted from an example in Chapter 14.

---

[9] For a definition of analytic scoring (as opposed to holistic scoring) and examples of more rigorous analytic and holistic rubrics, see Ishihara (in press, *a*).

Situation: John and Kevin are good friends at college. They arranged to meet in order to study together for an exam. Kevin arrives half an hour late for the meeting. (Learners respond in Kevin's role, below.)

Learner 1	Learner 2
John: (*annoyed*) I've been waiting at least half an hour for you! Kevin: So what! It's only an – a meeting for – to study. John: Well, I was standing here waiting. I could have been doing something else. Kevin: Yeah, I'm sorry. But don't make such a big deal of it. John: Well, it's pretty annoying. Try to come on time next time.	John: (*annoyed*) I've been waiting at least half an hour for you! Kevin: I am so sorry. . . . I studied until 3 in the morning last night and I couldn't get up this morning. I will buy your lunch for the compensation. John: Well, I was standing here waiting. I could have been doing something else. Kevin: I am very sorry for keeping you waiting. I should have called your cell phone. I won't do this again! John: Well, it's pretty annoying. Try to come on time next time.

Evaluation
4 – Very appropriate; 3 – Somewhat appropriate; 2 – Less appropriate; 1 – Inappropriate

1 Strategies of apologies	4	3	**2**	1
2 Vocabulary/phrases	**4**	3	2	1
3 Level of formality	**4**	3	2	1
4 Pragmatic tone	4	3	**2**	1

Teacher's comments:
Considering that Kevin and John are good friends, the language is appropriately informal and grammatically accurate. Kevin uses apologies minimally (and not until in the second turn), and even blames John for being upset. This makes Kevin sound less apologetic than John expects him to be. Maybe Kevin isn't feeling very sorry and is being a little confrontational with John.

Evaluation
4 – Very appropriate; 3 – Somewhat appropriate; 2 – Less appropriate; 1 – Inappropriate

1 Strategies of apologies	**4**	3	2	1
2 Vocabulary/phrases	4	**3**	2	1
3 Level of formality	4	**3**	2	1
4 Pragmatic tone	**4**	3	2	1

Teacher's comments:
Kevin sounds very apologetic – he uses multiple strategies of apologies well to express his sincerity. Because Kevin and John are good friends, Kevin's language could be less formal. For example, instead of "I will buy your lunch for compensation" he could say, "I'll make it up to you. How about if I bought you lunch?" or just "I'll buy you lunch."

As readers may have noticed, it is often difficult to make a clear distinction between language-related and culture-related aspects of pragmatics. This is precisely because both aspects are in many ways integrated, given that pragmatics occurs at the juncture of language and culture (see Chapter 1).

Another approach would be to assess learners' pragmatics more holistically and thus avoid distinguishing between what is a language and what is a cultural issue (as in most of the examples in this chapter). With this option in mind, we now turn to cultural aspects of pragmatics as a primary focus of assessment.

Focus on cultural aspects (assessing sociopragmatic ability)

The following are some of the questions that could be asked in assessing cultural aspects of learners' pragmatic awareness and use:

- To what extent do learners understand the use of the L2 and its likely consequence in the cultural and situational context?

- How are their intentions interpreted by members of the L2 community, given the dimensions of the culture listed below? What consequences might result from learners' L2 use in the L2 community?

- To what extent is the learners' pragmatic behavior effective in conveying their intention in this particular cultural context?

The specific dimensions of the culture include:

- the level of directness, formality, and/or politeness in the interaction: the extent to which these are appropriate in the given context;

- the choice and use of speech acts: whether the speakers' choice of speech acts is appropriate in the given context;

- the handling of cultural norms in the target language: the extent to which the speakers adhere to appropriate cultural norms (if in fact this is their intent); and

- the handling of the cultural reasoning or ideologies behind the L2 pragmatic norms: the extent to which learners adopt target culture ideologies (if this is their intent).

In assessing pragmatic ability, it would be important to include not only **productive** but also **receptive** skills. Along with learning what to say and how to say it, learners would also need to become able to interpret what others say as it is normally understood in the community. Assessment instruments of receptive skills can include elicitation of textual interpretation of intended meaning in context, and acceptability judgment in the multiple-choice format[10] or scaled-response questionnaires (see Chapter 14). Classroom-based assessments would inform teachers of learners' level of receptive pragmatic skills, and at the same time give feedback to learners as to their understanding of common interpretations of the speakers' pragmatic use in the L2 community.

The following are two examples of assessing cultural understanding (and some linguistic ability as well) in L2 pragmatics. The first example deals with comprehension of pragmatic tone in formative classroom assessment, and is applicable to younger learners. The second concerns the learners' interpretation of a simulated dialogue in a corporate setting, and thus may be most suitable for learners of business English.

Example 3

For adult learners: Watch a video clip (or take turns reading a transcript with emotions), and discuss the nuances being expressed (e.g., being serious, cynical, shocked, confrontational, pessimistic, joking, or sincere). Pay attention to the speaker's gestures, facial expressions, use of space, and eye contact, along with the tone of voice.

For young learners: Watch a video clip (or take turns acting out some sentences), and imagine how the speaker is feeling. Use one of the signs ☺ ☺ ☹ (printed separately on a poster board) to show the speaker's feeling.

Example 4

Listen to the following dialogue you overheard between your co-worker, Bill, and his boss at work. How would most English speakers understand Bill's message? What impression does Bill make by talking this way? Write a note to Bill regarding how he should probably speak to his boss.[11]

---

[10] Although valid and reliable multiple-choice questionnaires are time-consuming to develop and therefore may not be realistic for everyday practice, there have been vigorous efforts to construct a battery of tests for learners' pragmatic competence, e.g., Hudson *et al.* (1995); Liu (2007); Roever (2005). With further research, some of these measures could possibly be adapted for classroom assessment of learners' receptive pragmatic skills.

[11] Adapted from Anderson (2006).

Boss: Bill, can I talk to you for a minute?

Bill: Sure. What about?

Boss: Tomorrow's meeting. As you know, you and Sarah are both going to be presenting a sales pitch. I'd like to have Sarah present hers first, and then you can follow her, OK?

Bill: I don't think that's a good idea. Sarah doesn't make very good presentations, and I don't think she should speak first. I'd like to present first instead.

Sample answer:

Bill, you are logical and I can see you're trying to be convincing. However, even though you wish to communicate your strong preference, in order to sound more tactful to your boss, it may be good to tone down your message. Note that this is a formal job situation and you are speaking to your boss, who is higher in social status. In this case, you should probably 1) accept your boss's idea by stating something positive, and 2) suggest your counter-proposal in a more positive way. How about, for example: "OK, that sounds fine, but I was hoping that perhaps I would give the first presentation since I have come up with what I think are some strong arguments"? With this response, you are acknowledging the boss's authority by saying that her ideas are good, but still offering a counter-proposal without being negative about a co-worker or about your boss's idea.

Now we turn to the assessment of learners' **productive** skills with regard to language and culture. Below is an example of an analytic scoring instrument, learner language, and teacher feedback. Here again, if teachers have actual language samples from pragmatically competent target language speakers, they would be a useful yardstick in evaluation.

Example 5

This is adapted from an example in Chapter 14; learners can determine the boss's gender.

Situation: Michelle completely forgets a crucial meeting at the office with the boss at her new job. An hour later she shows up at her boss's office to apologize. The problem is that this is the second time she's forgotten such a meeting in the short time she has been working at

▶

this job. Her boss is clearly annoyed, "What happened to you this time?"

Learner 1	Learner 2
Michelle: So sorry, Mr Peterson. I have sleeping problems and then I missed the bus. I can make it up to you."	Michelle: Ms Peterson, I'm terribly sorry. It completely slipped out of my mind. I know this is my second time, but believe me, this never happened to me before. I'm really sorry, I'll be very careful and this won't happen again.

Evaluation
4 – Very appropriate; 3 – Somewhat appropriate; 2 – Less appropriate; 1 – Inappropriate

Evaluation
4 – Very appropriate; 3 – Somewhat appropriate; 2 – Less appropriate; 1 – Inappropriate

Learner 1		Learner 2	
1 Level of formality, directness, and politeness	4 **3** 2 1	1 Level of formality, directness, and politeness	**4** 3 2 1
2 Strategies of apologies	4 **3** 2 1	2 Strategies of apologies	**4** 3 2 1
3 Cultural norms	4 **3** 2 1	4 Cultural norms	**4** 3 2 1

Teacher's comments:
Michelle uses 3 apology strategies – expressing an apology, giving an explanation, and offering repair. The choice of these strategies is good in this situation. However, because the excuse provided is lacking detail, the apology may not sound very sincere. Her boss may appreciate more honesty here if Michelle is not being truthful.

Teacher's comments:
Michelle sounds very apologetic, and with good intonation can sound very sincere as well. She uses multiple apology strategies – expressing an apology, giving an explanation, and promising non-recurrence. She could also offer repair such as "I can meet with you right now or work overtime, whatever you want me to do to make it up."

Focus on analytic aspects (assessing metapragmatic ability)

Besides evaluating linguistic and cultural aspects of learners' pragmatics, it is also possible to assess learners' ability to analyze the pragmatics of the L2. If one of the primary goals of pragmatics-focused instruction is to equip learners with the skills required for independent learning of pragmatics beyond the immediate classroom, it would be important to assess the development of these skills.

The following two examples of assessment elicit learners' analysis of how L1 and L2 are used in authentic contexts. Example 6 below contains a set of prompts that facilitates analysis of the relationship between context and language, based on an earlier task in which learners collected samples of authentic request discourses in their L1 Japanese and in the L2 English. Learners analyze how relative social status, distance, and imposition can influence the language of request and the use of request strategies. Example 7 builds on a similar task but is part of an extended reflective journaling exercise. Through writing, learners observe naturally occurring language and reflect on the pragmatic norms and language forms of the data collected. These tasks come out of the "learners-as-researchers" approach[12] (see Chapter 6), in which learners are encouraged to conduct lay research through observation and analysis of the data they have gathered for themselves.

Example 6 – assessment of learners' analysis of contextual factors

You did an excellent job of collecting authentic requests! Now let's look back at how requests are really used in context in your English or Japanese data.

1   Comparing the dialogues you collected, analyze how **S** (social status, age, gender), **D** (social/psychological distance), and **I** (the level of imposition) influence the language of request.

> [Sample learner response, originally written in L1 Japanese]
>
> In Japanese, when **S** is equal and **D** is small (close relationship), the language is hardly honorific with small **I** and even with large **I**. But when the listener's **S** is high and **D** is large, honorifics are used regardless of the size of **I**. When **S** is large but **D** is small, I observed that speakers use informal honorifics rather than formal ones.

[Sample teacher feedback] Excellent observation!

2   Provide your hypothesis on how **S**, **D**, and **I** influence pre-request strategies and post-request strategies.

▶

---

[12] Tanaka (1997).

[Sample learner response, originally written in L1 Japanese]

In Japanese when S is equal and D is small, the larger I is, the higher the frequency of strategy use, and the smaller I is, the lower the frequency used. In contrast, when S is large and D is large, the chance of strategy use becomes high regardless of the size of I.

[Sample teacher feedback] Very good analysis. Now how does this apply to English? The influence of I in particular may be different in different cultures.

Example 7

In the coming week, listen to how people around you refuse invitations and jot down as many expressions as possible. In your journal, 1) report your observation, 2) discuss any cultural norms that you think exist in the community. Also, include in your writing 3) what you have seen/ heard people typically do/say to soften the blow of the refusals, and 4) why you think people do/say it that way.

Sample teacher's evaluation form

1) Report of observation	Excellent
Comments:	Good
	Needs more work
2) Understanding of cultural norms in the target language	Excellent
Comments:	Good
	Needs more work
3) Understanding of the language of refusal softeners	Excellent
Comments:	Good
	Needs more work
4) Analysis of cultural reasoning behind target culture norms (why people behave the way they do)	Excellent
	Good
Comments:	Needs more work

Teacher's comments:

This journal writing task can be adapted into a class discussion in which learners discuss critical incidents that they have experienced in interacting in the L2. Either through a written or a spoken channel, these reflective tasks can promote learners' critical thinking about cross-cultural issues (e.g., how social contexts are interpreted in the L2, what language is used to encode the social meaning, what cultural values and beliefs underlie the L2).[13] At the same time, they allow teachers to assess learners' pragmatic awareness.

So far, we have discussed the value of using research-based information not only in teaching, but also in assessing pragmatics, and have looked at examples of classroom-based assessment with a focus on language, culture, and analysis of L2 pragmatics. Here we might remind ourselves that not all learners' divergences from the acceptable range of community norms matter equally in authentic communicative interactions.[14] While some divergences (e.g., slightly awkward word choice) are unlikely to lead to misinterpretation of the learners' intent, others (e.g., no mitigating expressions in refusals) may cause unintended misunderstandings. In classroom assessment, we should make distinctions between more and less important features of pragmatics, and focus on the more important ones that are likely to cause serious pragmatic failure.

Also, as suggested in Chapters 5 and 6, learners may wish to model themselves after native speakers or follow culturally acceptable norms in the community. At other times the same learners may wish to intentionally behave rather uniquely in order to preserve their subjectivity. For example, learners may want to sound overly polite even in a fairly informal situation as a way of distancing themselves from a group of people they do not want to associate with, even though they are perfectly capable of speaking informally and amicably in other informal situations. In such cases, teachers may decide to respect those learners' intentions (i.e., how they want to present themselves) and support them in achieving their goals (i.e., what they want to achieve through their use of language). The next section shows how this culturally sensitive assessment might be realized in the classroom context.

---

[13] Shively (2008). This article provides an example of critical incidents and a useful discussion guide for learners that would particularly be useful for study-abroad students (pp. 420–2).

[14] For example, Kasper and Schmidt (1996).

Assessing pragmatics based on learners' goals and intentions

In assessment based on learners' goals and intentions, teachers would be asking:

- To what extent is the speaker's language use likely to achieve the goal (e.g., the match between what the speaker wants to achieve and the most probable consequence of the pragmatic use)?

- To what degree does the speaker's intention match the listener's most probable interpretation (e.g., the fit between how polite, direct, and formal the speaker wants to sound, and how s/he actually sounds to the listener)?

In this assessment, teachers could work with their students in detecting the nuances they are likely to convey intentionally or unintentionally in their pragmatic behavior. The teachers' role would include helping learners both to convey their intended messages and also to accurately interpret messages that they send and receive.[15] All the while, teachers need to take their learners' goals and intentions into consideration when engaging in assessment, since it is ultimately the learners' prerogative to decide to what extent they wish to emulate what they perceived as community norms in each situation. How, then, can learners' intentions be identified in every contextual situation where they use the L2? One answer may be to involve learners in somewhat of a partnership role in the assessment of pragmatics, as opposed to having teachers do it alone as in conventional classrooms. In such cases, teachers and learners co-construct the assessment of learners' pragmatic language use. This collaboration might in fact be a necessary component in the assessment of pragmatics, given its culturally sensitive nature.[16]

The following are two examples of teacher–student collaborative assessment of pragmatics. The items are intended to assess the extent to which the speaker's goal and intention match the listener's most probable interpretation and the consequence of the interaction. In these examples, the teacher's feedback is largely in narrative, so they may be more suitable for formative assessment. (More detailed assessment in numerical terms will appear in Example 10, and some other variations in Activity 15.1, below.) In order to ensure that learners are familiar with the instructions and the

---

[15] Thomas (1983).
[16] Ishihara (2008a), (2009).

requirements of the task, it is advised that the format and assessment criteria be clearly explained to learners (and if possible, presented to them bilingually). Because learners may need experience in order to use this format effectively, the same or similar format may well be used repeatedly during instruction.

Example 8

Situation: You are trying to do some homework but your roommate, Jenny is watching a sit com on TV and has the volume up so loud that it is distracting you and making it hard to concentrate. Write what you would say to her, if you decide to speak to her about this:

You say: [learner writes] Jenny, would you mind turning the volume down a little bit? Thanks.

(a) Your intention/goal as a speaker: How do you want to sound, and what do you want to achieve through your request?

[Learner writes] I want to sound politely and getting my wish granted.

(b) Most probable listener's interpretation:

[Teacher writes] The speaker made a fairly polite request. Most people in this situation would comply with this request.

(c) Match between (a) and (b): [Teacher marks]

(Excellent)   Good   Fair   Poor

Example 9

Situation: Same as in Example 1.

You say: [learner writes] Jenny, I'm trying to do my homework – I apologize to bother you but would you mind volume down a little bit?

(a) Check and/or circle one(s) that best describe your intention as a speaker. [Learner responds below.]

___ I want to make a request the way most people do in the community and get my request granted.

  __X__ I would want my request to sound ((a little)) more (formal/
  informal), ((polite)/impolite), (or _____) than most other
  people and get my wish granted, but still within the range of
  acceptable behavior.

  ___ I choose not to use common behavior because I want to
  communicate my intentions (or not communicate them at all)
  in my own way.

  Specify what community norms you decide not to use and why
  you don't want them: _____

  ___ Other (Specify: _____)

(b) Most probable listener's interpretation:

  [Teacher writes] The speaker made a very polite request. Most people
  in this situation would comply with this request but the request
  sounds so formal for a college student that it may seem fairly
  unfriendly or distant to the listener.

(c) Match between (a) and (b): [Teacher marks]

  Excellent   (Good)   Fair   Poor

For formative assessment, the largely narrative format used in Examples 8
and 9 would provide learners with individualized feedback. The evaluation
could be made in numerical terms if desired, as in the next example. A more
comprehensive assessment (Example 10) would include the following evaluative foci:

- linguistic ability to use community norms: assessed through a) and
  c) below;
- awareness of the most probable listener's interpretation: assessed
  through d); and
- the extent to which learner intentions match the most probable
  listener's interpretation based on b) and the teacher's judgment.

Example 10

Situation: Same as in Example 1.

(a) What would most English speakers say?

  [Learner writes] Hey, Jenny, can you turn the TV down little bit so
  that I can finish studying? It's kind of hard to concentrate, but I can
  probably take some time off afterwards.

(b) Your intention [learner responds below]

___ I want to make a request the way most people do in the community to get my request granted.

_X_ I would want my request to sound (a little) more ((formal/) informal), ((polite/)impolite), or _____ than most other people and get my wish granted, but still within the range of acceptable behavior.

___ I choose not to use common behavior because I want to communicate my intentions (or not communicate them at all) in my own way. Specify what community norms you decide not to use and why you don't want them: _____

_____

___ Other (Specify: _____)

(c) What would you say (if different from (a) above):

[Learner writes] I hope you don't mind my asking this big favor, I'm sorry if it trouble you but I am wondering if it is ever possible for you to turn the TV down just a little bit? I wish it is no problem for you. I very appreciate.

(d) How does your roommate most likely interpret your request?

[Learner writes] A little more polite than most Americans but considerate and nice.

Teacher's evaluation

1 Linguistic ability to use community norms (a and/or c above)	(4)	3	2	1
	Native-like	proficient	fair	poor
2 Awareness of most probable listener's interpretation (d)	4	(3)	2	1
	highly aware	aware	less aware	unaware
3 Match between (b) learner goal/ intention and most likely listener's interpretation	4	(3)	2	1
	excellent	good	fair	poor
Total Score	10/12			

Teacher's comments:

You made a very polite request and showed a high level of consideration for the roommate. She will probably comply with this request, but the request sounds a little too formal. It also sounds very verbose, a bit distancing or scholarly for this informal situation.

Example 10 shows how teachers could assess learners according to their intentions, while at the same time probing their linguistic ability to produce community norms. Ultimately the degree of success is assessed not just by way of community norms, but also by the learners' level of pragmatic awareness and their ability to align their language with its community interpretation.

In the examples 8–10 above, a range of L2 community norms becomes the baseline when learners attempt to speak according to the range of target community norms. Then, their language is assessed in terms of how closely it approximates the range of community norms. However, when learners do wish to divert from what they think is a community norm due to their subjectivity, community norms will no longer be the sole point of comparison.

Nonetheless, teacher readers may feel that this type of assessment is too complex for their particular learners or too time-consuming in their instructional context. If that is the case, teachers could consider using another approach, which is simpler, yet equally sensitive to learners' subjectivity. That would be to encourage learners to imagine a character – a typical member of the L2 community – and then to demonstrate the language that this character would be expected to use. For instance, instead of asking:

What would **you** say in this situation?

The questions could be rephrased as follows:

- What would **most speakers** say in this situation?
- What would **Mike** [an imaginary character] say in this situation?
- What could **Mike** say and couldn't say in this situation? or,
- What would be a **typical response** in this situation?

In this way, teachers can reconcile the wish to respect learners' (occasional) intention not to speak like other L2 community members, on the one hand, with the need to assess learners' pragmatic awareness and linguistic command on the other. Another culturally sensitive approach to pragmatics assessment would be to have learners assess their own language use for their own purposes, and we now turn to that approach.

Self-assessment

The role of reflection in self-assessment of pragmatic ability

Self-assessment affords learners an opportunity to take responsibility for assessing themselves, typically with some reflective prompts or evaluative criteria provided by their teachers (also see Chapters 7 and 11). In the spirit of a "learners-as-researchers" approach,[17] they do not just wait for their teacher's assessment of their language use, but conduct their own analysis of their L2 pragmatics. The process of making and renewing hypotheses about L2 pragmatics calls for an active monitoring and evaluating of pragmatic awareness and use. Reflection has already been identified elsewhere as potentially contributing to the effectiveness of L2 teaching and learning.[18] The reflection process entails having learners think deliberately about their own L2 production and comprehension, and can take the form of self-assessment along with other activities such as peer review and debriefing.

For L2 pragmatic learning, metapragmatic reflection (as in Examples 6 and 7 above) is likely to work to the learners' advantage as they gain more advanced pragmatic ability.[19] Learners can carefully observe other speakers' linguistic behavior and analyze contextual factors and L2 pragmatic forms. Extending this approach to the assessment process, learners can further be encouraged to reflect on their own L2 awareness and production, especially using the authentic feedback they obtain from their conversational partners in natural settings and from instructors in the classroom.

Teacher scaffolding in self-assessment

In order to make self-assessment an effective part of instruction, learners need varying levels of guidance in how to conduct systematic self-reflection and self-evaluation. Learners can be given a rubric or checklist with some clear examples. Teachers might routinely use the same self-assessment format during instruction before formally assessing learners' pragmatic language, so that learners know what to do and how to do it. In a self-assessment task, learners can be asked to compare their production with L2 models provided in order to evaluate key features of their own L2 pragmatic use. Depending on learners' characteristics and learning style preferences, self-assessment tasks such as this one might require various degrees of direction and feedback from the teacher.

Self-assessment might also be undertaken in collaboration with teachers. Unlike the case of assessment conducted by teachers alone, in collaborative

---

[17] Tanaka (1997).

[18] The *Proficiency-Oriented Language Instruction and Assessment (POLIA) Handbook* (Tedick 2002), a curriculum handbook adapting National Standards for Foreign Language Education has reflection as one of the six pillars of effective language learning. This resource is available online (http://www.carla.umn.edu/articulation/MNAP_handbook.html, accessed December 10, 2009).

[19] Kasper and Rose (2002).

assessment learners first reflect on and evaluate their own language. Then, teachers join to further evaluate learners' insights in self-assessment as well as the learner language itself (as in Examples 8 to 10). In developing assessment, teacher-driven assessment tools can be adapted to incorporate learners' self-assessment. For example, teachers can provide reflective prompts that direct learners' attention to key features of pragmatics. Learners' self-evaluation can be placed side-by-side with the teachers' so that they can compare them for further insights. Example 11 below is designed to facilitate learners' reflections concerning their own pragmatic awareness (marked as *1 below) and linguistic control (marked as *2). It includes a successful example of authentic learner language and self-assessment, along with a sample of teacher feedback (see Chapter 7 for instruction given before and after this self-assessment).

Example 11[20]

Situation: Karla takes a large class at a university in Minneapolis. A week before a course paper is due, she notices that she has three more long papers due the same week. She realizes that it is not possible to finish them all by their respective due dates. She decides to go to one of the instructors, Professor Johnson, to ask for an extension on the paper for his course. This is her first time talking to him in private. She approaches him after class is over and says:

Karla: [learner writes] Hi Professor Johnson. Um, will you do me a favor? I was wondering about the paper. Could I get an extension?

Prof. Johnson: But you knew the deadline, didn't you?

Karla: [learner writes] I knew it. But I have three other papers.

Self-evaluation

First, mark an X for status (S), distance (D), and imposition (I) below on the scale and then write what Karla would say to Professor Johnson after class.

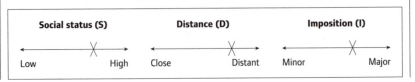

---

[20] Although it is best to assess learners' spoken language in a role-play (or in natural discourse if possible), analysis of written dialogue as it is illustrated here facilitates reflective analysis on the part of both teachers and learners. An example of role-play assessment can be found in Ishihara *et al.* (2008).

1   Given the context, how appropriate was Karla's request in terms of overall directness, formality, politeness, and the tone (e.g., intonation, gesture, eye contact)?

(a)   What part of Karla's language demonstrates appropriate levels of directness, politeness, and formality? (*1)

> [Learner writes] *I was wondering* . . . was a polite expression.

[Teacher feedback] Good.

(b)   What part of her language may need improvement, considering the appropriate level of directness, politeness, and formality called for by this situation? (*1) What should she have said? Write the actual expressions you think she could have used. (*2)

> [Learner writes] Could I get an extension? – I could have asked more politely here, for example: Do you think it'll be possible to get an extension? I was wondering if you could please, please extend the deadline for me.

[Teacher feedback] Yes, nice analysis and appropriate language!

2   Request strategies (supportive moves):

(a)   What requesting strategies did Karla use appropriately? Check the ones she used on the left column, and write out the expressions she used in the right. (*1)

	Requesting strategies	Karla's language
✓	Getting a pre-commitment	[Learner writes] *Um, will you do me a favor?*
✓	Giving a reason for the request	[Learner writes] *I have three other papers* [Teacher feedback] Give more details (e.g., *I have three other papers due the same week. I've been working very hard but . . .*)
	Showing consideration for the hearer/minimizing the imposition	
	Apologizing	
	Thanking/expressing gratitude	
	Sweetener	
	Promising to pay back	

(b) What other strategies could she have used? What might she have said? (*2)

> [Learner writes] I could have offered apologies or asked more humbly, for example:
>
> ■ *Thank you; that will be really helpful.* [Teacher feedback] Good!
>
> ■ *I was wondering if you could please extend the deadline for me. I'd appreciate it.* [Teacher feedback] Good.

3 Listener's interpretation: How do you think Karla's request sounds to Professor Johnson, considering the situation? Check the one that most likely represents the professor's reactions. Then, explain why you think that is the case. (*1)

__ Prof. Johnson would be willing to give her an extension because . . .

✓ He would give her an extension but may not be very happy with Karla's language because . . .

> [Learner writes] My language is not very polite and the reason is unclear. It's not convincing enough for the professor to happily extend the deadline. But I think he'll probably give her extension considering the fact that she came to ask him. [Teacher feedback] Excellent analysis!

__ He may not give her an extension because . . .

Teacher's assessment

*1: Assessment of awareness		*2: Assessment of language	
✓	Excellent analysis	✓	Excellent language
	Good analysis		Good language
	Need more work with the analysis		Need more work with the language

In the classroom setting, a teacher may identify the common misunderstandings among their learners and emphasize more commonly accepted interpretations of L2 pragmatic norms. Learners might need some assistance with linguistic scaffolding, such as grammar or vocabulary explanations, in order to understand the intended meaning accurately or to communicate ideas precisely as intended. Alternatively, learners may need cultural knowledge or want cultural reasoning behind certain L2 pragmatic uses. Teachers might also give learners individual feedback and provide related examples or more extended interactive practice.

Discussion

Successful instruction in pragmatics cannot be complete without assessing learners' receptive and productive ability in pragmatics, as well as their pragmatics-related analytic skills. This chapter has focused on teacher-based assessment of pragmatics in the everyday classroom context and has provided sample assessment instruments, learner language in those assessments, and sample teacher feedback. As has always been stressed in this book, pragmatic norms among competent L2 speakers encompass a healthy degree of variation, which is why they are simply norms and not rigid rules.

In order to use fairer judgment and enhance reliability, teachers may wish to call upon extra raters in assessing learners' pragmatic awareness or ability. Raters would require some sort of training or background information as to the interpretation of each of the rubric or checklist criteria. Raters would also need to reach some level of consensus on the ratings of anchor samples (even though it is unlikely that raters will reach perfect agreement because their appraisals of what constitutes acceptable pragmatic performance could vary). Although such a procedure is time-consuming and may not seem realistic for everyday practice, this process may work for a group of collaborating teachers.[21]

The evaluative efforts introduced in this chapter are still preliminary and should be further refined and researched. Readers are invited to join these assessment endeavors and help enhance effective future practices.

---

[21] This collaborative rating approach has been used successfully in writing portfolio assessment. Further details of the procedure for rater training (although not specifically about L2 pragmatics) can be found elsewhere (e.g., O'Malley and Valdez Pierce 1996).

Activity 15.1 Assessing learners' pragmatic skills

Objectives

1   You will be able to assess learner language and give feedback to students.

2   You will vary your assessment strategies by viewing how other participant teachers deal with learner language.

Suggested time: 30 minutes.

Materials: Task sheet: "Assessing learner language for pragmatics".

Directions

1   First, work individually at this task, as is probably the case with classroom-based assessment. Read the sample learner language given in the task sheet and write down what you would actually say in response to the learners. Consider learners' goals and intentions in evaluating their responses and inform learners of how their responses would be most likely interpreted in the target community (see Examples 8–10 in this chapter).

2   With someone next to you, discuss your written feedback to learners.

3   Each pair reports back to the whole group as to the similarities and differences between each others' assessment and feedback.

Discussion/wrap-up

Consider and discuss the insights and challenges that you may have gained or encountered while doing this task. What solutions might there be to the issues and challenges in assessing learners' pragmatic use of language?

Task sheet: Assessing learner language for pragmatics

Read the following authentic learner-language samples[22] **provided in comic font,** assess them, and give feedback under "Teacher's comments" as you would in your classroom setting.

---

[22] The actual learner language in samples 1 and 2 is adapted from Ishihara (2004: 47, 56) and sample 3 is from Bardovi-Harlig and Hartford (1991: 45–6).

Sample 1	Sample 2
Your friend, Kate, is giving you praise. Write your response as if you were talking to her.	Your friend, Steve, is complimenting you on your class presentation. Write your response as if you were talking to him.

Sample 1	Sample 2
Kate: I like your hat. You: **Keep liking**.	Steve: Nice job! You: **No, I didn't do well**.
Indicate your intention as a speaker.	Indicate your intention as a speaker.

Sample 1

_X_ I want to make a response the way most people do in the community.

___ I would want my response to sound (a little) more (formal/informal), (polite/ impolite), or _____ than most other people.

___ I choose not to use common behavior because _____

___ Other (Specify: _____)

Teachers' comments:

Sample 2

___ I want to make a response the way most people do in the community.

_X_ I would want my response to sound ((a little)) more (formal/informal), (polite/ impolite), or <u>humble</u> than most other people.

___ I choose not to use common behavior because _____

___ Other (Specify: _____)

Teachers' comments:

Sample 3

You are a graduate student in your academic advisor's office. You are discussing the courses you are going to take next semester. Your advisor recommends an ESL writing course but you really don't want to take it. Now role-play with the advisor.

Advisor (A): You do need to take a couple of English courses but . . .

Student (S): But I think this Sentence Writing may . . . Sentence Writing is too simple.

A: Well, why do you think it's too simple?

S: Because in Taiwan I do I did a lot of exercise on that . . .

A: Umm, do you know how it's taught here?

S: I don't know, but I think . . . because I understand fundamental of paragraph writing. The only deficiency I have is experience, so I think I can improve by myself·

Indicate your intention as a speaker.

 __X__ I want to make a refusal the way most people do in the community to avoid taking that course.

 ____ I would want my refusal to sound (a little) more (formal/informal), (polite/ impolite), or _____ than most other people, and avoid taking the course.

 ____ I do not wish to make a refusal, regardless of whether I end up having to take the course (reason: _____

 _____)

 ____ Other (Specify: _____

 _____)

Teachers' comments:

Possible assessment/feedback

Sample 1

Because you and Kate are friends, your level of formality is appropriate. Your response carries a humorous tone because your word choice, *keep liking*, is uncommon in American English (even though *keep -ing* is grammatical). However, Kate will most likely understand your message fine. Most people would say, "Thanks," "(I'm) glad you like it".

Sample 2

Because you and Steve are friends, your level of formality is appropriate. Steve may understand your modesty and politeness if he knows you well. Other people may feel rejected if you have a sharp or flat tone of voice; direct refusal of compliments is very strong and can be impolite. Most English speakers phrase their modesty this way: "Do you really think so?" "Well, I didn't think so myself, but thanks," or "I think it could have been better."

Sample 3

Your level of formality is appropriate in this dialogue, but your overall tone seems too direct and inappropriate. In American English, it's customary to soften your refusal a great deal, because you are speaking to your advisor (someone of higher social status). For example, *Yes, I've been thinking* about Sentence Writing but it *could in fact be a little bit basic* for me. You could also present your reasons for refusing her advice differently (e.g., *I've taken similar courses in Taiwan*) or use another reason (e.g., *that class conflicts with what I have to take*).

Activity 15.2 Adapting pragmatics assessment tools to incorporate self-evaluation and learner goals/intentions

Objectives

1   You will be able to construct assessment tools that utilize learners' self-evaluation.

2   You will be able to incorporate learners' goals and intentions as a basis of assessment.

Suggested time: 30 minutes.

Materials:

- Information: "Sample assessment tools";
- overhead projector transparencies and transparency pens (or large construction paper and felt pens).

Directions

1   Work in a small group of approximately three to adapt the sample rubrics originally designed for teacher use. For Sample 1, provide more linguistic and cultural scaffolding so that learners (high beginners) are able to assess their own pragmatics using your revised tool. For Sample 2, make some revision to the teacher's assessment to explicitly address learners' goals (what they want to achieve through their use of language) and intentions (how they want to present themselves). Using the assessment in its current form is likely to disregard the learners' actual intent for the given situation and assess learner language based on default community norms.[23] As a result, this assessment fails to elicit learners'

---

[23] As discussed earlier in this chapter, the practice of using native-speaker baseline data is appropriate as long as learners want to sound native-like on this task. However, it could be perceived as cultural imposition if the learners are actually attempting to express themselves in a way that distinguishes them from typical community members.

pragmatic awareness and production in its present status as the learner decides to "opt out" and say nothing. Look back at Examples 8–10 in this chapter for making revisions if necessary.

2   Each group transfers their finished rubrics to overhead transparencies or large construction paper.

3   Show your work and report your group discussion to the whole class.

Discussion/wrap-up

Self-evaluation supports students in becoming observant, reflective, and independent in their learning process. Employment of learners' goals is also an important component in culturally sensitive instruction and assessment of L2 pragmatics. Consider and discuss potential benefits and drawbacks of self-evaluation and assessment based on the learners' goals and intentions. Consider what could be done to maximize the benefits, and avoid or minimize the drawbacks.

Information: Sample assessment tools

Sample 1

Situation: James is trying to do some homework but his roommate, Sam, is watching a variety show on TV and has the volume up so loud that it is distracting James and making it hard to concentrate. James talks to Sam (learner language provided in comic font):

James: Hey Sam.

Sam: Yeah?

James: While I study, can you low a volume?

Sam: Come on, why don't you just take a break and watch this with me? It's an awesome show, you know.

James: Oh, . . . I want to study!!

Sam: Well, okay. No problem.

Teacher's evaluation
4 – Very appropriate; 3 – Somewhat appropriate; 2 – Less appropriate, 1 – Inappropriate

1 Level of formality, directness, and politeness	4 3 2 1
2 Strategies of requests	4 3 2 1
3 Vocabulary and phrases	4 3 2 1
4 Pragmatic tone	4 3 2 1

Sample 2

Situation: Your neighbors next door just moved in two weeks ago, and you have not met them yet. It is now midnight and you are just about ready to go to bed, but your new neighbors are playing loud music. You have a very important test tomorrow morning and need to get as much sleep as possible before your alarm starts ringing at six o'clock tomorrow morning.[24] You knock on their door:

[Learner says] I'll try to sleep with ear plugs and won't say anthing.

Choice and use of strategies of complaining

(a) Strategies of complaining used: _____

(b) Appropriateness of the choice of strategies (place an X below)

Very appropriate   Appropriate   Fair   Inappropriate

(c) Appropriateness/effectiveness of the strategies used

Very appropriate   Appropriate   Fair   Inappropriate

Tone of complaining

(a) Tone communicated by the complaint: _____

(b) Appropriateness of the tone in complaining

Very appropriate   Appropriate   Fair   Inappropriate

[24] Situation adapted from Arent (1996).

Conclusion

As can be seen from the thrust of this book, we feel strongly that the time has come for teachers to make even greater strides than they now do to extend their teaching beyond the presentation of decontextualized language forms. The aim of this book is to encourage teacher readers to support learners in interpreting what people really mean in the target language and in expressing themselves the way that they want to. Too frequently learners memorize words and phrases, and then find that they do not really know when and how to use them effectively. This book appears at a time when there is a wave of interest in enhancing learners' control over the pragmatics of the language. The book joins others that give special focus to the classroom, and views teachers as facilitators in the classroom. The material in this book is intended to be used both in teacher development programs and in direct implementation of L2 pragmatics instruction in the classroom.

The book started by defining terms in the field of pragmatics. It then addressed the issue of teachers' knowledge and beliefs about pragmatics, and how they may affect what teachers do or do not do in the language classroom. With the realization that no textbook could possibly provide all the relevant pragmatics material that a given learner needs, suggestions were provided as to how learners could collect and analyze the kinds of data they might need for successful communication and further independent learning. The spotlight was put on intentional and unintentional divergence from the perceived community's pragmatic norms, since there may be various reasons for why learners at times fail to achieve a desired outcome and why at other times they deliberately make individual pragmatic choices.

Needless to say, the successful integration of pragmatics instruction in the curriculum depends in no small part on the knowledge, understanding, and instructional prowess of classroom teachers and teacher educators. For this reason, the book has offered instructional principles, practical suggestions, and activities for engaging teacher readers in issues related to the teaching of L2 pragmatics at a genuinely operational level. We have described and illustrated various characteristics of pragmatics instruction, drawing both on published literature and on strategies-based internet sites for learner self-access. We have given attention both to classroom lessons and to websites specializing in pragmatics. We have also made efforts to illustrate practical strides that have been made to provide instruction in pragmatics to L2 learners.

The book has also dealt with two other dimensions that have a crucial bearing on the potential success of a pragmatics focus in the curriculum. The first is that of students' strategies for learning pragmatics and performing what they have learned. The intention is for teachers to encourage learners to review their repertoire of strategies, with an eye to enhancing their learning of pragmatics, a complex and challenging area for learners at all levels. The other dimension is that of assessment, which is an area inextricably intertwined with instruction. In our opinion, one means of boosting student motivation for learning is by getting them to understand the value of learning pragmatics, by making sure that their pragmatic ability is assessed, and by making sure that they get feedback regarding their use of pragmatics. So we have devoted Chapters 14 and 15 to issues of assessment in the classroom, an area that is largely neglected in many professional volumes on pragmatics, which usually focus on assessment for research purposes.

We would hope that exposure to the issues voiced in this volume has encouraged you to undertake this enterprise, or to take it on with renewed vigor. Your efforts might start small, such as by just asking learners to comment on the likely relationship between the conversational partners in dialogues. Learners could then be invited to consider how language might differ according to their given partner in a particular interaction, since degree of acquaintance, relative social position, and the context of the interaction can all influence the nature of the interaction (see Chapter 8). Or you may want to adapt currently available material quite extensively, or even design a new curriculum with pragmatics as an organizing principle. In any case, if explicit teaching of pragmatics is yet to be recognized or practiced systematically in your local context, there could be some challenges in the process.

In this conclusion, we would once again encourage those of you who are teacher readers to engage in focused reflection and goal-setting. First, in order to further organize your knowledge and beliefs about teaching pragmatics, it may be helpful to go back to the reflective prompts introduced in Activity 2.1 in Chapter 2. These prompts invite the teacher readers among you to articulate how your experience of learning L2 pragmatics and professional preparation may have shaped your beliefs as to how you teach pragmatics. The prompts also focus attention on certain logistical issues with regard to how to teach and assess pragmatics, as well as raising the fundamental question as to whose norms for pragmatics to use in the classroom. In the reflective portion of the exercise, it may be beneficial to review the thoughts and reflections that you have engaged in while working through Chapters 6, 10 and 11. As we have discussed in Chapter 2, teachers can benefit from becoming fully aware of the knowledge and beliefs that they have about pragmatics. Once they have heightened their awareness, they have a better chance of making informed choices about how to link their beliefs to daily practices. This process can be an empowering one, in which teachers find themselves better able to make decisions about whether or how to change their practice when necessary.

Next, we would like to suggest some goal-setting for pragmatics instruction, if it in fact is part of our teacher readers' ongoing professional pursuit. Incorporating pragmatics into the classroom (especially using research-based information) may require determination even on the part of a most committed teacher. This is because it is a multi-step process, which includes deciding on the L2 pragmatics content to teach, planning the instruction, preparing the materials, and conducting assessment to determine what has been learned. What is a realistic timeline for these efforts? What resources would be necessary, which would actually be available, and what instructional materials would assist this new teaching endeavor? What steps would need to be taken in order to access these resources and to obtain the necessary instructional materials? What issues might still need to be resolved before launching into the teaching of pragmatics?

In addition, there may be a need for institutional support in order to add a pragmatics focus to the curriculum. Those of you who are teacher readers may wish to enlist your colleagues' support in this endeavor. It facilitates this process if you have colleagues who already see the value of teaching appropriate language use in context. If this does not reflect the reality, then you might need to advocate for the integration of pragmatics into the existing curriculum. How can this begin? Is there some kind of collaborative group or task force to join, or would it be possible to form one? And again, what is a realistic timeline for such efforts?

At times you may have the impression that you are on your own in the efforts to develop a pragmatics component in the curriculum. In fact, a connection to a professional network may be effective in order to sustain the enthusiasm and commitment to teaching pragmatics. The good news is that the professional community does offer regional, national, and international support on a variety of subjects, including instruction in L2 pragmatics. For example, various professional organizations for language teaching have interest groups for pragmatics, intercultural communication, sociolinguistics, and other related areas. Annual conferences of these organizations typically have sessions on teaching pragmatics. If you already have experience teaching pragmatics or even in conducting classroom-based research on your instructional practices (as described in Activity 2.2 in Chapter 2), it would be fruitful to present at one of these sessions in the near future.

Workshops and summer institutes are another place where professionals sharing the same instructional and research interests congregate. In fact, the summer institute at the University of Minnesota's CARLA has been a productive and inspiring place since 2006, where interested teachers share their passion for advocating pragmatics in language education, learn from each other, and become part of this exciting professional community.

Finally, we would like to emphasize that the effort to promote systematic teaching of pragmatics in the L2 curriculum instruction is a relatively recent endeavor. This is precisely why there are challenges ahead and there are areas that were not covered in this volume that need to be dealt with in the future. For example, there are issues of authenticity to consider at multiple levels. How can we make efforts to teach pragmatics truly consistent with learners' genuine needs? What situations and whose norms are most relevant to the learners' purposes (especially in **foreign-language** contexts)? Furthermore, how can we teach authentic language use and authentic pragmatic variation if the bulk of the research-based information is based on elicited data?

There also are issues of teacher education. How prepared are teachers to provide pragmatics instruction? How can we better incorporate pragmatics into teacher education? Should we teach L2 pragmatics to learners at a young age, and if so, how might the instruction and teacher education be different from those for teaching adults? These issues of authenticity and teacher education are two of the questions voiced in professional conferences in the past few years. We need to address these issues by accumulating enhanced research results and by reconciling creative pedagogical innovations.

In closing, let us just reiterate our aim that this book serve as a springboard for active discussion regarding pragmatics. It is our hope that the book will foster the fruitful collaboration of teachers, curriculum writers, researchers, and teacher educators who are of like mind in their willingness to enhance the teaching of pragmatics. The empirically validated instruction of pragmatics can be truly possible only through the collaborative insights of all engaged in language education. Consequently, contributions of each of our readers can most definitely play a crucial role in the future development of instructional pragmatics.

References

ACTFL (1999) ACTFL proficiency guidelines: Speaking. (n.d.). Retrieved November 26, 2008, from http://www.sil.org/lingualinks/ LANGUAGELEARNING/OtherResources/ACTFLProficiencyGuidelines/ ACTFLGuidelinesSpeaking.htm.

Adolphs, S. (2006) *Introducing electronic text analysis: A practical guide for language and literary studies*. London: Routledge.

Akikawa, K., and Ishihara, N. (in press) "Please write a recommendation letter": Teaching to write e-mail requests to faculty. In D. Tatsuki and N. Houck (eds), *TESOL classroom practice series: Pragmatics volume*. Alexandria, VA: Teachers of English to Speakers of Other Languages.

Alcón, E. (2005) Does instruction work for learning pragmatics in the EFL context? *System*, 33(3), 417–35.

Allwright, D. (2001) Three major processes of teacher development and the appropriate design criteria for developing and using them. In B. Johnston and S. Irujo (eds) *Research and practice in language teacher education: Voices from the field*. Minneapolis, MN: Center for Advanced Research on Language Acquisition, 115–131.

Allwright, D. (2003) Exploratory practice: Rethinking practitioner research in language teaching. *Language Teaching Research*, 7(2), 113–41.

Anderson, J. (2006) Form, meaning, and use of English negation. Class handout at American University, Washington, DC.

Arcario, P. (1993) Criteria for selecting video materials. In S. Stempleski and P. Arcario (eds), *Video in second language teaching: Using, selecting, and producing video for the classroom*. Alexandria, VA: Teachers of English to Speakers of Other Languages, 109–121.

Archer, E. (in press) They made me an offer I couldn't refuse: Teaching refusal strategies for invitations. In D. Tatsuki and N. Houck (eds),

TESOL classroom practice series: Pragmatics volume. Alexandria, VA: Teachers of English to Speakers of Other Languages.

Arent, R. (1996) Sociopragmatic decisions regarding complaints by Chinese learners and NSs of American English. *Hong Kong Journal of Applied Linguistics*, 1(1), 125–47.

Armstrong, S. (2008) Desperate housewives in an EFL classroom. *Pragmatic Matters*, 9(1), 4–7.

Aston, G. (1993) Notes on the interlanguage of comity. In G. Kasper and S. Blum-Kulka (eds), *Interlanguage pragmatics.* Oxford, England: Oxford University Press, 224–50.

Bardovi-Harlig, K. (1992) Pragmatics as part of teacher education. *TESOL Journal*, 1(3), 28–32.

Bardovi-Harlig, K. (1996) Pragmatics and language teaching: Bringing pragmatics and pedagogy together. In L. F. Bouton (ed.), *Pragmatics and language learning* (Vol. 7). Urbana, IL: Division of English as an International Language, University of Illinois at Urbana-Champaign, 21–39.

Bardovi-Harlig, K. (1999) Exploring the interlanguage of interlanguage pragmatics: A research agenda for acquisitional pragmatics. *Language Learning*, 49(4), 677–713.

Bardovi-Harlig, K. (2001) Evaluating the empirical evidence: Grounds for instruction in pragmatics? In K. R. Rose and G. Kasper (eds), *Pragmatics in language teaching.* Cambridge, England: Cambridge University Press, 13–32.

Bardovi-Harlig, K. (2003) Understanding the role of grammar in the acquisition of L2 pragmatics. In A. M. Flor, E. U. Juan, and A. F. Guerra (eds), *Pragmatic competence and foreign language teaching.* Castellón, Spain: Servicio de publicaciones de la Universidad Jaume I, 25–44.

Bardovi-Harlig, K. (2006). On the role of formulas in the acquisition of L2 pragmatics. In K. Bardovi-Harlig, C. Félix-Brasdefer and A. Omar (eds), *Pragmatics and Language Learning*, (Vol. 11). Honolulu, MI: National Foreign Language Resource Center, University of Hawaii at Manua, 1–28.

Bardovi-Harlig, K., and Hartford, B. S. (1991) Saying "no" in English: Native and nonnative rejections. In L. Bouton and Y. Kachru (eds), *Pragmatics and language learning* (Vol. 2). Urbana, IL: Division of English as an International Language, University of Illinois at Urbana-Champaign, 41–57.

Bardovi-Harlig, K., and Hartford, B. S. (1993*a*) Learning the rules of academic talk: A longitudinal study of pragmatic change. *Studies in Second Language Acquisition*, 15(3), 279–304.

Bardovi-Harlig, K., and Hartford, B. S. (1993*b*) Refining the DCT: Comparing open questionnaires and dialogue completion tasks. In L. F. Bouton and Y. Kachru (eds), *Pragmatics and language learning* (Vol. 4). Urbana, IL: Division of English as an International Language, University of Illinois at Urbana-Champaign, 143–65.

Bardovi-Harlig, K., and Hartford, B. S. (2005) Institutional discourse and interlanguage pragmatics research. In K. Bardovi-Harlig and B. S. Hartford (eds), *Interlanguage pragmatics: Exploring institutional talk*. Mahwah, NJ: Lawrence Erlbaum Associates, 7–36.

Bardovi-Harlig, K., Hartford, B. S., Mahan-Taylor, R., Morgan, M. J., and Reynolds, D. W. (1991) Developing pragmatic awareness: Closing conversation. *ELT Journal,* 45(1), 4–15.

Bardovi-Harlig, K., and Mahan-Taylor, R. (eds). (2003) *Teaching pragmatics*. Washington, DC: Office of English Language Programs, US Department of State. Retrieved June 23, 2009, from http://exchanges. state.gov/englishteaching/resforteach/pragmatics.html.

Barkhuizen, G. (2008) A narrative approach to exploring context in language teaching. *ELT Journal*, 62(3), 231–9.

Barnlund, D. C., and Araki, S. (1985) Intercultural encounters: The management of compliments by Japanese and Americans. *Journal of Cross-Cultural Psychology*, 16(1), 9–26.

Barron, A. (2003) *Acquisition in interlanguage pragmatics: Learning how to do things with words in a study abroad context*. Amsterdam: John Benjamins Publishing Company.

Barron, A. (2005) Variational pragmatics in the foreign language classroom. *System,* 33(3), 519–36.

Barsony, O. (2003) "Actually, the deadline was Friday of last week, not this week." In K. Bardovi-Harlig and R. Mahan-Taylor (eds), *Teaching pragmatics*. Washington, DC: Office of English Programs, US Department of State. Retrieved June 23, 2009, from http://exchanges. state.gov/media/oelp/teaching-pragmatics/barsony.pdf.

Bayley, R., and Schecter, S. R. (2003) *Language socialization in bilingual and multilingual societies*. Clevedon, England: Multilingual Matters.

Béal, C. (1992) Did you have a good weekend?: Or why there is no such thing as a simple question in cross-cultural encounters? *Australian Review of Applied Linguistics*, 15(1), 23–52.

Beebe, L. M., and Cummings, M. C. (1996) Natural speech act data versus written questionnaire data: How data collection method affects speech act performance. In S. M. Gass and J. Neu (eds), *Speech acts across cultures: Challenges to communication in a second language*. Berlin, Germany: Mouton de Gruyter, 65–86.

Beebe, L. M., and Giles, H. (1984) Speech accommodation theories: A discussion in terms of second-language acquisition. *International Journal of the Sociology of Language*, 46(5), 5–32.

Beebe, L. M., Takahashi, T., and Uliss-Weltz, R. (1990) Pragmatic transfer in ESL refusals. In R. Scarcella, E. Andersen, and S. D. Krashen (eds), *On the development of communicative competence in a second language*. New York: Newbury House/HarperCollins, 55–73.

Beebe, L. M., and Waring, H. Z. (2004) The linguistic encoding of pragmatic tone: Adverbials as words that work. In D. Boxer and A. D. Cohen (eds), *Studying speaking to inform second language learning*. Clevedon: Multilingual Matters, 228–49.

Beebe, L. M., and Zuengler, J. (1983) Accommodation theory: An explanation for style shifting in second language dialects. In N. Wolfson and E. Judd (eds), *Sociolinguistics and language acquisition*. Rowley, MA: Newbury House Publishers, 195–213.

Bell, J. (2002) Narrative inquiry: More than just telling stories. *TESOL Quarterly*, 36(2), 278–87.

Belz, J. A. (2007) The role of computer mediation in the instruction and development of L2 pragmatic competence. *Annual Review of Applied Linguistics*, 27, 45–75.

Belz, J. A., and Kinginger, C. (2002) The cross-linguistic development of address form use in telecollaborative language learning: Two case studies. *Canadian Modern Language Review*, 59(2), 189–214.

Berger, P., and Luckmann, T. (1967) *The social construction of reality*. Garden City, NY: Doubleday.

Berry, A. (2003) Are you listening? (backchannel behaviors). In K. Bardovi-Harlig and R. Mahan-Taylor (eds), *Teaching pragmatics*. Washington, DC: Office of English Programs, US Department of State. Retrieved June 23, 2009, from http://exchanges.state.gov/media/oelp/teaching-pragmatics/berry.pdf.

Bialystok, E. (1993) Symbolic representation and attentional control in pragmatic competence. In G. Kasper and S. Blum-Kulka (eds), *Interlanguage pragmatics*. Oxford, England: Oxford University Press, 43–59.

Biber, D., Conrad, S., and Reppen, R. (1998) *Corpus linguistics investigating language structure and use*. Cambridge, England: Cambridge University Press.

Biber, D., Conrad, S., Reppen, R., Byrd, P., and Helt, M. (2002) Speaking and writing in the university: A multidimensional comparison. *TESOL Quarterly* 36(1), 9–48.

Billmyer, K. (1990) "I really like your lifestyle": ESL learners learning how to compliment. *Penn Working Papers in Educational Linguistics*, 6(2), 31–48.

Bloom, B. S. (ed.). (1956) *Taxonomy of educational objectives: The classification of educational goals. Handbook I: Cognitive domain*. New York: Longmans, Green.

Blum-Kulka, S., House, J., and Kasper, G. (eds). (1989) *Cross-cultural pragmatics: Requests and apologies*. Norwood, NJ: Ablex Publishing.

Blum-Kulka, S., and Olshtain, E. (1984) Requests and apologies: A cross-cultural study of speech act realization patterns (CCSARP). *Applied Linguistics*, 5(3), 196–214.

Borg, S. (2003) Teacher cognition in language teaching: A review of research on what language teachers think, know, believe, and do. *Language Teaching*, 36(2), 81–109.

Borg, S. (2006) *Teacher cognition and language education: Research and practice*. London: Continuum.

Bou-Franch, P., and Garcés-Conejos, P. (2003) Teaching linguistic politeness: A methodological proposal. *IRAL*, 41(1), 1–22.

Bouton, L. (1990) The effective use of implicature in English: Why and how it should be taught in the ESL classroom? In L. Bouton and Y. Kachru (eds), *Pragmatics and language learning* (Vol. 1). Urbana, IL: Division of English as an International Language, University of Illinois at Urbana-Champaign, 43–52.

Bouton, L. (1994*a*) Can NNS skill in interpreting implicature in American English be improved through explicit instruction: A pilot study. In L. Bouton and Y. Kachru (eds), *Pragmatics and language learning*

(Vol. 5). Urbana, IL: Division of English as an International Language, University of Illinois at Urbana-Champaign, 88–109.

Bouton, L. F. (1994*b*) Conversational implicature in a second language: Learned slowly when not deliberately taught. *Journal of Pragmatics*, 22(2), 157–67.

Bouton, L. F. (1999) Developing nonnative speaker skills in interpreting conversational implicatures in English: Explicit teaching can ease the process. In E. Hinkel (ed.), *Culture in second language teaching and learning*. Cambridge: Cambridge University Press, 43–70.

Boxer, D., and Pickering, L. (1995) Problems in the presentation of speech acts in ELT materials: The case of complaints. *ELT Journal*, 49(1), 44–58.

Brown, H. D. (2001) *Teaching by principles: An interactive approach to language pedagogy* (2nd edn). New York: Addison Wesley Longman.

Brown, H. D. (2004) *Language assessment: Principles and classroom practices*. New York: Longman.

Brown, H. D., and Hudson, T. (1998) The alternatives in language assessment. *TESOL Quarterly*, 32(4), 653–75.

Brown, J. D. (2001) Pragmatics tests: Different purposes, different tests. In K. R. Rose and G. Kasper (eds), *Pragmatics in language teaching*. Cambridge, England: Cambridge University Press, 301–25.

Brown, P., and Levinson, S. C. (1987) *Politeness: Some universals in language use*. Cambridge, England: Cambridge University Press.

Burns, A. (1999) Definitions and processes. In A. Burns (ed.), *Collaborative action research for English language teachers*. Cambridge, England: Cambridge University Press, 20–44.

Burt, S. M. (2001) Non-conventionalized blessings: Have a good rest of your life in Illinois. Paper presented at the Annual Conference of the American Association for Applied Linguistics, St. Louis, MO, February.

Byram, M., and Morgan, C. (1994) *Teaching and learning language and culture*. Clevedon, England: Multilingual Matters.

Calderhead, J. (1996) Teachers: Beliefs and knowledge. In D. C. Berliner and R. C. Calfee (eds), *Handbook of educational psychology*. New York: Macmillan, 709–25.

Campo, E., and Zuluaga, J. (2000) Complimenting: A matter of cultural constraints. *Colombian Applied Linguistics Journal*, 2(1), 27–41.

Canale, M., and Swain, M. (1980) Theoretical bases of communicative approaches to second language teaching and testing. *Applied Linguistics*, 1(1), 1–47.

Carter, R., and McCarthy, M. (1995) Grammar and spoken language. *Applied Linguistics*, 16(2), 141–58.

Carter, R., and McCarthy, M. (2004) Talking, creating: Interactional language, creativity, and context. *Applied Linguistics*, 25(1), 62–88.

Celce-Murcia, M., Brinton, D. M., and Goodwin, J. M. (1996) *Teaching pronunciation: A reference for teachers of English to speakers of other languages*. Cambridge, England: Cambridge University Press.

Celce-Murcia, M., and Larsen-Freeman, D. (1999). *The grammar book: An ESL/EFL teacher's course* (2nd edn). Boston: Heinle & Heinle.

Chamot, A. U. (2008) Strategy instruction and good language learners. In C. Griffiths (ed.), *Lessons from good language learners*. Cambridge, England: Cambridge University Press, 266–81.

Chen, R. (1993) Responding to compliments: A contrastive study of politeness strategies between American English and Chinese speakers. *Journal of Pragmatics*, 20(1), 49–75.

Chen, X., Ye, L., and Zhang, Y. (1995) Refusing in Chinese. In G. Kasper (ed.), *Pragmatics of Chinese as a native and target language*. Honolulu: University of Hawai'i Press, 119–63.

Clark, D. (2001) Learning domains or Bloom's taxonomy. Retrieved September 28, 2008, from http://www.nwlink.com/~donclark/hrd/bloom.html.

Cohen, A. D. (1998) *Strategies in learning and using a second language*. Harlow, England: Longman.

Cohen, A. D. (2004) Assessing speech acts in a second language. In B. Boxer and A. D. Cohen (eds), *Studying speaking to inform second language learning*. Clevedon, England: Multilingual Matters, 302–27.

Cohen, A. D. (2005) Strategies for learning and performing L2 speech acts. *Intercultural Pragmatics*, 2(3), 275–301.

Cohen, A. D. (2007a) Becoming a strategic language learner in CALL. *Applied Language Learning*, 17(1–2), 57–71.

Cohen, A. D. (2007b) Coming to terms with language learner strategies: Surveying the experts. In A. D. Cohen and E. Macaro (eds), *Language learner strategies: 30 years of research and practice*. Oxford, England: Oxford University Press, 29–45.

Cohen, A. D., and Ishihara, N. (2005) *A web-based approach to strategic learning of speech acts*. Minneapolis, MN: Center for Advanced Research on Language Acquisition, University of Minnesota. Retrieved November 30, 2008, from: http://www.carla.umn.edu/speechacts/ Japanese%20Speech%20Act%20Report%20Rev.%20June05.pdf.

Cohen, A. D., and Olshtain, E. (1981) Developing a measure of socio-cultural competence: The case of apology. *Language Learning*, 31(1), 113–34.

Cohen, A. D., and Olshtain, E. (1993) The production of speech acts by EFL learners. *TESOL Quarterly*, 27(1), 33–56.

Cohen, A. D., Olshtain, E., and Rosenstein, D. S. (1986) Advanced EFL apologies: What remains to be learned? *International Journal of the Sociology of Language*, 62(6), 51–74.

Cohen, A. D., Paige, R. M., Shively, R. L., Emert, H., and Hoff, J. (2005) Maximizing study abroad through language and culture strategies: Research on students, study abroad program professionals, and language instructors. *Final Report to the International Research and Studies Program, Office of International Education, DOE*. Minneapolis, MN: Center for Advanced Research on Language Acquisition, University of Minnesota. Retrieved November 30, 2008, from http:// www.carla.umn.edu/maxsa/documents/MAXSAResearchReport_000.pdf.

Cohen, A. D., and Shively, R., L. (2003) Measuring speech acts with multiple rejoinder DCTs. *Language Testing Update*, 32, 39–42.

Cohen, A. D., and Shively, R. L. (2007) Acquisition of requests and apologies in Spanish and French: Impact of study abroad and strategy-building intervention. *Modern Language Journal*, 91(2), 189–212.

Cohen, A. D., and Tarone, E. (1994) The effects of training on written speech act behavior: Stating and changing an opinion. *MinneTESOL Journal*, 12, 39–62.

Cohen, A. D., and Weaver, S. J. (2006) *Styles and strategies-based instruction: A teachers' guide*. Minneapolis, MN: Center for Advanced Research on Language Acquisition, University of Minnesota.

Cohen, A. D., Weaver, S. J., and Li, T.-Y. (1998) The impact of strategies-based instruction on speaking a foreign language. In A. D. Cohen, *Strategies in learning and using a second language*. Harlow, England: Longman, 107–56.

Coulmas, F. (1981) "Poison to your soul": Thanks and apologies contrastively viewed. In F. Coulmas (ed.), *Conversational routine:*

Explorations in standardized communication situations and prepatterned speech. The Hague, Netherlands: Mouton Publishers, 69–91.

Crandall, E., and Basturkmen, H. (2004) Evaluating pragmatics-focused materials. *ELT Journal*, 58(1), 38–49.

Daikuhara, M. (1986) A study of compliments from a cross-cultural perspective: Japanese vs American English. *Working Papers in Educational Linguistics*, 2(2), 103–34.

Daly, N., Holmes, J., Newton, J., and Stubbe, M. (2004) Expletives as solidarity signals in FTAs on the factory floor. *Journal of Pragmatics*, 36(5), 945–64.

Decco, W. (1996) The induction–deduction opposition: Ambiguities and complexities of the didactic reality. *IRAL*, 34(2), 95–118.

Derewianka, B. (2003) Developing electronic materials for language. In B. Tomlinson (ed.), *Developing materials for language teaching*. London: Continuum, 199–220.

Dewaele, J. M. (2005) Investigating the psychological and emotional dimensions in instructed language learning: Obstacles and possibilities. *Modern Language Journal*, 89(3), 367–80.

Di Vito, N. O. (1993) Second culture acquisition: A tentative step in determining hierarchies. In J. E. Alatis (ed.), *Georgetown University Round Table on Languages and Linguistics 1992: Language, communication, and social meaning*. Washington, DC: Georgetown University Press, 324–35.

Dörnyei, Z. (1995) On the teachability of communication strategies. *TESOL Quarterly*, 29(1), 55–85.

Dörnyei, Z., and Thurrell, S. (1998) Linguistics at work: A reader of applications. In D. D. Oaks (ed.), *Linguistics at work: A reader of applications*. Fort Worth, TX: Harcourt Brace, 674–86. (Original work published in 1994)

DuFon, M. A. (1999) The acquisition of linguistic politeness in Indonesian as a second language by sojourners in a naturalistic context. Unpublished doctoral dissertation, University of Hawaii, Honolulu.

DuFon, M. A. (2008) Language socialization theory and the acquisition of pragmatics in the foreign language classroom. In E. S. Alcón and A. Martínez-Flor (eds), *Investigating pragmatics in foreign language learning, teaching, and testing*. Bristol, England: Multilingual Matters, 25–44.

Dunham, P. (1992) Using compliments in the ESL classroom: An analysis of culture and gender. *MinneTESOL Journal,* 10, 75–85.

Edge, J. (2002) *Continuing cooperative development: A discourse framework for individuals as colleagues.* Ann Arbor, MI: University of Michigan Press.

Ellis, R. (1994) *The study of second language acquisition.* Oxford, England: Oxford University Press.

Eslami-Rasekh, Z. (2005) Raising the pragmatic awareness of language learners. *ELT Journal,* 59(3), 199–208.

Eslami, Z. R., and Eslami-Resekh, A. (2008) Enhancing the pragmatic competence of non-native English-speaking teacher candidates (NNESTCs) in an EFL context. In E. S. Alcón and M. P. Safont (eds), *Intercultural language use and language learning.* Dordrecht, The Netherlands: Springer, 178–97.

Estrada, A., Gates, S., and Ramsland, J. (2006) Pragmatics-focused lesson plan: Compliments. Course paper at the University of Minnesota, MN.

Félix-Brasdefer, J. C. (2003) Declining an invitation: A cross-cultural study of pragmatic strategies in American English and Latin American Spanish. *Multilingua,* 22(3), 225–55.

Félix-Brasdefer, J. C. (2005) Discourse pragmatics. Retrieved November 8, 2007, from http://www.indiana.edu/~discprag/index.html.

Félix-Brasdefer, J. C. (2006) Teaching the negotiation of multi-turn speech acts: Using conversation-analytic tools to teach pragmatics in the FL classroom. In K. Bardovi-Harlig, J. C. Félix-Brasdefer, and A. S. Omar (eds), *Pragmatics and language learning* (Vol. 11). Honolulu: University of Hawai'i Press, 167–97.

Firth, A. (1996) The discursive accomplishment of normality: On "lingua franca" English and conversation analysis. *Journal of Pragmatics,* 26(2), 237–59.

Fordyce, K. (2008) Japanese EFL learners' use and acquisition of epistemic stance forms: Focusing on descriptive and discursive spoken language. Paper presented at the Annual Conference of the Second Language Research Forum, Honolulu, HI, October.

Freeman, D. (2002) The hidden side of the work: Teacher knowledge and learning to teach. *Language Teaching,* 35(1), 1–13.

Freeman, D., and Johnson, K. E. (1998) Reconceptualizing the knowledge-base of language teacher education. *TESOL Quarterly,* 32(3), 397–417.

Fujioka, M. (2003) Raising pragmatic consciousness in the Japanese EFL classroom. *The Language Teacher*, 27(5), 12–14.

Fujioka, M. (2004) Film analysis: A way to raise Japanese EFL learners' sociolinguistic awareness. *Kinki University Multimedia Education*, 3, 15–25.

Fujioka, M. (2005) The speech act of suggesting as part of peer response activities. In D. Tatsuki (ed.), *Pragmatics in language learning, theory, and practice*. Tokyo: The Japan Association for Language Teaching Pragmatics Special Interest Group, 166–70.

Fukuya, Y. J., and Clark, M. K. (2001) A comparison of input enhancement and explicit instruction of mitigators. In L. F. Bouton and Y. Kachru (eds), *Pragmatics and language learning* (Vol. 10). Urbana, IL: Division of English as an International Language, University of Illinois at Urbana-Champaign, 111–30.

Gallow, S. (2003) Listen actively! You can keep that conversation going! In K. Bardovi-Harlig and R. Mahan-Taylor (eds), *Teaching pragmatics*. Washington, DC: Office of English Programs, US Department of State. Retrieved June 23, 2009, from http://exchanges.state.gov/media/oelp/teaching-pragmatics/sara-gallow.pdf.

Garfinkel, H. (1967) *Studies in ethnomethodology*. Englewood Cliffs, NJ: Prentice-Hall.

Garrett, P. B., and Baquedano-López, P. (2002) Language socialization: Reproduction and continuity, transformation and change. *Annual Review of Anthropology*, 31(1), 339–61.

Giles, H., Coupland, J., and Coupland, N. (1991) Accommodation theory: Communication, context, and consequence. In H. Giles, J. Coupland, and N. Coupland (eds), *Contexts of accommodation: Developments in applied sociolinguistics*. Cambridge, England: Cambridge University Press, 1–68.

Golato, A. (2002) German compliment responses. *Journal of Pragmatics*, 34(5), 547–71.

Golato, A. (2003) Studying compliment responses: A comparison of DCTs and recordings of naturally occurring talk. *Applied Linguistics*, 24(1), 90–121.

González-Lloret, M. (2008) Computer-mediated learning of L2 pragmatics. In E. Alcón and A. Martínez-Flor (eds), *Investigating pragmatics in foreign language learning, teaching and testing*. Clevedon, England: Multilingual Matters, 114–32.

Graves, K. (2000) *Designing language courses: A guide for teachers*. Boston: Heinle & Heinle.

Grenfell, M., and Harris, V. (1999) *Modern languages and learning strategies: In theory and practice*. London: Routledge.

Grice, H. P. (1975) Logic and conversation. In P. Cole and J. L. Morgan (eds), *Syntax and semantics 3: Speech acts*. New York: Academic Press, 41–58.

Griffiths, C. (2008) Strategies and good language learners. In C. Griffiths (ed.), *Lessons from good language learners*. Cambridge, England: Cambridge University Press, 83–98.

Griswold, O. (2003) How do you say good-bye? In K. Bardovi-Harlig and R. Mahan-Taylor (eds), *Teaching pragmatics*. Washington, DC: Office of English Language Programs, US Department of State. Retrieved June 23, 2009, from http://exchanges.state.gov/media/oelp/teaching-pragmatics/griswold.pdf.

Haley, M. H. (2005) Action research in language learning. *Academic Exchange Quarterly*, 9(3), 193–97.

Hall, J. K. (2002) *Teaching and researching language and culture*. London: Pearson Education.

Hancock, S. (2008) White lies or communicative competence? *Essential Teacher*, 5(2), 25–7.

Harris, V. and Grenfell, M. (2008) Learning to learn languages: The differential response of learners to strategy instruction. Paper presented at the 15th AILA World Congress, Essen, Germany, August 21–25, 2008.

Hartford, B. S., and Bardovi-Harlig, K. (1992) Experimental and observational data in the study of interlanguage pragmatics. In L. F. Bouton and Y. Kachru (eds), *Pragmatics and language learning* (Vol. 2). Urbana, IL: Division of English as an International Language, University of Illinois at Urbana-Champaign, 33–52.

Hayashi, A. (1999) Kaiwa tenkaino tameno sutorategi: "Kotowari" to "wabi" no shutsugen jokyoto kaiwa tenkaijono kino [Strategies for conversation: Analysis and functions of refusals and apologies]. *Bulletin of Tokyo Gakugei University Section II Humanities*, 50, 175–88.

Herbert, R. K. (1990) Sex-based differences in compliment behavior. *Language in Society*, 19(2), 201–24.

Herbert, R. K., and Straight, S. (1989) Compliment rejection versus compliment-avoidance: Listener-based versus speaker-based pragmatic strategies. *Language and Communication*, 9(1), 35–47.

Hinkel, E. (1997) Appropriateness of advice: DCT and multiple choice data. *Applied Linguistics*, 18(1), 1–26.

Hinkel, E. (2001) Building awareness and practical skills to facilitate cross-cultural communication. In M. Celce-Murcia (ed.), *Teaching English as a second or foreign language* (3rd edn). Boston: Heinle & Heinle, 443–58.

Holmes, J., and Brown, D. F. (1987) Teachers and students learning about compliments. *TESOL Quarterly*, 21(3), 523–46.

Horibe, H. (2008) The place of culture in teaching English as an international language (EIL). *JALT Journal*, 30(2), 241–53.

House, J. (2003) Teaching and learning pragmatic fluency in a foreign language: The case of English as a lingua franca. In A. Martínez, E. Usó and A. Fernández (eds), *Pragmatic competence and foreign language teaching*. Castellón, Spain: Servicio de publicaciones de la Universidad Jaume I, 133–59.

House, J. (2008) What is an "intercultural speaker"? In E. S. Alcón and M. P. Safont (eds), *Intercultural language use and language learning*. Dordrecht, The Netherlands: Springer, 7–21.

House, J., and Kasper, G. (2000) How to remain a nonnative speaker. In C. Riemer (ed.), *Kognitive Aspekte des Lehrens und Lernens von Fremdsprachen* [Cognitive aspects of foreign language teaching and learning]. *Festschrift für Willis J. Edmondson zum 60. Geburtstag* [Festschrift for Willis J. Edmondson on the occasion of his 60th birthday]. Tübingen, Germany: Narr, 101–18.

Howard, A. M. (2008) Message from the newsletter editor. *Pragmatic Matters: JALT Pragmatics SIG Newsletter*, 9(1), 1 (English), 1 (Japanese).

Hudson, T., Detmer, E., and Brown, J. D. (1995) *Developing prototypic measures of cross-cultural pragmatics* (Tech. Rep. No. 7). Honolulu: University of Hawai'i, Second Language Teaching and Curriculum Center.

Iino, M. (1996) "Excellent foreigner!" Gaijinization of Japanese language and culture in contact situations – An ethnographic study of dinner table conversations between Japanese host families and American students. Unpublished doctoral dissertation, University of Pennsylvania, Philadelphia.

Ikoma, T., and Shimura, A. (1993) Eigo kara nihongoeno puragumatikku toransufaa: "kotowari" toiu hatsuwa kouini tsuite [Pragmatic transfer from English to Japanese: The speech act of refusals]. *Nihongokyouiku [Journal of Japanese Language Teaching]*, 79, 41–52.

Ishida, K. (2005) Why shift forms when addressing the same person? Raising awareness about the pragmatic use of the Japanese plain and *desu/masu* forms. In D. Tatsuki (ed.), *Pragmatics in language learning, theory, and practice*. Tokyo: The Japan Association for Language Teaching Pragmatics Special Interest Group, 161–5.

Ishihara, N. (2003*a*) Giving and responding to compliments. In K. Bardovi-Harlig and R. Mahan-Taylor (eds), *Teaching pragmatics*. Washington, DC: Office of English Language Programs, US Department of State. Retrieved June 23, 2009, from http://exchanges.state.gov/media/oelp/teaching-pragmatics/giving.pdf.

Ishihara, N. (2003*b*) Identity and pragmatic performance of second language learners. Paper presented at the Annual Conference of the American Association for Applied Linguistics, Arlington, VA, March.

Ishihara, N. (2004) Exploring the immediate and delayed effects of formal instruction: Teaching giving and responding to compliments. *MinneWI TESOL Journal*, 21, 37–70.

Ishihara, N. (2006) Subjectivity, pragmatic use, and instruction: Evidence of accommodation and resistance. Unpublished doctoral dissertation, University of Minnesota, Minneapolis.

Ishihara, N. (2007*a*) Tracing the development of teacher's knowledge and beliefs about the instruction of L2 pragmatics: The effects of a summer institute. Paper presented at the Annual Conference of the American Association for Applied Linguistics, Costa Mesa, CA, April.

Ishihara, N. (2007*b*) Web-based curriculum for pragmatics instruction in Japanese as a foreign language: An explicit awareness-raising approach. *Language Awareness*, 16(1), 21–40.

Ishihara, N. (2008*a*) Incorporating instructional pragmatics into teacher education. Paper presented at the 42nd Annual TESOL Convention, New York, April.

Ishihara, N. (2008*b*) The pragmatics of identity negotiation: What is the relevance of native-speaker norms for L2 use? Paper presented at the Language Learning in and out of the Classroom Colloquium, Annual Conference of the Second Language Research Forum, Honolulu, HI, October.

Ishihara, N. (2008*c*) Transforming community norms: Potentials of L2 speakers' pragmatic resistance. In M. Hood (ed.), *Proceedings of the 2008 Temple University Japan colloquium on language learning*. Tokyo: Temple University Tokyo, 1–10.

Ishihara, N. (in press, *a*) Assessing pragmatic competence: A study of teacher-based assessment for foreign language pragmatics. In D. Tatsuki and N. Houck (eds), *Pragmatics from Research to Practice: Teaching Speech Acts*. Alexandria, VA: Teachers of English to Speakers of Other Languages.

Ishihara, N. (in press, *b*) Maintaining an optimal distance: Nonnative speakers' pragmatic choice. In A. Mahboob (ed.), *Non-native speakers of English in TESOL: Identity, politics, and perceptions*. Newcastle-upon-Tyne: Cambridge Scholars Press.

Ishihara, N. (2009) Teacher-based assessment for foreign language pragmatics. *TESOL Quarterly*, 43(3), 445–70.

Ishihara, N. (in press, *c*) Teaching communication in context: Giving and responding to compliments in English. In A. Martínez-Flor and E. Usó-Juan (eds), *Speech act performance: Theoretical groundings and methodological innovations*. Amsterdam, The Netherlands: John Benjamins.

Ishihara, N., Aoshima, S., and Akikawa, K. (2008) Assessing pragmatic competence: A study of authentic assessment for foreign language pragmatics. Paper presented at the Annual Conference of the American Association for Applied Linguistics, Washington, DC, April.

Ishihara, N., and Cohen, A. D. (2004) Strategies for learning speech acts in Japanese. Minneapolis, MN: Center for Advanced Research on Language Acquisition, University of Minnesota. Retrieved September 23, 2009, from http://www.carla.umn.edu/speechacts/ japanese/introtospeechacts/index.htm.

Ishihara, N., and Maeda, M. (2010) ことばと文化の交差点： 文化で読み解く 日本語 *[Kotobato bunkano kousaten: Bunkade yomitoku Nippongo]: Advanced Japanese: Communication in Context*. London: Routledge.

Ishihara, N., and Tarone, E. (2009) Emulating and resisting pragmatic norms: Learner subjectivity and foreign language pragmatic use. In N. Noguchi (ed.), *Pragmatic competence in Japanese as a second language*. Berlin, Germany: Mouton Pragmatics Series: Mouton de Gruyter, 101–28.

Jeon, E. H., and Kaya, T. (2006) Effects of L2 instruction on interlanguage pragmatic development: A meta-analysis. In J. M. Norris and L. Ortega (eds), *Synthesizing research on language learning and teaching*. Amsterdam: Benjamins, 165–211.

Jernigan, J., Yazdanpanah, R., Mendoza, M. B., and Lucas, T. (2007) Developing pragmatic competence through video based instruction. Video presentation at the 41st Annual TESOL Convention, Seattle, WA, March.

Jiang, X. (2006) Suggestions: What should ESL students know? *System*, 34(1), 36–54.

Johnson, K. A. (2002) Action for understanding: A study in teacher research with exploratory practice. In *Teachers' narrative inquiry as professional development*. Cambridge, England: Cambridge University Press, 60–75.

Johnson, K. E. (1999) *Understanding language teaching: Reasoning in action*. Boston: Heinle & Heinle.

Johnson, K. E., and Golombek, P. R. (2002) *Teacher's narrative inquiry as professional development*. Cambridge, England: Cambridge University Press.

Johnson, K. E., and Golombek, P. R. (2003) "Seeing" teacher learning. *TESOL Quarterly*, 37(4), 729–37.

Johnston, B. (2003) *Values in English language teaching*. Mahwah, NJ: Lawrence Erlbaum Associates.

Johnston, B., and Goettsch, K. (2000) In search of the knowledge base of language teaching: Explanations by experienced teachers. *The Canadian Modern Language Review*, 56(3), 437–68.

Judd, E. L. (1999) Some issues in the teaching of pragmatic competence. In E. Hinkel (ed.), *Culture in second language teaching and learning*. Cambridge, England: Cambridge University Press, 152–66.

Juker, A., Smith, S., and Lüdge, T. (2003) Interactive aspects of vagueness in conversation. *Journal of Pragmatics*, 35(12), 1737–69.

Kachru, B. B., and Nelson, C. L. (1996) World Englishes. In S. McKay and N. Hornberger (eds), *Sociolinguistics and language teaching*. Cambridge: Cambridge University Press, 72–102.

Kakiuchi, Y. (2005a) Greetings in English: Naturalistic speech versus textbook speech. In D. Tatsuki (ed.), *Pragmatics in language learning, theory, and practice.* Tokyo: The Japan Association for Language Teaching, Pragmatics Special Interest Group, 61–85.

Kakiuchi, Y. (2005*b*) Language variation analysis. In D. Tatsuki (ed.), *Pragmatics in language learning, theory, and practice.* Tokyo: The Japan Association for Language Teaching Pragmatics Special Interest Group, 157–60.

Kasper, G. (1992) Pragmatic transfer. *Second Language Research,* 8(3), 203–31.

Kasper, G. (1997) The role of pragmatics in language teacher education. In K. Bardovi-Harlig and B. Hartford (eds), *Beyond methods: Components of second language education.* New York: McGraw-Hill Company, 113–36.

Kasper, G. (1999) Data collection in pragmatics research. *University of Hawai'i Working Papers in ESL,* 18(1), 71–107.

Kasper, G. (2000) Data collection in pragmatic research. In H. Spencer-Oatey (ed.), *Culturally speaking: Managing rapport across cultures.* London: Continuum, 145–64.

Kasper, G. (2001) Four perspectives on L2 pragmatic development. *Applied Linguistics,* 22(4), 502–30.

Kasper, G. (2006) Speech acts in interaction: Towards discursive pragmatics. In K. Bardovi-Harlig, J. C. Félix-Brasdefer and A. S. Omar (eds), *Pragmatics and language learning* (Vol. 11). Honolulu: University of Hawai'i at Manoa, 280–314.

Kasper, G. (2007) Pragmatics in second language learning: An update. Paper presented at the Language Learning Roundtable, the Annual Conference of the American Association for Applied Linguistics, Costa Mesa, CA, April. Retrieved January 2, 2009, from http://www.aaal.org/index.php?id=53.

Kasper, G., and Dahl, M. (1991) Research methods in interlanguage pragmatics. *Studies in Second Language Acquisition,* 13(2), 215–47.

Kasper, G., and Rose, K. R. (1999) Pragmatics and SLA. *Annual Review of Applied Linguistics,* 19, 81–104.

Kasper, G., and Rose, K. R. (2002) *Pragmatic development in a second language.* Malden, MA: Blackwell.

Kasper, G., and Schmidt, R. W. (1996) Developmental issues in interlanguage pragmatics. *Studies in Second Language Acquisition,* 18(2), 149–69.

Kawate-Mierzejewska, M. (2005) Acceptance and ritual acceptance anticipated by prosodic features. In D. Tatsuki (ed.), *Pragmatics in language learning, theory, and practice*. Tokyo: The Japan Association for Language Teaching Pragmatics Special Interest Group, 45–59.

Kellerman, E. (1983) Now you see it, now you don't. In S. Gass and L. Selinker (eds), *Language transfer in language learning*. Rowley, MA: Newbury House, 112–34.

Kim, Y., Poonpon, K., and Biber, D. (2007). Preparing corpus-based grammar materials. Paper presented at the Effectiveness of Corpus Based Grammar Materials Colloquium, 41st Annual TESOL Convention, Seattle, WA, March.

Koester, A. (2002) The performance of speech acts in workplace conversations and the teaching of communicative functions. *System*, 30(2), 167–84.

Kondo, S. (1997) The development of pragmatic competence by Japanese learners of English: Longitudinal study of interlanguage apologies. *Sophia Linguistica*, 41, 265–84.

Kondo, S. (2008) Effects of pragmatic development through awareness-raising instruction: Refusals by Japanese EFL learners. In E. S. Alcón and A. Martínez-Flor (eds), *Investigating pragmatics in foreign language learning, teaching, and testing*. Bristol: Multilingual Matters, 153–77.

Kubota, Mikio (1995) Teachability of conversational implicature to Japanese EFL learners. *IRLT Bulletin*, 9, 35–67.

Kubota, Mitsuo (1996) Acquaintance or fiancée: Pragmatic differences in requests between Japanese and Americans. *Working Papers in Educational Linguistics*, 12(1), 23–38.

Kubota, R. (2008) Critical approaches to teaching Japanese language and culture. In J. Mori and A. S. Ohta (eds), *Japanese applied linguistics: Discourse and social perspectives*. London: Continuum, 327–52.

Kubota, R., and McKay, L. S. (2008) Language learning in rural Japan: EIL/EILF discourses and the local linguistic ecology. Paper presented at the Language Learning in and out of the Classroom Colloquium, Annual Conference of Second Language Research Forum, Honolulu, HI, October.

Kumagai, T. (1993) Remedial interactions as face-management: The case of Japanese and Americans. In S. Y. T. Matsuda, M. Sakurai, and A. Baba (eds), *In honor of Tokuichiro Matsuda: Papers contributed on the occasion of his sixtieth birthday*. Tokyo: Iwasaki Linguistic Circle, 278–300.

Laforest, M. (2002) Scenes of family life: Complaining in everyday conversation. *Journal of Pragmatics*, 34(10–11), 1595–620.

Lantolf, J. P. (2000) *Sociocultural theory and second language learning*. Oxford, England: Oxford University Press.

Lantolf, J. P., and Thorne, S. L. (2006) *Sociocultural theory and the genesis of second language development*. Oxford, England: Oxford University Press.

Lave, J., and Wenger, E. (1991) *Situated learning: Legitimate peripheral participation*. Cambridge, England: Cambridge University Press.

Lazaraton, A., and Ishihara, N. (2005) Understanding second language teacher practice using microanalysis and self-reflection: A collaborative case study. *Modern Language Journal*, 89(4), 529–42.

Lee, K. (2003) Discourse markers "well" and "oh." In K. Bardovi-Harlig and R. Mahan-Taylor (eds), *Teaching pragmatics*. Washington, DC: Office of English Programs, US Department of State. Retrieved June 23, 2009, from http://exchanges.state.gov/media/oelp/teaching-pragmatics/lee-well. pdf.

Lee, C. D., and Smagorinsky, P. (2000) Introduction: Constructing meaning through collaborative inquiry. In *Vygotskian perspectives on literacy research: Constructing meaning through collaborative inquiry*. New York: Cambridge University Press.

Leech, G. (1997) Teaching and language corpora: A convergence. In A. Wichmann, S. Fligelstone, T. McEnery, and G. Knowles (eds), *Teaching and language corpora*. Harlow, England: Addison Wesley Longman, 2–23.

Liddicoat, A. J., and Crozet, C. (2001) Acquiring French interactional norms through instruction. In K. R. Rose and G. Kasper (eds), *Pragmatics in language teaching*. Cambridge, England: Cambridge University Press, 125–44.

Liu, J. (2007) Developing a pragmatics test for Chinese EFL learners. *Language Testing*, 24(3), 391–415.

LoCastro, V. (1998). Learner subjectivity and pragmatic competence development. Paper presented at the Annual Conference of the American Association for Applied Linguistics, Seattle, WA, November. Retrieved November 11, 2008, from http://eric.ed.gov/ERICWebPortal/custom/portlets/recordDetails/detailmini.jsp?_nfpb=true&_&ERICExtSearch_SearchValue_0=ED420201&ERICExtSearch_SearchType_0=no&accno=ED420201.

LoCastro, V. (2000) Evidence of accommodation to L2 pragmatic norms in peer review tasks of Japanese learners of English. *JALT Journal*, 22(2), 245–70.

LoCastro, V. (2003) *An introduction to pragmatics: Social action for language teachers*. Ann Arbor, MI: The University of Michigan Press.

Long, M. (1985) Input and second language acquisition theory. In S. Gass and C. Madden (eds), *Input in second language acquisition*. Rowley, MA: Newbury House, 337–93.

Long, M. (1996) The role of linguistic environment in second language acquisition. In W. C. Ritchie and T. K. Bhatia (eds), *Handbook of second language acquisition*. San Diego, CA: Academic Press, 413–68.

Long, M., Inagaki, S., and Ortega, L. (1998) The role of implicit negative feedback in SLA: Models and recasts in Japanese and Spanish. *Modern Language Journal*, 82(3), 357–71.

Macaro, E. (2001) *Learning strategies in foreign and second language classrooms*. London: Continuum.

Mach, T., and Ridder, S. (2003) E-mail requests. In K. Bardovi-Harlig and R. Mahan-Taylor (eds), *Teaching pragmatics*. Washington, DC: Office of English Programs, US Department of State. Retrieved June 23, 2009, from http://exchanges.state.gov/media/oelp/teaching-pragmatics/mach.pdf.

Manes, J. (1983) Compliments: A mirror of cultural values. In N. Wolfson and E. Judd (eds), *Sociolinguistics and language acquisition*. Rowley, MA: Newbury House, 82–95.

Manes, J., and Wolfson, N. (1981) The compliment formula. In F. Coulmas (ed.), *Conversational routine: Explorations in standardized communication situations and prepatterned speech*. The Hague, The Netherlands: Mouton, 115–32.

Martínez-Flor, A. (2008) Analyzing request modification devices in films: Implications for pragmatic learning in instructed foreign language contexts. In E. S. Alcón and M. P. Safont (eds), *Intercultural language use and language learning*. Dordrecht, The Netherlands: Springer, 245–80.

Martínez-Flor, A., and Fukuya, Y. J. (2005) The effects of instruction on learners' production of appropriate and accurate suggestions. *System*, 33(3), 463–80.

Martínez-Flor, A., and Usó-Juan, E. (2006) A comprehensive pedagogical framework to develop pragmatics in the foreign language classroom: The 6R approach. *Applied Language Learning*, 16(2), 39–64.

Martínez-Flor, A., and Usó-Juan, E. (eds) (in press) *Speech act performance: Theoretical groundings and methodological innovations.*

Matsuura, H. (1998) Japanese EFL learners' perception of politeness in low imposition requests. *JALT Journal*, 20(1), 33–48.

McEnery, A., Baker, P., and Cheepen, C. (2001) Lexis, indirectness and politeness in operator calls. In P. Peters, P. Collins, and A. Smith (eds), *New frontiers of corpus research.* Amsterdam: Rodopi, 53–70.

McEnery, T., Xiao, R., and Tono, Y. (2006) *Corpus-based language studies: An advanced resource book.* London: Routledge.

McGroarty, M., and Taguchi, N. (2005) Evaluating the communicativeness of EFL textbooks for Japanese secondary students. In J. Frodesen and C. Holten (eds), *The power of context in language teaching and learning.* Boston: Thomson/Heinle, 211–24.

McKay, S. L. (2002) *Teaching English as an international language.* Oxford, England: Oxford University Press.

McKay, S. L. (in press) English as an international lingua franca. In N. Hornberger and S. L. McKay (eds), *Sociolinguistics and education.* Clevedon: Multilingual Matters.

McLean, T. (2005) "Why no tip?": Student-generated DCTs in the ESL classroom. In D. Tatsuki (ed.), *Pragmatics in language learning, theory, and practice.* Tokyo: Pragmatics Special Interest Group of the Japan Association for Language Teaching, 150–6.

McNamara, T. (2001) Language assessment as social practice: Challenges for research. *Language Testing*, 18(4), 333–49.

McNamara, T., and Roever, C. (2006) *Language testing: The social dimension.* Malden, MA: Blackwell.

Meier, A. J. (1997) Teaching the universals of politeness. *ELT Journal*, 51(1), 21–8.

Meier, A. J. (1999) Identifying and teaching the underlying cultural themes of pragmatics: A case for explanatory pragmatics. In L. F. Bouton and Y. Kachru (eds), *Pragmatics and language learning* (Vol. 9). Urbana, IL: Division of English as an International Language, University of Illinois at Urbana-Champaign, 113–27.

Meier, A. J. (2003) Posting the banns: A marriage of pragmatics and culture in foreign and second language pedagogy and beyond. In A. Martínez, E. Usó, and A. Fernández (eds), *Pragmatic competence and foreign language teaching*. Castellón, Spain: Servicio de publicaciones de la Universidad Jaume I, 185–210.

Meijer, P. C., Verloop, N., and Beijaard, D. (1999) Exploring language teachers' practical knowledge about teaching reading comprehension. *Teaching and Teacher Education*, 15(1), 59–84.

Mey, J. L. (2001) *Pragmatics: An introduction*. Malden, MA: Blackwell.

Mir, M. (2001) Un modelo didáctico para la enseñanza de la pragmática [A didactic model for the teaching of pragmatics]. *Hispania*, 84(3), 542–9.

Mishan, F. (2004) *Designing authenticity into language learning materials*. Bristol, England: Intellect Books.

Miura, A., and McGloin, N. H. (1994) *An integrated approach to intermediate Japanese*. Tokyo: *Japan Times*.

Möllering, M. (2004) *The acquisition of German modal particles*. Bern, Switzerland: Lang.

Morgan, C., and Cain, A. (2000) *Foreign language and culture learning from a dialogic perspective*. Clevedon, England: Multilingual Matters.

Mori, J. (2002) Task design, plan, and development of talk-in-interaction: An analysis of small group activity in a Japanese language classroom. *Applied Linguistics*, 23(3), 323–47.

Mori, J. (2004) Negotiating sequential boundaries and learning opportunities: A case from a Japanese language classroom. *The Modern Language Journal*, 88(4), 536–50.

Morita, N. (2002) Negotiating participation in second language academic communities: A study of identity, agency, and transformation. Unpublished doctoral dissertation, The University of British Columbia, Vancouver, Canada.

Morita, N. (2004) Negotiating participation and identity in second language academic communities. *TESOL Quarterly*, 38(4), 573–603.

Moriyama, T. (1990) 'Kotowari' no houryaku: Taijin kankei chouseito komyunikeishon [Strategies of refusals: Interpersonal adjustments and communication]. *Gengo*, 19(8), 59–66.

Nakatani, Y. (2005) The effects of awareness-raising training on oral communication strategy use. *The Modern Language Journal*, 89(1), 76–91.

Nelson, G., Al-Batal, M., and Echols, E. (1996). Arabic and English compliment responses: Potential for pragmatic failure. *Applied Linguistics*, 17(4), 411–32.

Nelson, G. L., Carson, J., Al-Batal, M., and El-Bakary, W. (2002) Cross-cultural pragmatics: Strategy use in Egyptian Arabic and American English refusals. *Applied Linguistics*, 23(2), 163–89.

Nelson, G. L., El-Bakary, W., and Al-Batal, M. (1993) Egyptian and American compliments: A cross cultural study. *International Journal of Intercultural Relations*, 17(3), 293–313.

Nonaka, K. (2000) Apology is not necessary: An in-depth analysis of my own intercultural and intracultural miscommunication. *Journal of Hokkaido University of Education at Kushiro*, 32, 155–86.

Norris, J. M., Brown, J. D., Hudson, T., and Yoshioka, J. (1998) *Designing second language performance assessments*. Honolulu: University of Hawai'i Press.

Norton, B. (1997) Language, identity, and the ownership of English. *TESOL Quarterly*, 31(3), 409–29.

Norton, B. (2000) *Identity and language learning*. Harlow, England: Pearson Education.

Norton, B. (2001) Non-participation, imagined communities and the language classroom. In M. P. Breen (ed.), *Learner contributions to language learning: New directions in research*. Harlow, England: Longman, 159–71.

Nunan, D. (1992) *Research methods in language learning*. Cambridge, England: Cambridge University Press.

Ochs, E. (1993) Constructing social identity: A language socialization perspective. *Research on Languages and Social Interaction*, 26(3), 287–306.

Ohara, Y., Saft, S., and Crookes, G. (2001) Toward a feminist critical pedagogy in a beginning Japanese-as-a-foreign-language class. *Japanese Language and Literature*, 35(2), 105–33.

Ohta, A. S. (2005) Interlanguage pragmatics in the zone of proximal development. *System*, 33(3), 503–17.

Olshtain, E., and Blum-Kulka, S. (1985) Degree of approximation: Nonnative reactions to native speech act behavior. In S. Gass and C. Madden (eds), *Input in second language acquisition*. Rowley, MA: Newbury House, 303–25.

Olshtain, E., and Cohen, A. D. (1983) Apology: A speech act set. In
N. Wolfson and E. Judd (eds), *Sociolinguistics and language acquisition*.
Rowley, MA: Newbury House, 18–35.

Olshtain, E., and Cohen, A. D. (1989) Speech act behavior across languages.
In H. W. Dechert and M. Raupach (eds), *Transfer in production*.
Norwood, NJ: Ablex, 53–67.

O'Malley, M., and Valdez Pierce, L. (1996) *Authentic assessment for English
language learners: Practical approaches for teachers*. Reading, MA:
Addison-Wesley.

Paige, R. M., Cohen, A. D., Kappler, B., Chi, J. C., and Lassegard, J. P.
(2006) *Maximizing study abroad: A students' guide to strategies for
language and culture learning and use* (2nd edn). Minneapolis, MN:
Center for Advanced Research on Language Acquisition.

Paige, R. M., Cohen, A. D., and Shively, R. L. (2004) Assessing the impact of
a strategies-based curriculum on language and culture learning abroad.
Frontiers: The Interdisciplinary Journal of Study Abroad, 10, 253–76.

Pajares, M. F. (1992) Teachers' beliefs and educational research: Cleaning
up a messy construct. *Review of Educational Research*, 62(3), 307–32.

Patton, M. Q. (2002) *Qualitative research and evaluation methods* (3rd edn).
Thousand Oaks, CA: Sage.

Pavlenko, A., and Blackledge, A. (eds). (2004) *Negotiation of identities in
multilingual contexts*. Clevedon, England: Multilingual Matters.

Pearson, E. (1986) Agreement/disagreement: An example of results of
discourse analysis applied to the oral English classroom. *International
Review of Applied Linguistics*, 74(1), 47–61.

Pennycook, A. (2001) *Critical applied linguistics: A critical introduction*.
Mahwah, NJ: Lawrence Erlbaum Associates.

Preston, D. R. (1989) *Sociolinguistics and second language acquisition*. Oxford,
England: Basil Blackwell.

Prosser, M. H. (1978) *The cultural dialogue: An introduction to intercultural
communication*. Boston: Houghton-Mifflin.

Rea-Dickins, P. (2008) Classroom-based language assessment. In
E. Shohamy and N. H. Hornberger (eds), *Encyclopedia of language and
education: Language testing and assessment* (2nd edn, Vol. 7). New York:
Springer Science & Business Media, 257–71.

Richards, J. C., and Lockhart, C. (1996) *Reflective teaching in second language
classrooms*. Cambridge, England: Cambridge University Press.

Richards, J. C., and Schmidt, R. W. (1983) *Language and communication.* Harlow, England: Longman.

Rinnert, C., and Kobayashi, H. (1999) Requestive hints in Japanese and English. *Journal of Pragmatics*, 31(9), 1173–201.

Roberts, C., Byram, M., Barro, A., Jordan, S., and Street, B. (2001) *Language learners as ethnographers.* Clevedon, England: Multilingual Matters.

Robins, J., and MacNeill, A. (2007) *Impact listening* (2nd edn). Hong Kong: Longman Asia ELT.

Roever, C. (2004) Difficulty and practicality in tests of interlanguage pragmatics. In B. Boxer and A. D. Cohen (eds), *Studying speaking to inform second language learning.* Clevedon, England: Multilingual Matters, 283–301.

Roever, C. (2005) *Testing ESL pragmatics: Development and validation of a web-based assessment battery (language testing and evaluation).* Frankfurt, Germany: Peter Lang.

Rose, K. R. (1994a) On the validity of discourse completion tests in non-western contexts. *Applied Linguistics*, 15(1), 1–14.

Rose, K. R. (1994b) Pragmatic consciousness-raising in an EFL context. In L. F. Bouton and Y. Kachru (eds), *Pragmatics and language learning* (Vol. 5, 52–63). Urbana, IL: Division of English as an International Language, University of Illinois at Urbana-Champaign.

Rose, K. R. (1997a) Pragmatics in teacher education for nonnative-speaking teachers: A consciousness-raising approach. *Language, Culture and Curriculum*, 10(2), 125–38.

Rose, K. R. (1997b) Pragmatics in the classroom: Theoretical concerns and practical possibilities. In L. F. Bouton and Y. Kachru (eds), *Pragmatics and language learning* (Vol. 8). Urbana, IL: Division of English as an International Language, University of Illinois at Urbana-Champaign, 267–95.

Rose, K. R. (1999) Teachers and students learning about requests in Hong Kong. In E. Hinkel (ed.), *Culture in second language teaching and learning.* Cambridge, England: Cambridge University Press, 167–80.

Rose, K. R. (2001) Compliments and compliment responses in film: Implications for pragmatics research and language teaching. *IRAL*, 39(4), 309–28.

Rose, K. R. (2005) On the effects of instruction in second language pragmatics. *System*, 33(3), 385–99.

Rose, K. R., and Kasper, G. (2001) *Pragmatics in language teaching*. New York: Cambridge University Press.

Rose, K. R., and Ng, C. K. (2001) Inductive and deductive teaching of compliments and compliment responses. In K. R. Rose and G. Kasper (eds), *Pragmatics in language teaching*. New York: Cambridge University Press, 145–70.

Rose, K. R., and Ono, R. (1995) Eliciting speech act data in Japanese: The effect of questionnaire type. *Language Learning*, 45(2), 191–223.

Rubin, J. (1975) What the "good language learner" can teach us. *TESOL Quarterly*, 9(1), 41–51.

Rubin, J., Chamot, A. U., Harris, V., and Anderson, N. J. (2007) Intervening in the use of strategies. In A. D. Cohen and E. Macaro (eds), *Language learner strategies: 30 years of research and practice*. Oxford, England: Oxford University Press, 141–60.

Schauer, G. A., and Adolphs, S. (2006) Expressions of gratitude in corpus and DCT data: Vocabulary, formulaic sequences, and pedagogy. *System*, 34(1), 119–34.

Schegloff, E. A. (2001) Getting serious: Joke -> serious "no." *Journal of Pragmatics*, 33(12), 1947–55.

Schegloff, E. A., Koshik, I., Jacoby, S., and Olsher, D. (2002) Conversation analysis and applied linguistics. *Annual Review of Applied Linguistics*, 22, 3–31.

Schegloff, E. A., and Sacks, H. (1973) Opening up closings. *Semiotica*, 8(4), 289–327.

Schieffelin, B. B., and Ochs, E. (1986a) Language socialization. *Annual Review of Anthropology*, 15, 163–91.

Schieffelin, B. B., and Ochs, E. (eds). (1986b) *Language socialization across cultures*. Cambridge, England: Cambridge University Press.

Schmidt, R. W. (1983) Interaction, acculturation, and the acquisition of communicative competence: A case study of an adult. In N. Wolfson and E. Judd (eds), *Sociolinguistics and language acquisition*. Rowley, MA: Newbury House, 137–74.

Schmidt, R. W. (1990) The role of consciousness in second language learning. *Applied Linguistics*, 11(2), 129–58.

Schmidt, R. W. (1993) Consciousness, learning, and interlanguage pragmatics. In G. Kasper and S. Blum-Kulka (eds), *Interlanguage pragmatics*. Oxford, England: Oxford University Press, 21–42.

Schmidt, R. W. (2001) Attention. In P. Robinson (ed.), *Cognition and second language instruction*. Cambridge, England: Cambridge University Press, 3–32.

Schneider, J., and von der Emde, S. (2006) Dialogue, conflict, and intercultural learning in online collaborations between language learners and native speakers. In J. A. Belz and S. L. Thorne (eds), *Internet-mediated intercultural foreign language education*. Boston: Heinle & Heinle, 178–206.

Schneider, K. P., and Barron, A. (eds). (2008) *Variational pragmatics*. Amsterdam: John Benjamins.

Scollon, R., and Scollon, S. W. (1995) Interpersonal politeness and power. In R. Scollon and S. W. Scollon (eds), *Intercultural communication*. Oxford: Blackwell, 33–49.

Scotton, C. M., and Bernsten, J. (1988) Natural conversations as a model for textbook dialogue. *Applied Linguistics*, 9(4), 372–84.

Selinker, L. (1972) Interlanguage. *IRAL*, 10(3), 209–31.

Shively, R. L. (2008) Politeness and social interaction in study abroad: Service encounters in L2 Spanish. Unpublished doctoral dissertation, University of Minnesota, Minneapolis.

Shohamy, E. (1996) Language testing: Matching assessment procedures with language knowledge. In M. Birenbaum and F. Dochy (eds), *Alternatives in assessment of achievements, learning processes and prior knowledge*. Boston: Kluwer Academic Publishers, 143–60.

Shrum, J. L., and Glisan, E. W. (2004) Using a story-based approach to teach grammar. In J. Shrum and E. Glisan (eds), *Teacher's handbook: Contextualized language instruction* (3rd edn). Boston: Heinle & Heinle, 189–213.

Shulman, L. S. (1987) Knowledge and teaching: Foundations of the new reform. *Harvard Educational Review*, 57(1), 1–22.

Shulman, L. S., and Shulman, J. H. (2004) How and what teachers learn: A shifting perspective. *Journal of Curriculum Studies*, 36(2), 257–71.

Siegal, M. (1996) The role of learner subjectivity in second language sociolinguistic competency: Western women learning Japanese. *Applied Linguistics*, 17(3), 356–82.

Siegal, M., and Okamoto, S. (1996) Imagined worlds: Language, gender, and socio-cultural "norms"; in Japanese language textbooks. In

Proceedings of the 4th Berkeley Women and Language Conference. Berkeley, CA: Berkeley Women and Language Group, 667–78.

Siegal, M., and Okamoto, S. (2003) Toward reconceptualizing the teaching and learning of gendered speech styles in Japanese as a foreign language. *Japanese Language and Literature*, 37(1), 49–66.

Sinclair, J. M. (1997) Corpus evidence in language description. In A. Wichmann, S. Fligelstone, T. McEnery, and G. Knowles (eds), *Teaching and language corpora*. Harlow, England: Addison Wesley Longman, 27–39.

Spencer-Oatey, H. (ed.) (2000) *Culturally speaking: Managing rapport through talk across cultures*. London: Continuum.

Swain, M. (1984) Large-scale communicative language testing: A case study. In S. J. Savignon and M. S. Berns (eds), *Initiatives in communicative language teaching*. Reading, MA: Addison-Wesley, 185–201.

Swain, M. (1998) Focus on form through conscious reflection. In C. Doughty and J. Williams (eds), *Focus on form in classroom second language acquisition*. Cambridge, England: Cambridge University Press, 64–81.

Swain, M., and Lapkin, S. (1995) Problems in output and the cognitive processes they generate: A step towards second language learning. *Applied Linguistics*, 16(3), 371–91.

Sykes, J. (2008) A dynamic approach to social interaction: Synthetic immersive environments and Spanish pragmatics. Unpublished doctoral dissertation, University of Minnesota, Minneapolis.

Sykes, J., and Cohen, A. D. (2006) *Dancing with words: Strategies for learning pragmatics in Spanish*. Retrieved September 28, 2008, from: http://www.carla.umn.edu/speechacts/sp_pragmatics/home.html.

Sykes, J. M., and Cohen, A. D. (2008) Observed learner behavior, reported use, and evaluation of a website for learning Spanish pragmatics. In M. Bowles, R. Foote, and S. Perpiñán (eds), *Second language acquisition and research: Focus on form and function. Selected proceedings of the 2007 Second Language Research Forum*. Somerville, MA: Cascadilla Press, 144–57.

Takahashi, S. (2001) The role of input enhancement in developing pragmatic competence. In K. R. Rose and G. Kasper (eds), *Pragmatics in language teaching*. Cambridge, England: Cambridge University Press, 171–99.

Takahashi, S. (2005) Noticing in task performance and learning outcomes: A qualitative analysis of instructional effects in interlanguage pragmatics. *System*, 33(3), 437–61.

Takahashi, S., Hardy, T., Negeshi, M., Hedei S., Mikami, N. *et al.* (2006) *New Crown 1: English series*, new edn. Tokyo: Sanseido.

Takenoya, M. (2003) Appropriateness in terms of address. In K. Bardovi-Harlig and R. Mahan-Taylor (eds), *Teaching pragmatics*. Washington, DC: Office of English Programs, US Department of State. Retrieved June 23, 2009, from http://exchanges.state.gov/media/oelp/teaching-pragmatics/takenoya-revised.pdf.

Takimoto, M. (2008) The effects of deductive and inductive instruction on the development of language learners' pragmatic competence. *The Modern Language Journal*, 92(3), 369–86.

Taleghani-Nikazm, C. (2002) A conversation-analytic study of telephone conversation opening between native and nonnative speakers. *Journal of Pragmatics*, 34(12), 1807–32.

Tanaka, K. (1997) Developing pragmatic competence: A learners-as-researchers approach. *TESOL Journal*, 6(3), 14–18.

Tarone, E. (2005) English for specific purposes and interlanguage pragmatics. In K. Bardovi-Harlig and B. S. Hartford (eds), *Interlanguage pragmatics: Exploring institutional talk*. Mahwah, NJ: Lawrence Erlbaum Associates, 157–73.

Tarone, E., and Yule, G. (1989) *Focus on the language learner*. Oxford, England: Oxford University Press.

Tatsuki, D. (ed.) (2005) *Pragmatics in language learning, theory, and practice*. Tokyo: Japan Association for Language Teaching Pragmatics Special Interest Group.

Tatsuki, D., and Houck, N. (eds) (in press) *TESOL classroom practice series: Pragmatics volume*. Alexandria, VA: Teachers of English to Speakers of Other Languages.

Tatsuki, D., and Nishizawa, M. (2005) A comparison of compliments and compliment responses in television interviews, film, and naturally occurring data. In D. Tatsuki (ed.), *Pragmatics in language learning, theory, and practice*. Tokyo: The Japan Association for Language Teaching Pragmatics Special Interest Group, 87–97.

Tedick, D. J. (2002) Proficiency-oriented language instruction and assessment: Standards, philosophies, and considerations for assessment. In D. J. Tedick (ed.), *Proficiency-oriented language instruction and assessment: A curriculum handbook for teachers. CARLA working paper series*. Minneapolis, MN: University of Minnesota, The Center for Advanced Research on Language Acquisition, 9–48. Retrieved November 29, 2008, from http://www.carla.umn.edu/articulation/polia_standards.html.

Thomas, J. (1983) Cross-cultural pragmatic failure. *Applied Linguistics*, 4(2), 91–109.

Thomas, J. (1995) *Meaning in interaction: An introduction to pragmatics*. London: Longman.

Thompson, A. G. (1992) Teachers' beliefs and conceptions: A synthesis of the research. In D. A. Grouws (ed.), *Handbook of research on mathematics teaching and learning*. New York: Macmillan, 127–46.

Tomlinson, B. (2003) Material development courses. In B. Tomlinson (ed.), *Developing materials for language teaching*. London: Continuum, 445–61.

Tsui, A. B. M. (1993) Helping teachers to conduct action research in ESL classrooms. In D. Freeman and S. Cornwell (eds), *New ways in teacher education*. Alexandria, VA: Teachers of English to Speakers of Other Languages, 171–5.

Usó-Juan, E. (2008) The presentation and practice of the communicative act of requesting in textbooks: Focusing on modifiers. In E. S. Alcón and M. P. Safont (eds), *Intercultural language use and language learning*. Dordrecht, The Netherlands: Springer, 223–43.

Usó-Juan, E., and Martínez-Flor, A. (2008) Teaching learners to appropriately mitigate requests. *ELT Journal*, 62(4), 349–57.

Vandergrift, L. (2003) Orchestrating strategy use: Toward a model of the skilled second language listener. *Language Learning*, 53(3), 463–96.

Vásquez, C., and Sharpless, D. (2009) The role of pragmatics in the master's TESOL curriculum: Findings from a nationwide survey. *TESOL Quarterly*, 43(1), 5–28.

Vellenga, H. (2004) Learning pragmatics from ESL & EFL textbooks: How likely? *TESL-EJ*, 8(2). Retrieved September 28, 2008, from http://www-writing.berkeley.edu/TESL-EJ/ej30/a3.html.

Vellenga, H., and Smith, C. (2008) Increasing effectiveness in ESL teacher training: Connecting theory to practice. Paper presented at the Annual

Conference of the American Association for Applied Linguistics, Washington, DC, April.

Vygotsky, L. S. (1978) *Mind in society*. Cambridge, MA: Harvard University Press.

Wallace, M. J. (1998) *Action research for language teachers*. Cambridge, England: Cambridge University Press.

Walsh, S., and O'Keeffe, A. (2007) Applying CA to a modes analysis of higher education spoken academic discourse. In H. Bowles and P. Seedhouse (eds), *Conversation analysis and language for specific purposes*. Bern, Switzerland: Peter Lang, 102–39.

Washburn, G. N. (2001) Using situational comedies for pragmatic language teaching and learning. *TESOL Journal*, 10(4), 21–6.

Watson-Gegeo, K. A., and Nielsen, S. (2003) Language socialization in SLA. In C. J. Doughty and M. H. Long (eds), *The handbook of second language acquisition*. Malden, MA: Blackwell, 155–77.

Weatherall, A., Watson, B. M., and Gallois, C. (eds) (2007) *Language, discourse and social psychology*. London: Palgrave Macmillan.

Weaver, S. J. and Cohen, A. D. (1997) *Strategies-based instruction: A teacher-training manual*. Minneapolis, MN: Center for Advanced Research on Language Acquisition, University of Minnesota.

Weedon, C. (1997) *Feminist practice and poststructuralist theory* (2nd edn). Malden, MA: Blackwell.

Wenger, E. (1998) *Communities of practice: Learning, meaning, and identity*. Cambridge, England: Cambridge University Press.

Wolfson, N. (1983) An empirically based analysis of complimenting in American English. In N. Wolfson and E. Judd (eds), *Sociolinguistics and language acquisition*. Rowley, MA: Newbury House, 82–95.

Wolfson, N. (1989) *Perspectives: Sociolinguistics and TESOL*. New York: Newbury House/HarperCollins.

Wolfson, N., and Judd, E. (eds) (1983) *Sociolinguistics and language acquisition*. Rowley, MA: Newbury House.

Wolfson, N., and Manes, J. (1980) The compliment as a social strategy. *Papers in Linguistics: International Journal of Human Communication*, 13(3), 410–51.

Wright, T. (2005) Teachers' knowledge and classroom management. In T. Wright (ed.), *Classroom management in language education*. Houndmills, England: Palgrave Macmillan, 256–86.

Yamashita, S. O. (2002) Cross-cultural pragmatics: Comparing Japanese, Korean, and English apologies. A study using picture response test (PRT). Paper presented at the Conference of the International Association of Applied Linguistics (AILA), Singapore, December.

Yamashita, S. (2008) Investigating interlanguage pragmatic ability: What are we testing? In E. Alcón Soler and A. Martínez-Flor (eds), *Investigating pragmatics in foreign language learning, teaching and testing*. Bristol, England: Multilingual Matters, 201–23.

Yates, L. (2003) Softening short requests. In K. Bardovi-Harlig and R. Mahan-Taylor (eds), *Teaching pragmatics*. Washington, DC: Office of English Programs, US Department of State. Retrieved June 23, 2009, from http://exchanges.state.gov/media/oelp/teaching-pragmatics/short.pdf.

Yoon, K. K. (1991) Bilingual pragmatic transfer in speech acts: Bi-directional responses to a compliment. In L. F. Bouton and Y. Kachru (eds), *Pragmatics and language learning* (Vol. 2). Urbana, IL: Division of English as an International Language, University of Illinois at Urbana-Champaign, 75–100.

Yu, M.-C. (2008) Teaching and learning sociolinguistic skills in university EFL classes in Taiwan. *TESOL Quarterly*, 42(1), 31–53.

Yule, G. (1996) *Pragmatics*. Oxford, England: Oxford University Press.

Zitzen, M., and Stein, D. (2004) Chat and conversation: A case of transmedial stability? *Linguistics,* 42(5), 983–1021.

Appendix A: Electronic resources for teaching pragmatics[1]

1 Information about pragmatics and speech acts

(a) *Description of speech acts* (CARLA, University of Minnesota): Research-based descriptions of six speech acts

http://www.carla.umn.edu/speechacts/descriptions.html

(b) *Discourse pragmatics (*Indiana University*): Language and culture resources for instructors, students, and researchers of Spanish linguistics*

http://www.indiana.edu/~discprag/index.html

(c) *MIMEA* (Center for Language Education and Research, Michigan State University): Multimedia Interactive Modules for Education and Assessment Interactive video language sample (natural data) in Arabic, Chinese, German, Korean, Russian, and Vietnamese:

http://clear.msu.edu/clear/store/moreinfo.php?product_ID=7

2 Lesson plans and pragmatics curriculum for learners

(a) *Teaching pragmatics* (Department of State): Online teacher's resource book with 30 chapters for teaching various pragmatic features

http://draft.eca.state.gov/education/engteaching/pragmatics.htm

(b) *Learning speech acts in Japanese* (University of Minnesota): Self-access learner modules for learning five speech acts

http://www.carla.umn.edu/speechacts/japanese/introtospeechacts/index.htm

---

[1] The web links listed here accessed December 10, 2009.

(c) *Dancing with words: Strategies of learning pragmatics in Spanish* (University of Minnesota): Self-access learner modules for learning eight speech acts

http://www.carla.umn.edu/speechacts/sp_pragmatics/home.html

(d) *Teaching pragmatics in the classroom* (Indiana University): Pedagogical model for teaching refusals in Spanish with teachers' resource manual and student handouts

http://www.indiana.edu/~discprag/teachrefusal.html

3 Research

(a) *Speech act bibliography* (University of Minnesota): Annotated bibliography of L2 pragmatics research

http://www.carla.umn.edu/speechacts/bibliography/index.html

(b) *Learner strategies in the development of pragmatic ability* (University of Minnesota): Research study about the impact of speech act strategy instruction

http://www.carla.umn.edu/speechacts/research.html

(c) *Politeness* (Indiana University): Manuscripts related to politeness and indirectness in Spanish

http://www.indiana.edu/~discprag/polite.html

Appendix B: Pedagogical resources in L2 pragmatics

NOTE. This list excludes the useful online resources listed in Appendix A. Below are some of the professional articles which teacher readers are likely to find resourceful because they contain specific and practical information about how pragmatics can be taught.

Armstrong, S. (2008) *Desperate housewives* in an EFL classroom. *Pragmatic Matters*, 9(1), 4–7.

Bardovi-Harlig, K., Hartford, B. S., Mahan-Taylor, R., Morgan, M. J., and Reynolds, D. W. (1991) Developing pragmatic awareness: Closing conversation. *ELT Journal*, 45(1), 4–15.

Billmyer, K. (1990) "I really like your lifestyle": ESL learners learning how to compliment. *Penn Working Papers in Educational Linguistics*, 6(2), 31–48.

Bouton, L. (1994*a*) Can NNS skill in interpreting implicature in American English be improved through explicit instruction: A pilot study. In L. Bouton and Y. Kachru (eds), *Pragmatics and language learning* (Vol. 5, 88–109). Urbana, IL: Division of English as an International Language, University of Illinois at Urbana-Champaign.

Boxer, D., and Pickering, L. (1995) Problems in the presentation of speech acts in ELT materials: The case of complaints. *ELT Journal*, 49(1), 44–58.

Crandall, E., and Basturkmen, H. (2004) Evaluating pragmatics-focused materials. *ELT Journal*, 58(1), 38–49.

Dunham, P. (1992) Using compliments in the ESL classroom: An analysis of culture and gender. *MinneTESOL Journal*, 10, 75–85.

Eslami-Rasekh, Z. (2005) Raising the pragmatic awareness of language learners. *ELT Journal,* 59(3), 199–208.

Félix-Brasdefer, J. C. (2006) Teaching the negotiation of multi-turn speech acts: Using conversation-analytic tools to teach pragmatics in the FL classroom. In K. Bardovi-Harlig, J. C. Félix-Brasdefer, and A. S. Omar (eds), *Pragmatics and language learning* (Vol. 11, 167–97). Honolulu: University of Hawai'i Press.

Fujioka, M. (2003) Raising pragmatic consciousness in the Japanese EFL classroom. *The Language Teacher,* 27(5), 12–14.

Holmes, J., and Brown, D. F. (1987) Teachers and students learning about compliments. *TESOL Quarterly,* 21(3), 523–46.

Ishihara, N. (2007) Web-based curriculum for pragmatics instruction in Japanese as a foreign language: An explicit awareness-raising approach. *Language Awareness,* 16(1), 21–40.

Jiang, X. (2006) Suggestions: What should ESL students know? *System,* 34(1), 36–54.

Liddicoat, A. J., and Crozet, C. (2001) Acquiring French interactional norms through instruction. In K. R. Rose and G. Kasper (eds), *Pragmatics in language teaching.* Cambridge: Cambridge University Press, 125–44.

Martínez-Flor, A., and Usó-Juan, E. (2006) A comprehensive pedagogical framework to develop pragmatics in the foreign language classroom: The 6R approach. *Applied Language Learning,* 16(2), 39–64.

Martínez-Flor, A., and Usó-Juan, E. (eds) (in preparation) *Speech act performance: Theoretical groundings and methodological innovations.*

Meier, A. J. (1997) Teaching the universals of politeness. *ELT Journal,* 51(1), 21–8.

Ohara, Y., Saft, S., and Crookes, G. (2001) Toward a feminist critical pedagogy in a beginning Japanese-as-a-foreign-language class. *Japanese Language and Literature,* 35(2), 105–33.

Rose, K. R. (1994) Pragmatic consciousness-raising in an EFL context. In L. Bouton and Y. Kachru (eds), *Pragmatics and language learning, monograph series* (Vol. 5, 52–63). Urbana, IL: Division of English as an International Language, University of Illinois at Urbana-Champaign.

Rose, K. R. (1997) Pragmatics in teacher education for nonnative-speaking teachers: A consciousness-raising approach. *Language, Culture and Curriculum,* 10(2), 125–38.

Rose, K. R. (1999) Teachers and students learning about requests in Hong Kong. In E. Hinkel (ed.), *Culture in second language teaching and learning*. Cambridge: Cambridge University Press, 167–80.

Tanaka, K. (1997) Developing pragmatic competence: A learners-as-researchers approach. *TESOL Journal*, 6(3), 14–18.

Tatsuki, D. (ed.) (2005) *Pragmatics in language learning, theory, and practice*. Tokyo: The Japan Association for Language Teaching Pragmatics Special Interest Group.

Sample chapters:

- Fujioka, M. (2005) The speech act of suggesting as part of peer response activities (pp. 166–70).

- Ishida, K. (2005) Why shift forms when addressing the same person? Raising awareness about the pragmatic use of the Japanese plain and *desu/masu* forms (pp. 161–5).

- Kakiuchi, Y. (2005) Language variation analysis (pp. 157–60).

- McLean, T. (2005) "Why no tip?": Student-generated DCTs in the ESL classroom (pp. 150–6).

Tatsuki, D., and Houck, N. (eds) (in press) *TESOL classroom practice series: Pragmatics volume*. Alexandria, VA: Teachers of English to Speakers of Other Languages.

Sample chapters:

- Akikawa, K., and Ishihara, N. (in press) "Please write a recommendation letter": Teaching to write e-mail requests to faculty.

- Archer, E. (in press) They made me an offer I couldn't refuse: Teaching refusal strategies for invitations.

Washburn, G. N. (2001) Using situational comedies for pragmatic language teaching and learning. *TESOL Journal*, 10(4), 21–6.

Index